Y0-DBX-538

No Time To Cry

No Time To Cry

Wilmer Cooksey Jr.

authorHOUSE®

AuthorHouse™ LLC
1663 Liberty Drive
Bloomington, IN 47403
www.authorhouse.com
Phone: 1-800-839-8640

© 2013 by Wilmer Cooksey Jr.. All rights reserved.

No part of this book may be reproduced, stored in a retrieval system, or transmitted by any means without the written permission of the author.

Published by AuthorHouse 09/10/2013

ISBN: 978-1-4918-0892-4 (sc)
ISBN: 978-1-4918-0890-0 (hc)
ISBN: 978-1-4918-0891-7 (e)

Library of Congress Control Number: 2013914854

Any people depicted in stock imagery provided by Thinkstock are models, and such images are being used for illustrative purposes only.
Certain stock imagery © Thinkstock.

This book is printed on acid-free paper.

Because of the dynamic nature of the Internet, any web addresses or links contained in this book may have changed since publication and may no longer be valid. The views expressed in this work are solely those of the author and do not necessarily reflect the views of the publisher, and the publisher hereby disclaims any responsibility for them.

Acknowledgements

Thanks to all the people who put up with my absence when I should have been there to do my part. You were my "Rock." Thanks to those who excused Liz and picked up her slack because she was with me. Above all, thanks to those whose books and publications jogged an unreliable memory about facts that I once knew. For those whose names have been misspelled or omitted because of that unreliable memory please forgive.

Listed below are the publications that were used:

Antonick, Mike. *Corvette Black Book, 1953-2013.* Ann Arbor, MI: Michael Bruce Associates, 2012.

Auto Editors of Consumer Guide. *Corvette 50th Anniversary.* Lincolnwood, IL: Publications International. 2003.

Heasley, Jerry. *Corvette Masterpieces.* Ed. John Gunnell. Iola, WI: Krause Publications. 2007.

Montgomery, Andrew. *Corvette: The Definitive Guide to the All-American Sports Car.* San Diego, CA: Thunder Bay Press. 2003.

Shefter, James. *All Corvettes Are Red: The Rebirth of an American Legend.* New York, NY: Simon & Schuster. 1996.

Yager, Mike. *Mike Yager's Corvette Bible.* Ed. Tom Collins. Iola, WI: Krause Publications. 2007.

Dedication

To my mother who is now deceased

To my daughter, Cristin and her daughter, Catrina

To my son, David and his family:
David, Jr., Keiara, and Kevin

To my brothers and sisters who have made this journey with me:
Barbara, Janet, Debra, David (Deceased), Gregory, Richard, and their families

To James Lundy (more a brother than a friend) and his family

Preface

At first you may think that my life has been just a series of nightmares, but I am sworn to be completely honest: my life has had more than a few ups and more than a few downs in its course. That is why I designed this book as a series of sequences of my night's sleep. When I look back over my past, I found that it could be very depressing to re-live some of those memories. Nevertheless, I recounted them with painful honesty within these pages. However, in doing so, I revealed the triumphs and the glories that life has brought to me with just as much honesty.

Nightmare Number 1. My life as an adolescent was far from perfect. In fact, life presented me with a series of very strong challenges each in its own place and at its own time. It made my heart ache when I recalled some of the stories of my childhood years that can be found here, but I tried to recall them honestly without a coat of fresh clean paint. I have never looked back to recall what I might have done differently.

REM/Nightmare Number 2. In real life no one episode is exclusive in one way or another throughout. I met "The Love of My Life" during this time, but nightmarish events occurred as a result, hence the title here. As I promised, I shall try to recount all of the events honestly. The Love of My Life had occasion to say to me for the first of many times:

"Wherever you go, I will go."

REM/ Number 3. This was my first foray into adulthood and true independence. I began my professional life at this time. It was wonderful and sweet and all too short but still a truly impactful episode.

Nightmare Number 4. For over forty years I have struggled to bury the memories of the war in Vietnam as deeply inside me as I could beneath life and living. I still cannot talk about some incidents, but I did try during the writing of this memoir to be honest about all that I am now able to talk about, as I promised. Especially, some of the veterans of the Vietnam War might be able to guess about some of those experiences. Recalling the war is part and parcel of the gut-wrenching nightmares that I still experience upon occasion—even until today. I discovered that recalling the faces of some of my fellow soldiers—my buddies—was not any easier for me now than it was when I lost those people. I have tried to relive that time truthfully. I was unable to do that without spilling some of my pain onto these pages.

REM Number 5. The healing process is never a small thing. I needed healing in several areas although I did not realize that I did at the time. All of the people who helped me to heal did not know how big a role they played in my life at that time—not then, but now they do.

REM/Nightmare Number 6. This is another of those mixed episodes. Only in reading it will you will be able to understand why I have classified it as I have. I spent some fruitful years at General Motors Institute and began work on my PhD in Systems Analysis and Design. The strikes I took in my family life can be seen here in painful detail.

Nightmare Number 7. This covers the years that I spent at the large General Motors complex in Saint Louis. What can I say? Losing all your teeth and cutting your permanent teeth all over again might make a fair analogy for that experience. Maybe I think so because I know that it was a life-changing experience with nothing to compare in my life either before or after. Now I know that it was more than a major setback in my personal and professional life—almost a disaster. You will know when you read it.

REM/Nightmare Number 8. The years that I spent at the General Motors plant in Doraville, Georgia were more than life-changing. I met friends that became my friends for life. There were good and bad episodes but that is what happens in real life. I learned so much and grew by leaps and bounds in my professional life there. I have to say that my time in Georgia set the standard for the rest of my life to a very large degree.

Dreamscape Number 9. I tell about my years at the GM Fairfax plant in Kansas City, Missouri. The people beside whom I worked in that plant made me believe that a person's working life can, indeed, be a blessed experience. I will never forget my time in Kansas City although it was my shortest work experience at any location. At that time I found some lost kinsmen and realized my human kinship with all of the people around me.

Awakening! Number 10. This is the book's longest chapter. This phase of my life will surely make my readers say: "Look, Wil, it wasn't all bad. It turned out pretty good for you, after all. You survived and finally thrived. You've built a legacy with **Corvette** that you can be very proud of."

How true.

I am well aware that I can be proud of all the challenges that I have faced and overcome. I can marvel at all of the hardships that I have endured and I have good reason to be very proud that I did not let them stop me. It has taken a long time for me to even think about writing this memoir, but here it is. I know that you will rejoice with me at the end of this, for it has proven to be very cathartic to me.

The Beginning—Fort Worth, Texas—Nightmare Number 1

I was born in Fort Worth, Texas on April 6, 1942. My father disappeared into the Texas countryside after my mother divorced him when I was around three years old and he never returned. He did not return when I graduated from high school. He did not show up when I graduated from college. He was not there for my wedding. He did not see me shipped off to war. He was not there when I claimed my graduate degree. He never met his grandchildren. He did not participate at all in any part of my life.

My father was unable to meet my eyes when at last he looked into my face. It must have been like looking into a younger version of his own face when he finally saw me because, by then, I had become a grown man, a husband, a college graduate, a Vietnam War veteran, a father, a successful electrical engineer, and a corporate executive.

I had been told many, many times by my mother (especially when she was angry at me) that my face looked just like my father's toast-brown face, straight down from the deep cowlicks, wide forehead, dark eyes, high-bridged nose, thin tight lips and stubborn chin. I could tell from looking at the photograph of him that his Aunt Fannie kept on display in her living room that he was very tall and big—a large boned, handsome man with bright eyes, a friendly-looking, smiling face, and coal-black hair brushed back from his wide forehead. It is very easy to understand from looking at his photo why members of the opposite sex were so attracted to him.

It was my father's Aunt, Fannie Mae Melton, who finally prevailed upon me to go to Corsicana, Texas to see him. Aunt Fannie had always talked to me about my father, but this time when she called me, she claimed that he desperately wanted to see me because he was terminally ill. It was already near the end when I walked into his hospital room. I suppose that he had been drowsing when I called his name. His eyes slid open. Hazy and bloodshot, his eyes very slowly focused on my face. Though I knew that he must have recognized me at last, I did not move toward the side of his bed. He had rejected me long ago. He had never been there for me at all when I had needed him most. I felt nothing but coldness toward this man—perhaps some amount of pity but none of the warmth of kinship. I could not bring myself to touch the feeble, trembling hand that he held out toward me.

He uttered but one word: "Junior . . ." Then he closed his eyes and wept as though his heart would surely break. I could tell that he already knew things about me, but he desperately wanted to ask me more questions and I did try to give him some of the answers that he was seeking. Finally, in a wheezy, clogged voice, he begged me not to go just yet, but I really needed to leave. I had an airplane to catch that evening. When I went back to Corsicana less than two weeks later, he was unable to look at me at all because his dark eyes were closed forever. He was laid out in his casket and his once-imposing body was wasted away—the final result of the ravages of pancreatic cancer.

Back in 1945, when I was three years old, my mother grew tired of my father's constant infidelity and womanizing ways. Their divorce was filled with anger and antagonism. She married another man, a sometimes-employed handyman with huge amounts of wit and charm, a flair for the dramatic, and not much else. They had six children together. That brought the total number of children in our house to seven. It meant that my family followed the inevitable downward spiral in life that led to a small, ramshackle, rental house on the other side of the tracks close by the stockyards of Fort Worth. It meant constant hunger for all of us, and constant doing without the necessities of life. It meant that the ever-present smell of the stockyards haunted us day and night. That smell seeped into our house, into our clothes, and into our everyday lives. In spite of such grave hardship, we remained an enduring, close-knit family.

The happiest time for us children was when Aunt Fannie's missionary society took us shopping for clothes during the generosity-inspiring yuletide season. My feet were always too large to fit into the shoes that fell within the youth grouping that was set aside for the charity children, but I made the shoes fit, although my feet sorely suffered and the shoes wore out much quicker than usual. My Mom often said that she would never take a dime of welfare, no matter what. Well, mother never did, but we were always dodging bill collectors because she had missed one or two monthly payments on this bill or that bill. The worse thing, though, was constantly getting evicted from our apartment because our family was far, far overdue on the rent.

Mom worked both daytime and nighttime jobs because her first priority was to keep food on our table. Her first job was as a nurse's aide. Later, she became a licensed practical nurse and that meant more overtime hours for her. In spite of that, life remained a constant struggle for us. My stepfather was a habitual gambler whose losses were legendary so there were hardly ever any "best of times" for our young family because of that.

I quickly learned that every able-bodied person in the house should keep busy trying to earn money for the family. Because I had inherited both my parents' size, wit and charm, I was always able to find work of some kind: sacking groceries at the local market, sweeping out the local barber shop, clearing debris from construction sites, removing trees and bushes from yards, tearing down derelict buildings—any kind of work that was available I did—no matter how hard or dirty it might have been.

Work kept me so busy that I cannot remember ever having time to just enjoy being a carefree kid. I would engage in an occasional football or basketball pick-up game, and everyone always said that I was athletic and very graceful to be such a tall, large-boned, and solidly-built individual. The school's football and basketball coaches constantly prevailed upon me to join their teams but I never had the time to play organized team sports at all when I was in junior high or high school.

In my neighborhood my dearest friends were the guys whom I had fought with when we were young. We never fought in anger—it was, rather, a form of entertainment. We took each other on singly with bare-knuckles and the selected combatants always fought until we saw blood: we gave each other nosebleeds, scrapes, scratches, and black eyes, but we never used knives or any other makeshift weapons although we all possessed them. Somehow our unspoken codes would not allow this, at least, not with each other.

Certainly I had the inclination for doing boyhood mischief but I did not have time to get into any *real* trouble as an adolescent. I *did* steal the hubcaps from the neighbors' cars parked along our street. I *did* throw rolls of toilet paper into the tall trees in the corner neighbor's yard at Halloween. I *did* throw dried dog poop in a brown paper bag onto the grumpy neighbor's concrete stoop down at the dead end of Cottey Street, light a match to it and hide to watch him cursing and snarling dire threats after he ran out, stomped out the fire, and saw what it was. However, I *did not* hang out under the street light on the corner until all hours after dark in the summertime harmonizing with my buddies or planning and participating in mischief. It was always the next day when I would hear about the *real* trouble that my friends had gotten into on the previous evening and what great fun it had been to run from our neighborhood police. I was always too busy working to join in with them. In fact, I worked a full-time job throughout junior high and high school.

Because I was always much taller and more solidly built than the other kids my age, my mother was able to secure a full-time job for me after school at John Peter Smith Hospital where she worked. I would leave school each day right after my last class and go straight to work. I can remember doing the job of a full grown man at the age of 14—cleaning hospital floors, transporting patients, holding patients in X-ray and other machines, helping to restrain unruly patients, removing soiled laundry, dumping bedpans—I did any kind of unskilled labor at the hospital to earn that much needed paycheck for my family. Because of my earnings, my mom and I were able to afford the payments on a small house in Stop Six and meet the payments on a used 1956 Chevrolet Bel Aire. That made it so much easier for us to get to and from work.

Surprisingly, I went to college in September, 1960. In those days, a career that required enrollment at an institution of higher learning seemed sorely out of my reach. During that time, all of the first-rate colleges and universities that would allow African Americans to enroll were located in the distant Northern cities—a long way from Fort Worth, Texas. I knew that if any southern university or college would accept me, it would have to be an HBCU (historically black college or university). God knows, I did not have a prayer—let alone a stray nickel—that would pay the tuition for me to get into ***any*** college anywhere.

However, during my senior year, Mr. H. L. King, the principal of I. M. Terrell High School, sat me down in his office and convinced me that college just might be possible for me. He was familiar with my family history and he knew what a hard worker that I always was. I was a better-than-average student, my grades were good, my cumulative average was more than adequate, but, above all, my record was clean. He convinced me that I should have an academic future. With his help, I completed the paperwork that secured the scholarships and student loans that I needed to get me into Tennessee State Agricultural and Industrial University (TSU) in Nashville, Tennessee.

I had once dreamed of studying medicine, but extreme lack of money has a way of quickly putting such dreams to rest. I knew that I had to be realistic. Eventually (I don't know exactly when), I found myself really believing that I needed to become an electrical engineer—no less of a career that required toughness of will, tenaciousness, and constant study. By the time I was a freshman at TSU, my dreams had finally solidified into rock-hard determination.

Tennessee State University—Nashville, TN—REM/Nightmare Number 2

When I first got to TSU in the fall of 1960, working toward my dream took all of my time as well as my attention. The day-to-day rigor of academics at TSU and the part-time work that I landed as an orderly at Meharry Medical College up the street from TSU gave me no free time at all. Still, I managed to enjoy a few rare moments of leisure with the friends I had made among my fellow electrical engineering students. Man! Could we ever make good use of even our smallest bit of freedom!

If we all had that rare, lucky, free week-end together, we would catch a football game or a basketball game depending on the season. Whenever we were able to scrape together the smallest amount of extra cash, we would pool it and buy cheap wine, mix it with beer and get absolutely, gloriously buzzed. Then, we would go and have a rollicking, boisterous good time in the bleachers of the gym at a basketball game or in the stands of the stadium at a football game. If the weather was warm enough, we would end our day sitting on the low wall outside the cafeteria ogling the beautiful co-eds who came walking down the hill from the female dormitories at dinner time. Thinking about that now, I can see how we must have really embarrassed those poor girls who dared to walk near us. Sometimes, our language could get pretty salty.

In reality, I had to spend as much time as I could buried in the library using the library's books to get my studying done. When I was working my job at Meharry I located several out-of-the-way places where I could be alone with my notes to cram when exams were coming up.

In 1962, during my sophomore year, something happened to completely change my life: a pretty little girl, Elizabeth Walton, caught my eye. I found out the reason that I had never seen her before: she had just arrived at TSU. She was a transfer student from a small institution in her hometown of Holly Springs, Mississippi. The school was Mississippi Industrial College, a college established by the

Christian Methodist Episcopal (CME) Church. Liz quickly became an academic star at TSU and was pledging a sorority, Delta Sigma Theta, when I first saw her. I watched her for a long time before I dared to speak to her. I always tied up with my steady girlfriend or some other date but still I tried to get near Liz and I found that she was as sweet and friendly as she appeared to be.

I was pledging Omega Psi Phi Fraternity and our two Greek groups found several occasions to get together: parties, fundraising, and academic study. It was purely by chance that I managed to get Liz alone at a house party given by one of the pledgees who lived in the city. I introduced myself and just so I could talk to her and get to know her, I questioned her thoroughly about herself and what she was studying (although I had found out almost everything about her already from some of her friends). I managed to work my way to her side and hold hands with her on a memorable civil rights march in downtown Nashville. We often sat together at numerous planning sessions after that.

Before long, I would smile when I thought of something that Liz had said or laugh at some trick she had pulled on her big sisters while we were pledgees. After a while, Liz was the only person that I constantly thought about and had the requisite amorous dreams about. I didn't think that it could ever happen to a sworn playboy like me but before I knew it, that little, laughing, brown-eyed girl had ensnared my heart completely. I found out that I was not alone—I soon recognized what had to be the light of love in her pretty, sparkling dark eyes whenever those eyes met mine and lingered for just a little too long. I would sometimes catch her watching me when we happened to be at the same place and I was with my steady girl. She would always look quickly away, but once I caught a roguish wink from her when I was clandestinely out on a date with some other female at a place where Liz and her friends happened to be.

I was thrilled beyond belief when Liz finally told me how much she wanted to be with me. I shall never forget that day.

It was a Sunday afternoon and nobody had any extra money to do anything or to go anywhere special. I whispered to Liz that I needed to talk to her at a place where we could be alone. Her eyes searched my face but she nodded solemnly as we sat across the table from each other in the cafeteria after a late lunch. She said softly:

"Library. Five o'clock."

It took a real effort but we managed to sneak away from all of our constant companions and we met at the library at five. We took a walk down the back way from the campus to the park down the street from the university where we might be alone. We were hoping that no one would come looking for either one of us. We sat on a bench together.

It was one of the first warm days of spring. The trees were just beginning to bud, and the sunlight was so golden that it drove all the memories of the past dreary winter days right out of our thoughts. I could not wait to put my arms around Liz. My heart was thundering like a runaway train when my lips touched her soft lips at last. I had never experienced such sweetness in my entire life. I told her truthfully that I had never wanted to be with any other woman as much as I wanted to be with her. Liz admitted that she really wanted to be with me, too, but each of us had very real difficulties.

Liz already had what she called "an obligation" meaning a ring on the third finger of her left hand put there on the past Christmas holiday by her long-time boyfriend back in her hometown. There was simply no way that I could respect her "obligation" when I wanted her so much for myself. Even more of a giant roadblock was my own well-known "obligation."

The absolute devotion of my steady girlfriend was known to almost everyone. She told anyone who would listen that she and I were going to be married and bragged that it was going to happen soon. I had never denied it, but even before I first held Liz in my arms I knew what I had to do. If I ever married anyone, I could not even imagine that it would be anyone else but Liz.

Certainly, I was in no position yet to ask anything of Liz but I could not stand looking at another man's ring on her finger and knowing that it gave him a legitimate claim on her. So, I told her one evening as we sat at a table in the library after we "happened" to meet there.

"Trust me. Give that ring back to him. Someday soon, I swear, I'm going to put my own ring on your finger. Just trust me."

Liz did not even blink. She took off her fiancé's ring on the spot and put it into the pocket of the short, white leather jacket that she always wore. It absolutely warmed my heart to know that she trusted in me that much. I knew that I had to get myself free of my "obligation" too, somehow and soon.

On a long week-end soon after we had talked, Liz took the bus home to Holly Springs, Mississippi. When she returned, she told me that she had tried to give the ring back to her high school sweetheart but he had become very difficult. He refused to take his ring back and it seemed that both their families had involved themselves.

Liz told me that her mother and many of her relatives spoke sternly about the grave mistake that Liz was surely making. I could well understand that breaking the engagement was not an easy thing for Liz to do. She told me that she and her boyfriend had been "exclusive" since high school and the guy seemed to believe that she belonged to him already. They had made promises of fidelity to each other. Her relatives seemed to want Liz to behave as if she were already married despite the fact that Liz had twice refused to go through with any formal ceremony.

So I held my silence and tried to be understanding when I learned later that the guy seemed ready to do anything and go to any lengths to try to keep Liz. He was anything but a rejected suitor and seemed to want to overwhelm Liz with his attentiveness. He would turn up on the campus almost every week-end driving a brand new black Pontiac Catalina. He would stay for the week-end at the motel down the street from the university and come up to the campus to ride Liz and her friends around in his car. He tried very hard to prevail upon Liz to keep her promise to him.

I had at various times made promises of fidelity to my steady girlfriend whenever it suited me. She pretended not to be aware of what everyone else already knew: I had a roving eye and no intention at all of settling down at any time soon. I had always been adept at engaging in various flirtations which I could be sure that she would quickly dispatch and willingly forgive. But when someone told her that I had been seeing Liz as much as I had, she did not take that news well at all. She knew that this was quite a different matter.

She became overly possessive and very difficult to deal with. She neglected her academics and dropped other things that she should have been doing so that she could keep a much closer eye on me. I never knew when she was going to show up outside my classroom door to walk with me to my next class. As she had done many times in the past, she would lie to her dormitory matrons, leave for the week-end pretending to go home, but of course she came straight to the apartment that I shared with three other roommates. She clung to me like a shadow on a sunny day and threatened any number of dire consequences including suicide if I did not stay with her. It was not at all easy to for me to disentangle myself from my past love interest but I knew that I had to do it because I wanted Liz so much.

One evening when Liz and my two roommates' girlfriends were visiting at the apartment, my constant girlfriend showed up at the door (it was bound to happen, as much as I dreaded it). We were all eating popcorn that the girls had brought for the occasion and watching a program on the finicky second-hand TV that we had pooled our limited finances to acquire. My roommates were at the door in a flash trying to run interference for me. They were hoping to convince my irate girlfriend that I was not inside. She refused to believe them. She was prepared to spend the week-end and loudly demanded to come in, so I went outside and told her that Liz was inside with me and that I intended to keep on seeing her. I also declared that she and I were finished. Of course she did not accept it readily nor did she leave immediately. When she finally left, it was with all-too public drama but I was more than relieved to come clean and have the double life that I was leading over. I didn't realize then that it was not yet done . . .

My problematic former girlfriend swallowed a bottle of aspirin or some kind of medication and wound up first at the infirmary on campus. When it happened for the second time she was taken to Meharry Hospital down on Jefferson Street. The doctors had to pump her stomach out, and then pump it again. She knew that I worked part-time at Meharry and she kept on asking for me.

When I went in to see her, she begged me to stay with her. I tried to talk reasonably to her and to make her see that she would not accomplish anything by harming herself, but she was relentless and determined to cling to me, while I was equally determined not to be ensnared that way. In spite of my grown-up facade, I really was not prepared at all to handle the trap of responsibility such as she was constructing. I had been forced into the full responsibilities of adulthood at age 14, but this was an experience unlike any soul-rending, titanic burden that I had ever carried. I knew that I had been very careful up to this point, and I felt that I had been extremely responsible by not ever leaving any element of protection in her hands at all. I did not recognize it at the time, but now I know that what I felt more than anything was the two-pronged, boiling anger and desperation of a hunted animal being forced unfairly into a corner. I think that it was more for my sake than for hers that the doctors decided that she needed to be totally confined. I was truly relieved when her parents came and took her back home to Arkansas.

I knew well enough that Liz had heard the flying rumors, enhanced greatly by the fertile imaginations of her sorority sisters and other females in her dorm, no doubt. I had found that young men whom I knew also had a real enjoyment of gossip and gab—they tended to add their own fiction to the facts. I hardly even recognized the story when my roommates related to me the various versions that they had heard around campus.

The long Thanksgiving holiday week-end had come by the time I finally went up to Hankal Hall to talk to Liz. It was no surprise that I had been drinking as much as my finances would allow. I was initially dismayed and then enraged to find that Liz had gone home to Holly Springs for the Thanksgiving week-end without telling me anything about her plans. It did not occur to me that I was being unreasonable or that I had been otherwise occupied and unreachable for a while. Fortunately, alcohol rendered me more silent and menacing than loud and boisterous, so I managed to get the information from one of Liz's sarcastic friends that Liz had gone home and I had vented my temper to her before the frowning and disapproving dorm matrons could make a real issue of it. Luckily, I got out of there but I knew that I had inadvertently caused more gossip to get started.

By Sunday evening, I was remorseful, subdued, and thoroughly hung over. Some unknown instinct told me to go to the library. I found that Liz had come back and she had not run home for comfort to her old flame as her sorority sister had so cattily insisted. I was overjoyed to find Liz sitting quietly, reading a book at the table in the library that had become "our table" by our own designation and frequent use.

Liz gave me the love and comfort that I needed without questions or recriminations. She had believed in me and trusted me from the first and she had been willing to stand aside and wait quietly without demands until I was able to get my dilemma resolved. There had never been any strings of any kind attached to her love. Now that I was free, I craved a sweet yoke of attachment to Liz. There was no reason anymore, but I felt ready to destroy anyone or anything that might threaten the fire-forged bond that had formed between the two of us.

In the summer of 1962, I went with my buddies, Napoleon Hornbuckle, Ulysses Williams, Edward Boyd and William Hampton to Bridgeton, New Jersey where we had heard that we might get jobs unloading tomatoes at Hunt's Ketchup factory. Luckily, we were all hired and we rented two rooms at Sweetie's Rooming House. We worked for twelve hours a day unloading crates of tomatoes from the trucks that brought them in. It was hard work but all of us were willing to stick it out because we all had goals in mind. I guess that some of the guys wanted to buy new clothes so that they could appeal to various ladies, but my motives were carved in stone. I wanted to earn enough money to finish up my leftover tuition assessments and to have enough money to put a down payment on a ring I had selected for Liz that had one perfect diamond in its setting.

When we returned to Nashville that fall, I was able to buy the engagement set that I wanted. Of course, there were monthly payments left after my initial down payment. I truly appreciated it when Ulysses' mother co-signed a note for me to be able to afford the rings. I took Liz to a night spot on Jefferson Street that was a favorite of ours because there was no cover charge at the door. I proposed to Liz with all my friends and their dates around us. There were tears in Liz's eyes when she said "yes" and we celebrated until curfew time when the girls had to get back to their dorm. I was really worried when I took Liz up to the front doors of Hankal Hall.

My buddies and I waited while Liz and the girls went inside the dorm because none of them were drinkers and their wobbliness from drinking our draft beer and wine mixture was really funny until they had to run the gamut of the two dormitory matrons at Hankal Hall. Liz told me later that she had distracted both the matrons by showing them her ring. While the matrons' backs were turned the other girls went shakily through the two heavy inner doors. Liz told me later that they all laughed like crazy at each other's efforts to make it up the flight of stairs to the second floor.

After her graduation that year, Liz got a job as an eleventh grade English teacher at Melrose High School in Memphis, Tennessee. She needed a car to get around, so her father helped her to buy a used four-door, blue and white Pontiac Catalina. She kept the highway hot between Memphis and Nashville running back and forth to be with me on weekends.

We were married in Holly Springs during the Christmas break of 1963. Liz made her own wedding gown. She and her sister, Florestine sewed all of the attendant's dresses: they stayed up every night sewing matching yellow dresses for three of Liz's cousins who were going to serve as her bridesmaids. I borrowed a coat from Liz's cousin Clara's husband Sylvester Ford. I was not at all comfortable in Liz's hometown nor was I in favor of having a formal wedding, but I agreed to being married by Liz's pastor Reverend Oree Broomfield in old Anderson Chapel Church on Memphis Street. I could not deny Liz her dream of wearing a white wedding gown and coming down the aisle in the church of her childhood while her family and friends looked on.

I went back to the university after the New Year, 1964, a newly married man with a new attitude about everything. I was already a serious student before then, but afterwards, I became even more determined to graduate and find myself a good, permanent job.

I kept my part-time job at Meharry and leased a one-bedroom apartment at the Jeffersonian apartments on Jefferson Street during my last year-and-a-half at TSU. Liz and I spent some happy times there in our apartment with the beat-up old television and the broken-down furniture that I had collected from numerous friends' apartments. The sagging couch had bricks for one of its legs and the matching chair had such loose springs that it was almost impossible to get out of it once a person had sat down because its weak springs allowed the seat to drop down between the arms almost to the floor.

I managed to graduate from Tennessee State a year later as a newly-minted electrical engineer. I was pleased and proud that I received several good job offers. The *Nashville Tennessean* newspaper in Nashville gave the graduating engineers from TSU a really good write-up. I saw my picture in the newspapers for the very first time in my life.

General Mills, Incorporated—Toledo, Ohio—REM Number 3

I was heavily recruited by General Mills, Incorporated of Toledo (the **other** GM—what a coincidence)! They manufactured Wheaties, Cheerios, and Cocoa Puffs breakfast cereals, along with Betty Crocker cake mixes and desserts. When I decided to take that job in January, it was then that I first heard these words from Liz's lips:

"Wherever you go, I will go."

Liz resigned from her job as a classroom teacher at Melrose in Memphis and we packed up and moved to Toledo, Ohio to finally start our lives together. I went to work for General Mills as a process engineer.

We found a one-bedroom apartment very near my work. Then, we bought a living room sofa, two chairs, a bed and a television set. We kept the old table and two iron chairs from the apartment in Nashville and we made those do for our small kitchenette. I traded Liz's Pontiac Catalina for a brand-new, dark–blue, four-speed Pontiac GTO which both of us loved to drive. Liz found a job as a social worker and she needed to use the car most of the time to visit her clients. We settled down to live the life of carefree newlyweds thinking that we might eventually save up enough money to buy a modest house with the extra income that Liz was bringing in.

Our carefree life ended in1966 when I was drafted by the United States Army during the infamous Vietnam conflict. I had to put my civilian career with General Mills on hold while I went off to serve my country. No one ever said so, but I knew that if I tried, I might find an alternative of some kind, or, at least, a way to put the inevitable on hold until the conflict might come to an end. If that happened, my military service might then not be needed. I refused to even consider any of that. After all, the people who had been my colleagues, classmates, fellow engineers, and lifetime friends were putting their lives on the line to go off to a foreign and hostile land to serve their country. How could I even consider doing anything less?

I went first to Fort Leonard Wood for basic training. After that, once again, Liz had occasion to say:

"Wherever you go, I will go."

Liz left her job as a social worker in Toledo, put the furniture that we had accumulated into storage and came with me to Fort Sill, Oklahoma to officer's candidate school. We found a fairly comfortable furnished trailer that an army sergeant had advertised for rent and Liz lived there while I had to live on post during Officer's Candidate School (OCS).

Liz quickly decided that she would not be idle. She took an Army aptitude test that yielded an excellent score. She was pleasantly surprised that the test showed she would do well with mathematical calculations because she often declared that she absolutely hated math and was no good at it. She took a job as a computer programmer with the Department of the Army. She told me that she really enjoyed her job and she was learning a lot about computers. When I had taken classes in engineering at TSU computers were huge room-sized contraptions using lights, whirling disks, magnetic tapes and trays of cards with strategic holes punched into them. Liz told me that the computers that the Army used were still just as big and complicated. I had always figured that most women would have a problem coping with that, but Liz laughed and said that most of the people who worked in her department were women who were married to servicemen.

OCS was rigorous. I thought many a time: If I drop out of this, then what?

Demerits were given to any cadet for lack of neatness, lack of academic attainment and other "slacking" as it was termed. We were allowed to go off post to visit our wives in the city on weekends if we had not collected any demerits. I never got enough demerits for "punishment" which meant a run up the hill and back. I became the corps honor man, but I did make a ceremonial run up the hill at the end of training.

I was allowed to visit Liz often which made her very happy. There were days set aside that our wives could drive onto the post and we were allowed to come out to talk to them through the car window while they sat in the car and we stood at ease outside. It was funny how those visiting days became so precious to us especially if the recruits were confined and not allowed to leave the post at all for some reason.

Liz made a beautiful, yellow dress shot with gold threads to wear at the graduating officers' ball. When they introduced the wives of the officers, I was very proud of her. My family all came up for my graduation: my mother, my brothers, my sisters and Aunt Fanny all came. I wanted my mother and Aunt Fannie to pin the Lieutenant's bars on my shoulders but the crowd was so large that my mother and the girls and Aunt Fannie got hung up in it and did not get a chance. Liz and my younger brother, David had to do it. We all went out to dinner and everyone raised a glass of wine to salute me as a newly minted Army artillery officer. Then, it was obvious that my training was over. It was time for me to go for intensive training for combat. And, it was time once again for Liz to say:

"Wherever you go, I will go."

Liz again left her job and moved with me to Barstow, California where I learned to be an Army artillery officer and a forward observer. Liz sent for our furniture and we moved into the Officers' Quarters which were two-story barracks on the post. We spent many happy week-ends running around the country side and into Los Angeles. We looked up old friends and relatives and we made connections with a few classmates who were living in California at the time. We did not remind any of our friends who had predicted that our marriage would not last that they were wrong. They had believed because of my somewhat carefree past that we would not still be together.

As soon as my training was over I moved Liz back to Memphis and I went off to Vietnam where I spent twelve full months on the DMZ (demilitarized zone) first as a forward observer, then as the commander of the First of the 40th Artillery Battalion.

The Vietnam War—DMZ, South/North Vietnam—Nightmare Number 4

I can still vividly remember the plane ride over to Vietnam. My Army aptitude tests had shown that one of my particular talents was survival skills (no surprise there). So, I was being sent to replace a Forward Observer who had been badly wounded when his company had been overrun by the North Vietnamese army. I looked every bit the part of a new, clean shaven, second lieutenant: my shoes were spit-shined and glowing; I was nattily dressed in freshly laundered, stiffly starched, pressed and creased dress khakis; my cap sat jauntily on my head sporting the shiny gold bar that signified my rank. I carried my garments and gear in a new, black, leather, zip-up valise.

I was being deployed with a number of soldiers who were returning into the combat zone from a rotation of rest and recuperation (R and R)—some from Hawaii and some from the mainland. They were already scruffily clad for combat in rough jungle gear and I noticed that they were already armed—pistols at their sides, rifles in their hands. They looked me up and down before saluting half-heartedly then they dismissed me completely as they joked and laughed loudly among themselves. I settled into the transport, made myself as comfortable as possible, and slept for most of the airplane ride. As we landed on our first stop in Vietnam, I sat up to notice that the joviality amongst the men had lowered in volume quite a bit. It was no more than a "Rest and Stretch" stop for us. Here our transport took on more fuel and supplies.

As we went deeper into the country in large Army transport trucks, and got closer to the DMZ, the joviality amongst the men disappeared completely—totally replaced by an air of tension that was thick enough to cut with the switchblade that long habit and living in Stop Six made me carry in my pocket into the combat zone.

By this time, the soldier's firearms were no longer loosely held, but clutched almost into the "ready" position. There was no banter now—their lips were flattened. If they spoke at all, they spoke in low, guttural, one-word whispers, and their eyes had become no more than glittering slits as their heads turned this way and that way toward the small openings on both sides of the transport. Damn! I thought. I could not help it—I felt my own muscles tightening and my nerves tensing up, too.

After the cargo was off-loaded, I was the last man to step out of one the transports and I hadn't made it down to the last step when I heard a deep-throated, hollow sound like thunder low to the ground or a gigantic finger being pulled out of an equally gigantic bottle sending deep reverberations into the air:

Thoooop!!

The low, oppressive sound alone seemed to shake the air for miles around and the reverberations seemed to suck our eardrums against the insides of our heads. That sound was destined to have a place in my worst nightmares for the rest of my life.

Our transports were hastily moved, they were trying to make it out of harm's way among the virtual storm of dust and trash while hell was belching up fire and brimstone all around us. Some of the scruffy vegetation that remained around the airstrip were blasted out and went flying wildly across the pock-marked ground. Dirt, sticks, and rocks flew high up into the air, and then rained back down on us. There it was again:

Thoooop!!

Like the rest of the men, I could only run for my life, ducking, dodging, and zigzagging across the cratered ground of the wide open airstrip toward some unfamiliar shelter just as I had learned to do back in basic training.

I was in totally unfamiliar territory plus I was being shot at! Somehow, in the flash and confusion (I do not know to this day how it happened) I stepped into the fortifications and a coil of unseen barbed wire snagged onto my foot. I went down like a ton of bricks into the muck that was the ground. The rope used for entrapment with the barbed wire encircled my ankle.

I surely was not going to linger out there in the open if there was to be another barrage of fire. I was all too aware of my un-armored state. I kicked and flailed like a madman until a large plug from the leg of my muddy pants was ripped out by the wire. My muddy left shoe was badly gouged and torn. I must have been acting on pure instinct now because, somehow—I really don't know just how—I pulled out the switchblade from my pocket, popped it open, and sliced through the rope that had ensnared my ankle. I had already dropped my bag and lost my cap, but I was not about to spend a minute more of time right then trying to locate or gather up either of them. Sheer panic got me onto my feet and moved me off that airstrip in record time.

"Too close!" I mumbled shakily as I thought about my family, "Just too damn close."

"Good job, Sir!" One of the men said with a buck-toothed grin. "You sure can run!"

Afterwards, I armored up. I outfitted myself with a bulletproof vest, two bandoliers of bullets to crisscross my body, a sidearm, two hand grenades, an almost—machete knife in a carrier on my belt, a rifle, a steel helmet, and pair of heavy boots. I was not about to be so utterly vulnerable when I went out on my first patrol into the Vietnam countryside.

I returned from my first patrol dragging tail like a plow horse at suppertime. Sweat poured down my body, drenching my clothing and gear right down to my combat boots. The heavy humidity mixed with my sweat was steaming off me like I was a hot, red lobster just pulled from a pot of boiling water. Our company's Non-Commissioned Officer, a gruff, battle-hardened, cigar chomping bear of a man, peered at me and gave out a loud, rumbling laugh.

"Sir, it ain't no need for you to wear all that shit," he said in his tobacco-roughened voice, "You get that close to them gooks, all you need is your sidearm and maybe a rifle. You get captured, you just gotta' make sure you got one goddam' bullet saved to put through your own temple."

I quickly learned how to make my big, 6' 6" body smaller and lighter any way that I could because as a forward observer, I often went on patrol alone or with a very small unit of South Vietnamese Army Regulars. The SVA regulars were all short enough in statue and thin enough to be covered and camouflaged by the tall, waving grass while I stood well above grass level like a giant California redwood tree—an easy and inviting target. Despite my size, when I was alone, my training kicked in: I avoided the open spaces and I knew just how to melt into the jungle or to fade into a stand of trees like a whiff of breath. If danger was near I was more than adept at hiding in plain sight. My training had taught me how to move silently, remain motionless, and to watch and listen.

When I was with the SVA regulars I made myself become one of them. When the regulars turned, I turned. If they ran, I ran with them. If they hit the dirt, so did I and in quick order. If they shot their guns, I fired my weapon, too, in the same general direction that they were shooting whether I had located or locked onto a target or not. I told myself sarcastically that if they shit or went blind, so would I.

When I think about it now, I believe that it had to be the fervent and constant prayers of my wife, my mother, and the rest of my family that kept me safe on more than one harrowing occasion. I prayed, too, and since I was pretty much a lapsed Christian living through the hell of Vietnam, I could only hope that God had not become totally unfamiliar with me.

I can well remember the armored convoy that we rode in from one place to another to place our large weapons and dig bunkers. The captain and I were leading the convoy in a jeep. When we stopped on the pitted, rough, dirt road, the Captain told me to run back and give the Sargent Major our new information and to tell the driver of the huge transport just behind the jeeps not to drive so closely. I jumped from the jeep with the information. Some strong feeling made me stop. I yelled the information to the Sargent Major and to the driver of the huge truck behind us. Both nodded acknowledgement. The minute we started our engines and the truck began to lumber forward, it happened. An IED exploded at just the spot that I imagined that I might have stepped to convey the information. Two of the huge tires of the transport exploded and debris and shrapnel landed all around us. Both the Captain and I had to wipe our sweaty faces and swallow hard. That could have been my end right there.

Even today, in the throes of a hot, sweaty nightmare, I relive our fierce battles there on the DMZ. I can still hear the buzzing whine of those bullets passing too close to my head. I admit it: I feel again that sheer and utter panic that I felt uncountable times on the DMZ and my body switches once again into sheer survival mode. I vividly remember each and every firefight that we had—each one different in some way, yet each one the very same in the basic way:

I smell the sizzling, hot, smoky smell of lead clogging and weighing the air as a round whizzes past me. I swallow hard, and I can taste the acid burn from my clenched-up stomach heaving bile up into my throat every time those shots come so agonizingly close. I get a dark, greasy, sweaty, heaviness settling over me like a thick blanket. That's when I know that one of those rounds has found its mark, but I realize that my heart is still thumping furiously and I need desperately to breathe because I am still alive. I do not realize it yet but it was a rocket blast that knocked me completely off my feet and the force of my fall has crushed the breath from my lungs. Then, I taste the mixture of bile, blood, and grit in my mouth and dust clogging my nose because dirt has smashed up to spray all over me. I don't have the slightest idea how long I have been down, but when I manage to lift my head, I can see one of my gunners through the still-swirling dust. He was getting ready to feed a round into gun number four. The large, unexploded metal round lies on the ground near our feet where he has dropped it. I come to fully realize then that both of us are on the ground side by side. I can see no sign at all of any of the other members of our company. Ironically, an enemy rocket has smashed down on our position in just that breath of time. I cannot speak but horror settles over me as I become aware that there is no need now to issue any orders. Not anymore. My gunner's blue/green eyes are wide open but they have no depth, no vision—they are sightless. I realize finally that I am only shaken up—slammed down hard off the gun stand and onto the ground. I have a few scratches and bruises. It is my gunner's blood and body mixed with the dirt that covers us both. Our big gun has somehow protected me. Shrapnel from the rocket has blown my gunner's right arm and most of his right side completely away.

That vivid nightmare and its vicious relatives have lived in my subconscious mind since Vietnam. My war experience has never become any less of a real presence, although it does not appear in my dreams quite the same each time or quite as often anymore.

My company fired 105 self-propelled artillery howitzers at all hours of the day and night. We constantly dodged the incoming North Vietnam missiles and rockets by taking cover in deeply hollowed-out ground bunkers. We had to be on the alert and ready to shoot at a moment's notice because the native enemy, the Viet Cong regulars had the capability to be anywhere and everywhere—all around us. But because we were so close to North Vietnam we were always their targets. They watched us continually through their binoculars and night scopes just like we constantly watched them. If we were standing in the chow line, the invisible Viet Cong would call in fire from the NVA point position nearest the DMZ and they would start shooting their Russian-made long range missiles and firing their rockets at us.

Thoooop!!

Food would go flying everywhere as we dropped our trays to duck and cover.

Anytime we felt like sitting outside to smoke or getting out on the court to have a little recreation by playing a game of pick-up basketball, we were sure to get a few mortar rounds right in the middle of our game to make us scatter like a flock of chickens to grab our weapons and scramble hard for the bunkers.

Thoooop!!

There could never be any peace at any time because the Viet Cong could often be expected to slip in close as they could and attack us with rifles and hand-held artillery. We had to constantly keep lookouts posted to stop them.

I can still see the face of the Captain, our company leader, who was scheduled to leave the company for home the very next day. His rotation was done. The NVA had been highly active all week. They had been shooting at our position for most of the day, so we were staying pretty close inside our bunkers. We broke out some warm beer to toast the coming departure of our CO. We were all happy for him. Then, Cap got up and stretched. He was such a soft-spoken and likeable guy. I guess he intended to step just outside the bunker to get fresh air or take a quick piss. We thought nothing of it; I suppose we all were just a little dull but still, the familiar, far away and hollow-sounding . . .

Thoooop!!

. . . that signaled incoming mortar fire would have spruced us all up and Cap would have had time to get back into the bunker. We hadn't heard anything—so we were not immediately concerned—all was pretty quiet. Then, we heard it: three quick shots, someone shouting, then some popping rifle shots followed by three or four more. It was only a second or two before reality dawned:

Cap was still outside.

The sergeant major was the first to jump up. He threw down the blunt that he was always chewing on and started cussin' like nobody's business. We grabbed our weapons and we all rushed out of the bunker, but we were too late. Cap was on the ground. His blood was already pooling around him. Obviously, a deadly Viet Cong suicide sniper had somehow made it past the changing watch. We couldn't know how the hell it happened but that Cong bastard had done his dirty work. It didn't help the Cap, but our base string had made the Cong pay the price. Small in stature, shirtless and painfully thin, he lay face down with his weapon next to his outstretched hand. Blood was still seeping onto the ground from his ruined head. There was a dirty, blood-soaked band that was still tied around his greasy, black hair.

It could have happened to any one of us. Any man could have been the first one to step outside at just that moment. We couldn't even look at one another. Some of the men, including me, got really sick to their stomachs and more than one of us turned aside to throw up. Everybody had tears in his eyes. The terrible irony was just too mind-crushing: Cap was due to go home tomorrow! We didn't know what to say, but we were all thinking the same thing:

"Oh, Damn! Damn! Damn! Aww Cap . . . If only he hadn't gone outside just then . . . Damn!"

Finally, the sergeant major said it for every one of us:

"Now we owe 'em—we really owe 'em, boys! We gotta' make 'em pay big time for the Cap! That's all this goddamn war is about for us right now . . ."

They were my men now and we made a rock-solid pact: we made sure to shoot first, ask questions later . . . if we asked questions at all. Most of all, we made sure to never, ever let our guards down. Not only was it "all for one and one for all," we swore to be super careful.

I was no longer the forward observer in command of the intelligence, I was fully in charge of the whole company now and I meant to take every one of those men home. We vowed that we would stay alert and get the hell off that DMZ. We damn well didn't intend to do it in a horizontal position either.

Truth be told, it was not always the NVA who caused more than a few American deaths: it was our own B-52 and stealth bombers.

They flew over the battle zones, stealthily and with less accuracy than anyone was willing to admit, they rained bombs and missiles down on enemy and ally alike. Their strafing runs were pure hell on earth. It was a deluge that destroyed all of the life and vegetation within their range: they changed the whole landscape and the courses of many an undecided battle. When we got intelligence that they had been called in, we welcomed them during the close, nasty firefights. But we were careful that our cover was deep enough and that our communication was good and as clear as possible with them. Needless to say, we welcomed their help but we feared their deadly mistakes pretty badly.

I do not think I will ever forget the wildlife in the countryside of Vietnam: the rare orange and black tigers that melted into the shadows of the jungles with their luminous, yellow, staring eyes looking as if they were in as much distress and fear of us as we were of them; the wild pigs with their long, dangerous-looking tusks and rims of foam at their lips; the roaming, savage-eyed packs of wild dogs looking as if they could never have been anyone's pets at any time; the skittering, chattering monkeys that might have been fun to watch if we had the time or inclination to watch them. We encountered them all at one time or another while we were out on patrol. I have to admit, the animals sometimes served as good target practice for us. But, for the most part, we had the good sense to stay alert for them, to stay away from them, and to never wander abroad alone because of them.

We absolutely hated the insects. Those buzzing gnats, the annoying flies, the stinging wasps, the biting fleas, and the ravenous mosquitos nearly drove us crazy! Malaria shots and other vaccinations protected us from the vast majority of the insect-borne diseases, thank God.

The rats were as bad as the insect pests. They seemed huge. They stayed out of our way—they were insidious. Scurrying off away from us, they looked like sorry mounds of dirt covered with hair, trailing their scaly, hairless tails behind them. We swore that they were able to chew their way into anything—any food supply that we stored—even foodstuffs that was stored in tin cans.

There was no protection for us from the absolute worst nightmare pest of them all.

Those were the horrible, red colored, giant centipedes with their six to ten inch, shiny, segmented, bodies. They crawled on their many, hairy legs right inside our bunkers especially during wet season—the monsoon rains. We went to extreme lengths to protect ourselves from them everywhere inside our bunkers. We especially feared that they would crawl onto us while we were trying to grab a few winks. We even went as far as wrapping ourselves in netting and swathing up in mosquito wraps to try to fend them off. A boot-clad man could stomp one of the creepy crawlers into the dirt and the thing would make a screeching noise loud enough for everyone sheltering in the bunker to hear. But, even that might not kill the giant crawling horror.

Often, a critter would keep right on running on its thousand legs even after a soldier had whaled the hell out of it with whatever makeshift weapon that was handy. The sting of the giant centipede could be really, really painful and the venom could make even the biggest, toughest man awfully sick. Viet Cong bullets didn't strike much more fear into our hearts than the Vietnam centipede did. Cong bullets seemed less insidious and seemed easier to dodge.

I was all too aware that we were not to discharge a weapon inside the close quarters of the bunker—I had issued such orders myself on more than one occasion. However, I shot a particularly large, hairy centipede that was crawling toward me inside the bunker with my sidearm—put two rounds right into it—I hated and feared those things that much. Even today, I still harbor some pretty vivid nightmares about being stung or bitten by one of those big, hairy, many-legged, crawly creatures. For me, those nightmarish menaces destroyed any notion that I might ever have entertained about camping out in the woods for fun.

After five and a half months on the DMZ, I realized that I was soon to be due for some R and R (Rest and Relaxation). I had written letters to my wife, to my mother and my family whenever I could but I never told them exactly when I might be pulled out of the war zone for R and R. There was a very good reason why I had not done so. The GIs on the demilitarized zone really had to be careful of any information that they might give out in writing. We all had been warned during briefings that we could not divulge our position or anything else in letters we wrote home. So, I always wrote that I was doing well; that I missed them all; and I reminisced about things that we had done together. I never told my family exactly where my unit was located, what we were doing, or anything else of any significance. I knew that all of our written communications had to be thoroughly censored because of the possibility that it might be intercepted by the enemy.

Then too, I was just busy trying to keep body and soul together. There were the day-to-day responsibilities that weighed upon me so heavily: keeping my men alert and safe; making sure that all the men looked after their health as well as keeping sharp eyes on their responsibilities; supervising the perimeter reinforcements; making sure the men kept our guns and equipment in good working order; making sure that the outer reinforcements were in place; and grabbing some sleep myself whenever and wherever I could.

I found myself constantly worried by the two-headed beast of my dilemma: I desperately wanted to see my wife when my turn came around for R and R, but I also desperately dreaded our meeting because I knew that Liz would be shocked when she laid eyes on me. The damn war had surely taken a toll on me physically. Like every GI who was charged with guarding the demilitarized zone, pushing the limits of personal grooming had become more than a way of life for me. When we were in the field we never gave a second thought to bathing, shaving or changing our clothes—that was not our main concern. We were just too damned busy trying to stay alive. I was unable to give much consideration to my personal hygiene for sometimes days on end. I had become more than adept at living on the line.

Our latrines were holes in the ground. We sometimes put open-ended cans over the holes so we could use tops over them. Sometimes we used drums that we would fill with diesel fuel and set on fire when they got filled up. The smell from that operation stunk to high heaven—it was enough to keep God as well as the enemy a long way away from our position for the duration.

Our showers were makeshift canvas enclosures jury-rigged with rain water or the water trucked in to our position by the huge water transports that brought in the drinking water that we needed. We would often bathe in the rain water that filled up the rock craters hollowed out by bomb blasts. Sometimes the water in the craters looked cleaner than any to be found anywhere else. My disreputable fatigue uniform was sometimes dampened by weather and sometimes by my sweat. It was more often than not crisscrossed with salty sweat lines and dirt. I felt like I could have wrung a river out of my thick socks at any given time. When we were in the field for days on end, I would have given anything for clean underwear and a dry pair of soft, cotton socks.

Most of the time, athlete's foot and crotch rot plagued us really badly. Those were fungus irritations that came from wearing the same clothes to deterioration by the constant exposure to wet and rain. We needed to keep athlete's foot medication in our packs to treat both of those damp weather maladies.

Bowel dysfunction was likely to be an everyday thing with us because of the regimen of medications that the field doctors pushed us to take. The docs always had their hands full treating us because of everyday occurrences, our living conditions, our beastly eating habits, and the effects on our nerves caused by the constant tension of living on high alert on the DMZ.

I had learned long ago which portions of the field rations were really nutritious and those that caused my stomach to fight back. Liz and my mother sent me dried fruit, candy bars, cookies and other well-wrapped goodies. My mother's wax-paper wrapped, homemade treats, fudge bars and brownies, were always welcomed by all of my soldiers. The downside was that the goodies were delivered so very sporadically. Liz had found post office employees who were sympathetic to her cause and would look the other way when she admitted to hiding small cans of alcoholic drinks in the boxes that she sent to me. Whenever I got those, the men all knew it because I would become suddenly very secretive and furtive. I was stingy with those little cans and was very reluctant to share. Sometimes, I would allow someone who had gone over and above to do a good job one sip . . . maybe.

Nothing kept me from losing weight. I was already lean—my usual weight was around 230 pounds. But now, after six months of living the life of a combat soldier, I knew I weighed much less than that. I was lucky if I weighed 190 pounds soaking wet. My huge frame looked close to skeletal. My face was so bony I had to blow air into my sunken cheeks in order to make the surface of my face smooth enough to shave. And here I was scheduled to go on R and R.

When I got off the transport that picked me up from the DMZ and brought me down to the army base at Da Nang, it was obvious that I had been living in the jungle because it seemed to me that the city around the base had become a fast-moving and much more densely populated metropolis—more urbane than I remembered it being before. I had become used to the occasional small villages with farmers using ox-carts for transportation.

When I got into a *real* hot shower, got myself a haircut and shaved my scraggly beard off, I looked more like my human self than I had in many months. When I retrieved one of my freshly laundered khaki uniforms that had been tailored to fit spiffily on me during basic training, the uniform hung on me as though it belonged to someone else. When I ate a *real* meal, at a *real* table using *real* silverware and *real* dinnerware, I had to stop to remember. It seemed like a long time and many worlds ago when it had been second nature for me to do this. I wondered if I was going to be able to make a real meal stay in my stomach because my insides had gotten too used to eating "chow in the rough" back on the DMZ.

We were headed to the city of Honolulu on the island of Oahu in Hawaii. I had finally gotten around to getting it set up for Liz to fly in from Memphis and meet me there for R and R, but I was dreading our meeting. I could hardly control my anxiety to see her, but I knew she would be shocked by my appearance. I got the idea to buy flowers and candy for her as a distraction before I left the base at Da Nang. My plan was to hold the goodies out in front of me in order to hide my emaciated frame behind them. Knowing Liz, I could make a safe bet that she wouldn't be sidetracked by either the flowers or the candy, but what else could I do?

When we landed at the airstrip on Honolulu, we were checked out and hustled onto a bus to take us to the other side of the base. We had no way of knowing that our wives and relatives had been told that our transport had been delayed yet again. The officials had informed them three days earlier that we would be arriving much later than scheduled, so when we got off the bus at the base, none of our relatives were there to greet us. Liz told me later that nobody thought we would be coming on this day either, so she had gotten up early, taken a shower, gotten dressed, had breakfast with the rest of the wives and relatives, and was sitting in the common room reading a mystery novel that she had found on a bookshelf.

The other guys and I grabbed our gear and decided to just walk on over to the quarters where they had put our wives and relatives up for the four days. When we were about a block away we saw one of the women standing outside of the barracks smoking a cigarette. The minute she saw us coming she started waving her arms, jumping up and down, and screaming the news of our arrival. We could not help but laugh at her antics. It seemed hardly a minute before the door burst open and everyone who had been waiting for us for almost a week seemed to fly out all at once.

When Liz jumped into my arms I dropped my bag, the candy and flowers went flying. She was crying and shaking so hard, I had one heck of a time just holding on to her. When she calmed, I thought I was ready. I had managed to dash the unmanly wetness from my own eyes, and I held her at arm's length so I could drink in the beautiful sight of my little wife. I did not consider right then that she was also looking at me. Her eyes immediately filled up again as she whispered:

"You look . . . so . . . so . . . skinny! What have they done to you?"

As I hugged her against me, I was conscious of the fact that she could feel every one of my ribs. I kissed the top of her head. "I've just been too busy to get in three squares a day sometimes," I said as an explanation.

One of the guys, a Captain, whom I had met on the plane coming over, retrieved my flowers and candy and handed them to Liz.

"Here you go, ma'am." He was laughing at us with his eyes shining. "Ol' Wil was so excited to see you that he dropped these."

I thanked the Captain and we shook hands. His name was Stover. We had spent a lot of time talking together on the plane on the way over. He told me that he was on his second tour of duty in Vietnam. He also confided to me that his wife had left him for another man during his first tour. Although his wife had stuck with him through Officers Candidate School in Oklahoma, she had gone back home when he had been sent to Vietnam that first time. That's when the guy who had been his wife's high school sweetheart had started to come around her folk's house again. That guy had eventually prevailed upon the captain's wife until he had persuaded her to begin an affair with him. Now, the captain and his wife were still in the process of getting a divorce.

"All for the best," he shrugged nonchalantly after he had related these details to me on the plane. He did not seem to be broken up at all about losing his wife, but I wondered if he was hiding his true feelings beneath that happy-go-lucky smile. If so, I had to admit, he had a pretty good act going.

Captain Stover was being met by his mother and sister. They were both read-headed, rosy-cheeked, and freckled just like he was. Both were overjoyed to see him and were all happy tears and laughter. We made introductions all around and Liz seemed to have regained her composure and was smiling a little, too. I figured that I had made it through the worst of our meeting, so I was starting to relax a bit.

Finally, the women were ready to go back inside to retrieve their suitcases and all the rest of their things. I had to go inside to help Liz because she always tended to over pack and her suitcase was always too heavy for her to easily handle alone. She had brought along some of my "civvies" too so I guess she had reason to be overloaded. I did not mind in any case because I wasn't about to be cranky with my lovely wife now. My mind was strictly focused on exercising my marital rights and privileges—I had one track going on—there was not a chance of being side-tracked.

I had been able to get a suite at the Ilikai Hotel on the beach on the day that I got into Da Nang. Such short notice was allowed by most hotels for the combat troops who needed to go on leave but had been out of touch in the field.

The cab ride seemed really long to me, but in truth it was actually only a short distance. We were awed as we pulled up to the tall, elegant, stone façade of the Ilikai Hotel. One of the many good things about the hotel was the fact that it was on the beach and we could smell and feel the warm sea breeze as soon as we were out of the cab. Inside, the lobby was splendid and we were checked in by a smiling young clerk who took care of his job quickly.

The clerk turned us over to a gangly porter, an older, black-haired, swarthy guy, who quickly loaded our suitcases onto his rolling cart, got us through the lobby, into the elevator and up to our rooms in almost no time. He set the bags beside the large bed, glanced at me and then it seemed as if he was moving in slow motion as he strolled over to fiddle around at the windows and slowly draw back the curtains. I went for the wallet in my back pocket and yanked out a tip for him. With the widest smile, he abandoned those curtains, reached for the money and was out the door in a flash. Liz told me later that the tip I had given him was too large but I did not care—I just wanted him gone!

The minute the door closed behind him, I had my wife in my arms. I did not notice until the sun came through those half-opened curtains the next morning how lovely the view was through the floor-to-ceiling windows in our rooms on the seventh floor on the sunrise side of the hotel right alongside the beach.

I could have sat on the balcony holding Liz on my lap, smoking and watching the sun sparkling out on the waves of the ocean forever. I was at peace. I was not proud of the fact that after almost four years as a non-smoker, I had started to smoke cigarettes again while I was in Vietnam. For a fact, the cigarettes were soothing to my nerves. I did not intend to smoke at all while I was on leave and I really did try hard not to do it, but I found that I had become really addicted to the nicotine again. I tried always to smoke outside but still it was likely that the aroma of smoking on my breath and in my clothes bothered Liz who has always been severely asthmatic. She never did complain.

I felt the need to explain to Liz that cigarettes were just as plentiful in our supplies as food. The soldiers all kept them in their mess kits in large supply. The locals absolutely loved our cigarettes. When we were out and about in the countryside we used cigarettes just like cash. We often bartered or traded them to the civilians and farmers for reconnaissance about the enemy. We also used food and aspirin and even cough syrup to bribe the civilians when we were in the field or when we came across the inhabitants of the small scattered villages.

I tried to hide it, but my body was still on high alert when I first got to Honolulu. I found myself looking at the trees thinking of hidden snipers when Liz and I were walking on the streets. The vacationing crowds that thronged the shops along the avenues of Honolulu bothered me terribly at first because my mind told me that there could have been traitors hiding among the civilians. When Liz dragged me into one of the shops so she could look at one thing or another, I would often wander back to the front windows while she was shopping so that I could be aware of what was happening outside. I would look around and check for alternate exits in every building because I could not let myself get trapped in any enclosed space without having some other exit readily available.

I felt vulnerable because I was not carrying my sidearm—by then, it had become an integral part of my body. At first, I felt an icy cold tickle of fear when we walked down to the beach—it was too much of an open space. I felt unarmed and exposed. Slowly though, I began to unwind somewhat and to enjoy the warm sand and the sun. I went into the water to swim a few laps each day. I had begun to really enjoy myself, but I found out the hard way that I had not totally let go.

Poor Liz, I know that it frightened her to death the first time the nightmares overtook me. In my dreams the 1st of the 40th Company was fighting off a particularly nasty attack from the NVA and the Viet Cong. Earlier in the war, the NVA/Cong had completely overrun the position that my company was now holding. The NVA/Cong had paid a heavy price but they had managed to overcome and kill the full squad of Marines who had been holding the position. We had better than average intelligence that informed us that the Viet Cong would try to launch another assault at midnight when they thought we would be sleeping. Sure enough it happened, and it had been one hell of a firefight. Now, here I was fighting that battle all over again in a horrible nightmare. I was drenched with sweat, firing my weapon as fast as I could with precision and accuracy while shouting encouragement and orders to my gunners:

"*They're running, goddammit! We got them fuckin' Gooks running! Drop it down! Drop it down on their goddam' asses! Keep firing! Keep firing! Load and shoot! Don't let a single one of 'em make it into them trees! Give 'em another fuckin' round! That oughta' teach them sneaky sonsabitches not to try that shit again!*"

I guess Liz knew better than to lay hands on me to try to wake me up. She got out of the way and called out my name until I jerked myself awake. She hurriedly got a towel from the bathroom to dry the sweat from my dripping face, and then she sat on the edge of the bed watching me silently with her dark eyes wet and wide with apprehension while I got up and walked around the bedroom until I calmed down. I walked over to the plate-glass windows, lit up a cigarette with shaky hands, smoked and watched the moonlight sparkling like diamonds on the dark, restless ocean until my mind was clear. Then, I was ready to get back into bed. With Liz's head on my shoulder, her arms around me, and her warm, soft breath against my chest, I slept soundly until morning.

I felt like my heart would be torn out completely when I had to put Liz on an airplane for home. She was crying without making any sound as was her way. Tears streamed down her face and she was shaking like a leaf. It was all that I could do not to cry, too, there in public. I just held her while she thoroughly wet the front of my shirt and I did my best to comfort her:

"Don't cry, Sugar," I whispered over and over. "Be a brave little wife now. Be brave for me, Sweetheart. I'll be home in a few."

After the passengers had been called for boarding, I walked over to the large plate glass windows and waited until the plane pulled away from its docking place, then I lit up a cigarette. I felt more than a little guilty about smoking because I had promised Liz that I would try to quit. Well, I intended to do that—just not yet.

I watched as the plane slowly taxied backwards around a corner and out of my sight. It appeared a few minutes later farther away rolling into position for takeoff. Soon, the big silver plane was speeding down the runway and then it lifted up into the air. I watched until the plane was lost from sight among the puffy white clouds floating against the blue sky. Then, I immediately turned my mind to being a soldier again.

This time, as we headed for Da Nang aboard the military transport I was one of those scruffily-clad, battle-ready combat soldiers laughing loudly, joking among ourselves and telling stories about leave-time. We did it to keep our spirits up and to make each other feel better. I understood it now—it was important and necessary to keep our minds off the absolute hell that we were going back to face.

In my turn, my story was about the sleek, black Corvette coupe that I had seen stopped at a traffic light while Liz and I were walking down the street in Honolulu. That Corvette had caught my eye and ensnared my heart forever as it purred like a crouching, sleek-muscled, black panther sitting still. When the light turned green, it leapt away with a roar leaving every other car in its wake. I could tell from the sound and the way it scooted that it had some good horsepower and it was a 4-speed, standard shift. The guy driving it could really handle those gears, too. I already knew all about Corvettes, I had read about them in the car magazines that we got with our rations back in Nam, but that little black beauty had taken my heart with it as it zoomed down the street, the exhaust pipes on both sides of the back end spitting like nobody's business.

The soldiers all listened quietly, nodding in understanding as I talked about that car.

"You gonna' get yourself a Vette when you get back." One of the guys stated solemnly. It was not a question.

"Righteous," I laughed, "black on black, wire wheel covers, 4-speed standard shift . . . all of the options . . ."

"Oh, yeah, Lieu," a corporal sighed. "That pretty 'Vette is gonna' be your baby. Here's what you do: buy yourself that 'Vette, love it hard, then treat it like you treat a woman—get off the old model and get on the new model as soon as she tails up."

Everybody laughed heartily at that as we slapped hands all around.

"Righteous, my brother!" I laughed heartily.

"Tell it to us while we listen!" a sergeant crowed in a warbling voice.

"You gonna' be *nothin'* if not a low rider!" the corporal hooted in affirmation. "Gonna' have a collection of Corvettes in your garage one day: that black one and every color of the rainbow too!"

How prophetic!

When we lifted away from Da Nang in our military transport we were much more subdued. By the time we reached the scarred and strafed airstrip on Dung Ha and boarded the transports to the DMZ, we were silent—stone cold warriors again, on high alert, staring out of the openings with eyes narrowed and unblinking, and our firearms held at the ready.

I won't say that we fought every day, but we stayed ready to fight every day. When other troops needed a rest they came to us. We protected miles of the DMZ as far as our big guns reached and as close as our handguns and rifles found enemy targets. My men and I were of one mind, one spirit, with one goal. The first of the 40th was fast becoming legendary.

We became so well known for the thoroughness and accuracy of our fire that we were re-assigned to provide the firepower for an important and top-secret time-on-target mission. We needed to put some rounds into certain territory previously off-limits in North Vietnam that was found to have become heavily occupied by the NVA. We needed to soften up the target so that the ground troops would be able to move in. I made sure that my men were really pumped for this. All six of our cannon were ready to go. So when the time came, I turned my men loose on the appointed mission. I gave them freedom to shoot at will. They fell to loading and shooting our six cannon, each man working like the machines that my intense training had made of them: load, fire, remove the empty shell, then do it again without missing a beat.

I moved between my six guns, changing coordinates when I needed to do it, shouting myself hoarse to give them encouragement, doing my best to keep them going, and keep each gun crew competitive with the other ones. We put down such heavy and accurate firepower that the operation command called for us to stop long before the time that we had agreed upon was over. The radio operator / forward observer was speechless. When the brigade commander finally asked for my report on how many actual rounds of artillery ammunition that we had expended, he could not believe my feedback.

"Whaaaat?" his voice crackled across the radio waves. He sounded purely dumbfounded.

I chuckled and gave the report again.

"*Dammmmn*!" he breathed. "Every goddam round came in here right on the target. You guys wiped up that fuckin' dog shit all by yourselves! Forty soldiers just walked in there without firin' a single shot!"

"Six guns, one mind, one spirit, one goal," I announced proudly as my sweating, exhausted troops gathered around me, back slapping each other, hugging and whooping triumphantly. We were the best and we were proud of it. That day, our nickname became the standard for precision and accuracy: "Automatic Alpha."

We were put on rotation down to Da Nang for an unscheduled R and R for our own sakes after that mission. The men found a little shop and bought a gold cigarette lighter to commemorate our spectacular accomplishment. They proudly presented it to me. They had it engraved to read: "Automatic Alpha." It still lives among the greatest treasures on the shelf in my den.

Immediately, when we got back from Da Nang, we got right back to taking care of our business the way that we always had—with vigilance and firepower.

When the final six months of my rotation were up, I was proud that I took every one of my original troops off the DMZ with me. I had received a bronze star, a field promotion to 1st lieutenant, and a commendation which stated that I would be promoted to Captain upon my re-enlistment. I was well aware that my leadership was needed by my country and, more importantly, by my soldiers. I also knew that my wife and my family wanted me to come home.

How could I tell my family that I intended to re-enlist?

My middle brother, Gregory, had enlisted in the Navy and was now stationed on the coast of California. Barbara and Janet, my twin sisters were both married now with children and Janet's husband, Ronald, was in the Navy stationed off the coast of Vietnam. My mother begged me not to re-enlist and so did my sisters.

Liz's sister's husband had enlisted after high school, done his time in the Marines and was now at home attending college on the GI Bill. A number of Liz's close relatives were presently members of the armed services and her family had a long history of service during past major wars including her grandfather, father, three of her uncles, and numerous cousins.

We made a trip out to the west coast just for the sake of driving. We visited Liz's and my relatives and saw many of my old college friends and roommates. They all thanked me for my service but to a man they prevailed upon me not take the promotion, not to return to my old company in Vietnam, not to stay in military service.

We spent a couple of days with my college roommate and fellow engineer, Napoleon Hornbuckle. He was working for Motorola in Phoenix, Arizona. He shook my hand, looked into my eyes, and profoundly thanked me for serving my country.

"Blood," he said (we used that family nickname for each other), "You've done your part for the country. Think of your own family now. They need you at home, Bro."

When we were returning from the trip to Arizona, we decided to make a trip through the Painted Desert. We were enjoying the desert scenery. But as usual, our conversation inevitably came back around to the same spot: arguing about my intention to re-enlist. It had become a very sore point of contention between Liz and me as the time came closer for me to make the decision. There was absolutely no normal communication, no peace, or harmony between us. I made my argument for what seemed like the 100th time, patiently explaining to Liz why I felt I had to go back. I knew that I would make less money in the Army overseas than I would in industry at home but I felt such a strong obligation—I felt duty-bound to be with my men. Liz was quiet for a long time as she stared out at the road ahead, and then she dropped a ton of lead on my position:

"I won't wait," she stated flatly. It was the first time that she had said something like this. "It's not fair for you to expect me to wait for you again."

"Just what are you saying, Liz?" I blustered furiously, "You can't mean that. I may not even be over there for the whole year. I could be back stateside in no time. Listen, I'm only asking . . ."

"No! I'm not going to try to compete with your sense of duty." Liz said shakily. "So don't you try to put me in a position like that because I won't do it! If you're so set on going back over there, maybe you and I aren't meant to be after all."

Something came over me then. Even then, I would not blame myself or accept that I was the one who was making a terrible mistake. Maybe I was remembering Captain Stover, because I said the worst thing that I possibly could have said to my wife:

"Ah, shit! Is there somebody . . . some guy? Have you been seeing somebody else while I was gone?"

Liz turned and stared at me. Then the shock seemed to seep slowly into her as if she had been slapped abruptly across her face and her reaction was delayed. She whirled away from me and curled up in the seat with her back to me. She shrank away from my touch and refused to say another word. I tried talking to her. I asked her if she needed to stop somewhere. I told her about Captain Stover as if to justify what I had just said. Then I tried cajoling, joking, anything to avoid accepting blame for the cruel hurt I had just inflicted upon my faithful little wife.

As soon as Liz shut me out, I could really feel that darkness again—it had been blurring the edges of my world from the first moment that I set foot in Vietnam. That dark coloring had not ceased to be there since I had heard that very first bullet whiz past my ear there on the DMZ; it had never faded—even by a little. Now, each time Liz and I argued it seemed to intensify and became more terrifying than any NVA or Cong assault. I didn't need to weigh my options against this—no way would I ever risk not having Liz to come back to.

"Well then, I guess you'd better get ready to head on back to Toledo," I said after we had been driving for a while.

Liz turned and stared at me with her eyes red and watery. "You mean that you're going to stay here—stay home?"

"Yep," I said.

Liz whooped happily and threw her arms around my neck while I continued to drive. We were lucky that no cars were approaching in the opposite lane just then. Her enthusiasm caused me to swerve dangerously as she surged against my arm like a playful puppy and planted kisses on the side of my face and mouth.

But, the most important thing of all was this: the weight seemed to lift from my shoulders and move the darkness back. It wasn't as if the whole world became instantly bright for me because I realized that would take time—lots of time. But when I had made that decision, the burden of duty did not clog so strongly in my heart or weigh so heavily on my soul like I had thought that it would. I was beginning to feel like there was some hope of knitting together the pieces of the fragmented parts that being a combat soldier had made of me.

"Look, I've got one condition, though," I said solemnly as I put Liz back into her own seat with my right arm.

"'*One condition*—?'" she started. "What is it?"

"I need to buy myself a Corvette."

Civilian Life—Toledo, Ohio—REM Number 5

I went back to my job at General Mills, Incorporated in Toledo, Ohio as a process engineer. Liz got a job as an eleventh grade English teacher at Scott High School with the public school system of Toledo. We bought a small, tidy, three—bedroom house on Cherry Valley Road very near the campus of the University of Toledo and our lives quickly became routine. We both decided to enroll in graduate classes at the university because I wanted to take advantage of the GI Bill and we were sure it would help to advance our careers.

We both loved our dark blue Pontiac GTO. It had served Liz faithfully while I was in Vietnam. It wasn't a shabby automobile by any stretch of the imagination. We were pretty content driving it when we first got back to Toledo. With the one car between us though, that routine of dropping each other off at work and picking each other up from work got old pretty quickly. So we paid cash to a dealer down the street from the university for a used, red and white Rambler.

The car was a good, cheap buy—a jaunty little convertible with a spare tire on the back. It had been in more than a few scrapes, and had more than a few rubs, dings, dents, and touch-ups—the paint job had long since seen its best days. Before we bought the Rambler, I checked to make sure that everything worked. The rag top was new but I checked to make sure it was not ripped anywhere along the seams; made sure that the salesman had someone to put a little oil put on the joints; and made sure that the re-worked convertible top lifted up and down easily. I inspected beneath the hood, did a bit of mechanical dabbling and turned a few wrenches. In spite of the fact that the car was already drivable the battery had some miles on it. I thought it best to replace the old battery with a new one from Sears in order to get Liz back and forth to work every day and to her classes at the university at night without any incident.

One Saturday morning, we were riding in the GTO down Bancroft Street on our way to stock up on a few necessities for our pantry that we hadn't had time to buy during the week. Neither of us was paying much attention as we passed several auto lots.

We probably saw it at the same time, a brand-new, shiny, Corvette coupe sitting elevated on a round dais and highlighted on a Chevrolet dealer's lot right in front of us. All that I can remember now is that the color was black and it had a black interior. The sun glinted on its sleek, rounded curves as it sat there. Both bumpers front and back were chrome just like I remembered and there were a few more touches of chrome on it than on my dream car. This was a newer version, the 1969 model, but in the most important ways it was the same car that had appealed to me while I was on leave in Hawaii. Some other features were different, perhaps, but the sleek styling and the color were the very same. It was one sassy little coupe.

I do not remember much of the details, except that there was a reluctant little guy who was our salesman. It was probably his turn—he must have pulled the duty to come out to talk to us when we drove in. But I was about to make his day because he had no idea how easy and lucky his job was going to be. Within the hour I had traded in my GTO and I was behind the wheel of my brand new Corvette. That little guy (I couldn't remember his name if I tried) almost broke his face he was laughing and smiling so much. He shook my hand over and over. He seemed barely able to restrain himself from gamboling around the office and jumping up and down. I figured that when we left, he probably did jump up and perform a fist pump in mid-air.

I do not remember if Liz and I did the errands that we had set out to do or not—whether we got the groceries and supplies that we needed that day or not—but I do remember driving all over Toledo, testing the four gears on every hill that I found, testing the cornering, and enjoying every minute of it. I was in my world.

One thing that I worried about was the snow and ice that was sure to come during the winter. I had heard too many times that Corvettes did not drive well on the ice and in the snow. The car simply slid and rode high no matter what the driver did or failed to do. I was not willing to risk it. Both Liz and I were inexperienced at driving during the Northern winters anyway, so I bit the bullet and purchased another car. Lured by the promise of a wide stance that guaranteed super stability in all kinds of weather, I bought a 4-door Pontiac demonstrator to get us through the icy times. Our little house had a two-car garage, so I parked the Corvette inside one bay of the garage and left it covered and stored for the winter. Liz argued that the poor little ol' Rambler could not possibly make it if it had to be parked outside. So, Liz got the other bay of the garage for the Rambler and I took it on the chin: I bought a car cover for the Pontiac and parked it outside.

Liz had been a top-notch dressmaker for a long time, sewing seriously since she was about ten years old. She made all the curtains and drapes for our whole house. She always sewed her own clothes even the winter coats and she often made clothes for her friends. At prom time, after she had made a gown for a girl in her English class, her reputation was set. She decided to make a pair of tailored pants for her father that Christmas. She scoured the fabric stores until she found the right menswear fabric and purchased it.

I watched Liz cutting and sewing each evening after she came home from work until, finally, she was at the point that she needed to check the fit. I had liked the fabric from the beginning. It was a deep charcoal grey menswear with a thin, subtle beige pinstripe that any good tailor might pick for a man's suit or dress pants. I had seen how well Liz had cut and sewn the pants. I was impressed with how professionally she had steam-pressed in the leg creases, sewn the belt loops flat across the waistband and made the pockets look store-bought with the inside finishing. What I really wanted to see was if the pants would look "homemade," if they hung lopsided, or if they had a real tailored appearance. I took off my shoes and jeans and stepped into the pants to become Liz's human mannequin. She held the pants together in back while I took a look in the mirror that was attached to our bedroom door.

"Ooh wee!!" I exclaimed, "I don't think your daddy will be getting these!"

Liz fussed a bit but I knew she was pleased by my back-handed compliment because she immediately set to work making adjustments. She changed the sewing lines at the back to make the pants smaller at the waistline so that they fit me perfectly. Since she had cut the legs of the pattern with extra length for cuffs which her daddy wanted, she only needed to turn up a single hem for them to fit my long legs. The next day she went back to the store and bought more fabric to sew another pair of slacks for her dad.

After that, Liz became my personal tailor. She made suits, sports shirts, dress shirts, ties, pajamas—she even tackled a leather coat. I was beginning to gain a reputation as a really well-dressed guy. All my friends said how lucky I was to have a real tailor for a wife. For my birthday and at Christmas, I simply told Liz what I needed next. When she told me that she wanted to trade her economical straight-stitch machine for a more heavy-duty sewing machine that had many built-in stitches and a blind hemmer there was no question from me at all, I bought one for her because I figured that it was a good investment toward my own wardrobe.

Before I knew it, it was time for me to graduate. Liz had finished all of the work on her master's degree a year ahead of me. It had taken me a bit longer to complete my courses because my undergraduate degree was in electrical engineering, but in order to make myself more versatile, I had decided to get a graduate degree in industrial engineering. I was sitting in one of my very last evening classes. I had already aced the final project for this class—I was all but done. One of the engineering professors with whom I had become friendly opened the door behind me, came up to where I was sitting and slipped a folded note into my hand. I opened the note and my eyes widened.

As soon as the lecture was finished I grabbed my books, told my friend and fellow IE student, Bob Dettinger, where I was headed and went over to the dean's office. The office was closed and locked by this time of the evening, but a tall man was sitting on one of the couches in the common area outside the door. I figured he was waiting for me. He unfolded his long frame from the couch as soon as he saw me coming and stuck out his hand. We shook as we greeted each other.

"Robert Morris," he said "From General Motors Institute up the road in Flint. You're Wil Cooksey?"

I nodded. "Pleased to meet you, sir," I said. His note had given no reason why he wanted to see me. It was not his name—it was the "from General Motors institute" written on the note that had me so intrigued.

"How's life been since you've been home from overseas?" He asked smiling.

I noticed then that he was holding a manila folder. I wondered if it could be my records that it contained.

"Been good—real good," I answered. "I've been home for almost three years now."

"You got right to work when you got back," he stated. "How do you like what you're doing over there at General Mills?"

"Right now I'm working on optimizing processes," I said. I was not sure how technical I might want to get with him but he was smiling and nodding, encouraging me to keep talking.

"I'm working on several projects to try to eliminate waste in our processes," I said. "I'm running the department that keeps the equipment at optimal production. You know that our cereal really is shot from guns like the ads claim that they are? We've gotten the process down from five guns to three in some cases. We're making real headway on that. Our production is almost doubled though."

"Sounds really interesting," Mr. Morris said, "You'll have to tell me all about that sometimes."

I could tell that there was something else on his mind. He was a very refined and professorial looking gentleman. In his tweed jacket and bow tie, he was real academia walking. I knew that he was probably a technician but I felt that his outlook on getting a job done in an industrial plant might differ in every way from mine. Nevertheless, I got the feeling that he already knew about me and understood my job much more than he was letting on.

"Let's sit for a minute," he said indicating the couch behind us on which he had been sitting.

I noticed then that Bob Dettinger had followed me out of the classroom and when we sat, he sat down on one of the couches across from us unabashedly listening to our conversation.

I figured that Bob was waiting for me. I gave him a grin and a nod. I liked him a lot. We had become good friends over the two years that we had classes together. We had pooled resources and worked on two really successful projects and we had found that we were a lot alike: we believed in doing our best at whatever project we tackled.

"I was asked to be a guest lecturer in a class where I met my namesake, Bob, here last week," Mr. Morris said indicating Dettinger who acknowledged his reference with a slight nod of his head.

"I've heard quite a bit about you from your professors." He began, "I like what I've heard, I'll tell you that. But I'll make no secret of the fact that we need more diversity in the ranks among our professors and you're just what we need. We want you to come to work for us. We want you to teach Applied Statistics and some Quality classes . . . maybe some Reliability classes, too,"

I stared at him. "I'm pretty well set at General Mills. Right now I'm deeply involved in working on . . ."

"I know," he said cutting me off, "I already know that you're not looking to move away from General Mills, but there are many advantages that we can offer you that you might find really appealing. First of all . . ."

He stopped, flipped the folder open, looked at a couple of pages in it then said coolly: "We can give you up to 30 percent over what you're making now as base salary with the possibility of outside consulting jobs and guest lecturing—that would be pay outside of your base salary . . ."

He was really stretching this out. I could see that he was really enjoying himself.

". . . and there are some pretty good discounts on the cars that you can purchase from General Motors." Here he looked up and gave me a lopsided grin.

"I've heard that you really love Corvettes." He went on, "What if I told you that you will be able to get a pretty substantial discount on any automobile purchase from General Motors . . . and . . . in a couple of years, if you still want to, we can let you to get some real technical automotive experience down in St. Louis—at the Corvette plant?"

I had begun to hold my breath at some point while Mr. Morris was talking. Now, I let my breath out slowly. He had me hooked like a fish on his line, and he knew it.

"My wife loves her job," I said, grimacing at the thought. "She's on track for a raise in salary this year. How will I ever get her to move to Flint with me?"

"I understand that your wife is a teacher in the public school system here," he said smoothly. "She'll find that the opportunities for her to teach in the public school system are quite good in Flint."

He leaned over and said to me conspiratorially, "Here's what you do: take your wife . . . her name's Liz, right? Take Liz out to dinner.

Talk it over and see if you can get her to see your point of view. I'm counting on you."

He stood up. I got to my feet and we shook hands. Dettinger quickly got to his feet and came over to shake hands with Mr. Morris.

"Bob here is looking to come with us, too," Mr. Morris said smiling.

I knew that Liz would not be happy, but luckily, she did not fight the move.

"Wherever you go, I will go," she said.

When we sat down to make our plans for moving to Flint Liz said to me:

"You're going to need a little different wardrobe, don't you think?"

So she set to work finding and buying more conservative pinstripes and subdued solid colors for the jackets and slacks that she made for me. I really hated to give up the casual and sometimes flashy slacks and shirts—I loved to wear them but they just would not do for the college classroom. I needed to dress more "professorially" now, Liz laughingly chided.

We hated to leave the friends that we had made in Toledo, the church that we had become accustomed to attending, and the activities connected with the university that we enjoyed. There were the people in our neighborhood, at Liz's job and at mine who had become very close to both of us. I was learning to play golf. Liz had begun to teach tailoring classes. An artist who taught at Scott High School with Liz, Ernie Jones, had also become one of our dearest friends. He said it better than anyone else:

"It's advancement, Bro," he said. "A man has to advance or he stagnates, you know?" Ernie laughed away our sadness and made us feel better by saying:

"Don't worry; we'll come to visit you and see that you're OK in your new place."

I can still see Ernie's face now and his jovial attitude always made me smile. He kept his word. Ernie, his wife, Gloria, and their little girl, Charvette, visited us many times and we visited them. After a long time, though, we lost contact with each other. I have two of his paintings that still hang in prominent positions in my home today.

General Motors Institute—
Flint, Michigan—
REM/Nightmare Number 6

We made three excursions up to Flint before we moved there. I went over to GMI to meet and talk to the engineering professors, tour the campus, and meet some of the officials in the city. Mr. Morris arranged for Liz to go the Flint Board of Education to meet and talk to their personnel people. I was happy that they immediately offered Liz a job at Holmes Junior High School as an English teacher. She seemed pleased that the salary was better than she was making in Toledo. I was glad to see that something about this move could make her happy.

It was not long before we found a house in a lovely neighborhood located right behind Northern High School and convenient to the shops and grocery stores. We were going to be the first of the three black families who moved into that neighborhood but that was of no real consequence to us. We were working people who fully intended to be good neighbors, who intended to keep the lawn neat and the snow removed in the winter. Anyway, our busy lives meant that we would both be gone from home all day. We would hardly have time to be very neighborly anyway.

It was an older house with spacious rooms and there was an unfinished basement that ran the full length of the house with vinyl tile already installed on the floor. My great concern was the wall leaks in the basement. Neither of us had ever lived in a house with a basement before, but both of us had heard stories of leaky basements in older houses. This basement had a small stream of water that ran down between the sill of one of the casement windows and the concrete wall. A contractor was hired to fix it and to install a system to deter future leaks all along the walls before we moved into the house.

The washer and dryer would be located down in the basement and we found that there was a laundry chute that came from upstairs between the bedrooms. There were three closets along the basement walls, a roughed-out bathroom area with a toilet and a sink already installed, and a place for a shower. The previous owner had begun to put a lot of work into the basement and he had gotten as far as putting in a bar in the corner on one side with mirrors all around it. It was really beautiful. Liz was enthusiastic about all the features of the house, but she loved the basement. She thought that we should try to finish the basement right away and make it into a downstairs living area.

I entered into one of the busiest times of my life. I was teaching some bright, talented industrial engineering students at GMI and I also lectured at other schools, junior college and college classrooms. Mr. Morris was very supportive and he helped me to make up my mind to begin work at Michigan State University on a doctorate in industrial engineering—systems analysis and design emphasis.

Since I had no time to help Liz with making the house livable, her older sister, Florestine, packed her three young children into their station wagon along with their mother and drove to Flint from Memphis that summer to help Liz out. The kids, Walter, Jr., Libby (named for her aunt Liz), and the youngest, Roger, kept the house alive with their antics and laughter up and down the steps and out onto the wide lawn until they collapsed at night completely exhausted. Liz missed her family terribly when they left to drive home to Memphis and, I admit, the house did seem pretty big and empty without them.

Luckily, my twin sisters Janet and her husband Ronald, their three kids Dawn, Ronnie, Jr., and Darren came to visit us. Barbara and her husband Rathel, and their sons Tim and Chris, came to visit to finish the summer with us before the kids had to go back to school. My sisters and brothers-in-law helped Liz with the cutting, sewing, re-upholstering, painting and curtain hanging while I labored through driving over to East Lansing to Michigan State for my summer classes. I was participating in numerous outside lectures and other activities and helping my students to complete their projects and in-plant assignments.

Rathel and Ronald did manage to get me out on the links to play golf a couple of times while they were visiting us. Rathel helped me straighten out my swing to the point that I was beginning to think that I might be making some real headway toward playing a pretty good game of golf.

Liz was depressed again after they had all gone home. One night at the dinner table I found out why her depression was so deep and had lasted so long.

"We need to think about adoption," she said out of nowhere.

"What?" I said. I was not thrilled to open that door again. The whole issue of children was more than a touchy subject with us. I had begun to believe that both of us had buried that pain deeply enough that it would not surface again. Not only were we both up to our ears in work, I felt that if we really wanted to, we could get a full dose of relatives' children anytime we felt like it.

"Adoption," Liz said emphatically. "We've had enough of the carefree life. We've traveled enough. Both our jobs are better than just decent. This is the second house that we've owned . . ."

"Adoption is not something that I want to think about right now," I said. "I'd rather just get a dog."

"We can adopt a kid **and** get a dog," Liz said drily. "Maybe it's time that we realized that we aren't getting any younger."

Truth be told both Liz and I had long since become adept at avoiding the truth or glossing it over. The pain and the disappointment had dulled somewhat, but it had never—would never—disappear completely. Our conversation had changed since the initial bouts of crying and depression after a pregnancy went wrong. We had been through it all: the tests that we both underwent that were too numerous to count; the crushing news that Liz's ovaries were her own worst enemies and needed to be removed; the hospital stays that Liz occasionally underwent for scraping to cut down on unexpected and excessive bleeding and the constant threat that the many medical procedures were thinning her uterus walls. It had worn us both down to what I thought was a completely exhausted acceptance that Liz and I would never have any children of our own.

Lillian Henry, our department secretary at GMI was firmly behind Liz's foray into finding the right adoption agency. She located an agency in Detroit and put us in touch with them. After the agency had completed a comprehensive study of our home and our backgrounds the news finally came: "We have a baby for you."

We picked up our baby girl in Detroit, Michigan on July 17, 1973. She was not quite a year old and she was seemed healthy, happy and high spirited. We named her Cristin Denise. When Cristin met the rest of the children in both our families it was Liz's sister Florestine's youngest son, Roger who started to call her "Crissy." So, Crissy she was.

Not long after Crissy became a part of our family, the agency contacted us again and we brought home a little brown-eyed baby boy. I thought that our little boy bore a strong resemblance to my younger brother when he was a child. So we named our son David Anthony. Not long after, we were glad that we had used his name because my younger brother, David, was killed in his apartment in Fort Worth.

We did get a dog, a sturdy little salt and pepper Miniature Schnauzer puppy with upright ears, a spiky white beard and the biggest, brightest, brown eyes in the world. We picked him from a litter that a breeder had advertised in the newspaper. His AKC registration papers showed a long formal name that indicated his parents and his lineage. "Ragamuffin" was part of his name, but we simply called him "Muffy." The kids loved him and it was not long before neither of them would go to bed unless Muffy had made the decision whose bed he was going to sleep beside. He was content to lie down anywhere near the kids when he was really sleepy but he actually preferred to sleep with his head on Liz's feet. No matter whose bed he had started his night's sleep beside, he would always make his way to the rug on Liz's side of the bed once she turned in for the night. His love for Liz was absolute. He was a little jewel who learned quickly how to indicate that he needed to go outside to make his toilet. He would stand stubbornly in front of his empty water bowl or supper dish and wait until someone noticed him. Lord help anyone who stepped foot onto our porch without his permission. We all loved that little guy just as much as he loved Liz, the kids, and me—in that order.

By June, 1975, I had finished all of my coursework at Michigan State in a rather short time. I had framed out my dissertation for my PhD, discussed it all with my committee chairman and had one meeting with the rest of my committee. I was really feeling that I was too beat-up to go any further. I just wanted to take a rest and do nothing at all, but I knew that I could not. I just hoped that it would not take me a whole semester to complete all of the preliminary writing before I had to tackle the rest. One afternoon, I was at my desk pouring over one of the countless books that were piled up in front of me, trying to make some headway on my reference search when the department secretary asked me to stop by Mr. Morris' office before I went home. I dragged my weary body into his office and fell into a chair across from his desk. He looked up from his writing, gave me his lopsided grin and said:

"Just how close are you to finishing up your lit search, do you think?"

I dragged my hand over my face. "It'd be hard for me to say, especially right now," I said, "I'm really hung up on this IE literature—not so much the mechanical. If I can get the IE part done—at least make more headway on it—I might say that I'm off to a fairly good start."

"Hmmm." Bob was rubbing his palms together with a pen between them as he sometimes did when he was in deep thought.

"You've completed certifications from the American Society for Quality Control in Quality Engineering, haven't you?" he asked.

"Both," I said, "Quality Engineering and Reliability Engineering."

"Right, right," he agreed, "Now, what else have you completed?"

"Well, my certificate just came from the state of California—my PE for Quality Engineering in the state of California . . ."

"Right, right" he said again, and he smiled. "And none of that is going to do you any good at all at the place where they want you to go."

"Where's that?" I asked caught completely off guard.

"The Corvette plant in Saint Louis. You know we promised you that you'd be able to go there, but I can tell you, that place is a snake pit—as poisonous as it can be. You have another choice—the AC Delco plant right here. That's what I would recommend."

"I want to go to the Corvette plant in Saint Louis," I said without any hesitation.

To Mr. Morris' credit, he kept trying. "You'd have to leave here immediately if you go there. They want you there like—yesterday. You'd have to be super-human to handle that and get your dissertation finished here. There's no guarantee you could get it finished at all if you go there. At least you'd be right here in Flint if you go to Delco.

Your dissertation is going to be hard enough. Your topic is excellent. I promise we'll all give you—"

But I was shaking my head stubbornly. My mind was made up. "I've been to that plant several times with my students. I'm not really . . . I wouldn't say I'm really familiar with it, but I know some things about it. I know enough about quality and quality control—in theory. I want to get in some practice. I want to get my foot in the door with real production. I really believe that's the place I need to go. I can't back down now. I need to get my teeth right into it. If I get started at a rough place . . . maybe—"

"Well, "Mr. Morris said, lopsided grin showing a bit of sadness. "We'll miss you. They'll look at you like fresh meat when you get to Saint Louis. Maybe they won't take too big of a bite out of your ass."

I laughed. "If they do, I'll pick up that piece of bit-off ass and come on back here with my tail between my legs. I can can't I?"

He laughed, heartily. "Sure you can. We'll take you back any day, any time." He leaned back in his chair smiling with his eyebrows raised. "I'd love to be a fly on your wall when you tell Liz this."

Liz was not happy about the move to Saint Louis. I saw how sad she was but I don't know if she cried about it or not, but she said what she had always said with a bit of modification:

"Wherever you go, the kids, Muffy and I will go."

We sold our house in Flint to the GMI engineering department secretary, Lillian Henry and her family. She and her husband had loved the house from the minute that they had seen it after we bought it. Their son was more than thrilled about the swimming pool that I had installed in the backyard and Lil's husband was really crazy about the pool table downstairs, so we sold them all of our basement furnishings. That was something that we did not have to bother to move to Saint Louis.

We found a house in Saint Louis County in the community of Olivette. The subdivision, Old Farm Estates, was so hilly that the streets were up and down like a washboard. The house was rather unusual because it had three small bedrooms, a larger master bedroom, and a large, finished basement. An elementary school was located quite near the neighborhood and a shopping center was just outside the subdivision on Olive Street. We bought the house and moved.

The back yard had a strong fence around it and that really was what sold us on the house. Back in Flint, Muffy had escaped through the rather weak wire fence that encircled the back yard a couple of times. When we found him that last time he was with a pack of other dogs taking his turn with a receptive female who must have been on the loose in the neighborhood. He had a couple of bloody gashes on his right side, probably from fighting for his chance to mate and he seemed to have suffered a bit from starvation and dehydration. We realized then that the little fellow was just doing the natural thing—finding a female to breed with. So we sold his services to a breeder of Miniature Schnauzers in Flint who was looking for fresh breeding stock and the arrangement proved to be fine all around. We knew that we'd soon have to do the same thing in Saint Louis.

GM Product Assembly Plant— Saint Louis, MO— Nightmare Number 6

If anyone wonders what makes a daytime nightmare, I could certainly speak to that issue as a lower level executive in an automotive assembly plant: labor problems on the assembly line, hostile working environment all over the plant, and the constant push and pull of management in conflict with the leaders and the rank and file of the labor union. There it is: the make-up of the world's worst daytime nightmare! That was the General Motors assembly plant in Saint Louis, Missouri during the 1970s.

I was not crazy about the fact that I had an hour's drive to get to work. I had found that after my training on the day shift, I would be placed permanently on the second shift. Then, with the evening rush out of the way, maybe I could make it to the plant in about forty minutes on the freeway.

The production facility was housed in an absolutely huge complex right in the heart of downtown Saint Louis—right alongside the river. There were three products running on three different assembly lines. The Chevrolet Caprice was assembled in one part of the complex; Chevy and GMC pickup trucks were done on the same assembly lines in another part; and the Chevrolet Corvette had its complete operation in a separate building. There was a huge building that held coal and other supplies that provided heat and energy for all of the assembly lines. Absolutely no one **wanted** to work there because it was dirty work, but since it came under UAW sanction with premium pay and rotation, absolutely everybody wanted to work there for a while. It was a strange phenomenon that did not make much sense to me until much later when I had learned more about the UAW.

Mr. Morris' epithet "snake pit" was putting it mildly. There were over 10,000 people working at the facility in 1976 when I arrived in June. I found out fairly quickly that the number of people working there and the number of people who actually **did** the work there were two entirely different things.

The plant manager, Cliff Vaughn, was an "old school" manager as he told me during our first sit down interview. My job description would be "trainee" and my pay grade was at the "general foreman" level to start. I was to be put on a training plan which would give me experience all over the complex and in every department. I was a bit disappointed because I wanted to go straight to Corvette, but Cliff asserted that I needed to have experience in all aspects of production all over the plant so I was to be put on a program called SEIT—Salaried Employee In Training.

General Motors was requiring me to learn about all kinds of production and, after some thought, I figured that it might be the best for me after all. Because I was coming from academia, I also knew that I needed to get acclimated to the plant, to the true rough-and-tumble of plant life and the push-and-pull of management/labor relationships if I was going to make it there.

I got myself a little pocket notebook which would be easy to carry and which would allow me to take notes on anything that I might want to review at night. I also went home after my first day on the job and dug out something that I intended to put into the pocket of my slacks: my old, trusty switchblade that I had always carried during my rough growing up years in Fort Worth and during my GI years during the war. I had no need of it while I was at General Mills or when I walked the academic halls of GMI, but here, in the "snake pit," I felt a little safer having it with me. I fully intended to follow the rules and I was fully aware that there were metal detectors at each entrance, but I was fairly certain from the first day that I walked into that plant, those metal detectors did not work. The union had sabotaged them long ago. Yet, there they stood right next to the guards at the doors of the plant, inoperable. I determined quite early that any protection that I needed would have to come from my own resources.

There were the things in my personal life that weighed so heavily upon me during the time that I was in Saint Louis that it was really hard on me both mentally and physically. My younger brother, David, was killed. The authorities vacillated between ruling it a suicide and murder. Although the police tried they could never find enough evidence to tie anyone to the crime. The case was never properly concluded.

My youngest brother, Richard, and his wife Felicia almost lost their youngest child due to a hospital error. The baby was permanently disabled because of it. Richard and his wife and two kids had to make adjustments to care for her. That event tragically and permanently affected their lives.

One of my twin sisters, Barbara and her husband Rathel lost both their two boys in a tragic house fire. When the building had begun to blaze and Rathel and the boys were safely outside, the children ran back into the burning building attempting to rescue their family pet, a little dog, when they had become trapped by falling debris. It was devastating—such a harsh blow. Our family had seen so much tragedy already, but this seemed as if it would crush our spirits like nothing else.

Those were dark times. My family was living through overwhelming, soul-rending events. We all had to stand up and to be as strong as we could to help each other to go on with our lives under such devastation.

At work, it helped to keep myself occupied. I walked so much every day, looked so much, wrote many notes on top of notes. It kept me really busy. I tried hard not to dwell on all of my family trouble, but it was impossible not to do it. I worried constantly. I had to really watch myself because I had started to lose weight again.

I saw as many management styles as I did managers. Everybody had his own method of getting the work done and I had decided after about a month of looking, judging and asking questions that I was going to have my own style of management. I knew that I was not going to let myself be buffaloed by the rough shod union leadership who were forever shouting threats, pulling mean, nasty tricks, and doing everything in their power to back management into an unsupported corner. I remained quiet, soft-spoken and watchful. I knew in my heart that I was going to be tested one day and I felt that it would be sooner rather than later. My first test came after I had been on the job for almost five months.

It was the end of the work day. I had spent all day working with the superintendents on problems on the Caprice side of the plant. It did not matter how long my day had been I always spent time before I went home watching the second shift start-up in the Corvette plant.

I loved watching that line move. I enjoyed watching all of the colors and styles of Corvettes go by. What I enjoyed most was watching the guys moving the raw, unpainted panels up to the end of the line to begin the process. But on this day, I was watching something that I had noticed the day before at the beginning of the process:

I was watching the melding of the fiberglass parts using glue which was mixed in huge cement mixers much like the ingredients for cereal dough was mixed back when I had worked at General Mills. The fiberglass parts had to be melded together using glue, then sanded like crazy to try to cover the seams and come out with a smooth, flawless finish before the paint could be applied. I was thinking that there had to be a better way than this for the job to be accomplished.

"You any kin to that nigger, Kirksey, over there in the break room?" a deep sarcastic voice behind me said.

I turned slightly until my eyes fell on the speaker. He was a rough-skinned white man with thick black hair done up in an Elvis-styled pompadour. He had long, bushy sideburns, a sharp-featured face, and a perpetual snarl on his full, red lips. I knew that his name was Donald Snodgress and I often heard that he was a very heavy drinker. His eyes were always red and glassy. I had gotten flak from him both directly and indirectly on several occasions. Once he had made fun of my dark blue striped slacks and the matching tie that Liz had made for me by calling me a "duded-up ghetto boy" within my hearing. Another time he had made some kind of disparaging comment about my afro hairstyle and expressed fear that I might start protesting something right there in the plant and getting other black people to start marching around in a protest group with signs or something.

I had been standing watching the Corvettes at the final line with my arms folded when he approached me. I actually smelled the liquor even before I turned and looked at him. My eyes held his glassy-eyed stare for a long moment.

"No." I said, "Why do you ask?"

He gave out a laugh that ended in a belch then a giggle before he said:

"Both y'all two niggers got pretty much the same names, both y'all are supervisors and y'all look just alike, you know. I was thinking since y'all both got that damn afro shit . . . Uggh!"

He was less than a head shorter than I and muscular. I unfolded my arms when he moved closer to me. Then, the smell of liquor got a whole lot stronger. I lifted both my hands and brought them down onto his shoulders, jerked my knee upwards with a quick, sharp snap and caught him squarely between the legs. I kept my hands on him to support him as he crumpled to the floor retching violently.

"Hey! Hey!!" I yelled loudly, "Got a sick man here!"

Kirksey rushed out of the break room and others came running over from the line. A couple of guys helped the pseudo Elvis to his feet and supported him as he staggered off toward the break room dry heaving all the way.

Kirksey looked at the ruined floor then he stared after the group. "I hate that rat bastard," he said. "Goddamn! That smell! That bastard drunk his goddam' lunch is why he's sick. He's always doin' that kinda' shit."

I re-folded my arms. "A knee in the nuts will do **that** kinda' shit, you know?"

It took a minute for Kirksey to get it. When he did, he turned and stared at me with wide eyes. I winked at him and grinned. He whirled and literally ran away toward the restrooms trying to contain his laughter.

I wish that I could say that everything was A-Okay and smooth as satin after that. It was not. Nothing changed except that as time went on some of the workers and much of management were willing to talk to me but no one seemed really comfortable around me.

Word quickly got around about the little "accident." It was given more embellishment and more details were added each time it was retold. I denied that I had anything to do with it every time someone asked me about it. No one had really witnessed anything and they wouldn't have said anything anyway because nobody really liked Snodgress very much. The black-haired "Elvis" gave me a particularly wide berth after that. He claimed to anyone who would listen that he had been drunk and had puked all over my fancy eel-skin shoes. That was OK with me. I figured that if I could finally get some of the labor group and much of management to see that I was willing to hold my own and pull my own weight without complaining, maybe I would get some amount of respect. Then, maybe, everything else just might have a chance of working out for me.

I became acquainted with many people during the time that I was in training. One of those was a guy who worked in the industrial engineering department named Sam Robinson. He made sure that he told me about many of the ins and outs of the plant culture and introduced me to many people at the plant who might be of some help to me. He took me to places outside the plant where I could find some of the things that we needed for the house and helped me work on my basement some week-ends. He and his wife Hazel were avid golfers and they succeeded in getting me out on the golf course on many weekends to play eighteen holes some Saturdays. Both Sam and I tried our best to do good work, but I suppose it was already wearing Sam down. We talked about it endlessly when our families got together on week-ends and when he, Hazel, and I were on the golf course, too.

If anything, union/management relations deteriorated even more while I was in training. I have to admit that in my heart of hearts I did not believe that there was even the slimmest chance of any improvement. As time went on, the tense, adversarial relationship between the UAW and GM management simmered, percolated and stormed hellishly forward.

When I had finished my year's training I moved to night shift. I started work as an assistant superintendent to Cliff Mitchell who was the department head of Chevrolet Caprice chassis. My responsibility was to take care of the superintendent's job at night. I found that with so many people all in one complex, truly dirty deeds were bound to be done on a regular basis, but night shift was its own particular hell.

One night after I had taken over the Caprice line, I was talking to Tracy Leon, a blond, baby-faced giant of a man who was a, bumper line supervisor. He had admonished me on numerous occasions to "get tough" or "lose my cool" and kick furniture around as he often did to let people know that he was tough. I laughed and said that I did not intend to do that because it was just not my style of management. Although Leon was fairly young, he was an "old style" manager who believed more in being a "boss" than a modern manager. I had just begun to explain my philosophy to him when all hell seemed to break loose on the chassis line.

By the time that Leon and I had pushed our way to the middle of the crowd, we found McKinnon, a supervisor, straddling a committeeman named Hinson who was on the floor trying hard to protect himself. McKinnon had all but made mincemeat of Hinson's face by the time we reached them. It seemed that Hinson had sprayed spittle into McKinnon's face while yelling obscenities at him. The dreaded slang terms "nigger" and "motherfucker," were included in Hinson's foul language and spit-spraying we were told later.

It fell to Leon and me to help in parting the two combatants. I pulled McKinnon's arms hard behind him but I spoke softly against his ear to calm him down and to remind him that he did not want to ruin his career. Although Hinson seemed to allow some members the crowd to hold him back, it was obvious that he wanted no more of the furious McKinnon.

We hated to do it to McKinnon, he was a good man, but both men had to be sent home. Upper management made the decision not to allow McKinnon to return, although I and other members of management spoke on his behalf. I later learned that he had filed suit against management seeking to be transferred to another plant. However, the committeeman, Hinson, was back on his job soon enough, courtesy of the UAW negotiations. The only retribution he suffered was that it took a while before he was able to speak very well. He had to have his mouth wired shut because McKinnon had broken his jaw during the fight. All too soon, it seemed, Hinson was back doing what he usually did—foul-talking to some other supervisor.

A lot of times it was outsiders who caused us trouble, but too many times they had inside accomplices. We had to post outside guards whose regular duty was to call police in if anyone attempted to cut the high chain link fence around the three storage yards. This was where the new cars and trucks were parked waiting to be loaded onto the car carriers and hauled away.

The guards that the plant hired were real armed professionals and off-duty policemen who could carry their own weapons on their hips or in their clothing. That was a good thing because the thieves were armed and they meant business. I was told that the thieves would give very specific orders to their accomplices working on the inside who would then scratch or damage any car or truck that met the thieves' specifications. Then, that car or truck would have to be sent to the repair yard. Sometimes, the car thieves would use whatever distraction that they could to keep the guards away from the repair area until they had safely moved in, swiped the cars or trucks and got them outside the yard. Often the distraction might be drugs, money or women—especially at night.

On one occasion I was called out into the yard because there had been a shooting. A guard, a line worker and a car thief had been shot. The thief had been wounded gravely by the guard and was bleeding but he had made it into the cab of the car hauler and had driven for some distance before he crashed and was caught. An hourly worker was wounded by a weapon as was the guard. We bandaged up the guard on the spot because his wounds were superficial, but the worker had to be put into an ambulance and taken to the downtown hospital because the guard had wounded him pretty seriously with his sidearm. The worker maintained that he was just out for a smoke and had not been involved in any way in the theft. He claimed that he was just caught up in unfortunate circumstances.

I was disgusted to learn that the hell-raising union reps fought to make us keep paying the wounded man while he was out on sick leave and demanded that we restore him to his job when he was finally well enough to return to work. The Labor Relations department fought the union on that, but finally after so much time had passed while GM was still paying the worker, they gave it up under WWOP (withdrawal without penalty). Everybody knew that the worker was guilty as sin but many times the labor relations department was just too short-handed, too swamped with all of the union's cases and too buried underneath everyone's demands that they just had to do the best that they could with what they had.

Not many honest people would go out into the yard at night because it was just too dangerous. Sometimes if an altercation between workers took place at the plant it just might have something to do with some incident that had been started elsewhere. Sometimes really bad incidents took place out in the yard or in the parking lot: fights, stabbings, and group rumbles. Many times a worker would need an armed escort to and from his car if things had gotten too much out of hand or if there was the threat of a group rumble. Fortunately, management was allowed to park in a fenced and gated lot presided over by the armed guards. Otherwise, managers might have been part of those parking lot rumbles all too often ourselves.

I remained soft-spoken just as I had decided that I would be. That did not keep me from issuing strict orders and expecting things to get done just the way that I wanted them to be done. I got constant push-back from the workers and from the union but I did not let up: I kept right on issuing orders and kept right on expecting things to be done my way.

Besides keeping the six–inch knife in my pocket, I kept an eight load handgun under the seat of my car out in the parking lot. Sometimes things got just that bad. My having access to a gun on plant property even outside of the building in my vehicle was surely contrary to the rules of management, but if I ever needed to use that gun it would be because of grave personal danger. That would certainly be outside of management's authority anyway. If I had encountered any trouble, I did not expect that anyone would be able to give me assistance until it was too late.

One evening after I had just come in to work, I was getting ready to get out on the floor. I had finished going over the notes left for me by Cliff and the supervisors telling me what the day shift had accomplished and what they had left that needed to be cleaned up during the second shift. I had already had the meeting with the second shift supervisors and they had gone off to attend to their duties.

Two of the items that were on my desk were from one of the supervisors. His name was Mike Fisher. "Hinds refused to work today," one note said. "Hinds cursed at me and refused to do assignment," said the other. It was not the first time that I had received notes from Fisher about Hinds for one infraction or another. I was damn sick and tired of Hinds and I was a bit annoyed at Fisher for reporting him so often, too. I was getting up to make my way out onto the floor when two people came through my open door. I stopped and sat back on the edge of my desk.

"So what the hell you think 'The Perfesser' gonna' do huh?" Hinds was grumbling too loudly as they walked in.

I was well aware that I was nicknamed alternately "Professor" "Big foot" "Swavee" "Big Dog" "Tall Jack" and such behind my back. I had also been called much worse names than those at one time or another I was pretty sure.

Alonzo Hinds was a black man, short and slim. He was a bouncy-walking popinjay with light skin and hair all the way around his mouth that ended in a scraggly goatee on his chin. He had large white teeth that his thick lips couldn't seem to cover quite properly. Every time I saw him out on the production line, his lips were always open.

Mike Fisher was a brown-skinned black guy who was a lot taller and heavier than Hinds. He was always clean-shaven with a low, neat haircut, and he was good-looking, with sleepy eyelids, and a rather sullen attitude. He was a good supervisor and was always ready to take anybody on if they were not getting their job done.

"He threatened me with a knife," Fisher grumbled to me in a low voice. "This is about the third time he's done that."

"Ain't got no goddam' knife!" Hinds spat. "You seen me wid a knife?"

"Nah, but you ***said*** you had one," Fisher said. "And you ***said*** you were gonna' cut me three ways from Sunday with it if I asked you to do anything else."

"You said you'd wipe the floor wid' my fuckin' ass, too, didn't you?" Hinds retorted.

"You threatened me first." Fisher's eyes glittered ominously beneath his sleepy eyelids. "What I said was: 'if you touch me it will surely make my day.' That's what I said. You're some kinda' fool if you think I'm gonna' just stand still and let you cut me—that's why we're in here right now."

"How about emptying your pockets for Mr. Fisher, then, to show him that you haven't got a knife?" I intervened.

"I ain't emptying my pockets, Perfesser! Your punk ass can't make me neither." His finger was pointed into my face straight at my nose.

Before I knew it, I had reverted to the old rough language from my boyhood neighborhood in Stop Six:

"You better get your goddam' finger outta' my face and settle your crazy ass down," I bristled sharply.

His hand dropped as our eyes locked. "I want my union rep," he snarled, "You better get him in here if y'all gonna' ack a fool up in here."

"Yeah, sure," Fisher said, "Union rep my left nut. Like they give a damn about your black ass. It'll be snowing in June before any of them crackers come in here for you."

I didn't take my eyes off Hinds. "Could you close the door, please, Mr. Fisher?"

Fisher quickly jerked the heavy door loose from the magnetic clamp that held it open, drew it shut and I heard him turn the latch although I had not asked him to do that.

I stood up to my full height and glared down at Hinds. "You want to point your finger in my face again?"

Hind's eyes went wide for a minute. He took a couple of quick steps backward watching me warily. "What you gonna' do if I . . ."

"Do it again," I growled, "You wanna' use that knife on somebody, use it right now. Go ahead and try. I'll break your goddam' hand off at the wrist and jam it straight up your ass."

He hesitated. His head swung around toward Fisher. Fisher's eyebrows were raised in surprise and his face was showing a real grin now. The look that he was giving me was definitely of a different sort.

Hinds turned back to me. Most of his bluster was fading. "They say you been in the war. You got that—that soldier thing where you all nice one minute then you just—you just go all crazy as shit the next minute . . . ?"

"Maybe so," I said. "That's got nothing to do with this. I'll show respect to any and everybody unless they don't deserve it. I'm not always nice."

I stared hard at him unblinking for a second or two more with my eyes narrowed. I tried to look as crazy as he thought I was. I pointed to my desk. "Empty your pockets right there."

He deflated dramatically like a punctured balloon. "Look, man, I—look, I got a blade, but it's . . . *necessary*, man. Shit, I ain't gonna' do nothing wid' it inside the plant. But—but I need it if somebody jump me in the parking lot or something. Hell, I promise, man. I—I didn't mean to threaten Fish, hell, he all right, but . . . look, I can't back down to nobody out there on that floor, man. I do and . . . guy like me, I'm subject to get my ass kicked every damn day in the week."

"I can understand that," I said, "But Fisher's not just anybody. He's your boss. He's the man who's got to see that the job gets done.

You can't go around bucking Fisher all the time. How do you think that makes him look? He's not going to tell you to do a thing that you're not supposed to be doing. If it's not in your job description, he won't tell you to do it. Anybody in Fisher's group is missing their job, then I'm gonna' get on Fisher's ass because he's responsible."

Hinds turned to look at Fisher again. Fisher had folded his arms across his chest in my style and stood nodding smugly at Hinds with that half-smile on his thin lips. Hinds turned back to me.

"Okay, look, if he leave me alone . . ."

"Ain't as if I don't have other shit to do every day," Fisher retorted.

"Well, how come you can't do it then and leave me the hell alone!" Hinds snapped.

"All of us have other things to do," I said reasonably. "Fisher and the rest of us are responsible to keep this whole line operating. You got one job to handle and obviously you're not taking care of that."

"Well, he always try to be—" Hinds started.

But I'd had enough.

"You're no fucking kid," I shot back. "Nobody needs to stand over you. It's not as if you don't get a day's pay for a day's work. You keep on bucking Fisher or anybody else and you're through. I already got nine goddam' write-ups on your ass. I get ten and you're upstairs and then you're on the street—union or no union. That's the rule. I could give one fuckin' damn about you or your goddam' knife! I get one more complaint like this on you, that's ten!"

I stepped around behind my desk and folded my arms to indicate that the interview was over, but I did not sit down. Fisher unlocked the door and held it open. Hinds glared from one of us to the other before he slunk through the door. Fisher continued to hold the door while he looked at me.

"Boss, he's still got the knife," Fisher reminded me softly.

"Yeah," I said. "If we take that blade, tomorrow he's got another. Just write his ass up. Bastard may go to his union rep and the assholes may make us prove that shit I just said."

"I only wrote him up maybe four or five times though," Fisher said a bit sheepishly, "Not nine times like you said I did."

"Then write up some more about . . . something when you get a chance and back-date them," I said impatiently, "I'll sign them. I've had enough from that prick. We can get rid of his ass for a while if not forever."

Fisher grinned. "Yes sir, Boss." He turned to go then stopped. "Bunch of us like to go to a club in East Saint Louis for an hour or two after work. It's right there just across the river. We have a beer or two, discuss the day. Want to go?"

"Sure," I said.

"We'll wait for you by the gate then."

That was the beginning. I had figured I would go just once. But, almost every night after the shift was over, a large group of supervisors, line superintendents, shift superintendents, other various members of upper management and vendors would stop at the club just across the river in East Saint Louis to have a few beers and discuss the happenings of the day. Fisher told the tale of Hinds during the course of that first evening to the hilarity of all of the others. Soon enough the "knee incident" was brought up and thoroughly analyzed. It was obvious that their ideas about me had modified a great deal. If I was not one of them before, I definitely got to be a bit of a minor celebrity as well as a "bearer of the common burdens" after that first night.

During the evening someone had news about what was happening elsewhere, and they talked endlessly about Detroit. I was more than glad that I could learn things from them that I did not have the time to learn when I was on my own job. The people from trucks seemed to have the least amount of problems. We Chevy Caprice people, without question, had the most. But it was the people from Corvette who (we all agreed) needed the most sympathy. They had the most production problems and their customers seemed, by far, to be the most discerning and the most critical in the world. The customers would aggravate the dealers to distraction about hood fits, bumper fits, top fits, seams in the body, paint, and even the little hardly discernible lines in the body finish. Then, the dealers had no choice but to aggravate the assembly plant.

I was already familiar with the Corvette operation. I owned a Corvette and I was on the Corvette side of the plant so much that everyone had become familiar with me. They knew how I felt about the car. The Corvette workers were a closer knit bunch than any group anywhere else in the factory. They had a culture that was unique to them and although I worked on the Caprice line, I felt that I was a part of that Corvette culture too. Their problems were unique and theirs was like no assembly line anywhere else in the complex. Almost everybody was willing to listen to them when they had a triumph or when they complained. Since it was well known that I was a die-hard Corvette lover who bought a new model each year my complaints were always solicited and listened to. In return, I felt free to ask them questions about Corvette assembly.

My disappointment had started with the 1973 Corvette when the chrome front bumper was replaced with a soft nose on the front of the car. I wondered if the people in headquarters in Detroit considered it to be just a cosmetic change or if they really considered that it was an improvement. I also wanted to know why they had not changed the back chrome bumper at the same time. They told me that the body-colored urethane plastic front bumper had seemed like a good idea when it had come from design, but they also shared that the front bumper was a disaster because color matching was such a problem. I wondered how design in Detroit could dump such problems on the people in the plant who were responsible for assembling and shipping the cars—how could they get away with that. I wondered if color mistakes were really the paint shop's fault. With the soft bumpers, things went wrong even before the cars could be shipped—soft indentations and ruffing appeared in the front bumper. I argued that continuous progress needed to be made, and that by now, studies should have been completed to tell whether the new design had really been a success or not. No one could dispute that.

But no matter the complaints, the Corvette people knew what they believed to be the real deal: really obvious changes were made from one model year to the next not to make improvements but because the company needed to sell more cars. Purists like me bought the car for the newness, the different sizes of the motor and for the performance aspect. It was not only for the sake of survival that the company made cosmetic changes to the body, but because more and more the customers were demanding more speed, more horsepower, less noise, better stability, higher revving engines, better tires. And the designers and builders of the Corvette were going to be forced to "come to the party." Yes! I thought. All of that made sense to me.

It was near 6:00 in the morning when I rolled home that first time. Every time after that, I only intended it to make just a short stop at the club over in East Saint Louis, have a beer and unwind from the pressures of the shift. The company and the camaraderie was so good and the atmosphere at the bar was so accommodating to the night shift, when we got together it was sure that the time would usually get away from us. Liz and the kids were always asleep when I got home. Usually, I tried to be as quiet as possible undressing and brushing my teeth before I crashed. I was always beyond tired from work and sometimes more than a little buzzed from my visit to the bar.

This pattern had gone on until one particular time when I came in a bit later than usual and a little more buzzed than usual. I hate to think that I might not have awakened when I did that afternoon if not for Muffy licking my fingers. He had his paws up on the side of the bed staring at me with his big round eyes and whimpering. I looked at the clock on the nightstand. It was only two hours before I had to be at work. I jumped up.

The house was far too quiet which meant that Liz and the kids were out somewhere—again. I was more than a little annoyed that Liz had not left a note this time and had left Muffy in the house so that I had to get up and let him go outside. I barely had the time that I needed to get up, clean up and get myself to work.

Liz always left my dinner prepared. This time, all that was needed was to pop it into the microwave but I did not even want to do that. I was still suffering the effects of last night's drinks. My mood was decidedly black. I felt that Liz should have been at home to help me by laying out my clothes, warming my food and putting my plate on the table for me as she usually did. It was not that I was incapable of taking care of myself, but since Liz did not have a job to go to, it was the least that she could do for me, I grumbled to myself, since I was the only working member of the household these days.

I had finished up the fried chicken, corn pudding, green beans, sweet potatoes and tossed salad that Liz had left covered in the refrigerator for me and was drinking another glass of sweet iced tea when the telephone rang. I was my middle brother, Gregory, who let me know that he had just gotten out of the Navy. He wanted to leave

San Diego. Were there any possibilities that General Motors would be interested in hiring a veteran, he wondered.

"Well, GM might be doing some hiring right about now," I said. "You could give it a shot."

"Man, I need to get out of here," Gregory said. "It's just too damned expensive to live out here. I love this place. The weather is gorgeous, but . . . Wow!"

While he had been stationed in San Diego Greg had met and married Betty who already had two young kids, a boy and girl. Everybody in our family had always thought that Greg was planning on the single, vagabond life and making a career of the Navy.

"I can check for you," I said, "I'll see what areas might need some people. You'll have to interview and have a medical exam if they hire you. You'd likely have to come up here for an interview . . .

"We've already packed up our stuff and given up the apartment," he said. "We're gonna' leave our furniture stored out here. Tonight we'll just put the bags in the car and start traveling. We ought to be there in a couple—maybe three days. Can we stay with you until we get straightened around about what we're gonna' do?"

"Sure," I said.

I had just agreed to let my brother and his family come to stay with us without checking first with Liz. I was pretty sure she'd say it was fine but, of course, she was not at home. My annoyance at my wife flared up again. She certainly had no real good reason not to be home, I told myself. So, what was she doing? Bowling? Shopping? We would have talked about this if she were here—maybe made some kind of a plan. What could have been more important to her than being at home anyway? It did not occur to me at that time, but I could sometimes be the most selfish and demanding person in the world.

I was still simmering when I stepped out of the shower. I got even more annoyed while I was getting ready for work. I was getting really, really tired of this whole thing. I told myself that I was lucky that Liz was still not home. If she had been, there was sure to be a fight. We hardly ever talked normally anymore and when we did, it usually ended in a heated argument about one thing or another.

Liz was not a fair fighter. Usually, she would quietly listen when I went on and on about this thing or that thing or whatever had stirred me up. These days, it happened pretty often and I could get pretty vocal but Liz might not even give her opinion about any point of contention or say how she felt unless I really pinned her down. If she got angry at me about something, she would snap at me initially but afterwards she had gotten to the point that she would clam up tighter than a drum. After that, she might walk around without speaking to me for days. She was really adept at avoiding contact with me in our modest little house in every way that she could find. Whenever I came into a room she would leave almost immediately.

On weekends when I was home, if Liz didn't go off with the kids early in the morning, she would retreat with the kids to the basement. The kids would play with their toys in front of the old television that I had set up for them next to the stairs while Liz would go into her sewing room in the back corner of the basement. If I wanted to talk to her at all I would have to make a special trip downstairs to the basement to trap her in down there. Lately, I felt like just shaking her until her teeth broke up into little ivory chips and rattled right out of her head. In truth though, I would have died before I put my big hands on my precious little wife in anger. I loved her far too much and had loved her far too long to ever think of doing a thing like that.

I really did need to talk to Liz about this new situation with Greg. It wasn't as if Gregory was not going to find himself a place as soon as he could get a job. He had said that if his job hunt in Saint Louis was unsuccessful, he intended to go on home to Fort Worth to look for a job. Because Liz was not home when I had to head out for work, I decided that I would have to call her as soon as I got a break to tell her all of this.

I fully intended to call Liz when I caught a break, but I had really gotten busy because as luck would have it the Caprice line went down around 7:00 that evening. I never even got the chance to call after that. By the time we got the line stabilized enough to run and started it back up, I decided that it was far too late to call Liz. It was almost the end of the shift. As it happened, a maintenance foreman, Eddie Jones, and a couple of Corvette general foremen, Sweeney and Hanson came by wanting me to go over to East Saint Louis with them when the shift ended. I knew that they wanted to talk about the Corvette move.

"Just for about an hour or so," I told them. "I need to get on home tonight."

As soon as we were settled at a table with our beer in front of us they began to talk about the Corvette move to Bowling Green. The whole place had been in an uproar about it for months now. Suddenly, people were leaving and the reality was all too tangible.

"We're moving with Corvette to Bowling Green!" Eddie Jones told the table at large. "This is my last day today fellows. Me and Carol are going, going, gone!"

We all cheerfully raised a glass to salute him.

"I heard that Bowling Green let them have all that land and there was already had a plant on it—they sold it to m for $1.00 per year just to get the Corvette operation to move down there," said Sweeney, "General Motors is really making out on that one."

"I don't believe it," Jones said, "They gotta' be paying the city more than that."

"No, no, it very well could be true," Sweeney argued. "Hell, the city will collect the taxes, and there will be more people moving to Bowling Green on account of the Corvette plant. Bowling Green's already done whatever they had to do to get the operation to move down there, believe me."

"Who else wants to re-locate down there now they got it set up?" Hanson asked.

Several voices among the Corvette supervisors said:

"Hell, I will"

"Do what I hafta' do to keep on working"

"Dang! I'd hate to leave Saint Louis, but, hell yes!"

"Shit, a job is a job."

I think everyone who worked in the Chevy and truck sections were actually disheartened now that it was really and truly done. It was common knowledge that the entire Saint Louis operation had seemed to be far too out of hand—too hard to be managed properly. None of the cars and trucks that were being made in the plant was selling as well as they had in the past. For years, the Corvette was not selling as well as some people thought that it should. It was common knowledge throughout the company that the Corvette project designers had worked very, very hard to keep costs down and yet keep the car competitive. There were people in upper management who were committed to saving the Corvette, but there were others who firmly believed that General Motors should stop manufacturing the car altogether. Most of the car magazines had some praise for the car and a few even stressed that someday it would be more of an icon than anyone could imagine. There was always the talk about Corvette being "America's Sports Car," and famous race car drivers were always willing to drive it on the track in "Name Brand" races, but it was obviously our customers, the everyday drivers, who bought and drove the cars who made the car viable and worthy of continued manufacture. These drivers were the ones who should have really mattered to upper management. It seemed that we were always discussing this.

"Oh, no, no, no," Sweeney argued, "If management cared at all about the customers, they would be manufacturing more of the cars that customers really want. Now you just look at the 1965 'fuelies.' Now that was a car! I'd love to have one of those cars in my garage right now."

The "fuelies" had been inspired, someone argued, maybe the move to Bowling Green would allow General Motors to begin building them again. Someone else argued that those cars would never make it into mass production because of the way that they had to be produced.

"No way we could keep 'em," Sweeney argued, "those cars almost have to be handmade. We can't bring them back. No way. Nothing that special is ever going to be easy to get out efficiently anymore the way production is running now."

Our talk went on and on. When I looked at my watch it was nearly 3:00. I had intended to head for home at no later than 1:30. I jumped up and rejected the offers to buy me another beer, turned down pleas from someone else to stay a little longer, and tried to shake off my beer buzz. I left the club and headed for my car.

If I am to be completely honest, I have to admit that the night club/bar across the river in East Saint Louis had become more than just a fair enticement for me. The management was determined to make the place welcoming for the workers on both the first and second shifts at the local factories. People from all over the plant could get together and share the news about what was going on in their part of the plant and give opinions about what was going on at HQ as well. All of us could share our problems in that atmosphere and help each other in any way that we could. Once the male workers staked out this certain bar as their place to relax and unwind, the female workers were sure to follow.

I have been a self-sufficient person for as long as I can remember. I had to be because my mother worked all hours of the day and at night. Seeing to my younger siblings and working to help to bring in money for the household made a man of me even when I was very young. I will only say that I have tried very hard to be my own man and make footprints around the lines that some men are very quick to step across.

I have always enjoyed looking at and admiring beautiful females just as much as any other healthy male. My quick and ready smile has often gleaned for me both wanted and unwanted attention from many women. But, even as a young, single man, I maintained strict limits. During my youthful years, most of my male friends who knew me well always said that making fortunate alliances with "real women" came much too easy for me. They claimed that I did not know just how hard it was to meet and connect with women. But true to my natural instincts and my own limits of decency, I never bragged or made boastful claims about my "conquests", and I tried never to encroach on any other man's territory. I have only made the one exception in my lifetime along that line—but it was a big one. I did what I had to do at that time only because the one true love of my life was engaged to marry another man when I met her.

That night I certainly had not intended to stay at the club as long as I had. I had no plans outside the one to get into my car and go home. I was heading into the darkened parking lot moving fast. I certainly did not intend for anyone to follow me out. It was always likely that someone might come out of the club with me and sometimes we would talk on the way out. Only occasionally did I walk out alone. I heard the quick, soft step and the rustle of movement. I turned around just as I reached my car. Just like she had on other occasions when we were alone she came up hard against me with her face against my bare throat inside my shirt collar. She felt and smelled wonderful and alluring. She knew just what her effect would be as her soft body pressed against me.

"You ignored all of us but I'm the one who's got you!" she laughed as she fitted her body against mine.

"Hey, hey," I said pulling her arms away, "Don't do this. You know I can't be fraternizing like this with the hourly—"

"Who's looking!" she countered. She stepped back. "Okay, then. My car is right over there. I know it's late but we can get in my car and we can go anywhere you say. We can be together any way you want. You won't have to worry about it. It'll be just you and me. Give me some time, Sugar. I want to be with you so much!"

She moved in on me again. Of all the single women that she always hung around with at the club, she was the most aggressive

She was a tall, large, shapely woman, less than a head shorter than I. I had told her many times not to do it, but she was very persistent. When I was at the club, she sometimes managed to insert herself next to me if we were at a table or in the bar. She always kept up a steady leg war with me at the table. I would spend the whole time doing everything that I could not to touch her

She was more than just good-looking and she knew it. She had brown skin, made smooth and flawless by expert make-up, short, curly hair and dark eyes that flashed an invitation every time she caught my eye. She and her former husband and her former boyfriend (who did not accept that he was "former") all worked at the Saint Louis GM complex. The boyfriend was a case. He had threatened several men, including me, just for looking at her. That did not stop her looking at me though. She worked on the first shift Caprice line. If I happened to be in the area or walked anywhere near her station, (which I studiously tried to avoid) she stopped what she was doing and just watched me to the point that it was all too obvious. Her whole face and demeanor would change when I came anywhere near where she was. A couple of the guys had told me she said that she was head over heels in love with me, but she wasn't the only one! After I had moved to second shift, someone was always leaving notes or gifts on my desk. I could admit to being flattered by the female attention, but that did not make me a fool. I had no desire to become a part of anyone's plots and schemes.

"I can't," I said. I was casting around for any excuse that I could find. "My brother is coming and I should have been home already."

She burrowed against me more if that were possible, and her arms were tight around me.

"You're always running away from me! Bet you don't run away from *her*! I've seen that bitch looking at you. She knows she'll never have you! I've got you now, even if it's just for a minute or two . . . put your arms around me, baby . . ."

I knew that I should refrain from letting her get that close even though I secretly enjoyed her avid admiration. I gave her a hug which I hoped would be satisfactory to her. I knew right away that I shouldn't have done it because as close as she was she had to feel my body's purely male reaction. She sighed, her hands came up onto my chest and she began to plant feathery kisses against my throat. I guess she was just that sure of herself. She probably figured that I was hooked and would no longer have the common sense to put her away from me . . . but I did. I disentangled myself from her avid hands and mouth despite her reluctance to let me go, and quickly folded myself into my Corvette.

When I got home, I was sure that everyone would be in bed, but just as I came in from the garage Muffy trotted sleepily into the kitchen to greet me with his stub of a tail twitching and the tags on his collar tinkling musically. He looked up at me so I bent down and gave him a pat on the head. He rubbed against my leg like a cat and then he headed for the back door. I followed to let him outside to do his business and waited leaning against the washing machine until he came back. I closed and locked the back door and when I walked back down the hall, Liz was standing in the doorway of the guest room with her arms folded. Her bright, dark eyes clearly said "*angry*" in their depths as she glared at me with downturned lips.

"So, she finally let you come home, did she?" Liz said drily. "One of these nights she just might not." She glared at me for a minute, then she said:

"Some crazy woman called and woke me up and said I better keep an eye on you if I wanted to keep you. Who ***is*** this woman she keeps on calling about?"

I frowned. All too often a man will pretend to be angry even when he knows that he has no right to be. I do not know of any truly guilty man who will not rely on anger as a defense when he feels that there is no other outlet readily available to him. I was feeling more than a little guilty remembering that previous encounter.

"Who is ***who***?" I snapped, frowning even more deeply. "What the hell are you talking about? I just went over to East Saint Louis with the guys for a little while like I always do. They were—"

"Sure you did. You think I believe you go over to East Saint Louis with the ***guys*** every night?"

"What are you asking me, then?" I snapped, "You know I don't go ***every*** night." I did not even consider whether or not I was telling the complete truth or I might have felt a twinge of guilt:

"I've told you before: I just get together with them once in a while and try to unwind a little. We always have some discussion about what's going on in everybody's—"

She ignored my explanation and held up her fingers as if she was numbering my sins.

"Now let's see . . . you claim that you've been playing golf with Sam and Hazel for the last two week-ends. You never gave a thought at all to your family. Then, you must have gone somewhere after you played golf because you ***still*** came home late on those nights, too. So, where do you go after you play golf? Whenever you get home you're always just *so* tired. You expect me to believe you're playing ***night*** golf? Off hand, I'd say that you're living your whole life somewhere else these days. You never have time for your family even on the weekends. You barely eat one meal a day here during your work week and last time you even ate dinner somewhere else—"

"What?" I growled again just to interrupt her. I really couldn't deny anything that she said, but I knew that I had to head off those accusations. So, I said what any guilty man might say because he believes that the best defense is to hurl a few accusations of his own at his accuser:

"What the hell do you want from me anyway? When I get up to go to work you're not even here. You've got the kids and you're gone every damn time I get up."

"What do *I* want from *you*?" she repeated as she stared at me, and the look that came across her face I could remember seeing there only one time before. I was feeling a bit of satisfaction about my stinging remark until she quickly turned her back to me. She hesitated, and then she dashed her hand across her eyes.

"So, you finally noticed that we aren't here when you get up," she said shakily with her back still turned. "That took you a long time so I'm surprised that you finally did notice. Not that you really care. As long as you have food ready when you want to eat, clean clothes when you need them, you could care less about the kids anymore or anything else that goes on in this house."

Muffy had already headed to his usual place on Liz's side of our bed. She called to him and he came out of our bedroom, looked up at her and followed her into the small guest room. I started after her intending somehow to mollify her or at least to refute her claims but when she turned around the wet shine in her narrowed eyes and the fury that was etched on her face stopped me cold.

"You've got some damn nerve coming in here so late smelling like a distillery. So now you've started coming home even later smelling like the perfume counter at some department store. What makes you think I want to smell ***her*** jasmine . . . or roses . . . or whatever that is all over you? So, what's next? Soon enough I guess you won't bother to come home at all. I know you don't expect me to wait around for that!"

I was stunned! There was absolutely nothing that I possibly ***could*** have said after that. Liz closed the guest room door in my face and I heard her turn the lock.

Good Grief! I hadn't even considered that I might have brought the remnants of her ***smell*** home on my clothes! I hastily went into the bathroom and stripped off my shirt. Sure enough it smelled strongly of a woman's sweet perfume. I wondered why I hadn't smelled it on me at any of those times when she or someone else had been that close to me before. There were red smudges on the front and one collar tip of my shirt and when I looked into the bathroom mirror with the bright fluorescent bulbs all around it I could see the smudges on the neck band of my undershirt where she had snuggled up against me with her lips against my throat. All this time when Liz had been washing my clothes and taking my pants, shirts and coats to the cleaners I had not even given a second thought to anything like that! Ah, dammit to hell! I swallowed hard. Liz had never said one word to me about this until right now. I tried to think: how many times ***had*** that happened before?

Angrily, I stripped off my clothes, got into the shower, turned the water on full spray and scrubbed. My rather pleasant alcohol-buzz was all but gone now replaced with a dark, simmering, self-sobering anger. Deep down, my common sense told me that I was being unreasonable and had no right to be angry at Liz, yet I was *very* angry because she had no right to be so hasty in her judgment. Didn't I deserve a rebuttal of some sort? In reality, since I had been faithfully married to her all this time and had never even ***considered*** being unfaithful, I figured that I was at least as good as some and better than most. Sure, like a lot of men, I tended to flirt a bit with the women, especially when I had had a drink or two, but, still, I deserved Liz's complete and utter trust no matter how things might have ***seemed*** to be!

I came out of the bathroom, put on clean PJs, turned back the covers, and fell onto the bed. Alone against the unwelcoming coldness of the sheets, I felt like I was a mile or more behind the lines into unfamiliar enemy territory and here was only bare, cold ground where I needed desperately to conceal myself. I could only stare up at the ceiling just as I had stared up at the flat black skies in Vietnam. I tried hard to make myself fall asleep but my body was on alert—my combat-trained hearing was at its keenest peak. I know that I must have heard it many times before—probably it was at this same time each morning but I hadn't consciously noticed it until I was alone in my bed like this:

Whump! Whump! Whump! Whump! Whump! Whump! Whump!

It was the hard, muffled sound of the rotor blades of a commercial helicopter or maybe a news chopper that was used by the TV stations for gathering reports about the weather. It was obviously headed toward the Saint Louis airport not too far away. Before the sound faded into the distance I realized that I had been holding my breath. I had to force myself to relax.

That sound brought back memories of the dark nights that I had spent alone under the foreign skies deeply hidden in North Vietnam territory watching the lights of reconnaissance helicopters flying over the ruined landscape. As soon as the lights passed my position, I would draw a quick bead it if it came within reach of my night scope. Depending upon the direction that the chopper was moving, I would whisper a hurried report to my nearest contact so he could radio the base. I can remember that I had to hold the radio very close to my mouth—so close that the wire mesh was right up against my lips. It took practice to learn to relax my muscles—it was a constantly tense situation. Mostly, I had to maintain complete silence inside my cover in the bush and rocks while still staying alert. The base camp needed to be alerted especially if I discovered that there was any troop movement or other activity at night. If I sent a report then I would have to move—and fast. As a Forward Observer (FO) hiding deep in enemy territory to gather reconnaissance information, I could not risk discovery. Even now (I hate to admit it) I can clearly remember my orders: if man, woman or child stumbled onto my position they could not be left with the ability to raise an alarm. If there were too many of them, then the FO had to determine if capture was eminent. An FO could never allow himself to be taken alive.

I heard the noises now; I had been asleep and nothing registered in my mind at first. I had spent an awful night tossing and turning with the nightmares goading me. Horrible images kept fading in and out of my dreams. They had come back once again and more often now since I had been working in the "snake pit" pressure cooker that was the Saint Louis complex. Even before this, I had never quite gotten over those sweat-drenched episodes. Most of those times, stress caused me to have a bit of a flashback, and sometimes if I was over-tired it might happen. Luckily, a beer or two before bed was strong enough to hold back the worst threat.

If anyone should ever wonder why a former combat veteran is very likely to be a drinker, it is because he has found that a good stiff drink of alcohol before going to bed will often assure him of clearing out his mind so that he is able to sleep deeply and peacefully. One might think that a cluttered mind would surely serve to fend off the threat of terrible nightmares—

Not true!

Oftentimes the close calls in which a soldier's life was spared while others were not mixes right in with other scenes in a war veteran's dreams and even a dream that started as either ordinary or pleasant has the potential to switch without warning into a horrible nightmare about the war.

One of my legs was twisted up in the sheets and I really thought I could smell the remnants of bomb blasts, burning foliage and that other unforgettable smell of burning flesh and vacated bowels. Then

I heard the sound again. I had left the bedroom door open and this time I recognized the sound of my brother's laughter. I realized that the smell that drifted into my nose came from the kitchen. This time, the faint, pleasant smells that reached my nose were from Liz's cooking.

I got up, took off my pajamas and pulled on fresh underwear and a tee shirt. I found the pair of soft cotton plaid Bermuda shorts that I usually wore around the house, got my slippers and stuck my feet into them. I went into the bathroom, wet my toothbrush, squeezed out a worm of toothpaste, washed the gritty sleep taste from my mouth and rinsed with stinging red mouthwash. Then, I got my face cloth, wet it and cleaned the remnants of my restless sleep from my face.

Greg jumped up and came over to hug me the moment I walked down the hallway. I had met his wife, Betty, only once before when she and Greg had flown down to Fort Worth the past Christmas so that Betty could meet the whole family on a rare occasion when everybody had been home for the holidays. I hugged everyone including Betty's two children, Trish and Walter. Crissy and David took their turns hugging my legs and I bent down to kiss their sweet little faces. I thought about what Liz had so harshly thrown at me the night before: I hardly ever saw the kids these days. But, that was completely Liz's fault I rationalized to myself with a surge of annoyance because Liz always had the kids out somewhere whenever I was at home.

Everyone was just finishing up lunch. The kids had already abandoned their half-eaten meals on the table. They ran off to the basement door and clattered down the stairs. I knew that they were headed for the corner in the basement where their toys and their old television were located. Trish and Walter remembered their manners: they brought their plates to the kitchen sink before they followed Crissy and David to the basement.

I remembered then that I had not had the opportunity at any time lately to tell Liz beforehand that Greg and his family were coming. I felt a twinge of guilt about that but I quickly shook it off remembering that eruption between Liz and me on the previous night. I was still bristling and smarting from that! Right now Liz seemed to be intent on making things seem "normal" for our visitors. She had gotten everyone fed it seemed, now she dished up a plate of food for me and brought it over to my place at the table. It was beef stew with a side of corn bread—one of my favorite meals. The delicious aroma of the stew stirred my taste buds but I resisted the urge to even look at the plate that Liz had prepared. When I think about it now, I realize that I could really be a stubborn ass in those days.

"I'm going to get ready because we need to get on over to the plant," I told Greg. "I've got your interviews set up as soon as we get in."

"Yeah, okay," Greg slid his chair back and looked at his watch. "I'll need to freshen up a bit but I'll be ready to go when you get ready." He grabbed two of the suitcases that they had brought into the kitchen. "Show me where to put these," he said.

I picked up the other two bags and led Greg down the hall to the small guest room. I did not even look at Liz, but I imagined the expression that was on her face. When I came out of the guest room where I had put Greg's suitcases I looked down the hall and saw Liz when she cleared the other plates from the table, quickly snatched up the plate that she had made for me and headed into the kitchen with it.

When I came back down the hallway dressed for work, Liz, Betty and Greg were huddled over a map of Saint Louis that they had spread out on the kitchen table. Liz had brought out a pad to write on and I presumed that they were mapping out the area so Greg could make his way back to the house after his interviews.

"Man! I'm just going to have to pray and hope I don't get lost coming back," Greg was laughing. He refolded the map and picked it up. "Y'all might have to come and get me off some street corner in some neighborhood somewhere."

Liz and Betty gave him assurances that he would be all right. Liz promised that she would come and get him and lead him back to the house if he got lost.

I went over to the basement door and yelled "goodbye" down to the kids. Their little voices echoed back up the basement stairs and I could imagine that they were busy showing off their toys to Trish and Walter. When I turned around Liz was gone from the kitchen and I again felt that surge of anger toward her that was becoming all too familiar. I knew my wife, she was fuming because I had not eaten the meal she had prepared for me and she wasn't about to give me the satisfaction of **not** saying "goodbye" to her.

"Do I look okay?" Greg fretted, "I haven't had to dress up in a while."

He was wearing a beige long-sleeved dress shirt and a beige, maroon, and grey striped tie with dark grey slacks. I couldn't have done better myself.

"You look good, Bro," I assured him. I was proud of my younger brother.

After a bit more discussion I pulled out of the driveway with Greg following behind me in his car and we headed for the plant in downtown Saint Louis. I figured that I would drive slowly enough for him to formulate some idea of the route that he would have to take to get back to the house.

I was hungry, but I was really, really dreading walking over to the cafeteria. For a brief moment I halfway considered stepping out to the vendors who always established themselves as near as they could to the back doors of the plant to sell food to the workers. By this time the plant was no longer allowing them to park as close to the back doors as they had in the past. Still, they were close enough so the workers could easily walk over to their trucks to buy food at lunchtime and take it back to the break room.

Those independent lunch truck vendors were really a competitive bunch. They never failed to give a good amount of food for the money that they charged, but at one time when there had been no controls at all on the vendors, they had become more of a problem than an asset for the plant. I had heard that a vendor had shot another over a desirable parking space close to the back door. According to whoever was telling the stories, any number of bloody rumbles, furious fist and knife fights, and all manner of altercations with baseball bats had broken out between the food vendors in the past. I had been told that there had been some of the worst kind of bloodletting going on right outside the back door of our complex.

Finally, the law enforcement team required the vendors to park further back away from the plant entrances but still they were permitted to be on General Motors territory. Anyway, nothing had stopped the ongoing competition and warfare among them. I had sworn that I would not patronize them even when I needed to grab a quick meal. I had more than one reason not to go over to the cafeteria and all of them involved aggressive females. I was thinking that if Fisher or someone intended to go out, I might prevail upon one of them to get a meal for me.

By the time that I got Greg situated in the personnel office, my stomach was really talking. When I got back downstairs to the Caprice offices Cliff was still there in his office next to mine with two of the general foremen from the day shift. We did not often get to talk between our shifts so I stepped into Cliff's office to see if there was anything that I needed to know before I met with the night shift personnel.

Of course the conversation was all about the Corvette move to Bowling Green, Kentucky. The move had begun and everyone was talking about it now. Surprisingly, after all the bellyaching and moaning, most of the workers had packed up and summarily moved their families out of Saint Louis. Surprisingly, those who were left and those not likely to be affected next seemed to be the most optimistic about it.

Everybody was talking about the two-toned Corvette coupe that was planned for the 25th anniversary. The hand-built prototype from Detroit had sat covered and taped up over in the Corvette area for several weeks before anyone was allowed to see it. I had been one of the many people who surreptitiously lifted the cover to take a peek. Everyone was impressed by the fact that it was supposed to have glass pop-out top panels wired right into the anti-theft system instead of a the normal body-colored roof. That had caused all kinds of talk and speculation for several weeks.

"I love the smoky glass tops on that job," said a paint guy named Jude Wolenski. "But that damned thing is just too small to have a two-toned paint job on it. I don't care what the damned desk jockeys up to Detroit say. They could fuck up a wet dream anyhow. Caprices will never have two-tones like that, and that's a fact. You know what though; at least the Caprice is big enough to handle the two-toned job if those damned fools ever catch a notion to do something like that. But the Corvette . . ." He shook his head, "Naaah!"

"Would you want to get that new one, Cooksey?" asked Steve Brandt.

"Sure," I said, "I like what they've done to that back bumper for this model. That thing's good looking! I love everything about that prototype even though the paint job is a mess. I squeezed a couple of those extra badges out of Frank to use on my desk as paperweights. Damned things are really big! He says that they're only going to put those on for the 25th. That car really has potential to be sweet."

"Whatcha' think Jude?" Brandt turned to Wolenski. "Think y'all could ever paint that thing in the plant here? That looks like a two or three process hand job to me. How the hell you gonna' mass produce something on an assembly line when you gotta' hand paint every last one of 'em?"

"We got an order to paint and stripe one or two of 'em, just to see what it really looks like," Wolenski said. "But, naaah, you know they're not thinking of hand painting all of the production. They won't be painting any of 'em here 'cause it wouldn't make sense. I understand they're setting up a system in Bowling Green to get that done right off the line using lacquer and—I guess—a clear coat. I haven't been down there to see what they got because nobody's said nothing to me about going. I really wouldn't mind taking a look at that new system they're getting set up."

Wolenski was a day shift foreman who was one of the best paint guys in the business. He was a through-and-through paint guy. He had his own paint shop on his property out in the country where he had been doing fancy and custom painting for the race car crowd for years. He had invited me out to see his operation. I had yet to make it. I figured that he would not even consider the move to Bowling Green because of his business.

"The 25th anniversary," Cliff sighed. "And here I didn't think Corvette would even make it to 15."

"That restyled back window is damned good-looking," Wolenski admitted. "They shoulda' had something like that long ago. That woulda' helped out a lot. Those cleaner lines will make it easier to paint."

"I bet it's going to be a damn good seller," I said. "Clean lines, stylish back bumper, two-tone paint if they can get it together. If not, one tone on it will still make a good seller. I don't know about that white leather wrapped steering wheel that they've got on the prototype over there but I bet that won't stay. They've tried that before and that white steering wheel gets dirty-looking real quick from people's hands. I guess it's like you say though, real Corvette people will go for it just because it's different. Anything different! They'll wrap the damned thing in plastic to keep it clean if they have to!"

"Them ol' race car boys love 'different', let me tell you," Wolenski said with a yawn. "I woulda' been outta' business long ago if they didn't like alla' that flash and dash."

Cliff stood up and stretched.

"I gotta' go home," he said. He looked at me. "Been rough as a cob today. We've been getting some bad door fits on and off, and I really don't think we've seen the end of that yet. We got some of those doors straightened around pretty good but we had to send the rest on out to repair. I left some notes on your desk." He flexed his shoulders. "Oh, yeah, while I had your office open, somebody came in with a box they wanted me to put on your desk. I think it's something for Liz."

"For Liz? But who—" I started. I stopped quickly because from the corner of my eye I caught a look that shot surreptitiously between Wolenski and Brandt. Ah, hell, I thought, now this shit is sure to start some talk. That will never do.

"Probably some sewing they want Liz to do," I said nonchalantly. "Liz is always sewing something for somebody."

I went next door to my own office. I unlocked the door and turned on the light. Sure enough a little square white gift box sat on my desk. Way too small to hold any sewing stuff despite what I had thrown out as a smoke screen to the guys. It had Liz's name written on the top of the box and I did not recognize the writing—I knew that I probably wouldn't have recognized it anyway.

I took out my knife and slit the tape that held the top to the rest of the box. I opened it and there sat a little round, chocolate cake with the name "Liz" written in cursive on the top of the cake in white icing that looked like it had been squeezed out of one of those cake decorators' tubes. The cake looked like a "quickie" similar to one Liz and I had bought once from a grocery store bake shop when we had almost forgotten a birthday for one of the kids.

I looked to see if a card or a note or something might be attached to the box. There was nothing. I knew I wouldn't take this home to Liz. She was beyond cautious about food because of some strange incident that had happened during her childhood—something about a feud where an entire farm family had died when their well water had been poisoned. I thought fleetingly about cutting a piece of the strange cake but something, some feeling about what Liz had said, made me change my mind.

I saw a couple of my foremen headed for my office for our meeting before the start of the shift and I still hadn't had time to get myself anything to eat. I closed the box, put in on the credenza behind my desk, and picked up the notes that Cliff had left for me. It was going to be a long night.

A little bit later, I saw Gregory coming toward me escorted by one of the guys from up in personnel. When they saw me, they spoke together for a few minutes then shook hands. The personnel guy headed back the way they had come.

We were still having big problems with door fits so I had been in discussions with Fisher, Grant, and Taylor the shift superintendents at the line where we had been since the shift had gotten started. I left them and walked over to meet Greg. He had good news. He said that Cliff had already told the people in personnel that he would use Greg on the frame line. I made a mental note to thank Cliff for that. I dreaded doing it, but I knew that I would have to go up to personnel to acknowledge the favor, too.

Greg was overjoyed at the prospect of getting a job so quickly.

"I just gotta' get a physical, Bro," Greg was saying excitedly as we walked over to my office. "They gave me a list of clinics and doctors who'll do the physicals. I just gotta' get to one of 'em. I had a hearing test not too long ago and I know I've got bad hearing, but this place would kill a man's hearing anyway with all of this noise! I was thinking that I might not be able to cut it but this is a factory, after all and I know it's not any worse than any other factory anywhere else.

"It's a different kind of noise than on that ship, man. You know being on a ship's out in the ocean is like nothing else. It's kinda'—it's kinda' muted below decks and everywhere else. There's only water noise sometimes. There's nothing else in the world like it. Hopefully I can get used to this real fast—in fact I know I can. Even if I gotta' use earplugs at first. Nobody seems to be affected by noise in this place. They're just going right on doing their jobs like nothing's happening.

I never thought I'd ever work in a factory but I bet I'm gonna' really like it. I already met some good, friendly folks, you know? The women who work upstairs are something else. Coupla' women seem to be crazy about you, you know. The woman in charge of personnel kept asking me all kinda' questions about you. When I get back to the house, I need to see what my clothes are looking like. I don't wanna' come out here dressed like I don't know what's going on."

I unlocked my office door, we walked in and I closed the door and stood against it for a moment. Because of his own talkative excitement, Greg probably hadn't noticed that I had been silent until now. His eyes followed me anxiously as I walked around behind my desk. I retrieved the cake and set it out onto my desk.

"What's up, Bro?" Greg said.

"Somebody sent this to Liz," I said opening the box.

Greg peered into the box. "A cake?" he asked incredulously. Then he said, "That's a cake!"

"Yeah," I said, "That's what it looks like. I don't know who sent this to Liz, but . . ."

We were both silent for a long moment as we looked at each other. It was as if I could see the wheels turning inside Greg's head. It was as if he could see right into my thoughts, too.

"You're not taking that thing home to Liz." He said softly.

I shook my head. "She wouldn't touch it anyway."

"Aw, man!" he stared at the cake. "Me neither. Wonder what's . . . ? You think it's from one of those women . . . I already heard that gossip from that guy up in personnel about that gal who's plum nuts over you, but . . . Aw, man!! Somebody thinks Liz is gonna' eat this?" He began to laugh. "Look Bro, maybe we should take this thing to a crime lab or someplace to see if there are razor blades in it or something—like crazy people give kids when they go trick or treating at Halloween. Maybe we better get it X-rayed or analyzed or—"

I laughed, too. "Now, how am I supposed to do that?" I closed the box. "What's it gonna' prove anyway. I'm just gonna' drop this thing into one of the garbage barrels around here. Come on, I'll walk you out. I'm so hungry, I could eat a bear. I guess I might as well stop by one of those damn criminals' lunch trucks . . ."

Later on that night, we had gotten a pretty good head up on the Caprice door fits. We narrowed the bad ones down to a particular supplier who was shipping Caprice doors and truck doors to the plant. We found way too many hit-or-miss products in his batches. I had enough evidence now to add to Cliff's findings. This company was going to have to be told to either tighten up the quality control methods or we would have to drop its doors off our supplier's list.

I finally had the chance to get back into my office. I sat down at my desk anxious to call home. I wanted to see if Greg had made it back to the house and figured that Liz would be forced to talk to me on the phone because she would have no choice since we had visitors in the house. I found myself badly wanting to hear the soft contralto of her voice, but even more now because of the constant anger between us. I figured Liz might even put the kids on the phone like she used to do. David did more breathing into the receiver than talking but Crissy was getting better and better at holding a pretty good telephone conversation.

I tried to think of the last time we had talked together on the phone. How long had it been? Two weeks? A month? More than that, I had to admit.

The last time, Liz had laughed as she told me how she had taken the kids to an ice cream parlor in the mall and just as they were walking away from the counter David had dropped his scoop of ice cream right out of the cone and onto the floor before he could even get a good lick from it. David had bawled so loudly that the clerk behind the counter had quickly given him an even bigger cone. Liz said that he was smiling with tears still rolling down his cheeks. I smiled a bit to myself thinking how Liz always had such amusing stories to tell me about the kids or Muffy's antics. What had happened lately? Why was I missing all of that?

I knew exactly why I did not call home as often as I had before. It was the almost constant fighting between Liz and me. I really wondered when had it started and what had caused it? Hadn't it started even before I had been going across the river after work? I had been going for a while, but no, it had been only lately that everything had really gone straight downhill between us. I knew that I had been finding excuses and avoiding it, but, it galled me to think that Liz might say that it was all my fault, so I was determined that I was not going to let her do that. I couldn't keep on avoiding it, though. Sooner or later we had to try to figure this thing out. I quickly punched in the numbers on the telephone.

It was Greg who answered and as soon as he heard my voice he launched into a run-down of things that he needed to get done before he started work next week. He laughed heartily as he told me how he had gotten his huge hand stuck in the kids' cookie jar earlier in the evening. Liz and Betty had laughed at him and put cooking oil on the rim of the jar to get his hand free. That reminded him:

"Gloves! Gloves!" he said, "I forgot to tell them I needed gloves. Oh, man!"

"We'll get you a pair of gloves here," I said. "Where's Liz?" I asked.

"Liz took Betty over to the mall to get me a couple of shirts and, maybe, a pair or two of jeans and maybe some khakis. The outfits I had in Cali won't do. I know they're too dressy for out there on that factory floor."

I bit down my disappointment. I had made myself believe that Liz and I might be able to talk sanely and more easily since Greg and his family were in the house.

"What did Liz say? Did she make dinner before they left?"

"Yeah. She made pork chops, some corn, rice and gravy for everybody else but I ate some more of that leftover stew and cornbread 'cause I really liked it at lunchtime. Liz sure can cook, Bro."

Yeah, I thought to myself, my talented little wife does many things very well. So why can't she get along with her husband anymore? I wondered.

"Say, Bro," Greg said as if he had read my mind. "What's going on between you guys? If you don't mind me asking . . ."

I should have known that Greg would sense the tension between Liz and me right away. Although he had always seemed like a happy-go-lucky kid growing up, quick to smile or laugh, Greg has always been the most perceptive and sensitive of us all, the hardest for outsiders to make friends with and get close to, and he was always the quickest one of us to bristle and react to perceived mistreatment.

"It's nothing," I said. "Just a little spat. Liz just gets too picky sometimes."

"Nothing to do with that person who sent Liz the cake? Or that real friendly woman in the personnel—"

"No! You didn't mention that cake to Liz, did you?"

"No way! That's **your** business, Bro. I am **not** getting into that. I do have an opinion, though, and a few questions. What about that one chick—that one that came up to you? She was something! Do you think she could have sent that cake—?"

I wasn't about to ask for his opinion nor answer his questions. That was the last thing that I wanted to do. So I immediately tried to throw him off track:

"What the hell are you crunching on?"

"Popcorn. Liz made a big bowl before they left. Man, it's good. She put some real butter on it and sprinkled some kinda' cheese seasoning on it, too. Me and the kids and Muffy have been eating—"

"You didn't give it to Muffy?"

"Well . . . yeah. He was begging me for it. He put his feet up in my chair so I gave him some. I put a little into his bowl for him and he ate it."

Greg did not know a thing about dogs, especially house dogs like Muffy. At first, I didn't either. We could never have afforded a pet when we were growing up even if we had wanted one. My family had too much of a hard time trying to feed ourselves let alone feeding and caring for a pet. Liz had to convince me to accept a house dog when we had gotten Muffy. We had found it really hard to believe that stand-offish little Muffy had taken quite a shine to Greg right from the first, but not at all to Betty and the kids. Liz had laughed and said that it must have had something to do with Greg and I having the same family smell.

"Dogs can't digest salted, buttered popcorn, Bro," I laughed. "You'd better get Muffy out to the back yard before he gets on Liz's blue and white carpet in the living room and starts throwing that buttered popcorn up."

"Aw, Man!" Greg ejected, "I don't see him anywhere—!"

I heard him calling Muffy as he was hanging up the telephone. I laughed harder. For his sake, I could only hope he got Muffy out to the back yard in time. I was pretty sure that he was going to be doing some clean-up.

I went with some of the guys to the club in East Saint Louis as usual. I bought two rounds of beer and kept myself surrounded by three of the foremen from Caprice as well as the superintendents and three of the guys from Corvette. We had sandwiches and conversation as usual. Most of the repair and maintenance people had already gone to Bowling Green, so we were missing them and one or two others were making plans to go. One thing was really interesting: some people were not planning to give up their homes in Saint Louis. They were planning to rent a small apartment or lease a room just to sleep in Bowling Green during the work week then they would drive back home to Saint Louis every weekend. They were going to have a regular wagon train going back and forth from Bowling Green—down and back on the weekends like clockwork. They would work in the small town and live in the city—they would be 20th Century nomads—nomads with damn good jobs in the auto industry that they were not about to let go of because of factors like time and distance.

She was there at the bar when I walked in. I was surprised to see her surrounded by other women I knew. They were all a mixed group that included attractive, unattached women who stayed at the bar while our rather large group of men sat at tables together. They watched us steadily as if they were waiting for something to happen. When I notice that she and one of the other women had left the bar probably to go to the ladies room, I made a dash for the door. I was in my Corvette and gone before anyone could have possibly stopped me.

I got home a bit earlier than I usually did. I was really anticipating a face to face confrontation with Liz. I was thinking that we would have to talk to each other quietly and civilly since the house was so crowded with people now. We'd **have** to sleep in the same bedroom now. Liz would have no choice because Greg and Betty now occupied the little guest room. Thus, we would have to sleep together and we would make up and all the anger would be forgotten. I felt myself tense with excitement like a bridegroom at the thought of that. My rash libido had already told me that it had been far too long.

When I found that our bedroom was empty, I was more than a little disappointed. I turned on my heel and went straight downstairs. Sure enough a strip of light was showing under the door of the room in the far corner of the basement—Liz's sewing room. A while ago, she had put the old recliner with its broken lever in the corner of that room. I had discarded it and replaced it with another. I knew that she and Muffy were in there and that she fully intended to spend the rest of the night in the old broken down chair rather than sleep with me.

"Goddammit!" I ground out. I was furious. I already knew that Liz had that door locked against me—I did not have to go completely down the stairs to know that. I felt like going down and kicking the door right off its hinges. If not for the fact that we had Greg's family in the house, I might have done just that. I got myself under control with an effort.

"If this is how she wants it," I said to myself, "I'll really show her that she can have it her own way. We'll see how long she can handle it!"

Things soon progressed from tense silence and ignoring each other to outright hostility between Liz and me over the next few days but I kept saying to myself that it was no fault of mine—I was just making the best of Liz's sulking. Surely she would cool off soon and speak to me. Somehow, my temperament had modified—still, as always, I wanted Liz to be the one to break the ice between us.

I stubbornly continued the ritual of going over to East Saint Louis for an hour or so after work, but I did try hard to make it home well before 4:00 in the morning. When I did call home from work in the evening, if I got hold of anyone it was Greg. On the few occasions that I chanced to speak to Liz, she managed to keep the conversation to "yes" and "no" and silence on her part no matter what subject I happened to bring up. She never spoke to me at all unless she was absolutely forced to do it.

I came home one night to find my wife asleep on the couch in the family room in front of the television with Muffy on the floor beside her. Muffy looked up at me with his big dark eyes shining and little stub of a tail twitching. He got up and turned around and around before lying back down again but Liz did not stir. I guessed that the limitations of sleeping in the sewing room had finally gotten to her. I watched her for a long time as she slept under a light coverlet and I marveled at how sweet and appealing she looked in her dishabille that left her feminine form exposed to my eyes. Her lips looked so soft and inviting that my heart rocked and I ached to lean over and kiss her mouth. I wanted very badly to hold her close and feel her soft and responsive in my arms. I walked over and switched off the television but Liz did not move or open her eyes, so I left her right there. Hardheaded, unreasonable female, I grumbled as I ground my jaw teeth together. How long is she planning to keep this up?

Greg and Betty soon found a suitable 3-bedroom apartment in a large complex in Olivette with easy access to the freeway. They called the moving and storage company to get their furniture from storage. Betty gave them the address to deliver it. On the day that the truck came into town, Betty and Liz took the kids and went to supervise while the workers from the moving company set the beds up in the apartment and did most of the heavy lifting.

On the evening that Betty and Greg moved out of our small guest room, Liz no more than changed the sheets on the bed than she moved herself right back into that room.

I played 18 holes of golf with Sam and Hazel on Saturday and followed my usual routine. Then I went over on Sunday to help Greg put up some shelves, hang curtains, blinds, and straighten out anything else that was necessary. Working with a few beers and lots of elbow grease, we had pretty much gotten everything to Betty's satisfaction by late afternoon.

The week-end had been really tense between Liz and me, so after work that Monday night I made a stop across the river in East Saint Louis and I stayed much later than I intended. All of the Corvette line supervisors and a few of the recruits from the other product lines were long gone by now. The Chevrolet Caprice people and the truck line folks who were left were a subdued bunch. We could only commiserate with each other and speculate on what was going to happen with our own product lines. The Caprice was not doing as well as it should have been and neither were the light trucks. American automobile purchases as a whole all over the country were way down. We hated to admit it but the cheaper imports were all but killing us. The freedom of the foreign cars to be sold in the United States was hurting all of the American based automobile lines but because of the size of General Motors, we were hurt somewhat less than any of the other American car makers. We speculated about that for about an hour all told.

It was only the beginning some argued. It was bound to get much worse everyone agreed. Some of us could even talk about the statistics and daily counts and what all of that meant.

I should not have stayed as late as I did. I guess it was because everyone was feeling down and we were all trying to shore each other up. I was no more buzzed on alcohol than I usually was so that was not a good excuse. I guess, every one of my numerous reasons might add up to just a bunch of self-serving excuses, though.

I knew that *she* had come out of the bar behind me when I walked out. Nobody else had followed us out. We stood and talked for a bit about the options that were available to all of the long-time employees of General Motors. We talked about a number of the workers in particular and what they would be wise to be doing to plan for their futures with or without the company. It would be awhile, but the employees would be wise to be thinking of that we agreed. We talked more and she was listening so avidly, I took the opportunity to tell her about my future employment aspirations at General Motors.

Finally, I said "good night" and unlocked the doors to my Corvette. Before I could even blink she had gone around and climbed in beside me without being invited. She claimed to want to talk some more, so I told her all that I had heard from the guys inside. Both of us speculated pro and con about the future of the operations in Saint Louis, but that was merely an artifice on her part—her real objective was soon all too obvious. She became more than amorous toward me. I was not surprised—a man can only plead ignorance until it appears to be stupidity. It was certainly without my consent that she slid her arms around my neck with one hand against my face and she was pulling my head toward her. After a second or two I gave in and passively let her kiss me. After a moment of selfish pleasure in her overeager upper body, hands and lips, I pulled back from her.

Fortunately, the construction of the Corvette does not accommodate to any kind of intimate action, but especially not for a man of my size. I was really glad that the parking lot was not well enough lit by the outside lights on the tall poles to allow people passing by to see into the car. She reached for my hands; obviously trying to get me to touch her but I was more than a little concerned about the possibility that someone could see that I was fraternizing intimately with that particular GM employee. It did not matter that we were both at management level, both of us were married—she to another GM employee. As unbelievable as it was, she breathlessly claimed that she had never done anything like this before. She claimed that she had really fallen for me—she said that being with me like this really overwhelmed her to the point that she was almost faint.

My eyes had become accustomed to the dimness inside the car and I could see the intense lines of passion on her face. I had already allowed this to go farther than I should have. When she licked her lips and reached over the center console the way she did, it made me think: she has to be wearing make-up and lipstick! What a disaster if it got on the light blue shirt that I was wearing or my khaki pants! That triggered my next action. I quickly fumbled the car door open, bent almost double, shot my long legs outside, and stood up.

"I'm feeling kinda' sick," I managed. "I just . . . I had too much to drink." I pretended to lean helplessly onto the car. "It's . . . it's catching up to me. Go on back inside, I don't . . . I might need to throw up. I'll feel better if you go on back inside. It's gonna' take me more than a minute . . ."

She got out of the car, came around and stood there protesting in a low passionate voice about what she could do to help me and saying that she did not want to leave me like this and that I shouldn't drive and that maybe I could get into her car which was right over there. She really tried and she must have thought that she had a good point given the acuteness of my "condition." Maybe I overdid it a bit, but I was guessing that she was thinking that she had made some progress. So, I gave her no choice. I stayed where I was outside of the car and wouldn't let her touch me again. She finally did as I asked and left me there. I waited until she had gone back inside before I got myself into my car, and drove home.

It must have been somewhere after 6:00 in the morning when I made it home and got inside. I walked down the hall and stood looking at the closed guest room door for a long time. I didn't try to kid myself: I was stirred up. I was no fool—I knew that unfulfilled desire could easily get the best of a man and cause him to do something that he would not ordinarily do. I knew I would feel so much better if Liz and I could put aside our long-standing disagreements just for a moment—long enough, maybe, for both our sakes . . . it was a ludicrous thought! What could I possible say to Liz that she would not angrily reject at this point? Our ongoing dispute had built up stone by stone and now stood like a solid wall between us. Both of us had drawn pretty deep lines in the sand. Everything had gotten way too far out of hand. I had asked myself a number of times how our relationship could have gotten so far off track and into such heated anger—such a bad, bad place. Unbelievable how I was able to side-step any thought at all that my actions and attitude could be blamed for at least some part of this strained and acutely estranged impasse between us.

I went into the master bedroom bath, checked my shirt and undershirt for lipstick stains as I habitually did now as I undressed, pulled on my PJs, brushed my teeth, and got into bed. As I lay there alone I couldn't help thinking about what I had just rejected. Was it only because it was forbidden to my mind and by my societal upbringing? I did not favor female aggression, I reasoned. As usual, in my mind, I had already made the logical excuses for myself both pro and con.

Really though, where was the surprise? Hadn't I respected my marriage vows from the very moment that I had first made them? Women had come onto me just as strongly before—certainly not one in a high-level position like *hers*. It was hard to believe that a person like her could put herself into a position to be so slavishly compliant. Every day at the plant, I never went to that area and I had made it a point to avoid anyplace that I thought she might be, especially the cafeteria and other commonly used places. I wasn't sure that she wouldn't find a way somehow to get next to me at work since she was so determined.

I had often pointed out to the guys at the club or at the plant that I was certainly not dead. Whenever they mentioned any over-interested female or talked about how they would certainly "hit that" if a woman came on to them like someone had come on to me, I did not attempt to plead ignorance or stupidity. I laughed and joked about it right along with them. I pretended that I might play the game if I had the right opportunity.

It didn't seem to be very "macho" so I never mentioned that the only woman I wanted or needed was my wife. Certainly, I never complained about the raw and ugly breach that had formed itself between my wife and me or tried to use it as an excuse. I never indicated that it pained me that we were fighting or that both of us were equally hard-headed and stubborn. I almost laughed aloud! I wondered if Liz would give in and come to me if she knew what I had just passed up for her sake tonight. Really, it was hard for me to believe. Just thinking of it did not give me any peace, though—it just seemed so . . . implausible. My behavior hadn't always been totally above reproach, but, certainly, I had never encouraged *her*. Before long, I fell asleep.

Liz must have gotten her things and the kids' clothes ready at some time during that weekend. Later, I wondered just when it was that she had packed up her suitcase and packed up the kids' suitcases. I figured later that she must have gotten it all done right after I left for work that previous afternoon. In any case, I had not noticed that anything was amiss when I had gotten home that morning. But my mind was centered so much upon ***me, myself***, and what ***I*** wanted and needed, it wasn't any question how I had so easily missed all the clues.

When I woke up on Tuesday afternoon, the house was empty, of course. But this time, when I went to warm up my meal, there was no food left for me in the microwave dishes in the refrigerator in my special spot—just leftovers in the usual refrigerator dishes. I was pretty annoyed as I tried to pull together a meal for myself from the leftovers. At first, I was a bit shocked that Liz had not prepared my meal. She needed to have cooked something for the kids, didn't she? I was willing to bet that she had taken them out for burgers and fries. Finally, I figured that this had to be a newer, harsher product of her ongoing angry attitude toward me. Well no matter. I decided that I would just grab a quick snack right now. I wouldn't let it bother me; I could get something decent to eat later on at work no matter how much I wanted to avoid going over to the cafeteria or outside to the vendors.

When I happened to look outside through the window, I noticed that Muffy was nowhere to be seen—he was not in the back yard at all. In any case, Liz had taken him with them in the car often enough so I really could not say that I thought anything was particularly amiss about Muffy's not being there. But In fact, when I began to put things together, I got the first feeling that something was more than a little off kilter. I do remember that while I was sitting at the table eating my pulled-together meal, I happened to notice that Muffy's bowls were gone, and the rubber floor mat that was usually underneath his bowls on the kitchen floor was gone, too.

It was then that I got up from the table and walked quickly back into our bedroom. Liz had not been sleeping there in a while but I was confident that all of her clothes were still hanging there on her side of the large bedroom closet that we shared. I slid Liz's side of the closet door open. Empty hangers dangled in the space that Liz's clothes usually filled. I opened Liz's lingerie drawer in the tall bureau. All three of the divided sections lined with scented, decorated tissue paper where Liz kept her lingerie were completely empty. I quickly walked across to each of the kids' rooms. The beds in both of their rooms were neatly made and the floor seemed far too clean—not a scrap of paper, no toys, nothing was scattered about. When I opened the top drawer in the chest in Crissy's room it, too, was empty, but in truth, I knew absolutely nothing about either of the kids' clothes, so I had no idea whether either of their small chests of drawers was ever completely full of clothes.

Then, it occurred to me to go downstairs and look in the closet where the suitcases were stored. I clicked on the basement light, hastened down the stairs, opened the double closet doors and caught my breath. Liz's old suitcase and both the kids' smaller red and blue pieces of luggage with the colorful cartoon characters on them were gone. The only pieces of luggage that were left neatly stacked there were my suit bag and my cowhide tote.

I went back upstairs with anger swirling around inside my head like snowflakes in winter, and the cold feeling that had begun to awaken in the space just below my ribcage was that explosive, raging spot that I had once been obliged to guard carefully after the war. Too bad that Gregory did not have a telephone hooked up in his apartment yet. That meant I couldn't call Betty to question her about this. Surely, Liz hadn't just taken the kids and left without telling anyone. I could not believe that my wife was capable of doing something as drastic as that!

Liz had complained off and on about the Pontiac Firebird that I had bought for her use. She had laughingly said that the glistening, golden Firebird decal that almost completely covered the hood of the black car was too big and far too flashy and gaudy for her. She drove the car constantly but she claimed that it had more power than she needed and since I had not asked her opinion beforehand, she knew that I bought it because I had wanted it for myself—I had *not* purchased it for her.

I went to work early and waited until Greg got off his job on the Caprice frame line. He assured me that neither he nor Betty had heard a thing from Liz in the last couple of days or so.

I was totally distracted but I went over to the office area and got to work. I did everything that was a part of my job the very best that I could. I performed my accustomed duties and dealt with my people as I usually did. Each hour or so, I called home. The telephone rang and rang. I wrapped things up, made some hasty notes for Cliff, left work hurriedly just before one o'clock and headed straight home.

Even though I knew better, still I was hoping against hope that Liz was just being over-dramatic and stubborn and she was just pretending to be gone. That was probably what it was: when I had called home previously, she had obstinately chosen not to answer the telephone. Maybe everything would be normal by the time I got home—even with Liz sleeping in the guest room. Deep down, I knew that I was lying to myself—saying to myself that we would put aside our ongoing disagreements this very night. Liz had always been the one to break the ice before, but, this time, after so long, I vowed that I would be the one to do it. I would even promise not to go across the river anymore, if that was what she wanted. I let myself envision how exquisite and sweet making up would be—better than ever before if that were at all possible. I tried to convince myself that everything was going to be all right when I got to the house.

It was not.

The Firebird was still not there when I pulled into the garage. It had been daylight still when I had left for work so I hadn't left any lights on. Now, the house was completely dark and empty.

I knew that all of Liz's folks in Memphis or in Holly Springs would surely be asleep at this time of the night but I had to call someone—this was far too important and much, much too necessary.

I looked on the bulletin board in the kitchen for the telephone numbers that Liz had copied on notepaper and kept tacked up there.

I immediately found Liz's sister Florestine's telephone number in Memphis.

When I called the number, Teen's husband, Walter, sleepily answered the telephone. I could hear a continuous sound that had to be the television in the background. I apologized for calling so late but Walter assured me that it was okay because he was in the house all by himself and he had fallen asleep hours ago while watching the late news. He laughed and said that he was glad my call had awakened him because he needed to get up and head off to bed.

Walter quickly told me that Liz had left the Firebird parked in their driveway and she and the kids had gone in the station wagon with Teen and their kids to their parents' house in Holly Springs earlier that evening. Teen had called him and said that they were planning to stay down there overnight. At least now I was able to still my fear about where Liz had gone and to know that she and the kids were safe. I didn't need anything else. When I got off the telephone, I poured myself a half-glass of bourbon and added some ice. No chance that it would help me to sleep restfully because I realized that my nerves still pretty stirred up.

That afternoon, as soon as I woke up, I called Liz's parents' telephone. Liz's mother said that Teen, Liz, and the kids had already gone to take Muffy back over to Memphis where there was a fence around the back yard. She told me pleasantly:

"They need to get a cage or some kind of stake for his leash so he can be safe when he's outdoors down here. We don't want to take a chance that he might somehow get loose and into the street. I've never been used to an inside dog, but Muffy is really clean and quiet. He'll growl but he only barks if he hears someone step on the porch. He's really good in the house."

Liz's mother was an elementary schoolteacher and she went on and on for a bit about how she was glad that school was out for the summer and how quickly the weather was getting hot.

I managed to get through the conversation, but I was sure that I must have sounded just as irritable and out-of-sorts as I was feeling.

About an hour later, I called Teen and Walter's house again. Again, Walter answered. I had almost missed him. He told me that he was on his way out of the door but came back when he heard his telephone ringing. He just happened to be at home because he had decided to stop by to grab himself a quick sandwich. He was a medical supplies salesman with flexible hours and he had planned to end his workday with sales calls at one or two doctors' offices at the hospital on the south side of town.

"Listen, Liz never called me," I complained.

"Damn!" he said, "I thought she did."

"No," I said.

"Well . . . I . . . well . . . I don't—"

He obviously did not know what else to say so I decided to confess:

"She never even told me she was going down home," I said.

He was silent for a long moment. "Damn!" He said again. "She didn't? So, you didn't know where she was when you called here last night? I kinda' figured something wasn't right 'cause you called so late. Damn! So she drove all the way down here by herself with the kids and the dog—"

"She needs to call me," I said cutting off his speculation. I was really hoping to avoid a complicated explanation. "I've got to go to work right now. I don't know if she brought my work number with her or not. Here, let me give you my number at work. Can you write it down for her . . . might be why she hasn't called: she forgot to bring it with her."

Whenever I caught a break at work, I went into my office. I had tried for the entire evening to stay close to my office in case the telephone rang but that had proven to be impossible to do. I had gotten far too caught up in solving problems on the line and far too concerned with absenteeism and hung up by other problems to accomplish that.

Stubbornly, I made up my mind that I would wait until Liz called me. My anger made me feel more than a little sorry for myself, so I went across the river for a quick drink after work but, of course, I stayed much longer than I should have. I found myself flirting outrageously with the over-eager GM women, but soon enough I broke away and headed for home.

I had to set the alarm clock to make sure that I would get up in time for work that next afternoon. There was still no word from Liz at all. I came home from work a little after two o'clock in the morning, promptly got into my chair in front of the television and fell asleep. Finally, I woke up around eight o'clock in the morning and went to bed. Yet another day had passed and I had not spoken with my wife. I was angry, but, in truth, I was much more hurt than anything. My wife should have, at least, called to tell me why she had seen fit to leave our house without waking me or leaving me a note. She should have had that much consideration. Even if she had called when I was not at home, I felt that she should have called back again until she reached me.

That afternoon, again I waited for the telephone to ring. When it did not happen, I got myself cleaned up and went to work.

During my break, I checked upstairs with the night shift clerk like I always did to see if any calls had come in for me. None of the three calls that the clerks had taken for me were from Liz. On that first day after she left, I had jotted down Liz's sister's telephone number and her parents' number on the back of one of my cards. I had brought the card with me to work and left it on my desk. During the break, I picked up the card and called Teen and Walter's telephone. Once again I got Walter on the line.

"I guess they've been gone for a while," he said. "They were gone when I got in from work. That's just teachers, man. They get plumb stir crazy in the summer and have to get out. Libby left Muffy in the back yard. He's out there chewing a rawhide bone. I bet our wives and kids are at some shopping mall somewhere running around to every sale at every store in there—" ("Libby" was Liz's childhood nickname that all of her relatives still often used).

"She still hasn't called me," I cut in.

"Well . . ." he said. He sounded uncertain again. "She said she was going to call—"

"Goddammit! She's sure playing hell doing it then!" I snapped. I immediately realized how angry I sounded. "I'm sorry," I said with an effort to calm myself. "I didn't mean to snap at you, Walter. I guess I'm all out of patience. I just—Liz is pretty angry at me."

"Sounds like you're both pretty angry at each other," he said on a long breath. "I—I really hate to tell you . . . she was talking about picking up a job application from the board of education. Last night she said something about finding a house to rent here in Memphis. Cooksey, she's **serious**!"

"No," I said with surety that I did not feel. "No. She is ***not*** serious."

"Hey wait!" he said suddenly with relief. "Here they come . . ."

I heard the kids' voices first: Teen and Walter's older kids' voices mixed with the high-pitched tones of our little tykes. Then, I heard more voices. Walter was talking to someone but I could not make out what they were saying. Then, he must have been holding the telephone receiver closer because I clearly heard him say:

"I told you . . . No, he's been worried—you knew he would be . . . Hell, no! I'm not gonna' tell him anything! You're not putting me in the middle like this! Take this phone—!"

"Hello," Liz's soft contralto voice said at last.

By that time, I was so angry at her that I could hardly control myself, but I was determined to keep my voice calm.

"Why did you leave this house without waking me up?" I asked too softly. "You never even said one ***word*** to me! Why haven't you called, Elizabeth?"

She did not reply.

"Why the hell—what's the matter with you? You know damn well you should have at least said ***something*** to me before you left!"

Still she said nothing.

"Suppose something had ***happened*** to you and the kids out there on that highway? I wouldn't have known that you were gone or where you were since you didn't leave me a note! What the hell were you thinking?"

"How long before you even noticed we were gone?" Liz asked stiffly. "I guess you finally noticed when I wasn't there to cook your meals and wash all that perfume and lipstick out of your clothes. I heard you when you came home the other morning. You just barely got home before we left. I guess you had such a big night with that . . . woman, you just didn't—"

"What woman?" I growled angrily, "You don't know what the hell you're talking about! I just went across the river for, maybe an hour or so like I always do. Then, I got to talking with . . . ah . . . I guess I did stay a little later because we were telling each other . . . I was finding out what everybody knew about those moves the company has been making lately. I—"

"Oh, sure, the big moves," Liz said dryly, sarcastically. "I'm sure those ***moves*** put that lipstick all over your clothes. What about ***your*** moves, may I ask? Were you about ready to make ***your*** big move? I beat you to it, didn't I?"

"Look, I told you where I was, dammit! Why are you talking like a—" I stopped myself, chewing down hard on my anger.

"'. . . *fool*?'" Liz finished calmly for me. "I'm a long way from being a fool! Remember when you asked me, '*What do you want from me*?' Do you remember when you asked me that?"

"No! I never asked you anything! So don't—ah, hell! I guess maybe I did say something like that . . . is that why you're acting like this? Look, you know I never meant that the way you're making it sound—"

"You meant exactly what you said!" she flared suddenly. "Here's your answer: there's ***nothing*** I want from you! I can take care of—"

"Ah, Liz," I protested reasonably, "Come on, now. You know I didn't mean it like that. I had a little too much to drink, that's all. I was just—"

"You can say whatever you want, but it's too late! How long did you think I was going to keep putting up with your crap—?"

"Look now, why don't you just finish up your visit with your folks and come on back home so we can talk—"

"Come ***home***?" Her voice had begun to tremble. "What's at home for me? You only drag yourself home when you need to change your clothes and eat. You never talk—at least not to me—you just mumble most of the time or you frown at me and glare. When you do open your mouth you're either snapping or complaining. You're not a real husband anymore and you never have time for the kids. You're too busy with your ***nighttime friends***! Well, I've had enough! You didn't really think I'd leave did you? Shows how wrong you can be, doesn't it?"

"Stop talking like a damn fool, Liz!" I snapped. I had gotten so angry, I couldn't think straight. Purely blind anger swept over me in waves. I was frustrated too. I didn't know how to cope with this. I took a deep breath, hoping to calm myself but that did not help at all. I said furiously:

"What do you mean: I'm not a ***real*** husband anymore? What the hell do you mean by ***that***? You're the one who started all this shit in the first place! You're always crazy and snapping at me like some . . . you never sleep in our room anymore! You're always crumpled up in that chair down there in the basement—or on the couch or you're locked up tight in the guest room! ***Hell!*** Whenever I'm at home you've always got the kids and gone! ***You're*** the reason for all this! ***You're*** the reason why I never see the kids! ***You're*** causing this whole—"

I did not immediately recognize that hard, abrupt sound until I heard the hollow hum of the dial tone in my ear. I was no longer talking to my wife. She had slammed the telephone receiver down.

The monstrous complex that was Saint Louis General Motors Assembly was beginning to look like a ruined battlefield now. The fierce, three-headed, Hydra-monster that was the UAW had rampaged for years and years throughout the collective Caprice, Chevy Trucks, and Corvette production areas. Now, finally, the monster had been joined in battle. The furious mauling that the labor union triad had been dealing to upper management in Detroit and to local management in Saint Louis for so long seemed to have finally brought out the backbone and the resolve in long-suffering upper management ranks in Detroit. One of the fierce heads of the UAW Hydra had been summarily lopped off when Corvette was moved away to Bowling Green, Kentucky.

Now, the death-dealing warriors from the Detroit headquarters were back and they were circling in tighter for another kill in Saint Louis. Caprice and truck production were both cut back to only one shift per day. That meant all of the production would be done on day shift. The night shift workers and all night shift management personnel had to find other places in the plant to be re-assigned. In a pre-emptive move, many in management had been transferred to other GM plants.

Cliff Vaughn, the plant manager, called me into his office and told me that personnel had already arranged for me to go over to see Joe Irwin in Materials. Since I was hoping that I would not have to leave Saint Louis under the present circumstances of my personal life, I was relieved to find that I was not being compelled to leave. I really needed to stay until my wife and family came back home.

Cliff told me that Joe Irwin had been operating without a superintendent for some time. It would be a step up he assured me. If I could work over there, it would give me a boost when I went elsewhere. So, quickly I agreed to do it. Everybody knew that Parts and Materials Supply was a tough department to work in and Joe Irwin was a hammer—a stickler and a tough guy to work for. However, it was the only department in the whole plant that was still up and running two shifts at full-tilt.

I went straight over to see Joe Irwin and he told me flatly that the job was not for me. "I hear you're an up-and-coming production guy," he said, "why would you want to get stuck in over here in supply? We're likely to be running for only a year or so longer with Corvette. They're gonna' be off and on until it gets moved completely down to Bowling Green. Caprice and truck will be our only lines then. Eventually, it will make a difference to us, but not right away—everybody's stuff comes through here. Well, anyway, what do you know about supply?"

"Only what I know from training," I said, "and I've got two years working over in Caprice. I used to teach Materials and Supply at GMI but I'm more than willing to learn whatever it is I need to know to work in this department. I'm a pretty fast learner."

He studied my face. I looked right back at him. Finally, he half-smiled at my frowning, stubborn expression. Then he nodded.

"All right then," he said, slowly getting up from behind his desk with his ghost-grey eyes still intent on my face. "Since you taught it you ought to know it. Let's get you right on it. I'll show you around myself. We'll see how you feel after a week or so at this, okay?"

"Okay," I said, meeting his steely stare evenly.

Despite what I had heard about him, I was determined that he was not going to intimidate me. Hell, after what I'd been through in production, I felt like I could work anywhere for anybody, so I was more than willing to reserve any judgment on this guy. He took me around, introduced his people to me, and talked on and on to me about his department and how things worked. Whenever he looked at me again or introduced me to one of the workers, I tried at least to look pleasant.

Once again I entered into an incredible state of learning and doing. I went right into Parts and Supply doing my very best and working my very hardest. It was just like it was when I took over the company in Vietnam: I was determined to do what I was obligated to do. My mind was set to be just as good, or better, than any other man at doing my job. I had built-in, inbred motivators. I grew up knowing the value of doing what I had to do to survive. I was back again to the same mantra that had been resonating in my heart since I was a hungry kid working at any job that I could get in order to earn some money to help put food on the table for my family: no time to stop, no time to rest, no time to feel, and no time to cry.

For the first time, I had to use the same methods that I had formerly taught at GMI about doing inventory, records keeping, building and comparing statistics, and going over pages and pages of logistics, records and plans. I pigeonholed all of the people who had jobs to do and pinned them down until I learned all about what their job requirements entailed. I learned about managing materials costs to budget. I learned about the "hot lists" and made sure I understood the importance of the materials on the lists. That meant knowing what materials should and could be located when and where and knowing what needed to be ordered and re-ordered.

Before long, I was familiar with suppliers, and I knew many facts that were not so well-known, too: I knew which suppliers' materials were suited for more than one of the products that we were building. I learned which questions to ask and which points that I had to check and re-check for myself. That one question was continuous though: were the materials from this or that supplier suitable for use on the Chevrolet, the Pontiac, the Oldsmobile or any other automobile that General Motors produced? Which suppliers would ship materials to us overnight if we needed them to do it. Could we get materials shipped to us quickly from another plant if we needed to do it? What means did we need to use? Air cargo? Big trucks? Small private planes? Individual's pickups? It was my decision and any decision I made in that regard could come back to bite me later.

I knew when to get the engineering department involved and when to make sure materials were suitable for interchanging. I knew when to determine whether they had the power to *make* certain parts fit: that is when my own judgment had to suffice. I also knew that my judgment could very well be second-guessed. If I made a mistake, I needed to be ready to take the lumps from the department head as well as from the area managers. But I found out soon enough that working for Joe meant that he was not about to let me take any lumps from anyone but him. He took the responsibility for everything that happened in his department right down to every nut and every bolt. He took our biggest and most tangled problems onto his own shoulders. He was a tough taskmaster but he was willing to fight for any one of the people who worked for him if he figured that person was on the right track. He had a gruff and tough façade but I had begun to suspect that it hid a soft side and good heart beneath all that. I was growing to respect him more and more.

I learned that the scrap heap and waste bins had to be checked thoroughly because it was the job of our department to be protective and guarded about our materials. There was always the possibility that parts could be mistakenly thrown away into the trash gondolas. So, I made sure to have someone to check regularly in case a worker accidentally or intentionally threw away a part that was desired for use on a product either inside the assembly operation. Theft of materials and parts was a very definite problem. More "lost materials" were charged to the materials department than all other departments combined. We used armed guards both inside and outside our department so I decided not to set it as a goal to try to get a real handle on thefts, but I tried to institute stronger methods for hard core accountability on all of our people, so we were dealing with such losses ourselves.

In those days "Just-in-Time" delivery of parts to the assembly line was just an idea in many people's heads including Joe's and mine. When Joe saw the commonality of our thinking, he enthusiastically sat me down to compare our points. We talked about it and we drew out charts and maps laying out how this or that might be accomplished. We saw it as a way of dealing with losses as well as cutting down on the amount of materials having to be stored at the line and even in the storage facility itself. The materials department was so huge; it was a monster to manage. Between the thefts, losses, and mistakes in proper identification, we were a river flowing in every direction. Nothing bothered Joe and me more than to know that our biggest and most nearly hopeless situation was putting up dams and locks up to stop that river.

At the end of each day, I was absolutely wiped out. I was chewed up by all of the walking around the huge department; trying to motivate the workers and the foremen and other personnel in all areas of the spread-out department to start keeping a better accounting of what seemed to me like acres of stuff; and trying to get the workers to put things of a kind together. I was sorely tempted to do as much inventory as the clerks and as much manual labor to drag stuff together as the hourly workers in the department. Of course, I could not do their jobs for them, but there were some seemingly un-important things that hadn't been properly accounted for in far too long a time, and there were always new supplies coming into the department in a constantly pouring stream. I refused to allow the new materials to be stacked right on top of the old stuff until I was sure that the differences had been accounted for and a count of the new materials had been properly taken and recorded. I insisted that a much better continuous and ongoing system be set up to accommodate and account for the incoming materials as well to keep track of outgoing materials.

It did not bother me at all to work so hard; it kept my mind off the fact that I would be going home at the end of my work day to an empty house. I was continually busy and that helped. Joe had quickly begun to leave me to my own devices. I had noticed that he would only advise me when I asked for advice. He was quick, however to let me know when something I had done was good or workable. I knew he would chew my ass if I made a mistake and I think he was pleased that I was trying so hard not to let that happen. He said what he meant and he meant what he said. I could live with that well enough. I was pretty pleased that Joe really did seem to like me and to like my work.

My sleep schedule had to change now because I was back to working on day shift again. It had taken me all of a week to get myself into the rhythm of working when I had previously been sleeping. I was out of sorts at first but I found myself beginning to relax at work and to feel better physically and even mentally as I became more comfortable with the openness, the easy-going atmosphere, and the complete lack of pressure that characterized Joe's department. I found that the only pressure came from what I put upon myself. I began to slowly throw off the protective film that I had learned to wrap around myself while I was on the production floor of Caprice assembly line. I found out how to ease up a whole lot.

Once in a while, I stopped by Greg's apartment to catch a meal, but only after Betty called me or Greg literally came by and dragged me to their place. I had gotten into the habit of stopping to pick up dinner at one of the fast food places in Creve Coeur or one of the restaurants along Olive Street just outside the neighborhood on my way home. Whenever I cooked anything it was always something simple like bacon and eggs because I ate breakfast food most of the time. Prodded by Betty's nagging me, I went to the grocery store and bought TV dinners that just needed heating up. I almost always ate any of my meals from a tray in front of the television.

After I cleaned up the kitchen, I would make my usual telephone calls. It was maddening and frustrating because Liz never returned my calls no matter how many messages I left for her. Sometimes it would take two to four calls and two hours or more before I finally located her. Some days I never got in touch with her at all because she was often on the move—driving from her sister's house in Memphis, Tennessee to her parents' home down highway 78 across the state line in Holly Springs, Mississippi some 35 miles away. It wasn't unlike her to stop somewhere in between. Sometimes she had gone shopping with the two cousins that she had grown up with in Holly Springs: Pauline and Nadine Scales, or she was visiting her Dowsing cousins, her Scales cousins, or Holland cousins. Other times I was told that she had gone to somebody's house who had been one of her high school friends or a classmate in college.

It really did upset me to think that Liz might be serious about staying away from home. It had finally sunk in that it did me no good to try to give her any orders or try to get her to come home to discuss our problems. For this reason, I did not speak to her at all about my job situation. It took all of the persistence and patience that I had just to get her to talk to me and tell me about the kids. She never kept me from speaking to them on the telephone because she said that they had been asking about me and she did not think that it was fair if she did not allow them to talk to me at all. It was in the interest of fairness to ***them***—not to ***me***. She made sure that I understood this point quite clearly.

I had finally gotten to the place that I was pretty well adept at hiding the volatile anger that naturally arose in me when I did get to talk to my wife. Most of the time, her dismissive attitude fairly infuriated me. I quickly realized that Liz was not going to argue with me or even discuss anything about why she had left me or the causes for our "disagreement." I found that very hard to accept.

Liz had always insisted that I never listened to her or regarded her opinion at all. Whenever we disagreed, she claimed that I always had to be right and I never admitted it even when facts proved that I was wrong. She insisted that I always declared that **she** was wrong no matter what. Thinking of this, I tried to pretend that I needed her help to sort out the bills and such or needed her input about a household concern but she was not fooled by that because she knew that in the past, I had always checked behind her whenever she had made any decision. So, I could not persuade her that I really needed her help with anything at all.

Still, I had to try. I was careful that I was not sharp or curt with my wife. If I pushed her too much, showed displeasure, or disagreed with her about anything, I needed to remember that she could simply hang up the telephone or refuse to talk to me at all. I suspected that she was already avoiding talking to me half the time.

I stubbornly would not let myself settle for the most simplistic answer. So what if I had gone across the river after work to have a drink with my colleagues? Did that mean that I was automatically guilty of adultery or some other horrible crime? Why in hell was that? There was no logical reasoning behind that at all.

I was just like any other grown man who had worked my ass off all my life to make a living—first for my mother's family and now for my own family. I'd been on my own, holding down a full-time job for so long that I was not about to allow anyone to dictate what I could or could not do or make *any* important decisions at all about my life. Hell! It was not as if I had not grown smart enough or tough enough by doing whatever I had to do to fend for myself in all this time!

However, it soon became clear to me that since Liz was refusing to participate at all in even the simplest of our household concerns and decisions, that she really meant to detach herself. That really brought me up short. I was even more disheartened and hurt. I finally admitted to myself what might be happening.

No surprise that I finally decided to at least curtail my visits to the club across the river. I knew well enough that I could find someone to commiserate about work but I did not seem to need that anymore. I had learned long ago to confine my personal problems to my own mental storehouse and to keep my own counsel about that. I took great pains now to ensure that what I said and did would not cause any entanglements or possibly create trouble for me later. I was not about to invite any other person into my life at this point. I was careful how I interacted with everyone now, especially those who solicited my attention just a little too avidly or persistently.

I made sure that I let Liz know that I was working for Joe on the day shift. I was careful not to mention anything at all about the club across the river. I kept in mind that she might call during the hours that I was not working and find that I was not at home for long periods of time. I was only too aware that could be the straw that completely broke the camel's back. I knew well enough that I could do what I wanted freely, but I was sensitive to what Liz's quick little mind might figure out. I did not want to give my wife any more ammunition. I needed her to believe that she could trust me. I knew that was the real issue that I needed to work on.

Really, when I began to look at the situation logically, I felt that Liz needed to have more understanding. I thought she should *automatically* believe in me and trust me because she always had been able to do that. I knew that it might have appeared that I was totally indifferent about Liz's opinion of me. I was not. Maybe I hadn't always used the best judgment about visiting the club in East Saint Louis so often or staying as late as I had, but the guys always welcomed my input and my opinion about things. They always seemed to wait for me just to be in my company and to talk to me. I always considered their opinions and valued their understanding just as much as they did mine. The bar in East Saint Louis had truly become a comfort zone for all of us who worked at the plant.

Call it lack of objectivity, male naivety, or whatever, but I never admitted that I had been pretty flattered by the female attention that I was always getting at the club or even when I was on the job at the plant as well. I simply did not look at that as a legitimate cause for

Liz's anger. In all of the years that I had been married, I had never sought any other female's admiration or encouraged any of it. Was *I* really to be blamed because of female aggression? I knew well enough that the lipstick on my clothes and the woman's perfume that my wife had smelled on my shirts a few times had been the ***real*** causes for her anger. What man in my position had never had at least ***one*** occasion that women hit on him? I knew well enough that I did not get any more of that than any other man.

I could hardly dispute the fact that I had always left the everyday work of raising our children pretty much up to Liz but I resented it when she condemned me for my "neglectful parenting." She had been really extreme when she claimed that I had never once changed a diaper or done any of the every-day work that being a parent required. Where was the surprise in that? I had done enough of that kind of thing with my younger siblings when I was growing up to last me for two lifetimes! Since I was the oldest child in my mother's house, I always had to help her with that. When I was but a child myself, I was the one who had to take care of my younger brothers and sisters while my mother worked two jobs. My stepdad was only around some of the time but basically, he was more of a big hinder than a help. Our aunts and uncles had often been the only help we had, and they couldn't be around all the time—they had their own jobs to occupy most of their time and their own families to take care of.

Since we had been in Saint Louis, I had been the only wage earner. We had always kept a good handle on our finances. Liz had chosen not to work—she didn't bother to look for a teaching job—she had chosen to stay at home until the kids were older. If she was dissatisfied with that, it was her own decision. I had always rather resented that we had never discussed it.

Certainly I could say that I should have thought more about how things had gone at home since we had been in Saint Louis. I could admit that I had been really preoccupied with work but I could blame the extreme stress of my job for that. These days, a black man in my position had to stay ahead of the curve—be twice the man on the job as any of his white counterparts were required to be in order to be considered *almost* as good. Being the first of my race to be in my position was not easy in any way. I did not want to be an example for all nor was I inclined to believe that I was chosen to bear the cross for all, either. I had learned the hard way how to work through racial prejudice as well as the regular ugliness of malice, discontent and pure evil stirring all around me each and every day at that plant plus all the other abnormal occurrences that every other superintendent had to endure just to get our jobs done. Those things constantly hung like a boulder over all the managers. With the UAW always butting up against management, my white counterparts quite regularly suffered through the very same kinds of uphill battles every day as I did.

So, was it surprising that I wasn't sunshine and roses most of the time? Too often I tended to be angry, worn down and more than a little out of sorts. So, maybe I hadn't always been an attentive, loving husband to Liz or an attentive, loving parent to the kids. When I had finally realized that Liz was keeping the kids away from me I figured that she was just trying to give me as much time as possible to rest, recuperate, and keep myself together. I guess I hadn't been very wise about that. I was really sorry that my wife had lost patience and run out of understanding. But, I couldn't help but be upset when Liz had disrupted our family so abruptly without even giving me half a chance to try to fix things between us. I knew that I deserved much more consideration than that!

I continued to re-think and rehash everything. Whenever I started to feel really down, then I considered that part of what had happened must have been caused by the manifestations of the damned war showing up in my attitude and personality even after all that time. I was not prone to admit that I had weaknesses or any failings even when my shortcomings were obvious and the truth was right in front of me. The war had more than hardened my resolve. I was strictly trained to never have feelings of regret and guilt for the decisions I made or any actions that I had to take. I had lived all my life never bowing to pressure or allowing myself to look back with regret about anything that I had done.

And yet, I was not completely hopeless . . .

For a fact, I had always loved my wife more than anything else in the world and I was more than confident in the fact that she loved me just as much. I felt very lucky to have her in my life. She was such a bright spot to us all: she was a very loving wife and mother, she was always generous, and she always tried to make her family happy. Everyone who knew her usually liked her a lot.

I had to face the fact that Liz must have stopped being happy some time ago. I had never taken one minute to think about how she might have felt. We had never talked about her feelings; therefore, I should not be blamed because I had never really tried to do anything about her unhappiness or discontent before now.

No matter. There was no way that I was going to allow what we'd had together for nearly fifteen years to become just a footnote in both our lives. It hurt like hell to think that Liz did not want to work through this just as much as I did. That couldn't be! Maybe I **had** been overly distracted lately, selfish (okay, I admitted it) but none of that meant that I did not love and need my wife and my family just as much as I always had.

I continued to call Liz every day even though not once had she ever called me. That is why I was so certain that it was Liz who had kept us at that angry impasse for all this time—not me. ***I*** was surely trying as hard as I could, wasn't I?

She had not hung up on me anymore since that first time because I was careful about what I said to her. I was relieved that she had begun to talk to me more easily whenever I caught up with her. I never admitted that I felt Liz and the kids were not truly safe without me. I never had thought about how much just hearing my wife's voice each day meant to me. I just felt that I *wanted* to assure myself that Liz was okay. I never admitted that I really *needed* to check on her and the kids.

Our conversations were all too short, artificial, and dissatisfying: I asked questions and she answered what I had asked but she never volunteered anything more. I was angry because I did not know just how to prod my wife. I wanted to hear her say that she was coming home. I knew that she had to miss me and I was confident that she needed me. I was on edge waiting for her to say it. When I finally confessed that I missed her, the kids, and Muffy, she responded that the kids missed me, too. What a stubborn little thing she was! She would not admit that **she** missed me, even when I came right out and asked her! It was maddening!

After work and on the weekends, there were chores around the house that had to be done and that kept me occupied. The summer growing season meant that the grass needed cutting every week-end, lawn food needed spreading and the spikes of growth on the bushes needed pruning back to level pretty often. Greg helped me to re-attach the downspouts where a few of the screws had come loose from the house during the previous winter; we cleaned the gutters and re-placed the wire mesh covering on them that was meant to keep the leaves out; we did some touch-up painting; and replaced some broken stepping stones right off the patio.

I spent a lot of time cleaning and polishing my Corvette and I did a bit of tinkering under the hood. I even got out my manual for the car and learned a lot of the information that I had neglected to learn when I had first purchased it.

I went to Greg's apartment to help him out with whatever project he had going, but most of the time, when I was by myself after I had eaten the meal that I had made, I would get myself a cold beer, get into my easy chair in the den, crank up the foot rest and watch a program or two on television. Then, I would fix myself a nightcap, move to the bedroom, sit in the chair next to the foot of the bed, put my feet up on the ottoman and have my drink while watching the evening news on the bedroom television. Then, I would, brush my teeth, wash my face, and go to bed.

For almost a month, I strictly maintained the routine that I had finally gotten established for myself. I got into the habit of sleeping with the television on for the whole night. Sometimes, depending upon the station that I had been watching when I had fallen asleep, I woke up in the early mornings, with static and a grey, bulls-eye test pattern covering the screen. Being in the house all alone was really hard to take. Nights and week-ends, especially if it was raining outside, I really hated the emptiness of the house. I realized that it wouldn't have seemed empty at all if my family had been there.

Summer was coming closer to the down side of the season. The daylight seemed to stay around forever. It was that time of the year when dusk would be creeping in from the east while the sun's illumination still hung on to reflect red hues against the clouds in the western sky until 8 o'clock or so in the evening.

I had left work only a bit later than I usually did and I exited the freeway farther down on Olive Street in a neighborhood section of Creve Coeur. There was a tall, sandy-haired guy with a buzz-cut standing on a corner as I was cruising slowly through a school zone on a neighborhood street. He wasn't doing anything particularly—he was simply standing there on the deserted street corner watching the passing cars. He was wearing an army fatigue shirt open over a snow-white athletic shirt. He was square of jaw and upright—all Army. When I recognized the insignia on the shirt that he was wearing, I immediately pulled over, stopped the car, and got out. He turned toward me, and watched as I approached where he was standing. He grinned broadly and said:

"Nice ride! That's one of the new Corvettes, isn't it?" Before I could answer he laughed out loud. "How do you fold up your big ol' body to get into that little ol' car?"

I smiled. "Not hard. You sit, lean your head in, bring your feet and legs around, drop 'em in, and then you straighten yourself up."

"Righteous!" he exploded, still laughing. "That's the way to do it! I love that car but I guess I could never get into one that low to the ground anymore."

I introduced myself and held out my hand. His hand came up quickly and as he took a step toward me the hitching movement of his body was obvious. I had a pretty good idea then just what the neat khaki slacks that he was wearing were covering from sight.

"Royce Whittaker," he said.

"You were Army," I said. "Artillery."

"Yeah. You?"

"Same. That's why I stopped. I saw the patch on your arm. I was commander of the First of the Fortieth. We were stationed on the DMZ for twelve."

"Righteous! I was stationed there for twelve, too!" He said. "Corporal, Sir, Third of the Forty-fourth. I was on the howitzers." Then, patting his leg, he said: "Got my right leg crushed under a gun stand when we took a bad hit. Damn freaky! Blood vessels got choked up, messed this leg up pretty bad. Gangrene right down this side before they knew it. The docs couldn't save it then. Coulda' been worse though—much worse. I might've lost 'em both."

I nodded. I told him how our gun stand had protected me that one time. There had been only three of us in that area who had made it. The sarge had shot a Cong who had almost stepped right on me trying to get to the gunney while I was out. That was freaky, too. I found that remembering it was not as bad as it could have been since I was talking about it with someone like him.

He listened attentively, interjecting, and nodding, then he said:

"My father-in-law's a veteran. He was an Army grunt in Korea and he's really proud of his service. He's always onto me to be proud of my service, too. But hell, ours was a nasty war—too ugly to be proud of. Ugly here, ugly there. Nothing's ever good about any war, whether it's a declared war or not . . . like 'Nam was." He smiled, "Pop's a good man. Guess I'm trying to show some pride now, for him. You know what, I never wore this shirt until today . . . been packed up in a trunk with the rest of my gear 'til we moved down here last week."

"Righteous!" I affirmed. I was surprised how easily I used the lingo again. "Mine's still stored down in the basement in a trunk, too." I considered for a minute. "Well, I guess I'll say I'm proud of my service. We did what we had to do and we were serving the country the best we could—no matter what anybody can say."

He nodded and we stood quietly for a few minutes, each of us mulling over our memories as we looked toward the passing traffic. Both of us had served our country. We had done our duty. Thank God, neither of us had paid the ultimate price, but he had paid a dear price indeed—he had lost his leg. I had surely paid a dear price because I had lost something just like he had. I had looked at too many pairs of dead eyes and seen too many mangled bodies of my own soldiers and too many of theirs, too. Way too many dead men—too many that we had caused to pay the ultimate price while they were trying to do the very same to us. It was the memories that caused my longing to go back—to exact more of a price from the enemy. That was what I had felt so strongly: the weight of obligation to finish the job. He understood that—that longing. Over the years I had begun to realize that the job could not be finished and God had seen fit to let me and my soldiers do what our country had asked of us. Maybe that was enough. I found I was able to accept that more and more easily as the years went by.

Surely this man's life was sorely affected by the loss of his limb. My life was sorely affected by unapparent and mental injuries—my memories and my nightmares. There were many of us who were unable to accept what it was or how it had been. I hated to think that their military lives would never be finished—not during this lifetime. Some would be forever lost because they had fallen among the collateral damage from that war when they had come home—they were mere existing in some mental limbo and would never get over it.

It was hard to believe that despite our personal sacrifice, when we veterans had come back to our beloved country, we had been spat upon, denounced, and called "baby killers." We were blamed for an "undeclared war" by our fellow Americans who were activists against our actions in Vietnam. They behaved as though we had acted on our own as individual mercenaries—without US military orders. That had caused a lot of anger and so much bitterness at that time. It was a very tough pill that we US veterans of the Vietnam War had to swallow. I was more than sure that every one of us still carried that anger and bitterness like hard rocks inside of us.

But this Vietnam veteran was brave enough to wear his military shirt. I certainly would never have worn mine under any circumstances—not now—not after all the marches and protests and the violence against us and our actions that had been so prominent every day on the 6 o'clock news. Every bit of my Army gear was stored in a trunk under the stairs in the basement and there it would stay. I never stopped to think about why I hadn't—no—I **couldn't** get rid of any of my Army gear. I had earned every one of the dried edges of salt as my sweat stains had been renewed one right on top of the other. I had bought every splatter of mess and gore that soiled my military uniforms. I had paid the forever price too, I realized. My pain and rage and fear of death had been internalized and had become the solid stuff that lived inside my brain to re-awaken unbidden as gut-wrenching nightmares.

I had first figured that maybe this soldier was in distress of some kind, too. But after I had gotten closer and assessed his appearance I knew better: he was clean-shaven and the khaki pants that he was wearing were neatly pressed. He was okay. Our conversation let me know that as we stood there talking and reminiscing with each other. We were both survivors. It had been really good for me to talk to him and I could tell that he was pleased that I had stopped, pleased to be able to talk—really talk to someone who had been there, too. We understood each other completely.

In a matter of a few minutes, he told me that he joined the Army intending to be a lifer, but he had gotten out soon after he had been injured. He and his wife were parents to a daughter and a younger son. Since he had been back home, he and his wife had both been working on the post at Fort Leonard Wood. His wife had been a financial officer there since before they were married. She had been killed in a car accident over a year ago on her way home from work. How ironic! His wife's parents had never gotten over the death of their only daughter. Soon after his wife's death, her mother had a devastating stroke and had to be put in a permanent care facility. Since then, his father-in-law had become very lonely living in the big house by himself. So, the soldier had sold his own modest house, and he and his kids had moved to Saint Louis. Right now they were staying with his father-in-law until he found a house in Saint Louis. He intended to buy an interest in his father-in-law's heavy equipment rental business, maybe even become an equal partner. So far, so good, he said, but the hardest thing for him was trying to learn the business. It was going to involve making himself familiar with the day-to-day operations and he planned on using the bookkeeping skills that he had started to learn. He figured that was where the real work lay.

When I asked why he was out walking, he laughed and said that he really hadn't gone very far. He pointed to indicate where we could see the neat lawn, the ornamental trees, shrubs and the corner of his father-in-law's house (his home now) only one street over. With his artificial leg, he just needed to get out walking a little for the exercise since he had been sitting down all day at the office. Anyway, he said, he had promised himself that he would become more familiar with the neighborhood.

This soldier was a real hero. He had put his life on the line for his country and now he seemed to be taking another sacrifice onto his broad shoulders for the sakes of his father-in-law as well as for his children. Well, he had done some more good on another front today because he had all but told me where I should look to find the strong ally that I needed. When I told him that, he seemed really pleased that he had helped me.

I was grateful to this soldier for making me remember. I gave him one of my cards and asked him to call me sometime so we could talk again. We parted with a combat soldier's handshake but it did not mean as much as the brotherly hug of encouragement that we gave to each other. It did not know why I hadn't thought of it myself—this soldier had made me remember that the strong ally who could really help me to get a handle on my problems had been there all along.

I stopped by a fast-food drive-in and hastily got myself something to eat. I was pumped up, really anxious to put my new plan into motion. As soon as I was inside the house, I forgot all about my food. I set it down on the kitchen counter, went to the den, picked up the telephone, sat down in my chair, and dialed the number.

I was calling my father-in-law.

My mother-in-law answered the telephone. Our conversation was not as amicable as it had been the first time I had called. Maybe I was just imagining it, but I thought I could feel a bit of a strain between us. She seemed surprised or maybe she was relieved when I asked to speak to my father-in-law. It was a minute or two before he came on the telephone.

"Well, hey there, Cooksey," he said. "I've been thinkin' about you."

I really had to smile. Liz's voice was the same as his—that same soft, mellow tone; only his voice was deeper—masculine. I had never thought about that before because I just hadn't had any reason to. Even when I had spoken to him over the telephone on occasion during the years that Liz and I had been married I hadn't ever realized the similarity.

He was a very talented bricklayer and in later years he had become a brick contractor. He must have had a natural eye for lines and angles because after looking at plans and assessing a job, he seemed automatically to know just how bricks needed to fit on any building. What seemed to come so easily and naturally for him could pose a problem for others. The orders that he issued to the people who worked for him seemed to come from his natural knowledge. He took fierce pride in owing money to no one or being beholden to no one. I had gone to work with him one or two times when Liz and I were visiting. I knew that he did not really need my help because he hired numerous workers and unskilled laborers to do all of the more menial jobs. I could well remember their friendly grins and slaps on my back while I pitched in beside them and did some of the work that would have fallen to them.

My father-in-law always offered to pay me, but I never took payment for my work. I had not forgotten that he stood up for me and took my part when Liz's mother had so angrily refused to even participate in our wedding. He had given Liz away at our wedding while Liz's mother had never really forgiven Liz for breaking her engagement to her former fiancé and marrying an "unknown" like me.

"How are you, Sir," I said.

"I'm doin' fine—just fine," he said. "What about you?"

"I'm all right . . . I guess." I hesitated for a moment, then I said: "Liz says that she's not coming back home."

There was a long silence after that. Finally, he said: "Well, she didn't tell me herself but her mama said something to me about that. Why do you reckon she don't want to come back?"

"I . . . well, I guess it's because we had such a bad misunderstanding. I think she—"

"'. . . *bad misunderstanding*,'" he repeated gruffly, cutting me off, "Nobody said nothing to me about that. How bad was it? Y'all didn't do no fightin'—?"

Very suddenly, his voice had an icy cold edge to it.

"No! No!" I said quickly when I understood what he meant. "Mr. Walton, your daughter is my heart. I would never fight with her! Not like . . . ***fight***! Ask her yourself if you don't believe me!"

He chuckled softly, then he said: "I figured I knew you better'n that. I guess you woulda' sent her on back home before you'd hurt her or anything like that."

"Yes, Sir," I said tersely, "I would."

"Their momma would smack both of 'em on their butts sometimes, but I never did. A man don't never need to be hittin' his woman or his babies."

"Yes, Sir," I agreed. "A man should never hit his woman or his babies."

"So . . . what caused y'all to fall out? Is it ***somebody*** she's mad at you about, then?"

I froze. What had Liz said to her parents? I refused to believe she had said anything about ***that!*** Good God! What nasty turn might this take? Suddenly, I was unsure and wondered if it had been a mistake to call him. I refused to believe that, so I took a deep breath and rushed ahead:

"Work has really been getting me down. Liz claimed I was mad and hard to get along with all the time and . . . well, she said she was fed up with that. She got to where she wouldn't talk to me at all. That's what she always does—she won't talk when she's upset. I'm on the day shift now, but I was on the night shift when she left, so I was sleeping during the day and working at night. Soon as Crissy's school got out for the summer, Liz took the kids and the dog and just took off while I was sleeping. She left here without saying one word to me."

"Say she did?" He seemed to be considering what I had said. "She just up and left home and didn't say nothing a 'tall, hunh?"

"Yes sir, she sure did." I said flatly.

"Any more to it than that?" He asked softly. He sounded thoroughly amused.

I still hesitated to be completely honest with him.

"I would stop by a club over in East Saint Louis with some of the guys after work once in a while. That's all. We'd have a few beers; we would talk and unwind for a bit; we would all discuss our problems at work. I guess maybe I stayed a little too late sometimes, so Liz got really angry . . . ah . . . about the drinking . . . who I was drinking with . . . all that. She just mixed everything all up that way . . . everything. She left here without saying one word to me."

He did not speak right away. My roundabout move to evade the question caused my heart to thunder like crazy. I did not like to lie so I would always try to evade rather than to lie. I waited until, finally, he said:

"Well . . . it's always about drinking ain't it? I can't say if she had good enough reason to leave because of that or not, but I always figured she had a pretty good head on her shoulders."

Now ***he*** was being evasive rather than saying what he was thinking. I could hear pride in his voice right along with his amusement though. It was obvious how he felt about his daughter. I couldn't blame him, but I had hoped that he would see my side of things with what I had told him. However, he gave me no indication that was the case as he continued slowly:

"You know . . . some of the kin folks got real upset back when y'all first got married. They didn't know nothing about you or your folks—that was true, but it wasn't just that. That boy my baby girl was engaged to marry . . . we been knowing him and all his folks for a long time. They live down the street from us. It was a real mess 'round here after she quit him because everybody could see his side of things. But . . . you were the one she wanted—that was plain. After y'all got married . . . she followed you all over—everywhere you went. When you went overseas during the war, she came on back home . . . but she wasn't herself. She was sick with worry the whole time you was over there. You know that?"

"Yes, Sir, I know . . ." I was starting to grow disheartened because he had said far more than I had ever heard him say at any one time. I thought I understood his meaning all too well: maybe he didn't intend to take my part as I had hoped. Well . . . no matter, I still felt like it had been worth it to talk to him.

"I'd say it's time for her to get herself on back home where she belongs," he said after a minute. "She keep saying she's gonna' go to work over there in Memphis and put the kids in school over there. Who's she think she's fooling? Everybody got sense enough to know she don't mean none of that. That's nothing but talk."

If I had been holding my breath at all, I hadn't realized it until just then. Suddenly, I felt like I could breathe again.

"Yes, Sir," was all that I was able to say at the moment.

"I gave her to you at your wedding and I'm satisfied with that. I'd say y'all been doin' pretty well. Things might not always go just the way neither one of y'all want ***all*** the time, but my baby girl, she know she got herself a good man in you."

My heart lifted then. I began to feel much, much better. I gave an easy chuckle.

"You think I need to come down and bring her on back home, then?" I asked.

"Naaah," he said immediately, "When a man work as hard as you do, he don't have time to go runnin' around behind his wife on account of she's poutin' and goin' on and showin' her temper. You been keeping a decent home and some decent transportation for her. No need to spoil her no more'n that. She can get on back home by herself—same way she come down here. I'm just gonna' tell her to be careful on that road especially since she got them kids in the car."

"Yes, Sir," I laughed. "Well, thank you for talking to me—"

"One more thing," he said.

"Yes, Sir?"

"Stop callin' me '**Sir**,'" he laughed, "And y'all call me more often y' hear?"

He was "Dad" to me from that very minute.

Walter called me that next evening to give me a "heads up." He wanted me to know that Liz was coming home. He said that she had packed her bags and gathered up the kids' things and intended to leave early the next morning. I thanked him for letting me know.

I slept mighty well that night. In fact, I had slept a whole lot better since I had spoken with Liz's dad. He was a man whose few words really meant something and I was confident that I could count on whatever he had to say.

I was on pins and needles from the moment that I got out of bed on the morning that Liz was supposed to come back home. I was distracted at work and too impatient. I decided to just leave early. I really wanted to be there when my family got home. I went over to Joe's office to tell him that I was leaving.

Joe had suspected that something was wrong in my life weeks ago, because he had persistently asked me about it in his stony, gruff way. I knew that he was honestly concerned about me, but I kept on denying that I had any personal "troubles," as he put it.

One time, when he found me giving our three cowering clerks hell about keeping better records after not a single one of them could account for four huge boxes of door pads that records showed were supposed to be in our inventory, Joe tried hard to soothe my nerves. Todd Snowden, a superintendent for Caprice supply, had complained that he needed to send the pads over to the Caprice line. After Joe had told me to calm down, he waited with Todd and me while we made telephone calls ourselves for several minutes until we finally found the proof that the door pads had been sent over to the truck line. No one had bothered to record the transfer or write orders to replace the inventory for the Caprice line. That was a major screw-up, not to mention bone-headed, slip-shod records keeping that nobody had caught. The clerks had no excuses at all as far as I was concerned. It was their jobs to keep all the records about our materials in order so that all of our stocks could be kept up-to-date.

Most of the time when everybody except the heavy equipment operators, electricians and maintenance men had gone home after our work day was over, if Joe found me still at my desk working on a problem or if something unexpected had come up and was needed right away for night shift or needed to be somewhere for tomorrow, he sometimes hung around with me himself until I got all of the problems resolved. He'd pitch in to help Todd or Kenny with anything left over—even going over the inventory delivery sheets if the facts and figures didn't jibe. Sometimes, he would just sit around talking while I did a check on the counts they had brought in or double-checked all of the forms for the day. I knew that Joe really stayed around to keep me from being in the half-deserted department all by myself.

So, on the day that I decided to leave early, Joe seemed to be really glad to see me get out of there for a change even though it was well before the first shift was scheduled to end.

I had already cleaned the old and spoiled food out of the refrigerator a while back. Now the refrigerator was pretty much empty except for what I had put into it recently: bacon, eggs, a loaf of bread, sliced ham, lunchmeat and cheese, plus there were jars of mayonnaise, mustard, pickles and the usual condiments in there.

I stopped by the grocery store and picked up a couple of steaks, some baking potatoes, salad makings, a case of already-cold beer, some sodas in the large bottles, a couple of cans of frozen, concentrated lemonade mix of the kind that Liz always bought, and packages of frozen green beans, lima beans, English peas, and mixed vegetables that I knew Liz would want. I went by McDonalds and bought hamburgers and fries for the kids because I knew well enough that was what they would want.

As soon as I got everything out of the car, inside the house, into the refrigerator or into the freezer, I picked up the telephone and called Florestine and Walter's house in Memphis.

"She left here about 6:30 this morning," Teen said, "so she ought to be there pretty soon. The kids were ***so*** excited to be going home to their daddy."

"I've really missed them," I said.

"They've really missed you," she said, "And I'll bet Muffy's missed you, too. He's such a great-looking dog. Libby keeps him all groomed and cleaned up so he can stay with the family in the house. My kids are crazy about him. He's a mean little bugger but I bet he loved all the kids paying attention to him all the time. Roger really wanted to keep him."

"He would never leave Liz," I laughed. "He's her dog through and through."

"I know! It's so cute how he likes to sleep with his head on her feet when she sits down. I think he does it to keep her from going anywhere without taking him along. He's so funny! We need to get our kids a dog like Muffy."

We talked for a while longer. Teen and Liz were alike in so many ways. Both she and Liz had the same great sense of humor—Teen really made me laugh out loud a couple of times. I was surprised how good it felt to really laugh again. I hadn't felt a shred of humor in what seemed like many, many months.

I must have paced restlessly to the kitchen door at least two or three times, opened it and looked out into the garage at the empty bay where Liz always parked the Firebird. Finally, I got into my recliner in the den in front of the television, cranked up my feet, and half-watched the final minutes of a science show about the planets and space exploration. I started to watch the news but after a while, I got up and turned off the television. I was thinking of calling Teen and Walter's telephone again when I heard the garage door going up. I quickly got back into my chair and turned the television back on. I made myself sit still, but I kept my eyes on the door that led into the kitchen from the garage.

In a few minutes, the kitchen door opened and I heard the muffled patter of little feet and the jingle of Muffy's dog tags. He ran right into the den and came straight to me. I petted him and allowed him to jump into my lap and lick my hands. I didn't try too hard to hold him back, and he managed to stretch up onto my chest and get in a lick or two under my chin. I put him to the floor just as the kids ran in, piling into me and throwing their arms around my neck. I kissed and hugged them both in turn. My eyes were still on the doorway even while I held the kids on my lap and listened to their chatter:

"Daddy! Daddy! . . . We didn't stop for nothing coming home . . ." "Daddy! Daddy! We went out in the country . . ." ". . . we saw some cows . . ." ". . . we saw some horses, too . . ." ". . . Daddy! We saw a whole lot of folks—they were our kin folks . . ." ". . . Daddy, we saw lotsa' chigs and pickens . . ."

"'*Chigs and pickens*?'" I laughed. "Don't you mean 'pigs and chickens,' David?"

"That's what I said," David insisted.

Liz walked into the house and unrolled Muffy's rubber pad back onto the kitchen floor and placed the rack and bowls back where they belonged on the pad. I watched her as she walked over to the kitchen sink with one of Muffy's bowls and ran some water into it. She stood there while Muffy lapped up water then she walked to the back door and let him go outside into the back yard. Then, without a word, she went back out into the garage.

The kids slid down my legs, onto the floor, then they headed straight for the basement to the toys and the old television that they hadn't seen in a while.

I figured Liz would have a struggle getting their suitcases out of the car so I got up and walked to the doorway of the garage, folded my arms and stood watching her as she poured Muffy's dry dog food out of a bag and into the larger covered plastic tub that we kept in a corner of the garage.

I said, "Hello," but Liz did not look up at me and she mumbled her answer.

"Want some help?" I asked.

I stepped down into the garage, got Liz's big suitcase out of the trunk of the car then I set out the kids' two suitcases. I took Liz's suitcase up into the kitchen and made an exaggerated comment about its weight while behind me she brought the kids' suitcases up to the step and inside. She gave a short, sharp answer when I asked casually about her trip and a single response to my numerous questions about the long drive she'd just made. She went back out again and brought back a large canvas bag that must have contained kids' toys and set it on the floor next to the basement door.

As soon as she got the garage door down and I was sure that she was inside the house for good, I blocked her passage and stood looking down at her as she was attempting to take the kids' bags down the hall to their bedrooms. She still wouldn't look up at me and tried to step around me. I reached out and caught her shoulders in both my hands as gently as I could.

"Okay, Mrs. Cooksey," I said with an effort to keep my voice normal. "We're going to talk right now."

She set the bags down and just stood there like a statue. My anger at her had revved up the minute I had my hands on her. I really wanted to shake her until she couldn't talk at all. It might well have made up for her absence and cooled my anger if I had done that, but, of course, I held myself back and tried my best to control the tone of my voice:

"Don't you realize how this has been for me? I was terrified to have my family travelling all alone like that. If anything had happened to you and the kids out there on that highway how do you think I would have felt . . . just tell me that, Elizabeth!"

"All your problems would have been solved," she said without moving. "Then you could have that woman right out in the open. You wouldn't need to be sneaking around—"

"Dammit!" I growled as my anger surged up, "How do you sound? Don't you ***ever*** say anything like that to me again!"

"Well, here we go!" Liz said sounding both resigned and angry. She attempted to move back from my grasp and away. "Nothing's changed I see. You're snapping at me just like you always do. I **knew** better—I **knew** I shouldn't have come back! I wouldn't have come back if my daddy hadn't kept on—"

I cut her off, "I snapped at you because of what you said! And you know it! You'd better not leave me like that again! I mean it! You hear me?"

I dragged her back in front of me and I shook her—but only a little. I restrained myself because didn't aim to frighten her and I would never have harmed her—not in a million years—no matter how angry she made me. I only meant for her to look up at me so that she could see how acutely disturbed I was. It had to be plain all over my face.

She raised her eyes finally and met my heated stare reluctantly. She was smart enough not to try to pull away again. I wished fervently that we could just forget everything. She had no idea how badly I wanted to hold her tightly in my arms. I wanted to take her straight back to our bedroom for all that meant. If not for the kids, I would have done just that.

Instead I took her hand and led her to my chair in the den, sat down, and drew her down on my lap. She pulled back from me and perched like a bird on my knee. She was determined to resist me. That did not keep me from touching her, though. She should have known better than to attempt to thwart a husband bent upon enjoying long overdue marital privileges. I knew her only too well and I knew just what I was doing. I took my time and drew her back onto my lap against my chest. She tried once to wiggle away from me, but I took pleasure in overpowering her then. Afterwards, I carefully smoothed and straightened her clothes and ruffled her hair playfully. She made another annoyed attempt to thwart my touch, but I persisted patiently until she finally gave in. Her only option was to relax into my arms. She laid her head against my shoulder.

"This is *not* fair," she mumbled.

"What's not fair?" I asked in smug amusement with my face against her thick, soft hair. I had really missed the soft feel of her skin and her warm, spicy smell that I knew so well. She could not know how good it felt to have her back in my arms.

"You just think you can do whatever you please no matter what," She exaggerated dramatically, "And you expect me to—"

"Now, you listen to me, Elizabeth" I said sternly, "You had no right to leave home like that without a word because of what you *believed* or how things *seemed* to be. I've told you, and told you: I haven't done a thing! I'm innocent! This all started because I came in here with a little lipstick on my shirt—some woman had hugged me. Women will hug men sometimes because that's some women's way of being nice. Somebody needs to tell them that heavy make-up and red lipstick and perfume and other stuff can get all over the front of a man's shirt. You women never think about that at all, and I'm not the kind of guy to be rude. You know that! I can't believe something so . . . ***meaningless*** could make you want to break up our family!"

"No!" she insisted, "It wasn't ***meaningless***! You can't tell me that you didn't—"

I cut her off again:

"You had no right to do what you did! I want you to think about this: What have I ever said or done to make you do something so extreme like that? You took the kids and you left me. You never said one word. We never talked about anything. It wasn't right and it wasn't fair because you didn't give me a chance to defend myself! Running off like that was just plain ***childish***!"

She stiffened rebelliously. I could tell she was really steamed about what I had just said. She closed her lips tightly and wouldn't say anything else.

But I was only thinking of myself and how I felt, so I failed to check the harsh words that I said to her then:

"We've been married all this time and you don't have any more faith in me than that? You knew well enough that I was stressed out at work! You knew I was under pressure, but you never tried to help me. All of a sudden you started snapping at me and getting all puffed up and not saying anything at all. You stayed angry all the time. You never gave me the least bit of encouragement. Well, somebody needed to encourage me! Other people were trying to be nice to me when you weren't! So, how did you expect me to feel—what did you expect me to do? You just got ***jealous***, that's all you did, and you acted really, really ***foolish***!"

I was still absolutely furious that she had left me like that. All I was thinking was: *How dare she run away without giving me a chance!*

Suddenly, it hit me then, like a ton of bricks and I realized how harsh and hurtful my words must be to her: Liz had done nothing but follow me around all over the country ever since we had been married. She had encouraged me and she had always stood by me. She had more than held her own and done her part to support our family. She was smart, accomplished and self-sufficient, but she had already abandoned five or six really good jobs without a qualm just to be with me and support me from the day that we married, everywhere my career had taken me.

She had gone completely still on my lap. I saw the lines tightening her lips and the too-bright shine in her eyes. It was that deep hurt on her face that she couldn't hide. She must have really been convinced that I was hopelessly self-centered and selfish. She looked resigned. What would I do if she decided that she wasn't going to take any more and left me again—this time to go somewhere else?

There were a few things I needed to face up to and admit to myself:

I had never once admitted to myself how much the extreme problems at work had caused my relationship with my wife and my family to be affected.

When I had gone across the river to the club, I had found such understanding there because those were men just like me—my comrades—and they had the same troubles at work as I did. I felt free to talk to them and I listened to their complaints too. We shared things that affected all of our jobs—therefore, we could provide uplift and support for one another.

I had never admitted that I really secretly enjoyed the rivalry between the women at work for my attention and I had more than enjoyed the extremely aggressive behavior of one in particular. She had gone overboard trying to get next to me. I had enjoyed seeing the longing in her eyes. I had to admit that I had let it inflate my male ego. I had almost let it go too far!

There was no discounting the implications of the lipstick and the perfume I had carelessly brought home on my clothes. Surely Liz must have found that damming evidence on more than one occasion, but true to my wife's inherently reticent nature, she had only mentioned it to me one time. Then, my angry, negative response to her just proved that I was totally aware and more than a little flattered by it all. Liz had known that then, because she knew me.

When had I stopped behaving like the loving husband that Liz was accustomed to? The daily pressure that I was working under had changed me pretty drastically. I had grown to think only of myself, my own feelings, and too much about my own self-important ego. I had trampled on the feelings of my precious wife one time too many. It had taken the shock of her leaving and taking the kids away to make me see just how self-centered I had become. I had taken my family far too much for granted and I had never once put their needs before my own egotistical selfishness.

I needed to try to somehow get my wife to believe in me again. She had to know that her trust in me was not misplaced. I realized my mistake now, but, what could I say? What could I do? I said to myself that it would be far, far better to talk about the past than to say anything about what had just happened between us. That was too fresh and would be just too painful. I cast around in my mind until I thought of the time long ago when we almost had our greatest disaster even before we began:

"Remember that freaky ol' headache I used to get when we were in school? Whenever times were so hard for me, I'd get that ol' headache—remember that? Linda showed up at the apartment that time when you were there . . . then she went and pulled that fool stunt with those pills. I had stopped seeing her but she just wouldn't give up. You knew it—you believed me. But, I guess I really felt guilty. I felt like it was my fault that she just kept on and on. I had let her believe she could have her way and she believed that I would come around and do what she wanted me to do. She thought everybody would blame me for what ***she*** did . . . and they did. But they were all wrong. Finally, I just made my mind up! I was determined not to let it take me down. Everything seemed to be going straight to hell until Linda's folks took her on back home. Afterwards, I looked for you, you were gone . . . it was just too much. I thought for sure that I had really lost you. It was hard to take. But, when you came back . . . I'll never forget when I saw you sitting there in the library at ***our*** table! All I wanted was to prove to myself that you belonged to me. You understood that, I know you did. God! You were so sweet! Just so, so sweet how you trusted in me . . . You never once blamed me—for anything. You always trusted in the love we had for each other . . ."

I saw that her face had softened as she looked up at me. I had been rambling—trying hard to say the right thing. I knew that mixed up in all the stuff I said, I must have somehow got something right!

Long ago, when both of us had finally broken from the people who had tried so hard to bind us to them, they had tried to make us feel guilt, fear and they had shamelessly tried to exploit any weakness. They wanted us to think that we were so wrong to leave them to be with each other. They put us through hell. When the war had separated us—that was hell, too. We went through our own special kind of hell trying to have kids of our own. What else was **this** misunderstanding but another hell: a breakdown of trust that had very nearly destroyed our marriage . . .

I had always said that I was not an optimist. I knew that there would be other circumstances and other people who were going to give us more hell in the future, but I figured that if we stayed together, trusted in each other, we could live through the worst of it again . . . and again . . . and again if we had to. We both knew that together, we could survive anything!

Liz sat up then, put her hands against both sides of my face, pulled my head down and pressed her lips softly against my left temple, then my right. That sweet gesture meant everything in the world to me.

"This serious pain in my jaw's been bothering me the whole time . . ." I complained. I was confident now though I tried hard not to sound that way.

Liz patiently turned my face and kissed my left cheek then my right. She paused, smiled sweetly, "Better?"

"Oh yeah, so much better," I whispered. "What about my lips . . ."

Her arms went around my neck. Her soft lips touched mine. I did not try to hold myself in check any longer. It all fell away then—all that had happened to us, even the misunderstanding and harsh words that had passed between us recently—none of that mattered at all anymore when we kissed each other.

"I'll make you a promise," I said fiercely. "I won't ***let*** this happen to us again! Anybody who—"

"Stop that!"

It was Crissy. We hadn't heard her come up the basement steps. She was standing in the doorway of the den frowning at us with her little hands fisted on her hips authoritatively.

"Stop all that ol' kissing stuff and all that ol' being in love!" she said haughtily. "Y'all are ***married***!"

She turned, grabbed up their bag of toys, and went righteously clumping and bumping across the hall and back down the steps to the basement while we tried to muffle our laughter.

"Your daughter thinks just like you do" Liz said still laughing, "Married people don't need all that ol' being in love and all that ol' kissing stuff. You don't think married folks need that ol' forgiveness stuff either, do you?"

I refused to answer that. I kissed her again—once just for myself; again like a husband might; then again with a roguish threat of, "just you wait until later!"

Liz laughed at that. God! It was so good to hear her laughing again!

"I have to tell you something right now," I said, "Every day the Saint Louis assembly operation is thrashing around on spindly legs and big club feet like a camel tied to a tree in a thunderstorm. The labor union—some of the radicals—they've been gouging that plant to death for a long time. I guess they never figured that Detroit would just gear up and absolutely get rid of the plant altogether. For the sake of my career I can't afford to stay around here while this place is going straight to hell. I hate to do this to Joe, because he's really been good to me. I've always been straight with him though, so he knows that I have to go so I can do the best I can for myself—try to find some stability. I've located three places with openings that I might look into. All of them seem pretty promising: materials management in Fremont, California—Joe's giving me a leg up on that one; production superintendent in Doraville, Georgia—that's near Atlanta; and production superintendent in Arlington—that's close by Fort Worth and Dallas. Every one of those openings seems suited to me."

Liz had grown very still against my shoulder while I was talking. I could almost hear the wheels turning in her head. "So, you've been making plans to leave here without us?" she asked quietly. "And if we hadn't come back—?"

"I told you every day that you needed to come home!" I scolded. "I told you things were changing! You should have come on back, but **no-o-o**! You went and you stayed for the whole summer!"

Liz grinned up at me with her pretty dark eyes twinkling. "You're saying that you told me all this and I just wouldn't listen, right? And you're also saying that you were going to leave here without us if we hadn't come back home when we did. That's what you're saying, right?"

"That's right!" I huffed grumpily. "I was going to—"

"Oh, nonsense! You mean, growly ol' bear!" Liz said laughing, "No such thing! You were going to stay right here waiting for us to come home. You weren't about to leave without us. I know that!"

I hung on for a bit longer. I swore mightily that I intended to leave Saint Louis with or without them. Finally, though, there was no use to keep up the lying or the denying. She was right and she knew it. I planted a kiss on her forehead to smooth out the frown lines between her eyebrows and said:

"I really need to get a move on if I expect to save my career in production at General Motors. I really hate to leave Joe in the lurch—he's gotten to where he depends on me a whole lot—but I have to be thinking about my career. I don't want to take the 'safe' way out by staying in Materials. Production is way more important in manufacturing than anything else. I really need to be in Production."

I caught her chin and held her face up to make her look into my eyes. I still hadn't asked her forgiveness but since I had put my heart into her hands nearly fifteen years ago, she did not need any words from me at all. After our near-mishap, I was the one who needed to hear words of assurance from her.

"You know what I want to hear," I said softly, frowning down at her.

She smiled smugly and made me wait while she took her own sweet time. She caught my hand, entwined her fingers with mine, pressed her lips against the back of my hairy hand and held it against her heart. Then, finally, she said the only words in the world that I needed to hear:

"Wherever you go, the kids, Muffy and I will go."

While Liz went into the kitchen to cook the food that I had brought home, I took all the suitcases back to the bedrooms. I left both the kids' suitcases in Crissy's room against the wall because I didn't remember which was which. Then, I made sure that I put Liz's suitcase at the foot of the bed in our bedroom. I rubbed my palms together like a cartoon villain trying to curb my anticipation. Then, I walked back down the hall to watch Liz as she moved efficiently around the small kitchen.

Liz had already put the steaks in a foil-covered pan. She sprinkled seasoning on them and put them under the grill in the oven, talking steadily while she got plastic plates from the cabinet and handed them to me to put on the table. She told me about things that she had done while she was in Memphis and Holly Springs. We mulled over the death and sadness that had plagued both our families during the last few years that had made our hearts ache.

"Why does it have to happen like this?" Liz asked sighing. "We hardly get over one thing before another thing comes along and mows us right down. What is the old saying: 'very bad things always come in threes?'"

"Nah, that's superstition," I said. "Death is a part of life and living. We're getting older—our folks are getting even older. If we stop to worry about it, it can really get us down. We've got the kids coming up, so we have to go on now—do things for their sakes."

"I hate to say this," Liz looked at me as she took the kids' hamburger patties out of the buns and put them into a plate and covered them to warm in the microwave oven, "I really hope that they don't want you to go to California. We're born and bred southern people and California is just too far away from your family and mine, too. I'd hate to think if anybody really needed us and we were way out there. It would be such a long trip to get back over to this side of the country where they are."

"I'm going to set the California interview up first," I said, "Joe thinks I'm really good at materials management. I've learned a whole lot in just these last few weeks or so, but I don't want to stay in it. I really, really want to get back into production. That's where I need to be. The position in Georgia is in production. It sounds ideal. I'm going to try to get that interview set up for next week. Texas is in production, too—smaller plant and all. I still have to get that one set up."

"I'm pulling for Atlanta!" Liz said fervently. "You have to try your best there! You have to make them see that you'd be so much better suited for the position in Atlanta! That's about halfway between both our folks, too."

"You know I told you that it's in Doraville, now—not Atlanta. Doraville is North of Atlanta. Have we got a map of Georgia or Atlanta? I'll show you where it is after dinner."

"I don't care!" Liz said stubbornly, "You said Doraville is close to Atlanta. All that really matters is that it's in the South! It's closer to home. I'm pulling for Doraville!"

"Suppose I don't like the place at all, though," I speculated. "That's one of General Motor's biggest plants. What if they've got a bad workforce? There's the southern thing, too. Those workers could be real assholes and the union could be ball-busters just like they are right here in Saint Louis. They might be inclined to give a black superintendent like me holy hell . . ."

"No! No, they won't," Liz insisted, "The workers in Doraville couldn't be any worse than they are here in Saint Louis. You cut your teeth in this hell-hole, didn't you? And you've survived. You've got the battle scars to prove it, haven't you? Nothing in life is ever promised to be all good for anybody. Anyway, I've heard that the Atlanta area is a good place to live and there are lots of good schools for the kids."

"Sam and Hazel have finally gotten moved down to Bowling Green," I said.

Liz paused for a minute and looked hard at me. "I know that's where you really want to go."

"Yeah, I do," I admitted. I got a cold beer from the refrigerator and popped it open. "You know I've wanted to work at Corvette since before I left GMI. That's why I went to Saint Louis in the first place. Then, GM moved the Corvette plant to Bowling Green but that still doesn't make the Corvette brand safe. It's really a small plant—small setup. I didn't have a chance of going when they moved because all the people who went there have the most seniority in production. I'm too new to even hope to get what I want. With all the cutbacks, I guess I'm lucky I still have a job. I'm gonna' be at the mercy of Detroit until I get some 'legs' under me. I'll just have to be patient."

Liz made a face with one eyebrow raised. "You could never be '*patient*.' Not you!"

I took a drink of the ice-cold beer, then I strolled over, pinned her hard against the refrigerator, trapping her with my body, and glared down at her with my most intimidating face. "And just what do you mean by ***that,*** Mrs. Cooksey? Are you saying that I have ***no*** patience?"

Far from being the least bit intimidated, Liz grinned up at me.

"You know exactly what I'm saying, *Mr. Cooksey*! Both of us know. You have no patience ***at all*** . . . unless something is really important to ***you***."

I took another long, deliberate drink of the cold beer before I leaned down, and nipped her on the nose with my ice-cold lips. She tried to squirm away, but I chuckled at the catch in her breath, thwarting her escape, thoroughly enjoying her efforts. Finally, I stepped back and unpinned her, and then I said:

"You're right: I don't have a lot of patience, so I guess I gotta' suck it up and wait. You mark my words though—I'm gonna' get to Corvette!"

It had been a long, long time since we sat had down to dinner as a family, but I found I didn't have to work too hard to make my conversation child-friendly. Both Crissy and David were overly talkative. Now that they had visited a farm, they had to tell me all about the woods, the trees, and the big, big open fields where all the crops were growing. That's why it was called "the country" Crissy explained. They talked about the young relatives they had met, what they had done and how much fun it had been. Cousin Andrea and Crissy had hand-feed furry baby chicks. The chicks were yellow because they were born from the *real* eggs and *real* eggs from hens were yellow inside—not like the ones Mom bought at the grocery store. David explained how he and Cousin, Kevin, had *almost* climbed up a tree. David had skinned his leg. The scar was right here! See? Kevin had said that David was too big to cry. It had hurt ***really*** bad when Mom had cleaned it with some red stuff and bandaged it up but he ***still*** did not cry . . . except only a little.

I was more than content to sit and listen to the kids as they talked. When Liz's eyes met mine, her soft, patient smile meant that she already knew what I was feeling. It has never been a part of my basic personality to use over-done, sentimental words to express myself. But later, as soon as we were alone, I meant to show her just how ***complete*** I felt now that my family was home.

At work the next day Joe walked in and stopped at my desk in the upstairs office. He leaned over, and peered across at me.

"What?" I grinned, looking up at him.

"You're actually smiling, that's what!" he growled. "You look relaxed! Your face looks . . . happy! Thank God! So it means your wife's come back! You were always frowning and so damn intense and grumpy—for a while I thought I was going to have to buy some horse tranquilizers or something and slip 'em into your coffee cup. Maybe everybody around here can settle down now and stop running away and hiding every time they see you coming."

I attempted to look just as solemn as he did.

"Grumpy?" I said, "Look who's calling me 'grumpy!' I never said my wife was gone—?"

"Aha!" He tapped his temple and said dramatically in his low rumbling voice, "Swami sees all and knows everything."

I couldn't help it—I laughed out loud, and he did too. Then he sobered:

"Well, it was something you said a coupla' weeks ago. You were never in any big hurry to go home—not until yesterday."

"Yeah," I conceded finally, "Liz has been a little miffed at me. She's been at her folks' in Mississippi most of the summer. She brought the kids on back home yesterday."

"I knew it!" he said still smiling, "from the way you tore outta' here, I knew it had to be something good like that. Good! Good!" He dragged a chair up to my desk and sat down and abruptly, his stony, grey eyes became fiercely serious. His mind had already switched gears. That was Joe.

"Now, when you get out there to Freemont, make sure you contact Jesse Goodhue. Tell him he can call me anytime. I've already seen to it that most of the guys in materials at the plant know all about you. You can probably use Jesse to seal the deal for you though. We got acquainted at GMI. We weren't close friends or anything but I knew him well enough. Lewinsky's another one I forgot to tell you about. I always forget that he's out there. I knew him at GMI, too. He's a good man. It won't hurt to talk to him. They might even talk to you together, I reckon."

I looked down at the bulky folder full of green inventory sheets that I had prodded the clerks to straighten around to make them easier to work on. Joe had told me many of the same things already. Joe could be hard-nosed, really straight-line, and stand-offish. But I had found that if he liked somebody, he could be a really good friend—and totally trustworthy. In spite of what people had said about him, I knew that he was really a good-hearted, very sensitive and down-to-earth guy. As much as it disturbed me and I balked at it, I had to be truly thankful for the personnel intervention on my behalf that had brought me into his department.

"Okay," I agreed. "I sure do appreciate your help, Joe."

"Aw sure," he said, "That's about all I can think of right now besides what I already told you. We know that the rest of 'em will really want you out there because of the reports I already made to them about you, so your shot is better than good. It's all up to you now."

I planned on giving that interview my best shot even though I already knew that Liz did not want to move to California again unless absolutely **nothing** else came my way. As it was, I would only be going for this interview to please Joe. Both Liz and I really did have our hearts set on going back south but I was far more flexible than Liz was. However badly I wanted to get back into production, I was not about to disappoint Joe by letting him know that.

"Know what," Joe said, "I wasn't so sure when you had that desk put down there on the floor. Now I can see the sense in making yourself more easily available for the counts and cataloging by being down there. It's a really good idea. I never had anybody who was willing to do it that way before. The rest of them prima donnas wanted stay stuck up here on their asses in the office all the time not doing a damn thing. That's why I wanted them the hell outta' here."

I nodded slowly without saying anything. I wondered if Joe knew about the harsh abrasions I had suffered from the mind-bending push and pull over on the production floor. Those scars were practically all healed up now and the healing had begun soon after I had gotten to Joe's department. It had helped me to be able to escape from the pressure from the union workers and leaders to come over here in this relaxed atmosphere and to work for a good man. People claimed that Joe was some sort of an ogre, and that his department was so awfully tough, but that was not true at all. Dealing with the plant's materials and accounting for resources just meant ***work***. It wasn't hazardous like producing a finished product had been every day. Working with Joe's people was **not** like pulling the teeth out of a dragon's mouth—working with the union people on the production floor had been every bit that bad, and worse, each and every day.

Thinking back over my career at General Motors, the academic atmosphere at GMI had really coddled me, but supervision out on the production floor had put me through the fire. It was constant, intense pressure. After the workers did the work, then I was the one who was held responsible for the work ***they*** did or did not do. That had been ***rough***! I was ultimately responsible for getting the final product done. That took special know-how—special talent—I had learned all those special lessons. That had toughened me, whether I looked like it on the outside or not. I could step back and look at it critically now, analyze it and figure out just how to use those hard lessons I had learned. Now, working for Joe had smoothed me out.

Joe slapped his open palms onto his knees and stood up.

"It's a long way over here from the main floor," he said as if reading my thoughts. "We're kinda' out of the way over here, but that's what I've always liked about it. I feel like being away from all that pressure over there in production for a time has helped you some, too, hunh?"

"Yeah, it has," I said. "I was never gonna' feel comfortable working with some of those people on the line—always battling with them—trying to get things done with people who were constantly pushing back, pulling tricks, and hiding out. It was purest hell. Working with the folks over here has really settled me down a whole lot. You told me that I would feel better over here."

"Well, you took up a lot of my load." Joe said pensively, "Y'know I've really gotten spoiled since you've been over here. You're damn good at this stuff, Cooksey. I'm going to play hell getting somebody as good as you to replace you when you're gone."

We both laughed at that.

"Thanks for all your help," I said. "You don't know how much I appreciate it." I put my hand out. We shook warmly, and then Joe went on down the hall to his office.

I went to Fremont and I found that the weather was wonderful—it actually felt soft and filled with sunshine like the songs and stories claimed. It was even better than I expected. A visitor like me could be tempted to eat practically every meal on the outside if not for the flies and other insects. The hotel that General Motors put me up in was really something. It was on the bay and only four stories high but it was a very spread out. Most of the buildings in the area were the same—no more than two or three stories high but they covered a lot of ground.

Since I had gotten into Fremont in the late afternoon before I had to go in for my interview, I spent some time after dinner sitting at a table under an umbrella on the lower balcony that jutted out into the surf, drinking draft beer because it was a lot less expensive. I sat enjoying the spectacular sundown on the water, watching the gulls wheeling and screeching over the rocky shoreline. I saw small crabs and some other spider-like water creatures climbing out of the surf onto the rocks down around the pier in the dying softness of the sunlight.

As an inland bred Texan, I was more accustomed to harsh sunlight, heat, dust, dry winds, tumbleweeds, armadillos, and jackrabbits. I had never been able to spend much time on either ocean shore of the country but Gregory had told me a lot about the balmy, humid weather on this south end of California. I was glad to be able to get close enough to the ocean beach to see for myself how strongly the waves lapped against the Western shoreline. I thought a little about gravitational pull, the directional turn of the earth and all that, but the engineer in me had to be even more concerned about the aggressive waves causing constant erosion of the soil along the shoreline. I went down the steps and walked along the sandy beach. I rolled up my pants legs, took off my shoes and socks, let the foamy, restless surf slosh up onto my feet, and looked for shells.

When I got back to my room that evening, I called Liz on the telephone and told her in great and elaborate detail all about the gulls, the crabs and the strong movement of the ocean currents on the West Coast. I talked about the weather, and all that I had seen on the beach. I talked about the people and how carefree and relaxed they all seemed. But I had to laugh at my droll little wife: none of what I told her changed her mind one bit. I could tell that she wasn't the least bit impressed by my colorful descriptions of the Southern California lifestyle.

The plant was absolutely huge. It sat on a typical California plain with dark hills and mountain ranges out in the distance. The hills seemed to very close, surrounding the plant just like the pictures that I had seen of the Freemont before. I was told that those mountains were not nearly as close as they seemed and there were more than 400 acres out there that belonged to the General Motors operations.

This massive plant assembled the Chevrolet Impalas, Pontiacs, Buicks and the big, impressive Oldsmobile 442. It was very hard to assess the culture and working life of the massive plant in just a couple of days but I tried to get the best estimate that I could of how things were done and who did what. I knew that they were sure to show me the production lines and the more impressive parts of the production operation but I also wanted to see the final line and to get out to the repair yard to catch a handle on how much and what kinds of repair that they were putting out. I also wanted to see how the departments were actually divided with the various cars and trucks that they were producing but I did not forget that I was there for materials and supply, so we never needed to go into the actual nuts and bolts of any other department.

I spent most of the time in the materials department with the supervisors looking at how the materials were stored, how much they kept on hand and the methods that were used to transport materials up to the production lines. Their operation was absolutely huge, impressive and nicely separated, but I couldn't help but wonder how much slack there was in their department inventory, how the records were kept, and so forth. I knew that there had to be deeper secrets and slack just like Joe's department back in Saint Louis. I knew that I would never find out on this visit and I had no right to speculate about anything unless I was on the job in the plant.

I met Joe's old friends and his General Motors Institute acquaintances and I told them how fondly Joe had spoken of them when he was reminiscing about their days as students at GMI. They were very nice to me and seemed to think I would commit to taking the position right away. I thought that honesty might be the best policy and told them frankly that I had two more interviews to go to. Before I left for home they reluctantly promised me that they would wait for my answer.

When I got back to Saint Louis, Greg and Betty immediately came over to hear what I had to say about the interview. Their new baby girl had been born only a few weeks ago. We talked about raising children, life in California and we spent time comparing our thoughts about Southern California over dinner. I was surprised to find that neither of them seemed to miss being on the West Coast at all.

"It's way too expensive to live out there" Greg said. "There's no comparison at all to Saint Louis. Food costs so much, clothes, furniture, apartments. Everything costs much less here than it does out there."

Betty was quick to agree.

I had to agree, too. The price of beer and even simple things like orange juice and soda had set me on my ear in the short time that I was there. I really figured it was because I was in such an expensive hotel. But the real estate prices really got to me most: they were steep enough to seriously choke me right up. I could not imagine a really simple, small house costing so much money!

When I went for my next interview to Doraville, Georgia I found that the weather was really warm. But I have always really liked warm weather. The temperature in Georgia seemed to be very much like the weather back home in Texas—only a lot less dry. It was morning, but I felt myself beginning to sweat as soon as I stepped out of the air-conditioning of the hotel.

The location of the plant was right off the busy I-285 freeway. I admitted to myself that in spite of the unknowns and possibilities, this just might be a good place to work. No matter what I had previously speculated about the workforce, Liz was right: the UAW in Georgia couldn't be any worse here than that hellish—workforce in Saint Louis had been. I was already feeling hopeful and upbeat as I drove up to the front of the huge complex.

I parked the rental car in the visitor's spot in front of the building and as I approached the doorway, I saw Alex McNeil standing just inside. He opened the heavy glass door to greet me. It was really good to be met by his smiling face. I had missed seeing him for quite some time at the Saint Louis plant. For several years he had been a supervisor there in trim. It was a while ago that I had heard he'd transferred down to the plant in Doraville. I guessed that he had heard that I would be coming and he had made it a point to be out in the lobby when I came in.

Someone had told me once that Alex was the one who had started the department heads and supervisors going across the river to the club in East Saint Louis after the night shift was over, to relax, unwind, discuss what had happened on the job that day, have a beer or two and, sometimes, do a little dancing. There was always a large racially mixed group of us who would go over to the club, but even at the plant when there happened to be only blacks together in a group, Alex would often mix right in. He seemed to be comfortable and able to be at his ease with anybody, anywhere. He was among the few of the GM bunch whose wives sometimes came over and met them at the club after work. Alex and his red-headed wife, Gloria, would try to teach us the steps for the latest dances. The old bias about white people not being able to dance as well as black people wasn't true with Alex or his wife. They were the only real dancers among us and together they could practically dance everybody else's feet off.

As always, Alex's thick blonde hair was impressively permed into a longish and swept-back style that complimented his boyish face, and he looked the picture of contentment and good cheer.

We shook hands and gave each other a "Bro Hug" ending with a pat on the back.

"Cooks, my man," he greeted me effusively, smiling, "I'm so glad to see you! You're lookin' great, man!"

"You look great as usual," I laughed, "I'm glad to see you, too. How're you making it down here?"

He grinned and threw up his arms.

"I knew I had to get out of 'The Louie,' man. I still got my friends at HQ and they told me beforehand what the 'wigs' in Detroit were planning to do: absolutely kill that Saint Louis plant. I admit it: I cut and ran like a fat rat deserting a sinking ship. I was ***not*** waiting around for disaster to happen. I didn't want to come under any pressure later on and absolutely ***have*** to get outta' there. When I heard a job was open at this plant, I came on down to interview—got the job. Man, I'm so glad I made that move when I did! I love it here!"

"Are you and Gloria still dancing?" I asked.

"You know it! They got clubs all over the place where we can dance. Just last weekend me and Glo went down to South Atlanta to get with a couple we went to high school with who are living here now. We all met up at a shopping center that's got a really nice club—it's a new one in a place that used to be a department store, I think. It's huge but the place was still crowded. They got that thing all set up with these three big dance floors with lights moving around 'em: spots, strobes—the whole works! One of the smaller dance floors looks terrific! It's like dancing on a cloud! It's got those little white sparkly lights under a Plexiglas floor. Really something else! The music was mellow, man. We had a ball! We all gotta' go down there sometime after you guys move down here."

We laughed and knocked fists enthusiastically. I was really hoping that he was right and fate would spin things in my favor.

We talked a bit longer and filled each other in on all the news that we knew about the whereabouts of some of our mutual friends but I had to get to my interview. I was a few minutes early but I always planned to be a bit ahead of schedule in case something came up.

"I'm gonna' be seeing you, good buddy," Alex said as we parted. "I know you'll get the job. Good thoughts often win the day."

How true.

Sure enough, I was offered the job on the spot—right in the first meeting while we were sitting at the table—even before I was finished seeing everyone who had intended to interview me. I knew that they had already looked at my records but Mike Hillmeyer, the production manager, consulted for a few minutes with Bill Canning, the plant manager, then they both turned in their chairs and smiled at me. Mike did not mince words:

"Wil, I'm gonna' tell you right out, we like you. We've heard nothing but good things about you. We don't usually do this, but we decided we'd go ahead. Now that we've met you, we know you're just the guy we need to help us start up and run this second shift we're going to put on. Will you do it Wil?"

We all laughed at his little play on words.

I said a silent prayer of thanks. This was beyond the expected and more than satisfactory to me. I took a calming breath and nodded until I felt confident to speak.

"Sure," I agreed. "I'd be excited to get the second shift going for you. I'm real anxious to get it built up."

It was the right thing for me to say. Before I knew it, I was shaking hands with everyone in the room, trying hard to memorize names, already wondering where my office was going to be.

Bobby Hall, the superintendent of first shift, took me right under his wing from that very moment. He walked me up to the department production offices.

"Here are our offices," he told me as we walked through the office complex. "Your desk," he pointed a neat oaken desk inside a large office in the glassed-in complex. We walked back to another office and he waved his hand casually to a cluttered desk that looked weighed down with paper and other items: "and mine."

We walked further into the offices and he showed me where the clerks and the rest of the office staff would be located. I met so many people, I realized that I had no chance at all of remembering their names.

We had lunch at a closed facility in the dining room. Afterwards, I did more touring of the offices and some touring of the assembly lines. As it was, there were three main products that they were assembling at that time: the Buick, the Oldsmobile and some light GMC trucks. I felt right at home at the assembly line.

I called Liz with the news as soon as I got back to my hotel room. I was pumped and I knew that Liz would be more than happy, too. I was taken aback when she said:

"That same woman called to tell me that I should have brains enough to keep a closer eye on you. She said you took your girlfriend with you to Doraville."

"What!" I was taken completely aback.

Liz gave a mirthless little snort. "I can only guess at her intentions. Maybe she was mad because you didn't take her instead. I guess she wanted me to think that I should be angry and—"

"Liz, look," I said as reasonably as I could, "I want you to think about this for a minute. Just think! Why would anyone call you? What would they gain by telling you anything like that if it was actually true? Do you really think this is someone who has your best interests at heart? Don't you think they're plain ol' evil and want to hurt you—hurt us?"

Liz groaned aloud. Then, she said:

"I know you're right. It's just hard to believe that anyone could be so . . . I'm sorry that I ruined your news. I'm so happy for you. I'm happy for us! I knew you would get the job. I just knew it! Both of us really had our fingers and toes crossed didn't we?"

"Yeah, we did," I laughed.

I gave her as much of the details of the morning as I could remember. Then I asked about the kids and we talked for a while longer. Liz promised to call Betty to come over to stay with the kids and Muffy while we came back down to Georgia to look for a house in the next few days. I told her that the plant manager's secretary had already given me the name of a realtor who was scheduled to see me tomorrow before noon. Neither of us mentioned the telephone call again. We left each other on a really upbeat note when we finally said good night.

However, I was still pretty angry when I hung up the telephone after talking to Liz. No doubt, I would be leaving Saint Louis, still, I had to think that it was just human nature for someone to call and try to upset my wife at this point. Why now? People are likely to blame you when you don't turn out to be the way that they wanted or expected you to be. Some women expect all men to be aggressive in attitude and womanizers whether or not they are single. Many women seem to count heavily on that fact of male nature—the inherent desire to make new conquests.

I jumped up. I was determined to get out of my hotel room before anyone could catch up with me there. Yes, I did know who else from the Saint Louis plant just "happened" to be at the Doraville plant right now. I was determined to do all that I could to avoid any more "accidental" meetings between us.

When I got back to the Saint Louis plant I worked hard to finish some of the projects that I had gotten started so that the materials department would be able to get and keep a handle on most of the new things that we had finally put into place. Joe already had too much to do. Instilling workforce quality, "just-in-time" delivery and individual accountability for only the areas where we had decided to start was going be difficult to keep up. I wondered how they would continue it without me spearheading that project. I had to think that they would continue. All I could think at this point was that I had certainly tried to get it started right.

Finally, it was my very last day at the Saint Louis plant, I was sitting at the desk down on the floor doing what I could to get some of my paperwork wrapped up before I gave my keys to Joe, picked up the last of my belongings and walked out of the Saint Louis plant for good.

I was startled when I saw *her* coming but I did my best not to show my surprise. She had gotten close to my desk before I looked up and made it obvious that I knew that she was approaching my desk.

Over the course of the time that we had known each other, the tension between us had become more and more uncomfortable for me. I had always figured that she had been the perpetrator from the very beginning. She was good at carefully using her friends and trusted sycophants. Someone had secretly placed a pair of bookends with the sculptured form of a golfer on them on my desk when I had first taken up golf. Another time there was a beautiful pair of African statuettes left on my desk. More recently, an expensive silk tie had been left and an enclosed note declared that it matched something I had worn. Those things had never been acknowledged by me to anyone—I did not attempt to pull the lid off Pandora's Box and allow trouble to roam abroad freely. I simply behaved as if I had not received any of them. The gifts were still in their beautifully embossed boxes and all of them had moved with me when I had moved my desk from the Caprice line over to Materials and Supply. Only yesterday, I had put all of the boxes into my car. They would go with me to my desk in Atlanta. I would eventually take them home one by one over a long period of time. Maybe it was not quite honest, but it was my way of keeping an iron lid on top of a simmering situation.

Her body was clad in a high fashion khaki-colored suit over an open-collared, jade green blouse that looked like silk or some other fabric equally as soft. She had on medium high beige heels that did not deter her confident stride. She was carrying several manila folders in one of her hands, clutched against her breast. She stopped before me, laid down the folders and bent slightly toward me with her hands resting on my desk. My practical mind couldn't help but wonder how she could do anything effectively with those long, iridescent red fingernails.

"What are you doing over here with the slaves?" I joked by way of greeting.

"I'm chasing a dream. I came to see you, of course," she purred, "Since I can never get you to come up to the office. You're always sending someone else—even your ol' grumpy boss." She looked around. "Ooh, this is one big ol' junky place. I've *never* been way over here before. There's just too much stuff all over and not enough people around. What's a beautiful thing like you doing here among all of this clutter? I was hoping to catch you in your office."

"I'm down here a lot more often than I'm up in my office," I said. "I'm here now because I've got some people coming back to give me the reports on some final counts. If I catch them right here and they don't have to walk all the way up there." I did not have to tell her that I planned to be around just long enough to organize those reports for the clerks upstairs and then I would be gone from this place for good.

She looked up toward the busy offices behind and above us, then she laughed.

"You are so strange," she said glancing around again. "You never do what is expected."

She studied me for a moment. I looked back at her waiting.

"I wouldn't have come over here," she said softly, "But I missed catching you at the Doraville plant. I really thought I'd be able to see you there—"

"Yeah," I said slowly. "I know. I got hung up with the guys from Saint Louis who are working there now and I just couldn't get away." I smiled at her again. "Were you working . . . or . . . ?"

"Of course I was working," she said as her eyes locked with mine once more. She smiled, too. "I work hard in more than one place because I need to make sure everything is right and things always go the way that's expected."

"I guess it's good that you're in a position to do that," I said.

"I haven't been able to get to the club lately," She said changing the subject abruptly. "I hear that you haven't been over there at all-even on the week-ends"

"Some of the day shift people can pull that off during the week," I said. "I can't seem to do any socializing anymore because I've been so tired after work." I leaned back in my chair, tossed my pen onto the desk, folded my arms, and let myself smile at her again. "The only time I get to rest is on the week-ends."

"You can rest when you can't do anything else." She raised her head looking away and glancing around, but her eyes snapped back to me. "We never got the chance to really . . . be with each other like we wanted . . . things just never worked out at all. We came close a couple of times. I know that we would have been wonderful together wouldn't we?"

I gave her what I hoped was a "Too bad!" resigned look.

She watched me levelly. "Weren't you scheduled to interview at the Arlington plant next week?" She asked. She already knew the answer to that, too.

"Yeah, I was supposed to go down there on Wednesday," I said.

"You can still say that you have to go for another interview," she whispered. Her eyes watched me steadily and she licked her small full red lips in a more than provocative manner. "We can find a way . . . we can even stay here . . . somewhere outside of the city . . ."

I gave her what I hoped was a pensive frown and looked away without answering. When I looked back to her, she was still watching me, undeterred.

"You promised me last time that you'd try to get away sometime." Her voice was a bit querulous, "it just never did happen. Maybe we didn't try hard enough or maybe the plans I made just never quite suited you."

I had to admit how surprised I really was. She was always stepping over the line of limitations and by now I had come to expect it. She had almost breached my personal limits the last time I had gone to the club. When a man feels lonely, and if he is drinking, he can sometimes get careless enough to compromise his position. More than once, she had tried to get me to do that. Maybe she really got a thrill from taking reckless, forbidden chances. Maybe she was hoping that she might finally succeed in breaking down the *de facto* barriers that separated us but *I* had *never* intended to let that happen. Not in this lifetime. While a man may tend to flirt recklessly while he is drinking, following through with any of his alcohol-induced recklessness is yet another matter.

"I've tried to make it happen," she stated softly with her eyes intent upon my face. "I've really tried, but something or someone has always gotten in our way." Finally, she smiled. "It's too bad because I know just what you want, don't I? I can see it in your eyes."

She surely must have *thought* she could see it in my eyes, but I was not about to make any moves on her. Apparently, she did not know that. I gave her another one of my patented, devilish smiles, not saying anything at all.

She knew that I was leaving the Saint Louis plant today. That had to be the ***real*** reason she was here. The people in personnel knew things before everyone else did. Getting and using information was their chosen profession.

I smiled at her again. Up to now, I was satisfied that I had managed to artfully avoid all of her strong sexual forays in my direction. I changed the subject thinking that it would be best to stay on a level road:

"You'll still occasionally get to spend an evening across the river?" I asked.

"I could only go once in a while. I went there just so I could see you." There was real sadness on her face and she said suddenly: "Stop pretending you don't know that! You're going to break my heart. What about tonight? Can we get together for a drink after work?"

She sounded as though she was prepared to be more than a little reckless again. But then, I should have known this since she was here.

"I guess I can make it over to the club for a quick drink," I lied knowing it would not pacify her. I dropped my voice to a near-whisper and said: "Joe is coming."

"I'm still determined to take you to your greatest heaven," she whispered. "We've let too many people get in our way. I haven't given up yet . . ."

She picked up her folders and paged through one of them elaborately, smiled at me again, nodded purposefully before she turned and walked swiftly away. She smiled and spoke brightly to Joe as she passed him. Joe nodded curtly in return and his eyes followed her as she made her way past the huge boxes and piles of materials to run the gamut that blocked a smooth passage in and out of our area.

"She really stands out like a peacock over here, doesn't she?" He said incredulously. "Since when do hoity-toity front office people come over here? We usually have to go upstairs and hunt them down like running quail whenever we need them."

I shrugged. Joe fully understood my preferred method of keeping my cards close to my vest. He was a straightforward and decent guy, but he was a man, so he could appreciate that men would be men. I had been completely honest with him from my very first day in his department. But I was not about to be honest about this! I could only hope that he had no idea.

Finally his grey eyes studied me and he raised his eyebrows. "So what's the deal: caviar, roe, or just fish eggs?"

He was using the quirky informal scale that I had made up to describe a really sticky situation that had developed between a supervisor and a female clerk in our department. The supervisor had transferred to another plant and not a moment too soon to avert a real situation with his irate and suspicious wife. We hadn't used it between us since then. I should have known that Joe would remember, but I wasn't happy that he was applying it to this situation.

"None of the above," I answered meeting his grey eyes levelly.

Joe snorted a laugh. "So, why was she here then? Anything I need to know about?"

"Nope," I said.

I knew that the rumor mill might have already ground its way to this. I had asked Joe to take my final papers up to personnel to avoid having to go up there myself. I was already over and done with this place. I had vowed to take no prisoners. I had no scores to settle nor did I feel any obligations.

"There was something she needed for my file," I lied blatantly "that's why she was here."

"What else could she need?" Joe asked. "I've turned in all your papers."

"No worries, now," I said, "I gave her the answers that she needs."

I hoped to cut off his speculation. I fully intended to leave it at that.

Liz and I packed just enough clothes to tide us over for our three-day trip to Doraville, Georgia. Betty came over early that morning and brought Walter, Trish and the baby with her to stay with our kids and Muffy until we got back.

We flew to Atlanta International Airport, rented a car, drove up I-85 to Doraville, and checked into the huge Hampton Inn intending to start house hunting the next day. I had met our realtor on my previous visit. She was a self-assured, sprightly, middle aged woman named Marsha Swenson. She had red hair, bright blue eyes and a riot of freckles across her nose. She picked us up in a light blue Olds 442 early the next morning. She said immediately:

"I've got just what you want! It's not too far from the General Motors plant and it's near good schools just like you said you needed. This subdivision is so new the builder still hasn't finished building on some of the lots in there. He's going to meet us with the keys. He can get started with the finishing on the house just as soon as we give him the word. Bet me that you won't like this place . . . just bet me!"

Liz absolutely fell in love with the house just like Marsha said she would. It was in the township of Sandy Springs in Fulton County. It was two-story, all-brick, with a large walk-out, daylight basement that ran the full length of the house. There was a three-car garage with plenty of space.

The rooms of the house were a lot larger than we were accustomed to having in all of our other three houses. There were three large bedrooms and a common room on the top floor. Three full bathrooms were also on the top floor with a half-bath on the first floor and half-bath in the basement. The family room was the highlight of the house. It was two stories high with a huge fireplace built into the outside wall with a tall, two-story chimney made of what looked like native stones. The chimney ran all the way up and through the two-story beamed ceiling. The wall around the chimney was all windows topped by two triangular windows at the peak of the high ceiling. The beams across the ceiling were highly polished and made of oak. Matching polished wood cabinets filled the wall opposite the fireplace and chimney. Another set of stairs came down from the second floor hallway behind the cabinets and into the family room.

The kitchen was huge and Liz loved it. She worked the tall sliding patio door's latch. I knew she wanted to assure herself that she would be able to conveniently let Muffy outside. We hardly looked at the formal living room with its small stone fireplace or the formal dining room across the hall from it. Both were located at the front of the house on either sides of the front door

I told Liz that I thought that the house was expensive after I heard the price, but she was adamant because the location was so convenient for me to get to work. The realtor had already pointed out several times that the Doraville General Motors plant was no more than maybe fifteen minutes away. This neighborhood was very secluded and the shopping centers were close by. Liz was impressed to hear that she would not have to drive a long way to get to the grocery stores and dry cleaners in Sandy Springs. I mentioned again that we had never spent this much for a house before and I said that we needed to look at some others. Liz turned and gave me a thoroughly assessing look before she said:

"David will be in kindergarten in the fall. I'm going back to work."

I was taken by surprise and couldn't help but feel more than a little guilty knowing that my initial reaction must have had something to do with the closed-off, determined attitude that Liz was displaying. I refused to think of that. I had never once mentioned anything about wanting her to return to work. So, I tried again:

"Isn't David still too young for you to go back to work right now? He'll only be in school for half the day. What about the rest of the day?"

"He'll be in school for a half-day, then I'll find a day care where he can play for the rest of the day," Liz said. "I know he'll be just fine because he's either outside with other kids or in the basement all day anyway. David is not spoiled and he's no crybaby. When he's out in the yard he comes into the house only when he has to use the bathroom. I almost have to force-feed him whenever I can get him to stop playing long enough to eat."

"You're seriously going to look for a job?" I asked incredulously.

"Yes," Liz said tersely still looking at me. "I'm already in touch with the places closest around Atlanta: Fulton County Public Schools, Atlanta City Schools and I didn't know we'd be this close to DeKalb County or any of the rest but I do now. I'm going to apply anywhere else that's close and I'll go to any of the junior colleges around here to see if there are any openings that I might be suited for."

She met my eyes levelly. "I want this house! And anyway, I didn't get my teaching degree and work my tail off to get my master's degree because I intended to stay at home. I'm going back to work whether we buy this house or any other house somewhere else."

I could see that there was no use arguing.

I had never admitted it to anyone, but in all of the cities where we had lived, all of the three houses that Liz and I had bought had always struck a similar chord of absolute dread in me. Every one of our previous houses had either been much smaller in size, much older, or cheaper in price than this one. Anytime there were papers to be signed, there was just something that basically un-nerved me. I had to think that maybe everyone had that same overwhelming fear of obligating themselves to pay for so large a purchase as a house. In my heart-of-hearts I was well aware of one of the real reasons why I felt as I did:

I would always be that hard-working kid from the big city forced to grow up early because I had to struggle to help my mother to keep a stable place for us to live. How could I feel comfortable purchasing a large, two-story brick house on more than a half-acre of land when I could still so vividly remember when I was a kid living in places where we could put a hand on our ramshackle rental house and easily touch the ramshackle rental house next door? Or we could stand on the porch and look straight down at the ground through our porch and through our neighbor's porch floor as well because the run-down houses where we were living were just that close together. I could also remember being evicted during my childhood when the slumlords who collected the rents determined that we were too far behind on the rent payments to ever catch up.

Maybe some people could easily get over those kinds of memories with the passage of time and eventually I might, too. True, I could say that the heartaches from those memories were part of yesterday, but I could still remember them . . . all too vividly.

I decided to make a lower offer for the house than the builder was asking. But, as I talked to him, I discovered that he was really just a negotiator. He just wanted to sell the house and could have cared less to whom he was selling it. Then, I became a lot less stiff. Since I would finish the basement myself, he used that to reduce the price. And since the large common room upstairs was not yet painted we considered that, too. All in all, we came to some pretty good terms.

We agreed, along with the real estate agent, to meet in a room upstairs in First National Bank in Sandy Springs to complete the deal on the morning the day after tomorrow. After that, Liz and I planned to catch an afternoon flight back to Saint Louis.

I left Liz picking out wallpaper for the breakfast room and strolled out into the "oversized" garage. It was big enough to fit three cars with enough room for the lawnmower and a few more tools. I was more than a little surprised to find that the garage had air conditioning and could be electrically heated. I inspected the bran-new heating set-up and laughed to myself thinking that I sure could have used this during previous winter snows, blizzards and power outages in Ohio, Michigan, and Missouri. But here during the mild winters of Georgia, a heated garage was truly a luxury. I had a feeling that I had better try to sell my snow-blower, too, before I moved away from St. Louis because I didn't expect that I would need it here.

There were electronic garage door openers installed on both the double and the single garage doors. I pushed a button and the single door opened.

I stopped for a minute to inspect the box that controlled the underground sprinkler system for the lush green lawn. When we had first driven up to the house, I had noticed how neatly the lawn had been trimmed. Now it would be my responsibility to see that it stayed just this neat.

I soon discovered that the back yard was separated from the thick woods behind it by a chain-link fence. I had to consider where we could allow Muffy to roam about. I needed to check out some fence companies to see how quickly we could get a fence put up around our back yard so that we wouldn't have to chain Muffy up all the time.

I walked a short way down the long driveway. I could see that the whole neighborhood was built on a steep hillside. The street went straight uphill to a hilltop cul-de-sac where a large, red brick house sat at the apex. What an all-American picture of beauty and tranquility that was! A large grey stone fountain was languidly spraying water in the middle of the dead-end turnaround on the top of the hill.

The houses on both sides of the street were all brick buildings that looked magazine perfect. The house that we were buying was on a large, flat yard a stair step above the next flat empty lot going downhill. The back yards of all the houses on this side of the street sloped gently back to a long, continuous chain link fence edging the surrounding thick forest of trees. This neighborhood was only accessible by way of the one long street that came in and one cross street that connected just in front of the house that sat on an uphill grade diagonally across the street.

Despite the fact that the houses were upscale and sat back on wide lawns, I could already see little kids like ours riding bicycles and playing games right in the middle of the street. They were doing it because they wanted to. I could well remember playing in the street, too, but that was because there were no lush wide lawns—no place for kids to play at all. Maybe buying this house could finally help me to get over my very personal heartache of growing up in the crowded, chronically depressed slum neighborhoods of Fort Worth, Texas.

I was determined that my kids would grow up without any such experience binding on them like my childhood had been. They were going to have a sweet life that was as good as any that I could give them. Yes, I admitted to myself with a secret smile—I was proud to be able to buy this house in this neighborhood for my family.

Promptly at 8 o'clock the next day, the realtor picked Liz up from the hotel where we were staying. With just a few artful telephone calls, Liz had arranged interviews for herself at both the Boards of Education of Fulton and DeKalb counties but she was unable to get in to see anyone at Atlanta City Schools so soon. I could only guess that since our realtor did not have to drive us around to look any further for houses, she must have felt obliged to give Liz a lift. She had breezily promised to drive Liz to and from both of her interviews.

So, I took the rental car and drove over to the General Motors plant in Doraville. I was just in time for a meeting of the management team. One of the headquarters guys visiting the plant for this meeting was a very tall, large man who stood up immediately, came around to the side of the table where I was about to sit down and extended his hand to me. He could have easily been a linebacker for the Atlanta Falcons or some other pro football team. This guy was half a head taller than I.

I shook his proffered hand.

"Joe Spielman," he said smiling.

"Wil Cooksey," I said. I had heard a lot about Joe Spielman who was a headquarters executive but I had not met him before now.

"Bobby Hall told me you like Corvettes, too," he said.

"Love 'em," I said surprised that he knew that about me. "I've got a red '80 that's got to be the best one I've ever had."

"Oh, yeah, no doubt," Joe said, "They're going to get better and better, I'm working to see to that. That's my goal. Continuous improvement has got to be the key—I'm sure of it. When I get my '81 I'll hang onto it until about the middle of production of the '82. I always get out and drive all the different promos at the track but I always wait for a bit until production gets going and everything settles down before I buy one. I have to wait until I know they've got it right."

"Do you drive a Vette as your company car?" I asked in amazement. He seemed too tall and too big to fit into a Corvette as an everyday driver.

"Always," he said casually as if he was surprised that I had asked, "Why would I ever want to drive anything else?"

"Oh, I agree," I laughed. "I just thought—"

He laughed, too. "I always tell everybody this: 'if you see me driving something else, it's because every one of my Vettes is in the shop and I can't get my hands on another one.' I told my wife that I intend to be buried in one of my Corvettes. I need to have something decent to drive when I get to heaven, don't I?"

"I know that's right," I laughed. I understood this guy completely.

Thus began a friendship between Joe Spielman and me that has been a lasting one. We saw that we had more than one point of commonality between us from the day that we first met. Both of us were much larger and taller than average guys and both of us loved Corvettes. Joe was a collector of Corvettes. Already he had driven well over ten and still owned three of those. I was not yet a collector when we first met. I had driven only five different Corvettes in my lifetime. At that time, the bank owned quite a large piece of the one I was currently driving. Joe had been a student at GMI in the past, and I had been a professor at GMI before I went to work in Saint Louis. Joe had come up through the ranks to his current position at headquarters in Detroit. I was working at plant level, only hoping that I might work my way up one day.

Joe Spielman and I gravitated together to talk Corvettes at every break and we went off to lunch in the executive dining room still talking Corvettes. We were both real dyed-in-the-wool car guys. We also talked about his wife and boys and I told him about my family, too. By the end of the day, I knew Joe was a down-to—earth human being that I liked very much and I surely hoped that we would become friends someday.

That afternoon, I drove back to the hotel where we were staying thinking that surely Liz would be back by now and we could go for dinner somewhere. I picked up the Atlanta Journal Constitution newspaper from the front desk and went on up to our room. Liz was not there yet, so I sat down in the easy chair in the corner, took off my shoes, put my feet up on the ottoman, turned on the television and scrolled through the channels until I found two people sitting at a desk giving the day's news. I was intending to read at least the front page of the newspaper while I half-listened, but it didn't happen. I was so comfortable I fell fast asleep in no time at all.

Liz came bouncing through the door and woke me up. She was practically jumping up and down and dancing a jig around the room. She was so cute; she made me smile watching her antics.

"Okay, what's going on?" I asked sleepily.

"I got a Job!" she chanted sing-song laughing.

"Great!" I said.

"Guess where I'll be work-king!" she sang.

Knowing Liz she fully intended to drag this out. "So, where will you be *work-king*?" I mimicked.

"First, we went to the Board of Education of Fulton County. They wanted me to finish my application and I told them that I would. But—guess what!—we went over to the DeKalb County board offices before lunch. They made me an offer on the spot! Oh, it was so great! You'll never believe it! They considered all but two years of my past experience!"

"I believe it." I said laughing along with her. "What else?"

She sat down on the edge of the bed and continued bouncing up and down. "We had lunch at O'Charlie's, then we came back up here to Dunwoody High School to meet with the principal, Mr. Stegall. He was a very nice man. He told me right away that he wants me to work there. The people in the Dekalb County office were wonderful and considerate in placing me there. They considered where we're looking to buy a house. You won't believe where Dunwoody High School is located!"

"So where is it?" I asked still following her lead.

"I marked it on the map. Here, let me show you."

She jumped up from the side of the bed and got the map of Atlanta out of the absolutely huge purse that she always carried with her. That purse was almost as big as she was.

Each of us had maps of Atlanta and vicinity that we had gotten from the gas station to help us to get around, to know where we were, and keep up with where things were located. She spread her map out on the bed and I got up and came over to look at the place that she pointed out. I had already put a red circle around where the plant was located on both our maps and another one around the street where our prospective house was located. She pointed to where she had circled Dunwoody High School on her map with a green marker. It was in DeKalb County just across the Fulton/ DeKalb county line.

"Wow! That couldn't be more than twenty minutes away from the house we're buying," I said tracing with my finger between the house and the school. Now I knew why she was so hyped.

"Aww, you don't even have to get on the freeway to get there. You should never be late for work!" I laughed.

"Isn't it great?" Liz was practically jumping up and down. "All I need to do is get the final papers filled out and signed."

She picked up the folder that she had brought in and fanned through the papers. "There are two here I need to get notarized then I'll mail them all back to them. I want to make sure I've got all this stuff back in plenty of time."

"Why were you gone so long?" I asked.

"Well . . . after we left the DeKalb County Board of Education we came back up here to the school to see Mr. Stegall. We took the freeway back down there to pick up the papers. We took interstate 285 down there and back both times. The traffic on that thing is murder! It was really packed coming back this way but it was fun for me because Marsha was doing the driving and she loves to drive in that horrendous traffic."

She was almost jumping up and down again. "Oh! I'm so happy that I'm going to be working again!" she said.

I could tell from her animation that she was happy about her success. She laughed merrily and grabbed me around the waist with her head against my chest.

"I could tell you didn't want to buy that house," she said softly, "I hope you'll start to feel better about it since I'll be working, too," Her voice was muffled against my shirt.

I put my arms around her, leaned down and kissed the top of her head. I was really sorry that Liz was disturbed by my reluctance to buy the house. I was relieved that she did not know the ***real*** reasons behind it, though.

"I'm glad about your job," I said, "I know you're happy."

Along with my old, hidden feelings, there was a less-familiar one that I was not sure about . . . jealousy? Now, home would not be the center of Liz's world anymore. I had to admit to myself that I had always been a little jealous because I knew that I stacked up in fourth place on her scale of importance behind both the kids and Muffy. Maybe I had grudgingly grown to accept that. But, now, we were all going to have a giant rival for her time: her new job.

When we got back home to Saint Louis, we found that Betty had locked up our house and taken the kids and Muffy over to her and Greg's apartment. The realtor that we had picked to sell the house had already put a sign in the yard. Betty told us she had left when there had been two or three couples who were just out riding around in the neighborhood looking at houses and they had come ringing our doorbell. After that, the realtor brought some people by who wanted to look at the house, so Betty knew it was time to lock up and get out. She was not about to let anybody go through our house with or without the realtor while we were gone. Both Liz and I could certainly see her point. Although our realtor was scheduled to handle all the details it was still going to be a pretty nerve-wracking time whenever he brought people by to look at our house before we could move out.

On the evening that we got back from Atlanta, we were emptying our suitcases on the bed in our bedroom when the telephone rang. Liz answered and I heard her say sharply:

"No, he's here. Do you want to speak to him? Okay . . . then, did you call to speak to me?"

Liz listened for a long moment, then she said: "No, I don't know anything about a cake."

Again Liz listened and I had become suspicious by this time. I came to stand near her. "Really?" I heard Liz say in an oddly false, too-bright tone, then "Really," again and "I think I know him better than that."

"Oh?" she said after a while, and then she quietly put the telephone back into its cradle. She turned and looked at me.

"What?" I asked.

"That was the woman who's always calling here with little bits of ***helpful*** information for me," Liz said.

"So . . . ?" I said.

"Even when you're here if I answer the phone she doesn't want to speak to you," Liz raised her eyebrows. "She keeps calling herself ***my*** friend . . . she said something about a cake. She claimed that you and your girlfriend were planning to poison me with it. I told her I didn't know anything about it and I didn't believe her. She must have gotten frustrated with me. She just hung up."

"Dammit!" I spat before I could stop myself. I felt like pulling the plug on the telephone right now. "Maybe they'll be satisfied when I finally get the hell out of here!"

At last, it was moving day. By now, we knew well enough how to stay out of the way while the men from the moving company packed everything up. General Motors always used the same company whose home base was in Flint. The movers would always drive trucks to any city to move the GM executives from place to place.

Liz and I were really pleased when we recognized two of the moving men who came to pack up our house as the same guys who had moved us from Toledo to Flint and from Flint to Saint Louis. Now they were moving us down to Sandy Springs in Georgia. They were really getting to be familiar. Back when they had moved us from Flint to Saint Louis, Liz had let the youngest of the moving guys keep and haul away our first, inexpensive, no-name brand washing machine because the guy told her then that he was a newlywed and that he and his wife were trying to get set up in their first house. The washer had two cycles but had only worked on one cycle. Nevertheless, the guy was glad to get it at the time. He claimed that he still had it and that he had repaired it twice himself. We all got a good laugh out of that.

Our beds were the last things that the movers were to take out of the house. We packed Liz's suitcase with our bare essentials and the movers gave us a big plastic bag to hold our sheets and towels. We slept in the empty house for the last night, got up the next morning, showered and cleaned up the stalls and washed down the walls in each bathroom.

All that was left for the movers to do now was to collect our beds. When the moving truck finally pulled away, we locked up the house, put a few things in the small trunk of the Corvette and put everything that was left into the trunk of the Firebird. Crissy and I got into the Corvette. Liz took David and Muffy in the Firebird. We went first to the realtor's office to drop off the keys. Greg was at work but we went to Greg's apartment to have lunch with Betty and the family before we hit the road for Memphis.

We intended to make a stop in Memphis at Liz's sister's house, and then we figured we would drive the 35 miles down into Holly Springs to spend the night at Liz's parents' house. We knew that we needed to get up well before daybreak the next morning to try to be at our new house in Georgia by the time the movers got there.

It took less than two weeks or so from the time that we had the house in Saint Louis on the market for our real estate agent to get a buyer for it. Wonder of wonders, we got a higher selling price than the price that we had originally paid for the house. We knew, of course, that we could have turned the house over to Argonaut Realty, the real estate arm of General Motors. We only planned to use them as our last resort. Luckily though, we never had to do that. The realty company sent Liz and me the final papers in a large mail packet that we needed to read and sign. Liz mailed the papers back to them the next day. When we got the check in the mail after the sale of the house, after all the residual payments had been made, we were able to consider the Saint Louis chapter of our lives closed for good.

I do not think that either Liz or I was unhappy that our sojourn in Saint Louis was over. It was truly life-changing. Both of us had learned lessons about ourselves and about each other. I certainly hoped that I had honed my job skills to a keener edge. During these years, we agreed that while we were in Saint Louis, we had matured a great deal more and learned a whole lot more about human nature. We had been through an awful lot together, but our commitment to each other became even stronger.

GM Assembly Plant—Doraville, Georgia—REM/ Nightmare Number 8

My first full day at work in the Doraville plant went fairy smoothly. I spent most of the day planning for setting up the production line. First, I met with two supervisors whom I had previously known and dealt with on a professional as well as a social level in Saint Louis, Mike Fisher and Alex McNeil. It was purely by chance that one guy was black and the other was white. I let them know that I intended to surround myself with a significant support group of like-minded individuals like the two of them. I knew that they were thoroughly dedicated and planned to do a top-notch job of getting things done. We were together in our ideas about many things, particularly our ideas about how people should be treated and just what needed to be done to get things up and running on the new night shift.

It was not too long before Farrell Walker and Bill Wilkie came in to meet with me. They were also looking to make the move to night shift. They were a part of the small cadre of black supervisors who made it known very early that they could be trusted to do their best work all the time and they, too, soon became my closest allies and very best friends.

I was determined to gather around myself a large multicultural group of men and women supervisors for the night shift. I only wanted supervisors who wanted to do their best. I left it to Alex McNeil to identify others to join with us because I knew that he was a guy who would be willing to make choices based on objectivity. Alex could be trusted to choose people with whom he wanted to work and to decide quickly who to trust. Alex was one I felt I could really depend on to convince everybody that they were all going to have to survive on trust. I soon found out that Alex was not the only white supervisor who was willing to make a move toward progress. I think they all soon began to feel the same way that Alex did. They believed what they had heard about me: that my word could be trusted, that I was willing to go above and beyond for them and that I would recognize them for the good work that they did. Soon enough, there were numerous supervisors as well as hourly workers who were willing to join the new order on night shift under my leadership.

I tried to learn who was really in my corner, who was less than hostile to me, and who seemed to resent that I was in the position that I was in. I figured that getting to know all of the people who worked for me, both hourly and salaried, had to be on my agenda. As my first order of business, I needed to get together quickly with the supervisors who had applied to be on the new night shift, and to try to draw them together into a close knit team.

Two people that I can remember most stood out among those who applied to be on night shift.

One was what we called in the professional vernacular a "two pointer" on the minority scale, that is, black and female. She was an intense woman, a hard worker, and a strict perfectionist. She was known to drive herself and everyone who worked for her really hard. She was enrolled in a graduate program at Georgia State University in downtown Atlanta and was a part of numerous community and church-related activities. When she expressed interest in working the night shift I questioned her motives. I had been told that on several occasions someone in a level above hers had tried to get her to slow down a little for her own sake and to go at a more moderate pace. But, their words to her fell on deaf ears because she seemed convinced that she was not being given the proper respect and credit that she deserved. She was working overtime trying to show herself to be worthy to move up. I had a feeling that she felt that she should have had my job. I did not accept her for my team because I just did not feel that she would be a good fit. I could not take a chance that she might be a disruption to the rest of the team.

There was an older white guy, a committee man, who, even though he had years of experience on the docket, surprised me when he put in to move to nights while we were in the process of setting up the second shift. He came into the office one afternoon before the beginning of the shift to tell me in confidence that he felt that he was slowly heading for a battle with memory loss. Neither of us mentioned Alzheimer's or anything like that even though that horrible disease was the elephant in the room between us as we talked. As a method of coping, he had adopted a style of calling everyone "partner" to cover the fact that he could not easily remember names anymore. I accepted him on my shift and assured him that we were happy to have him. We decided between us that we would keep a check to make sure his memory loss was not getting the best of him. I decided that I would use the designation "partner" for anyone who worked co-operatively with us to get the job done. Soon enough, the idea was adopted by all of us and everyone in our circle was known as "partner" from that day on.

Experience had taught me how to listen and learn, and to move quietly and decisively. I had also learned to move carefully but decisively. Soon enough, some of the decisions that I made proved themselves. I would listen to anyone who was willing to talk to me. I do not think that there was anyone who thought that I did not have an opinion just because I was quiet and listening. However, if I was issuing orders, it meant that my mind was made up. Then, I did not want anyone's opinion—I wanted my orders followed, period. It took some people longer than it did others to learn this about me, but when they did understand that point, things began work out and go smoothly for everybody.

Upper management of General Motors seemed to be making a system-wide effort to ensure that the workforce was upgraded according to generally held accountability standards of race, gender and education. Many of the blue-collar workforce members who had previously held their positions by virtue of their longevity with the company were being bypassed for promotion for more educated people with less in-plant experience. Despite the previous cliquish make up of upper management, I couldn't help but think that I represented one of those signs of change.

Certainly we had our share of detractors, people who were not willing to let go of old ideas, old prejudices, old ways of getting things done, and the "good ol' boy" system in general. I couldn't help but feel that what was happening on night shift was unique. Saint Louis had toughened me and taught me. But I hoped that it had not made me cynical. I had to believe that my sense of fairness and the inherent good attitudes of management and workers alike had a lot to do with the progressiveness that abounded on night shift. We still had our share of absenteeism, especially on Fridays; we still had people who would fight and push back on the orders given to them by foremen and supervisors because of UAW encouragement; and we had a bit of a hard time getting many of the hourly workers to train on more than one job. We kept on hoping to insure more flexibility among the workers. They nearly flat-out refused our requests for them to get any further training. That was my highest hurdle to overcome.

I really can't remember who initially asked me whether I was driving a company car or not. I had already learned in Saint Louis that company policy decreed that all of the managers at my level and above were to be given a company car to use as a daily driver and the car was to be given gas and weekly washing at the plant. I did not push for it because this was a huge plant. I was the newest manager and the lowest man on the totem pole. It was Bobby Hall, my counterpart on the day shift, who told me that a big shipment of company cars had just come in and that I should see Dick Zolecki so that I could be assigned a company car of my own.

The company car garage was a large building located just inside the plant where the executive offices were located. I was more than anxious to become a participant in the program. Being able to park inside the building was one of management's perks. Having my very own spot to park was another. Round-the-clock attendants in the garage, union workers who kept the company cars washed, waxed, and filled up with gas was also something that I was really pleased to have.

The keys for a company car were in an envelope on my desk when I came back into the office to wrap up before I left work at midnight. "Chevette" was written on the envelope.

"Aw, hell no!" I said to myself, "They've got to be kidding!"

I went out to the company car garage and headed straight over to the office where the parking garage attendant sat.

"Where's this thing?" I asked.

He got up from the chair in the glassed-in enclosure and took me right over to it. It was a pretty little red subcompact—a two-door hatchback with a rally package. The guy looked at me and I waited for him to fall on the floor laughing, but to his credit, he kept a straight face.

"You gotta' be shitting me," I growled.

"It's got pretty good pick-up for a four liter," he said. "It's nothing like your Corvette, though."

I glared at him and snorted. Initiation prank, maybe? Well, I wouldn't disappoint them.

I left my Corvette in my parking space and climbed into the Chevette. I had more room than I had first thought, but my big size 15 feet did not really have enough room to manipulate in a standard shift like this one. The seat mechanism would not allow me to move back far enough to accommodate my big body and long legs behind the steering wheel. I hated the car with a purple passion even before I pulled out of the parking space. I felt like I was crammed into a cement mixer. The thing had no juice and it moved like a turtle compared to my Corvette. In the rear-view mirror I could see the attendant laughing as I pulled out of the garage. I guess he was unable to hold it in any longer.

When I got home, I was glad to see that some of the lights were still on. More than likely Liz was still up and was down in the basement where the movers had put her sewing machine and the boxes of cloth that she had accumulated. I figured that she was working late to finish making curtains for the house. I walked toward the basement stairs intending to go down to where she was when she came up the steps and clicked off the basement lights.

"What is it?" she asked. I suppose the look on my face must have been really telling.

"You should see this little Chevette that they gave me for a company car," I complained. "I had a hard time just getting my foot on the right pedal. It's like they meant to screw me around. You could put an elephant into a kids' red wagon easier than I got into that thing. I might have killed myself in traffic if I hadn't been super careful."

Liz walked over to the garage door, unlocked and opened it. She clicked on the garage lights, looked out and started laughing. She said:

"Oh, wow! It's cute but it's really small. It might be alright for somebody my size but not for you. Where's your Corvette?"

"I left it parked in my slot in the company car garage," I said. I watched as Liz turned out the garage lights and locked the door. She was still laughing.

"The way I see it, I've got a choice here," I said. "I can raise hell or I can laugh and pretend I think it's a joke. Maybe I'll act like it never happened and just drive my own car from now on and have them to put gas in it over there at the plant."

"I like every option except number one," Liz said, "The 'raise hell' one—I don't like that one. You don't want to let them know they got to you, do you?"

"Nah," I said, "it'll be hard, but I'm gonna' pretend it was a joke and laugh about it harder than they do."

And laugh I did. I went in early the next day so that everyone could know that they were laughing **with** me—not **at** me. Bobby Hall and our clerks laughed when I told harrowing stories about stopping at traffic lights and having giant trucks barreling down on me. I said how my foot would not fit between the brake pedal and the gas. When Roz Hendricks found out that I was laughing about it, he came to my office and both of us had a big hearty laugh together as I told him about it.

But there were two people who were **not** amused when they heard about it: Bill Canning, the plant manager and Mike Hillmeyer, the production manager. They were furious at both Dick and Roz threatening to have both their heads on a stick. Bobby Hall told me that they were saying that I might have been killed on the freeway in such an ill-fitting car. I was surprised. I wasn't counting on having the plant manager or the production manager as my champions.

Bill Canning immediately called me in for a sit-down with Mike, Dick and Roz. When they questioned me about it, I was adamant that neither Dick nor Roz had given the keys to me. It was neither of their faults, I lied, but the car was the only one that had been left in the company car garage. I refused to blame anyone except myself since I was the one who wanted to take the car out in the first place on a lark just to see how it would drive and to see if I could fit into it. It hadn't been a good idea, I admitted elaborately; maybe I shouldn't have done that. Both Dick and Roz stared at me in surprise. I was not sure if Bill and Mike knew the truth but what could they say given my big falsehood? The relief on Dick and Roz's faces seemed to show that they were grateful that I was lying to save their necks.

I knew that I was doing the right thing. I think they all guessed that I was unwilling to put the finger on anyone. I could see some respect in their eyes even though I did not fit the pattern for their "good ol' boy" clique. Maybe they saw that I intended to be a team player . . . just as I had hoped that they would.

I was out on the line for start-up of the second shift when Roz himself brought me the keys to a big, full-sized Oldsmobile 442. He offered to get someone to drive my Corvette home for me before my shift started if I wanted. I refused that, because I had decided to bring Liz out to the plant and have her to take the Corvette back home and park it in the middle bay of the garage. I was adamant that he had done enough—no need to cause anyone to go through any extra trouble. I thought maybe I had scored points on all of their tally sheets that day. They would know soon enough that they owed me big time for that one.

Liz had to go for a week of orientation before school started and she barely managed to get home before I had to go to work each day. She had enrolled David in the ideal pre-school/after school day care facility right down the street from the public elementary school where she enrolled Crissy. From what Liz told me, the day care only seemed to be affiliated with the public elementary school but it really was not. It was run by a Presbyterian church.

The big yellow public school bus came right down our street in our neighborhood and circled around the fountain up the hill and came back out. Nevertheless, Liz planned to drive Crissy to school each day because she had already planned to drop David off at the day care before she went to her job.

Liz was able to sign up to have Crissy dropped off by the school bus at the same facility as David for the after-school program. Once Liz had gotten everything squared away for the kids, she was very relieved and enthusiastic that the arrangements had worked out so perfectly all around.

When school got started that fall, an open house was held one evening, so I took off for two hours during my shift so that I could tour both of the Kids' school facilities. I was pleased with the principal and I really did like Crissy's teacher. We went down the street to the day care center that David was enrolled in. It had been kept open that night during the school's open house because so many of the families had children in both of the facilities. It was good for new parents to be able to meet the teachers who would be running the pre-school, too. After I had seen the facilities, I really approved of the arrangements that Liz had made for our children.

I was glad that Liz and the kids got home most afternoons before I had to go to work each day. Crissy and David came downstairs to sit and play if I was still at work on finishing the basement. David would sometimes follow me around outside if I was planting shrubs or trimming the bushes in the yard. I insisted that he stay on the porch or in the driveway whenever I mowed the yard on weekends and whenever I manned the outdoor grill on the patio outside the back door. It turned out that there were two or three little kids around David's age who lived in the neighborhood and they would come down to our flat yard to toss a football around in the afternoon before dinner or on the week-ends. They would ride their bicycles up and down our flat driveway. Many of the parents in the neighborhood allowed their kids to ride in the street and coast all the way down the big hill, but I refused to allow David to ride out in the street unless Liz or I was there to watch him.

Crissy found a companion, too—the little girl who lived on the corner of the cross street. They spent endless hours playing together: dressing, combing and primping their Barbie dolls until Crissy came home furious one Saturday morning when they had been playing at the little girl's house. After a bit of questioning, Crissy finally told us that the girl had said that she wanted one of Crissy's dolls to be the maid because she was black. Liz's eyebrows shot up but neither of us said anything. I could see that Liz felt as I did: Crissy seemed to have handled that herself by coming home to play with her dolls on the den floor in front of the television. Soon enough, we heard knocking on the door that led from the garage. Liz got up and went to the door. I heard the little girl's voice asking if she could come into the house to play with Crissy.

"My doll is not a maid!" Crissy huffed jumping up to put her hands on her hips, "Her name is Crissy like me an' I told you, she's a princess!"

"My mommy says they both gots pretty dresses and they both can be the princess sometime and they both can be the maid sometimes," the little girl said around the door defensively. "That's what my mommy says."

"Your mommy is a very wise woman," I heard Liz say. "Why do you need to have a maid at all?"

"A princess gots to have a maid," the girl protested in her soft voice.

I didn't hear what else the little girl said but I saw that Liz held the door open to let her come inside from the garage.

Crissy seemed to be mollified. Arm in arm the two girls headed for the basement where the rest of the kid's toys were located and Liz came back into the den where we had been drinking coffee and reading the Saturday morning newspapers.

I had learned many, many lessons during my time in Saint Louis that I found I could apply very effectively at the plant in Doraville. This discovery was very gratifying to me. It was hard to believe that I was able to accomplish so much more with the cooperation of the workforce at the Doraville plant than I was ever able to get accomplished in Saint Louis. I had no real physical fear in Doraville. Now that I was no longer constantly fighting lack of cooperation and physical evil, it seemed almost too easy to see and feel things come together. I had long ago learned how to treat the people who worked for me and now I learned how real co-operation from them could make worlds of difference towards getting the job done.

One of the big things that I had to contend with was the fact that while the leaders of the company and the plant supervisors expressed great interest in implementing the "Team Concept" the older union members and leaders dug in their heels most of the time and fought against it. After much investigation I learned from the union members on the night shift that their perception of "Team Concept" was that the team leaders among the hourly workers would seem to be placed above others on the imaginary approval rating scale. As far as the union was concerned, that would never do. The union members had a great fear of anything new that they had never tried before. They were afraid of change but especially they were afraid of anything that had a chance of eroding their collective power. That was going my longest and most constant fight.

My primary task for the night shift was this: we all had to learn how to put man and machines together for the best fit that would accomplish our goal to set up the end of the assembly line. As it was, we were really the final line: the end of the production line. Because we were the night shift, many times we were held responsible to finish up the jobs that the day shift had gotten started and could not get finished before their shift was over.

Often enough, when we first started up, arguments and finger-pointing would happen between the day shift and the night shift. The day shift seemed to feel that the primary job of the night shift was to clean up whatever could not be finished before their shift was over. I made it clear many times to Bobby Hall and others that this was not the case. My people felt responsibility for their own jobs. I had made sure that my people felt that it was their mission not just to do a job, but to do a good job of getting as many cars effectively assembled as possible. They did not feel that they were accomplishing their mission when they had to spend so much time finishing up the assembly, and repairing and adjusting what day shift had left behind. If they did not move a certain amount of finished product from the line, then my people did not feel that they were accomplishing their mission at all.

When the guys from headquarters were in the plant they made it clear that they were firmly on our side of the fence in these disagreements, but that did no good. When the "suits" would go back to Detroit, we seemed to be stuck at the same place we were stuck before they came. Nothing changed but I made sure that my people knew that I fully supported their position. The best that we could do was to let our car parts assemblers on the line know that we were going to leave them to their own devices and we would not second-guess them. They were on their own to get their jobs done. We refused to hold them responsible for repair. We would not fault them, however, if they fell behind while picking up the repair that the day shift simply could not get finished.

I considered selling my 1980 red Corvette—not because there was anything wrong with it—quite the contrary. It was a pampered, garage-kept jewel. I just wanted the newest model. Because Liz would never have allowed me to have two Corvettes in those days, especially since we needed to have a family car for transporting the family, I reluctantly agreed to let my "baby" go.

I put an advertisement in the Atlanta Journal Constitution just to see if the car would sell. It was not long before I got a call from a lady identifying herself as Betty Lee. She lived in Atlanta and she wanted to come up to see the car. I invited her to come on the following Saturday.

Betty was a lovely and personable lady who absolutely loved the car. She agreed to my asking price and wanted to buy the car on the spot. We shook hands on the deal. All that was needed was for her to put a cashier's check into my hands and I agreed that I would have the papers ready for her when she did.

Betty was accompanied by a tall, dark-skinned, good-looking man named Ralph Brown who had driven her up to my house in his own Corvette. Right away, Ralph began to recruit me for his organization. We sat down in the den and talked about the organization of which Ralph was the national vice president. There were local clubs in the regions of North, South, East, and West of the United States, Ralph informed me, and all of these clubs were organized under the banner of the United Council of Corvette Clubs (UCCC). They informally called it the "U-triple-C." They held regional meetings by quarterly time periods in each geographic section, and then the regions would come together for the large annual meeting of the entire council in July of each year. They met in different cities around the United States for their annual convention and held numerous competitions, races, family social events and a large national car show. The convention had just been held in Atlanta, Ralph said, and it had gone really well. I was intrigued. I told him that I very much wanted to be a part of the organization.

"You have to own a Corvette to be a member of the club though," Ralph laughed. "And you just sold yours to Betty."

"Yes, you did," Betty chimed in. "You promised me, now. Don't take it back!"

"Not to worry," I said confidently. "I'm going to get another one soon."

Some days later, it was with great reluctance that I took a cashier's check for my Corvette from Betty; she took the notarized bill of sale from me and drove away in my Corvette—her car now. For the first time in nearly ten years I did not have a Corvette in my garage. I did not know that I would feel so absolutely bereft. I really did miss cleaning, waxing, polishing and tinkering under the hood of my Corvette. Liz saw how much I missed having my prized car and she encouraged me to go and find a replacement as quickly as I could.

Since most of the Chevrolet cars that were in our plant's company car fleet came through Tom Jumper Chevrolet on Roswell Road, I always took my personal cars to Tom Jumper for servicing. Many of the salesmen there had already somewhat familiar with me. But after I had sold my Corvette, I haunted the dealership waiting for a new Corvette to come in. It was then that even more of the salesmen came to know me. Finally, one of them called me at the plant to tell me that a car had come in that night and I might want to come down to take a look at it tomorrow.

At first glance, I was not overly impressed when I first saw the car. There was a two-toned paint job on it: white on the body and fenders with silver along the bottom. Silver striping edged the middle of the hood to simulate the raised stinger. For many years the Corvette had been nicknamed the "Sting Ray" which the car was said to resemble. From a distance, the car was quite striking but I couldn't help but remember the two-toned paint job on the Corvette that I had first seen back in Saint Louis. The paint job on that prototype had been a pure disaster to look at with overspray and missing edging. But the longer I looked at this car it was clear that the paint was a pretty good job. It became more and more appealing to me as I walked around and inspected it more closely. The sticker in the window told me the MSRP and that the car had been assembled in Bowling Green. The paint job on this car would have made my old Saint Louis friend, the expert painter, Jude Wolenski, very proud. I made up my mind to tell Liz that I wanted this car.

The next day as soon as Liz got home after she had picked up the kids, I asked her to drive me over to Tom Jumper before the time that I had to be at work. Bill Scott, the fleet manager, knew that I had to get to work so he handed me the keys and said that we would get the paper work done later since he still had to work out my company discount. He would bring the papers over to the plant for me. I was back in business again.

I called Ralph Brown that Friday night. He said that he was happy to hear that I had a Corvette once more. We made a date for the members of Metro Vettes Unlimited of Atlanta to drive up to my house on Sunday evening of the next week to decide whether or not I would be allowed to join their car club. Obviously, the people in his club were travelers, always ready to drive their cars from one destination to another.

The convoy was led by Ralph followed by Betty. A long string of Corvettes driven by the rest of the club members pulled into the neighborhood at about 4 o'clock that next Sunday afternoon. The neighborhood was completely stirred up. People came out into their yards to view the spectacle as the Corvettes filled up our driveway then parked along the street almost all the way up to the fountain at the top of the hill. Chaz Cone and his friend from down the street, two Corvette owners who lived in our neighborhood cruised up in their cars to meet the Corvette owners as they gathered out in the yard. The members of Metro Vettes spent time walking around our two neighbors' cars, thoroughly inspecting and admiring them.

I had pulled my car out into the driveway and as soon as our neighbors left everybody gathered around to inspect and comment on my brand new two-toned vehicle. Betty and Ralph introduced me to the other club members who were true Corvette lovers like me. Besides Ralph and Betty these people were the ones who became my closest friends:

Walter Brown, my fraternity brother and an insurance man; Emory Anderson a Vietnam vet and mechanic at postal services; Jesse Jones, a Vietnam veteran and service station owner; Phillip Hardeman, a General Motors supervisor at the Lakewood plant in Atlanta; Charles Hinton, a Vietnam vet and ambulance driver; Jerry Parker, a long-haul truck driver; Eleanor Arnold, a secretary, and Ruby Clark, a beauty shop owner.

They and the rest of the club members sat down on the sofa on chairs and on the floor of the den to take a vote on whether or not to allow me to become a member of their club. Everyone consented except Charles Hinton. He argued not too convincingly that the proceedings could not be legitimate unless there was at least one dissenting vote. No one took him seriously.

The alliance that Liz and I forged with those people that day constituted a life-long bond. We spent the next few years going on automobile trips with the club, going to picnics and other outings, meeting new people as we went to meetings with other clubs throughout the South, and making extended road trips over many, many miles.

The kids really enjoyed the trips and the camaraderie with the other kids their age. Liz would drive the Pontiac whenever we went on the trips and she would take other members' kids along with Crissy and David. Sometimes other members would drive their full sized cars or vans and our kids would ride along with theirs. Then, Liz and I could enjoy riding together in the Corvette. Our kids and the other children always took some souvenir from the places that we visited to show to their classmates for show and tell. All of them seemed to really love regaling their school friends about their adventures with the Corvette Club.

The people we met in the clubs were Corvette lovers who truly appreciated the beauty of the car and the raw horsepower that it already had when it initially came out of the factory. When we were down in New Orleans, Roy Barnes, James Landry and Paul Coulon took us to the racetrack so that we all could see what our cars could do. For the first time, I saw Lester Matthews push his car hard then run it down the track even harder with a shot of nitrous oxide.

In Birmingham, Alvin Holston, Melvin Henderson, Tom Ford, Bill Eaton, and Farnsworth Robinson challenged us all to get our cars out with their cars on one of the quarter-mile drag racing tracks that they had leased for the day.

Nobody was more daring than Phillip Gatson over in Shreveport, Louisiana. He was a true lover of speed and raw horsepower. We all sat around until far into the night, having a few drinks and talking about cars, engines and racing. Walter Braggs, who worked on transmissions and engines in his own auto shop, was always encouraging us to test our cars on the nearby racetrack. We joked that Walter just wanted us to break something on our cars so that he would have to repair it for us.

It was not until the next summer that we all went up to Indianapolis for the big convention of the United Council of Corvette Clubs (UCCC). It was there that Liz and I met Dr. Lonnie Marsh and his wife Vivian who were real, dyed-in-the-wool race car drivers. Dr. Marsh brought five cars to the convention. He and his wife Vivian raced all five of the cars. Their competitiveness was the reason that

Liz and I were caught up so completely in the excitement at the race track.

Usually, the men who were racers competed against other men in different classes of cars and the women raced against each other. I was finally persuaded to compete in a "Head's Up" race with a car in the same class as mine. I was surprised that I won rather handily. I won by a hair in the next race. The third time I lost against a driver who was more experienced with the light tree. By that time I was completely hooked on the speed my car would get, the adrenalin rush, and the thrill of finishing first in a race on a sanctioned track.

When we returned home from the convention, I was determined that I would find an older Corvette that I could work on myself just to race it. Jesse Jones and Phil Hardeman, and the rest of the racers in Metro Vettes, encouraged me and said that they would help me in any way that I needed if I was really serious about competing.

For the next few weeks Jesse, Phil and I poured over the latest issues of the Auto Trader. Other members of the club who knew we were looking for a car to race let us know when they had come across anything interesting through their acquaintances. We checked out everything that we heard about.

At last we found what I was seeking. A young man down in Conyers, Georgia had bought himself a Corvette and had traded his pick-up truck for it. Soon after, he figured that he had made a grave mistake. He missed his pick-up so badly that he had gone out and bought himself another one. After that, he drove the pick-up all the time and never drove the Corvette at all.

The paint was perfect on the car because the guy had left it covered under his carport for over two years before he had decided to advertise it for sale. It was a 1972 Elkhart Green convertible with a 454 big block engine. Phil, Jesse and I figured that we could really do a lot with that car.

With a bit of shuffling of money and dipping into Liz's and my savings account I was able to afford the car. Liz drove me down to pick it up on the next Saturday. The young man had gotten a new battery and had the car all ready to go when I came for it. When I heard the engine of that car start up for the first time I decided that I was really partial to the big block engine.

Jesse let me use an old trailer that had sat for a year outside his shop and I borrowed a pickup with a trailer hitch from the motor pool at the plant. I bought new tie-down straps from a hardware store, and I thought for sure that I was well on the way to hauling my car to the races like the pros did.

Not so!

It took a lot more experience than I had to be a real race car driver, let alone a car hauler. A lightweight pickup truck is not suited to pull a trailer as low and heavy as the one I had borrowed from Jesse. There were a lot more contingencies about hauling that I had not figured into my initial plan.

The next Saturday after I had gotten the green Vette home the racers in the club agreed to meet at the drag racing track in Covington, Georgia to test their cars.

On our way to the track, Crissy was riding in the truck with me while Liz and David were following us down Interstate 285 in the grey and white Corvette. As soon as I got going on the freeway, the trailer and car started to dance all over the place. The trailer would twist and the pickup was being flung like a plastic toy across at least two lanes of traffic. Other drivers on the freeway had to use all of their skills to avoid me. The green Corvette slipped loose from one of the tie-downs and a wheel had dropped over the side of the trailer by the time I finally steered the truck and trailer safely to the side of the freeway. Crissy was a trooper, she held on for dear life in the truck with me while David and Liz were frightened to tears in the grey and white Corvette behind us. Two guys in a pick-up truck that had been behind us stopped and they got out and helped me to get the car back onto the trailer.

I managed to get the pickup started again and get to the racetrack by driving slowly in the right lane for the entire trip. When we arrived, it was more than a relief. I vowed that I would get myself a real racing set-up as soon as I could.

I made multiple passes on the track and began to feel more and more confident about my abilities as the day wore on. I learned a whole lot about how to read the light tree, get off on the green light and get down the track as fast as I possibly could. Even Liz felt like she might be making progress toward becoming a true drag racer although she drove on the track a lot fewer times than I did. She was more adept at cutting the light tree just right and at shifting the gears faster than she thought that she could.

I found a Chevrolet Suburban Outdoorsman with a trailer hitch already attached at Tom Jumper Chevrolet and I traded Liz's Pontiac for it. It soon became the centerpiece of our little collection of cars. Liz had to get used to driving such a large vehicle on an everyday basis.

We used the Outdoorsman to take the kids for a visit to Disney World in Orlando, Florida. We bought a small television and I wired it into the raised center console in the middle of the suburban. I ran the wires through the headliners, drilled a hole and put an antenna on the outside so the kids could be fully occupied as they took turns sitting in the two bucket seats or lying on the back bench watching television all the way to Orlando. We also invested in some time sharing while we were in Orlando just so we could take the kids to Disney World each spring. We made plans to visit the Bahamas so the kids could enjoy the beach when we found that we could exchange our time sharing for places at other island resorts, too.

Many people had been talking about getting a group together to stop by and visit the Corvette plant in Bowling Green Kentucky on our way to Maryland for the next UCCC convention. So, by the time that the convention rolled around, a large group of us from the Southern Region got together in the parking lot of Greenbrier mall in order to drive up to Bowling Green together before going on to the convention in Maryland.

I have to admit that even though I was in an automobile plant every day of my working life and I had seen the Corvette being assembled often enough in Saint Louis, I was still thrilled to see all those Corvettes coming down the assembly line in Bowling Green. I stayed among the group as we moved along in the areas where visitors were allowed to go.

It didn't work.

It was not long before someone spotted me and before long I was surrounded by my old friends from the plant in Saint Louis. We were really glad to see each other. Word got around among the workers in the plant that I was there and soon enough many more of the workers who had known me in Saint Louis came off the line to greet and talk to me. I introduced the rest of the group with me and we got a longer and more in-depth tour than ordinary. Everybody in our tour group seemed to be as pleased as I was to see the Corvettes on the line.

Liz and I had a huge surprise for those real Corvette racers in Maryland. The new car won a couple of trophies in the car show, then Liz won second in the grey car and took home a trophy for racing it in her class of the women's division and a top trophy for racing the green car.

I made it to the finals in the 'ol famous "Heads Up" showdown. A racer named Perry Washington was in the final contest against me. I was hyped. I really intended to win. I had been cutting good lights all day. The entire Southern Region had formed a cheering squad in one corner of the bleachers and they were making such a concerted racket that I became even more excited.

Perry stayed away from the starting line for long minutes after the race was supposed to start, effectively "icing" me or making me cold. He had been watching me closely and he knew that his only chance to beat me was to come off the light within a split second and maintain the lead. When Perry finally came to his car and drove up to the light, I was ready to go. I was so excited that I had to take a series of deep breaths to calm myself down.

Finally, we were away. I cut one of the best lights of the day. The green Corvette squatted and shot away from the light like a race car should. I was ahead by a nose and beginning to pull away when the worst happened: "wheel hop."

There is no second place trophy that will suffice for the "Heads Up" racer. He can only lick his wounds and think about every "what if" in the books. He can only say: "Wait until next year!" and hope that everyone believes him. I knew that I was going to correct the "wheel hop" problem that had manifested itself at the most crucial moment of the race if it took everything that I had.

I had read about "wheel hop" in racing magazines and knew what it was but I hadn't experienced any of it during all my trials and previous passes. Now I needed to try to find out the best way to correct it.

Once we were home from Indianapolis, Phil, Jesse and I got our heads together and agreed that we needed to put a stabilizer bar on the wheels to prevent them from breaking loose again. I found what I was looking for in an auto supply store. We took the green Vette to Jesse's garage to install it.

On the advice of a new friend that I had met at the Covington track, Lamar Walden, I bought new racing tires, or slicks, to assure that the car would stick to the track. Lamar owned and operated a garage and speed shop just down the street from the Doraville assembly plant so Jesse, Phil and I solicited his advice and took every opportunity to visit his shop and tap into his knowledge about racing. Lamar and his friends had watched both Liz and me at the track and they felt that our racing skills were pretty good but they also told me that I might need to put more work into the car. I finally turned the car over to him and let him work on "sweetening up" the engine, that is, to build it up and bore it out a little. Then I decided after a little reading that it might also be a good idea to put a launch control bar on the drive shafts going to the wheels to cut down on the metal stress and help to keep the wheels on the track.

I left the green Corvette in Lamar Walden's shop for over 2 months during the winter months. I had some idea that I might not be able to drive it anywhere anymore except on a racetrack but when I got it back, it was obvious that Lamar had fully intended to make a real race car out of it. He had put in harnessing seat belts and did a few more things to make it a better, safer vehicle.

I couldn't wait for winter to be over. Finally, spring came and the Covington racetrack opened for the season.

Jesse, Phil and I took turns driving and we drew the crowd's attention every time we raced. We agreed that Lamar had truly done a good job. We were standing in the shade of some trees alongside the track, winding down between runs. Phil was calmly smoking a cigarette, Jesse was drinking a lite beer, and since I was the last one to drive, I was still trying to dry myself down after some serious sweating. A short, stocky, freckled-faced, red-headed guy came up to where we were standing.

"I want that car," the little guy said, "You don't know me, so I know you won't let me test drive it . . . will you?" He was simpering as if he was trying to be cute.

"No, Buddy, we sure won't," Phil said in an equally condescending voice.

"Name your price," the little guy said then, staring straight at me with unblinking blue eyes. He was suddenly all hard business.

"It will be for sale in July maybe," I said. "Check back with me then."

"We'll be back here after we kick some serious ass at the UCCC convention this summer," Jesse said laughing.

"Lamar flat refused to work on my engine," the young man said tightly, "But he did a hell of a good job on yours. I want to buy your car 'cause it's just what I need."

He lit up a cigarette not looking at us but thoroughly inspecting the car. The three of us stared at him. He walked away without saying another word.

"Damn," Phil said softly. "What was *that* about?"

"Well . . ." I said, "maybe the man just knows a good thing when he sees it."

The UCCC Convention was held in Birmingham that summer. Jesse was right: we "kicked some serious ass." As a matter of fact, all of the Southern Region represented well in the races and in the car show. Liz and I loaded up so many trophies with the new red car that we had bought after we sold the two-toned grey and white car that we were about to decide that we didn't want any more trophies.

The "Heads Up" showdown was between me and Evangeline (Van) Rickman whose husband Lance was a race official. Both Lance and Van had driven their car to victory in numerous previous races. Because the Rickman's car had more racing changes than mine, I was given a bit of lead time. Van had to overtake and pass me but it didn't happen. This time there was no "wheel hop" to thwart me. I never gave up the lead all the way to the finish line.

Van and Lance shook my hand and congratulated me on the win as did the rest of the participants in the drag racing venue. We racers were a part of an elite little group within the larger club and we knew it. It was the nature of what we liked to do that made us feel special and be treated with respect by the rest of the club members.

The green corvette and I were well on our way to making a name for ourselves. Within the next two years, I raced the car in every venue that Jesse, Phil and I could make.

Finally, I did sell the car to that little red-headed guy at the Covington track. By then, I guess he and Lamar Walden had become friends again. He was every bit as good as his word and although I hated to let the green Corvette go, he made me an offer that I could not refuse. Even adding the money that I had spent to make improvements, I still made a small profit when I sold him the car.

I had been elected head of the Southern Region of the UCCC during the last quarterly meeting. I really liked the way the members of the Southern Region gathered around each other to support whatever each of the clubs had going on in their communities. Members of the Atlanta club always enjoyed hosting a Christmas party and as many other community-based and charity benefits as we could manage. We often traveled to Louisiana where the members of the New Orleans club hosted a Labor Day event as well as other charitable gatherings. We went to Huntsville, Alabama to be with the Untouchables Corvette Club and even down into Florida to meet and socialize with the clubs there. We got together to inspect each other's cars, offer ideas, help to change interior trappings and race as often as we could find a track that allowed us to run our cars for a reasonable fee. Liz and I were having a far better time with our new Corvette than we could have ever imagined. The southern clubs found that they could run a far more organized program without any of the harsh and bitter rivalry that was present in the larger group of the UCCC. We simply got together to have fun within the Southern Region. Without any hard and fast effort, our members kept drawing in others who seemed to feel the same way as we did.

Always when we met at even the most informal of gatherings, talk would always come around to the same old griping and complaining about how we felt that the South had been totally marginalized by the Northern clubs. I, too, had seen many things that I did not like to see happening at that last UCCC convention. First of all, there seemed to be more clannishness and a tightening of the ranks among the members of the Northern Region. The Southern Region had become so powerful, so coalesced and single-minded that the same kind of thing never seemed to happen amongst our ranks in the South.

When we drove up to Washington for an election meeting, we discovered that the members of the Northern Region had obviously gotten together and decided to curtail any ambitions of the Southern group by strictly limiting their voting power in the UCCC. Someone from the North had let it slip out to us that the North had already decided on the slate of officers for the national slots without any consultation with any of the other groups. The members of the Southern Region, especially those who wanted to run for a couple of the national offices became incensed. As president of the Southern Region I registered a protest and tried to bring up the point for discussion on the floor, but the sitting president made an effort to suppress our protests by huffily declaring that there would **not** be any discussion about this at all in the open meeting. What was done was **done**, he stated.

"Let the record show—" he started.

James Britton from Birmingham angrily stood up. "Let the record show that I'm tired of this kinda' shit. I'm walking the hell out of here and I won't be back here or anyplace else with this group," he stated.

He did not walk out alone. Every member of the Southern Region and more than a few other members from the Northern region and various places stood up immediately and followed him out of the room. There were grumbles and rumbles from all quarters as we gathered in the hall outside the meeting room of the hotel where we were all staying.

"Look," Phil Gatson said in his self-assured manner, "we don't need these people. We've got enough clubs in the South. Let's start our own organization."

"I say so, too!" James Lundy from Huntsville said, "We don't need them! We can have more fun without all this kind of hassle."

"Let's see who's willing to make a true commitment to start our own organization." Carolyn Lundy said. "Who wants to do our activities in the South?"

There seemed to be an equal mix of those who wanted to leave the UCCC, those who did not want to leave the UCCC and those who wanted only to register a protest and stay with the UCCC.

It was a very hard decision to have to make. I think that all of us felt that we did not really want to leave the UCCC, but more than a few of us could see the handwriting on the wall. We did not think that the UCCC would ever see us as more than upstarts trying to take over power from the established, more stable group. Maybe that was not entirely true, but in the minds of some of the members in the Southern Region, the dictatorial methods of the UCCC were the uppermost irritants in our minds. The existing attitudes were more than the members of the Southern Region were willing to keep on allowing.

"Well then, let's meet in Atlanta in another three months," I said. "We'll consider that all who attend the meeting will be making a commitment."

One of the ladies, Eleanor Arnold, decided to make an address and telephone list so that it would be easy to notify everyone when a hotel for the meeting had been secured.

We did meet in Atlanta in the meeting room of a Sheraton hotel in April of 1986. We started with about sixty people at that meeting. Our word-of-mouth method of spreading the word about the initial meeting seemed to have worked pretty well.

Some of the people who were present hadn't ever attended a UCCC meeting at all because they simply did not want to go all the way to the northern part of the United States, but they seemed happy enough to come to our meeting. All of the people who attended really seemed to be fired up and ready to begin our own Corvette Council. It was even better than any of us had envisioned it would be.

We had the hotel to set up some chairs and we sat down in the smaller meeting room with me acting as moderator. We decided on the things that we really needed to have as the major tenets of our new group.

There would be no one making decisions that affected the whole group without input from all of the clubs. We would allow individuals to join the organization without being affiliated with any club as long as they owned a Corvette. In order to make our association of individuals viable, we decided that a modest fee should be charged to each individual who wished to participate—rather than to the clubs to which they belonged—for membership in the group.

We worked on the details of our association until far into the night, but everyone stuck it out until most of us were satisfied. For the most part, I really believe that all of us felt deep down that we had formed something that was viable and would be lasting.

"We need officers," James Lundy proposed.

"Yes, we do," Eleanor Arnold said. "And I want to nominate Wil Cooksey for president of this group."

James Landry from New Orleans reminded us that we needed a name and a definition for the group before we should think of electing officers.

"You're right," Carolyn Lundy said. "We need to give ourselves a name first,"

John Williams from South Carolina whose wife Deborah was an avid racer spoke up to say that we should name ourselves The International Council of Corvette Clubs. That would make us the ICCC. Needless to say, there were various comments about that suggestion:

". . . What's international about us . . . ?"

". . . That name is just too close to UCCC's name . . ."

". . . Won't it seem like we're copying their name . . ."

". . . I do like it a lot . . ."

". . . We **are** a spin-off . . ."

". . . Yeah, why not just admit that . . . ?"

Finally, we accepted the name, International Council of Corvette Clubs (ICCC) and I was elected as president of the group. Paul Mitchel from New Orleans was elected vice-president; Eleanor Arnold from Atlanta was elected secretary; and Phil Hardeman from Atlanta was elected treasurer. John Williams and Warren Gambrel agreed that their group, Stingray of Greenville, would be responsible to design the logo for the newly formed ICCC. Phillip Gatson from Shreveport, Louisiana agreed to start work on the convention right away.

We all were really tired when we finally got the business of setting up our organization done, but I gave a quick speech to thank everyone for their hard work and to assure them that I was committed to make it work. I hoped that they all were just as committed. Before we adjourned we voted to hold our first annual convention in Atlanta at the Sheraton Inn near the airport. We planned to race in Covington for a certainty on a Thursday or Friday of our convention, but we would only hold the convention from Wednesday to Saturday night—not for the entire week. We needed people to plan for the car show, for the hospitality room, for the races, and for the final banquet. These were the things that we were sure that were needed. Many of those people sitting there at that time volunteered to do the jobs. We all seemed to know that we were all going to have to work hard to see that everything went the way we planned.

At that time, none of us could have envisioned how important our efforts in that room and on that late evening really were.

Everyone seemed to be waiting with baited breath for the very first convention of the ICCC. We knew that the work would be hard, that things were bound to get extremely difficult at some point, and that some things would go wrong no matter how much we had tried to anticipate everything and prepare for the worst. Some gloom and doom naysayers who were following the new ICCC worried that our defection from the UCCC would prove to be disastrous in every way.

We knew that we were going to have a problem with identification of our members because we had no way of making sure that we quickly took care to separate those who wanted to become members from those who simply wanted to mix with us at the moment. Too late we learned that we needed to make sure we had secured some official method of identification and protection against outside people coming into the rooms that we were using for our hospitality. Some people who had no intentions of joining our group came in and ate and drank to their heart's content.

We learned the hard way that we were going to need official police protection after one of Gary Dawkins' powerful raised twin carburetors that stood up high from the hood of his car was removed and stolen right out of the parking lot. After that a few of us decided to stay overnight in the lot where we parked our cars to make sure that no one did any more malicious damage to our vehicles.

One thing that gave us a real boost was that we received recognition from a national segment publication, Vette Vues Magazine. Ed Tillirson who wrote articles for the magazine had come to the track in Covington to watch our races and wrote up a very nice article about our organization which appeared in the publication. He and a number of members of the Peach State Corvette Club brought their cars to our 1st annual car show and that impressed potential members who were visiting the track. It helped to convince them that we were serious and that we meant business.

When the first Annual Convention of the ICCC was finally over, many of us needed to just get home and catch up on some badly needed rest. We had worked our tails off at the convention, at the races, and at the car show. Inez Martin from Detroit was a firm supporter of ICCC. She worked hard at the racetrack to make sure that everything went as we had planned.

We did not know how well we had done but we knew that we would just have to wait and see. There was no way that we could possibly stop the river that was running through our finances and taking money away in a steady stream. Many of us had simply paid the money out of our own pockets just to make sure things went smoothly. We had no hope of putting a stop to our mistakes because it was too late to put a real organized program into place and financial checks and locks at that point. We were determined to simply stagger on and hope to finally get to a good place where we might set up an organized program and accumulate some money in the bank to work with.

At the next quarterly meeting the executive board of the ICCC soon discovered that things were not going well with some of the individual or local clubs. At that time we had only a few clubs and not as many individual members as we had thought we would have. It was really hard to try to run the organization when we had so many disgruntled members who had so many different ideas about how things were supposed to go. However, we were determined to stick to the rules that we had made at the inaugural meeting of the group and simply keep trying to slog forward step by step.

It really broke my heart when Metro Vettes of Atlanta finally dissolved after so much push and pull and disagreement. The original members of the club eventually formed themselves into four different clubs in the Atlanta area alone. Many of us formed Unique Corvettes of Atlanta. Others started Atlanta Corvette Society.

Many of the clubs in other cities were doing the same as we were. About the only clubs that did not break up and re-form were Jazz City of New Orleans, Untouchables of Huntsville, Vette Sette of Memphis, and Smoke City of Birmingham.

We knew that retention of membership in all of the clubs making up the ICCC was going to present a very real problem because so many of our members were young in their careers and upwardly mobile. Movement in and out of the cities where they were employed was bound to cause swift and sometimes harsh changes to every single organization.

Still, the end of our first year of existence, the fledgling ICCC was ready to congratulate ourselves.

The entire original group now formed the solid core of the organization. We had each other's backs. We had survived the first convention and we were more than proud of that. We were laden with a few financial debts and we had more than a few battle scars but the rock-hard determination on the part of the original members to keep our organization alive and viable remained strong during our first year.

The final meeting of the year was held in Birmingham. We had learned from our mistakes and each one of us swore to each other that as an organization, the newly formed ICCC, would not make the same mistakes all over again.

I had been promoted to Superintendent of chassis, so I was running my own department at work. That meant I was working on day shift now and although I had to go to work before the crack of dawn each day, I was glad to be around for dinner when Liz brought the kids home from school.

The day shift people in chassis really knew their jobs and working with them was purely a joy. We worked some long, hard hours, but there were hardly any complaints at all. Because I had started up the night shift, I kept the night shift workers in mind and strongly encouraged the day shift workers to try to have as little as possible catch-up work to hand to the next shift at the nightly shift change. That went a long way toward keeping everybody, especially my night shift guys, more satisfied with their jobs.

At first I kept waiting for the other shoe to fall—for some big disaster to happen. After so long when it had not happened, I began to relax and to let myself feel real satisfaction that both shifts were really doing good jobs.

Two ladies who were members of a group called Jack and Jill of America came to the house to recruit Liz and the kids for their group. The chapter, North Suburban Atlanta was formed by a number of professional ladies who lived in other subdivisions around us. Nancy Bishop and Terri Smith were two ladies who came to our house to talk to Liz. Although the fathers were encouraged to help out, the general feeling was that single parents should not be discouraged from joining. When Liz asked me about it I encouraged her to join. I figured that the more contact and with other kids in a social settings that our kids had as they were growing up, the better.

A guy named Starr Rogers, a utility man that I met when I came on day shift, told me one day about a flying club that he belonged to. He told me that he was one of the flying instructors for the club and they owned two planes, a Cessna 152 high wing and a Beechcraft Musketeer low-winged plane which they kept at Fulton County Airport, Charlie Brown Field. I was intrigued when he asked me if I would like to receive flying instructions from him.

When I was a youngster, I dreamed of one day flying an airplane like a lot of young kids do, but I always figured that I would never get a chance to do it. I grew too big and too tall. I was a member of the AFROTC in college and had learned a lot about the mechanics and engineering of airplanes before I graduated. Of course, I was unable to join the Air Force as a pilot before I was drafted by the Army. So, flying was just another dream of mine that seemed outside of reality—until that time. Most of the domestic propeller driven small planes that were privately owned were too small for me to fit into, so I had figured that I would never fly my own aircraft until Starr had come to talk to me. Now, here I was really considering taking flying lessons and actually learning to take a plane up into the air. I was really intending to become a pilot of an aircraft.

Every day after I had first talked to Starr, I would leave work, get onto Interstate 285 around the city of Atlanta then I went South on the west side of the city to Charley Brown Airfield to take instructions from Starr Rogers and some of his fellow members of the flying club.

I used the manuals and textbooks to learn about the basic instruments of airplanes and how a pilot uses those instruments. Then I had to learn how to actually manipulate the instruments for a number of hours on the flight simulator. I had to take various tests on the simulator as well as written tests. Finally, I was ready to actually get into the plane with the instructor and take tests in the air.

Starr and I went up in the Cessna 152 because I simply could not fit into the Beechcraft. If the Cessna was in use, I had to wait until it was free. Sometimes, it was pretty late when we finished doing the "touch and go" sessions around the vicinity of the airport. I figured it was worth it to get the sessions done and to get that much closer to getting my pilot's license.

I got my pilots license at the beginning of summer of 1987. I was anxious to go on my first solo flight. Starr was anxious for me to go, too.

I took off smoothly in the 152 intending to fly to the next closest non-commercial airport, touch down there and come back. I followed all of the ground markings on my chart but still I promptly got lost!

I was determined not to panic. I turned 180 degrees and went back until I found a ground marker that I was familiar with. Then I performed the actions that I had been assigned. I was relieved to get back to Charlie Brown Airport just after dark. I think that if I had kept going until I couldn't see the ground, I might have wound up going way past the next town and turning up somewhere totally distant and unfamiliar. I refused to even think about running out of gas or some of the other more frightening options. I knew how to coast down and keep the nose of the plane up but I was certainly not going to use that unless I was really in dire straits. Landing on a freeway was an option that I had heard about distressed pilots using but I was determined not to have to use it myself. That would have really been too much. But as I became bolder and more experienced, using the radio came more easily to me. Then, I found that being able to make ground contact gave me much more confidence and made being in the air much more comfortable.

Later that year, another of Starr Rogers' student pilots crashed the Beechcraft. The guy simply failed to get the nose up in time and he landed badly. Then, there was just too much demand for the Cessna so I began to look around to find an airplane of my own. Everyone in the club was willing to help and to offer whatever advice that they could.

Pretty soon I had found a Cessna 172 that seemed promising. The dealer who was selling it was located on Saint Simons Island right off the coast of Georgia. One of the airplane mechanics who was a member of our club offered to fly down with me to Malcolm McKinnon Airport on the island and thoroughly check out the plane. I could fly it back home if we found that it was a good enough buy.

We made our flight plan and flew down in the mechanic's Cessna 182 and found the guy who was selling the plane. It was pretty late in the evening by the time the mechanic had thoroughly inspected the plane, declared it A-ok and approved the buy. By the time I had negotiated a deal to pay the dealer for the plane, it was getting dark. We didn't waste any time though; we got into the air with the mechanic leading and me following in my new Cessna 172. It was nearly midnight when we finally returned home. I had gotten in some real night-time flying experience and I was feeling like I could fly anywhere at any time as long as I had fuel enough in the plane to do it.

I took everybody who came to visit us that summer for a ride to the next airstrip and back. Only Liz and one other person got air sick: my youngest brother, Richard was nearly wiped out. He said that flying that near to the ground just purely did him in. Liz could really sympathize with him.

Soon enough, I got to thinking that the Cessna 172 had weight limits that prevented taking too long a trip in it. I started to look around for another plane. I found a Cessna 182 that a guy wanted to sell, so I sold my 172 and bought that plane in fairly quick order. I told Liz that the new plane would make all of the difference in the world. It would be like riding in a commercial jet, I promised.

I planned a trip to Mississippi and got Liz's buy-in. I had plotted the trip out with my charts to the small airport in Holly Springs and we were ready to go. As soon as we took off, Liz became really air sick. I thought it might spruce her up if I got her to help me with spotting rivers, stands of trees or looking for landmarks. It did not. It only made her that much sicker. Liz fell asleep and did not wake up until after we had landed. We flew to Holly Springs and stayed for a few days. After we took off from Holly Springs, Liz slept all the way back to my tie-down at Charlie Brown Airfield.

Liz did not fly down to Alabama with me to the Negro Airman's International reunion in Tuskegee, Alabama. I called back home to tell her how much fun she was missing out on because of all the games, flying contests and picnics that we took part in. She said that she hated that she had not come with me but she sure did not sound very sorry at all.

Still, Liz would not go with me back to Saint Simons Island or to Key West. In fact, I never got Liz up in that plane again. She claimed that she was not frightened and I knew that she was not but she was never going to be able to be comfortable because she was so convinced that her stomach would become unsettled in that small plane. I showed her how to use the barf bag and assured her that it was not an embarrassment to do so. It was to no avail—she still would not go flying with me again.

I guess I could plead pure male blindness but the passage of time really can go unnoticed by anyone who keeps themselves as busy as I was each day. I was promoted from superintendent of chassis to full superintendent of night shift. That meant that I was in charge of the whole plant in the evenings. I did not hold that job for very long before I went to full superintendent on the day shift. I was taking care of my professional life pretty well, that is, I was doing very well at my job and I was receiving promotions in a timely manner.

It was not long before I was promoted to General Superintendent. This meant that I had responsibility for the two shifts, day shift and night shift, both of which I had worked. I knew the people well who worked on both the shifts. I tried to get out into the plant and out onto the lines of both day and night shifts. I was reporting directly to the production manager whose was responsible for total plant production. I did, indeed, have my eye on the job of production manager. I knew that I could do it, perhaps with a whole lot more effort, but with the knowledge of production that I had gained, I figured I had a pretty good leg up on it. I worked as hard as I could to do my job and do it well and still keep my eye on moving up to the next level.

I had already moved up the ladder salary-wise to the ranks of "Unclassified." That meant that I was eligible to receive bonuses in salary, too, but that was not my main goal. I now knew that I had the knowledge and capability to be in charge of all production in the whole plant. It was really a matter of time and circumstance, I reasoned.

My personal life was also full to the brim. I was flying my plane and enjoying leisure hours with my Corvette Club buddies and going on regular vacations with my family. I suppose the passage of time was not a distraction to me because of my extremely busy schedule.

Like kids will do, our kids were growing up and did not need our constant attention any more. Somewhere along the line they had become almost self-sufficient. We gave them jobs like cleaning up the kitchen after meals, supplying food and water for Muffy, running the vacuum cleaner, dusting, and putting their own clothes away after Liz had washed them.

When I thought about it later, I felt like I should have noticed the obvious signs that were there for me to see.

Liz lost her Aunt Cleva, who was Nadine and Pauline's mother. Then, not long afterward, Liz's father died, too. Liz was devastated. I was heartbroken, too. When her father had visited us that last time, he and I had shared many a lazy evening on the back patio enjoying a glass of sipping whiskey while he indulged in a good cigar. He always smoked on the job, but he had never been able to smoke in his house because his wife and daughters were all asthmatic.

I said to Liz at that time that I did not think that he looked well, but Liz did not share my concern. Since her father was still working full time and keeping his books as usual I guess Liz thought that meant that he was still in good physical shape, too. He would not see a doctor. He was pretty hard-headed about that and he never complained. He never once let on what was going on with him. So, no one suspected anything.

After he died, it took a long time before Liz, her sister or their mother could talk to each other on the telephone without reminiscing about things that he had said or done and beating themselves up because they had not insisted that he see a doctor. Their conversations always wound up with sadness seeming to weigh Liz down for a long time afterward.

When I finally noticed the dark circles underneath Liz's eyes and suggested that she needed to see a doctor herself, she claimed that she was just tired because of work at school and the two evening graduate classes she had enrolled in at Georgia State University. She had to take one of the classes in order to renew her teaching license and she was taking another class to begin work on her doctorate degree.

Liz finally, admitted to me that the professor of the class that she was taking to get license renewal had made an open and considerably racist remark about the academic abilities of black people. Liz said that when she had all but chided him about the remark he had snapped at her there in the class and had cornered her when the class was over in order to inform her that she would never pass his class and to tell her that she needed to get herself out of his class. Liz was shocked and she said that she had told him that she needed the class to renew her teacher's license; otherwise she would gladly drop it. Liz said he had smiled and told her that her problems were of no concern to him.

I knew that Liz's situation was important but I really did not feel it should have been enough to wear her down the way it seemed to be doing. I encouraged her to go to the department head at Georgia State and complain but she said that her classmates had warned her not to go to the department head because he was known by many of the students to be a particularly virulent racist and that he would probably automatically side with the professor anyway.

The kids and I tried to take some of the load off Liz by doing more of the chores around the house while she studied for her class and wrote the papers needed. Liz seemed to be doing exceptionally well, despite the fact that she said that the professor all but ignored her in class, but at the very end of the semester, the professor called her in to the department head's office and said that since she hadn't done all the work necessary, she had failed the class. The department head supported the professor's decision.

I was enraged on Liz's behalf because of the injustice of it all, but without anyone's knowledge Liz had already done what she needed to do to protect herself. She had gone to the Georgia state licensing officials when the incident had initially happened and promised to keep them informed of her progress in the class. She had also sat down with the Board of Education of DeKalb County to let them know what was going on. She had made copies of all of the papers that she had written for the class; given them copies of all of the work that she had done, including her lecture notes; and she had asked others in the class to sign a sheet stating that she had attended every class. The officials of Dekalb County helped to protect Liz's license and decided to take the initiative to put the classes that were needed by their probationary teachers under their own jurisdiction.

I really became concerned after I finally started to pay attention to the way that Liz seemed to have to drag herself through her day. She had begun to lose weight, and she sometimes seemed not to have any energy at all. If we drove a pretty good distance to an ICCC meeting, it purely wiped Liz out and she would stay in the bed at the hotel and sleep even when the club hosting the event had planned to do a really fun activity out in the city that I knew that Liz would have surely enjoyed.

One Saturday morning a month or so before the end of school, I went off on one of my flying excursions with one of my buddies. The kids had gone off into the neighborhood with a group of their schoolmates to sell candy for their school. Crissy told me later that she did not know why she had decided to go back to the house just then, but as she approached, she noticed that the sheer curtains over the living room windows and on the sidelights at the front door were moving in succession and seemed to be shredded and torn. She heard Muffy barking and heard his frantic scratching on the windows as she ran down the driveway toward the house. When she got inside she saw why Muffy had been trying to get attention from outside. Liz had collapsed on the kitchen floor.

Muffy had all but exhausted himself but when Crissy came in, she said that Muffy got right back to Liz, lay down beside her and began to gently lick the side of her face and the upturned palm of one of her hands. Crissy told me later how frightened she had been but she had called the 911 health services to send an ambulance the way Liz and I had taught her and David to do in a case of emergency.

When I think about it now, I'm sure that an ambulance coming into our quiet, serene neighborhood with its sirens screaming must have really gotten all of the residents stirred up. The neighborhood moms quickly rallied around the kids. One neighbor from across the street rode in the ambulance to the hospital with Liz. Because I didn't get in from the airport until nearly dinnertime, three of the neighborhood ladies had alternated turns staying with the kids and Muffy and waiting for me. The kids met me at the door with the news. I thanked the neighbor who was at the house and she went back home while the kids and I tore out for the hospital.

Our neighbor, Mrs. Lisa Marsden met us when we got to Northside Hospital. She had been there the whole time. She told us what she had found out: that Liz was stabilized; that she was on an IV drip; that they had gotten her asthma under control; and that she was very weak from blood loss. I was shocked. I knew how severely Liz suffered during the spring from seasonal allergies and asthma. She had suffered severely through the pine pollen seasons in the region since our very first spring in Georgia. But what was this about her having lost blood?

Liz's doctor was already with her when we got to the hospital. The nurse went to let him know that I was waiting. When he came out to talk to me, I was surprised to find out that the attending doctor was Liz's gynecologist. He told me that he had not seen Liz in a while but a tumor that he had been concerned about inside Liz's uterus had started to grow quite suddenly since he had seen her last. The tumor had made its way through the thick uterine wall after consuming much of the surrounding tissue and causing heavy blood loss. He asked me if I had noticed Liz's heavy bleeding and more cycles in the month than usual. I thought about it and admitted that I had. Twice when Liz had been at school and once when she had been at a meeting she had rushed home, overwhelmed by the heavy bleeding. Liz's gynecologist and the hospital surgeons who were on call were prepared to operate immediately.

We got to see Liz for only a moment or two after the surgery. The doctor told me that the operation was successful and he had gotten the tumor out cleanly. He had to perform a complete hysterectomy in the process. He told me to take the kids on home because Liz would have round-the-clock nurses and she would likely be asleep for the rest of the night and most of the next day. Her biggest problem was loss of blood but since Liz had not put blood aside for the operation and had refused a transfusion, it might just take a longer recuperation time. He assured me that there was nothing more to fear, however.

I have many, many regrets from that day, but one thing will haunt me for the rest of my life. I really wish that I would have thought about our loyal little Muffy and made some arrangements to leave him with someone. I wish I could have made sure that he knew that Liz was still alive. I truly believe that if I hadn't been so upset and so unthinking, what happened might never have happened.

Muffy did not meet us at the door when we got home as he always did. I expected to find him upstairs on his rug next to Liz's side of the bed. But he was in the den lying on one of Liz's house shoes next to the sofa. When David tried to arouse him, he did not move. Both of the kids were terribly upset and both of them started to wail and cry. I called the veterinarian's office that Liz had always used for Muffy's shots and treatments. Luckily, someone was still in the office. I got a towel from the closet, wrapped Muffy up, laid him on the backseat of the car and we took him over to the veterinarian's office. The vet took Muffy and laid him carefully on the steel table in his surgery and took the towel off his body. It was not long before he wrapped Muffy in the towel again, and laid him in a basket for cremation that next day. Both the kids and I cried all the way back home.

I was able to bring Liz home on Thursday of that next week. The kids wanted to stay home but I insisted that they should go to school. For Liz's own good we did not tell her about Muffy while she was still in the hospital. I knew well enough that Liz would be looking for Muffy to come running as soon as she was inside the house, so I immediately sat her down on the sofa and took her into my arms. I told her the entire story just as Crissy had told it to me—I told her how Muffy had shredded the curtains trying to get attention from outside. Liz was absolutely heartbroken. I left Liz crying in wrenching sobs on the couch while I went into the kitchen and made toddy for her and for myself. I knew that Liz must have felt physically cold and bereft just then, because we had lost a member of our family who was very dear to our hearts.

I knew that I was ready to be promoted to Production Manager long before I got the job. The guy who was promoted ahead of me had the proper amount of seniority and experience but he was just not getting the job done. I did not hesitate to work behind him, but I was not at all pleased to have to clean up when he had allowed the workers to leave something that had not been properly attended to. I was beginning to feel that maybe I had hit a brick wall in my career at

General Motors. I was not yet at my peak of productivity and I knew that I could really stretch my talents even farther. I hated to do it, but I pulled out my old resume that I had not even looked at since I was in graduate school. When I started to work on updating my resume I was reminded that I had talents that I had not been obliged to use at all up to that point. I had made some excellent contacts among my colleagues from other companies and I figured that I would surely get a bite from some of them.

I had to smile to myself when Tom Brady who had replaced Bill Canning as plant manager of the Doraville plant came to me and told me that I would be promoted effective immediately to Production Manager of the Doraville Plant. I had not meant to make it a motivator but updating my resume for a job search seemed to have an effect upon upper management that I could very well appreciate. Now I could feel that I was recognized as productive and valuable as a GM executive as anyone else.

After a few years, owning my own airplane and flying myself and occasionally someone else in it completely lost its luster for me. It was not something that Liz and I shared and neither of the kids really wanted to fly with me, so I just didn't get the joy from it that I had gotten when I was first learning how to handle an airplane. I resolved that I would sell the plane if I could because I wanted to build a custom house for Liz and the kids. It was not long before I found a buyer for the plane. I kept my membership in the flying club just in case I ever got the urge to fly again.

We retained the builder who had built our house in Sandy Springs because we were already familiar with the excellent work that he did. We looked around for a long time until we found an ideal spot for a house in a new neighborhood just off the Chattahoochee River in Roswell. Our builder showed us the plans for a house that he and his wife had designed and built in a smaller subdivision and proposed that it would fit wonderfully on the beautiful wooded lot that we had selected. The lot was right across the street from the neighborhood club house and the builder proposed to build on a wooded lot on the hilltop just above the river.

The house that our builder wanted us to inspect was located in subdivision in Atlanta, so we drove down one Saturday to see it. The house was already sold and the people who had bought it had not moved down from Cleveland yet. Since the builder still had a set of keys he was able to let us inside the house. We approved his plan immediately since that house gave us a true picture of how our house would actually look once it was completed. The only additions that we made to the builder's plans was a full basement that included a below ground garage for me where I might tinker on weekends and turn a few wrenches on my cars; and a sewing room for Liz where she could have room to design clothes and store fabrics.

While our house was under construction, we used the subdivision's club house to host a Christmas party for North Suburban Chapter of Jack and Jill. We invited the members of the Atlanta chapter, and hired a DJ. On the night of the party, the kids socialized, danced, had snacks, and had a wonderful time. We were looking forward to inviting the members of our Corvette Club for our annual spring party there, too.

It was not to be. Tom Brady called me to his office one afternoon just before I was getting ready to leave work. After we had talked for a bit, he informed me that there was a big problem at the Fairfax plant in Kansas City: Bud Darnell, the plant manager there was a friend of Tom's. Bud had said that he needed someone to take over as production manager as soon as possible because his present production manager at the Kansas City plant was not working out at all. I quickly declined the offer even though Tom assured me that it would mean an upward move in the unclassified pay ranks at General Motors. That meant an increase in salary. I was happy being the production manager in Doraville, I told him, why would I want to make a lateral move to a smaller, unfamiliar plant even if it meant more money? I had many other factors to consider including my wife and family so I simply said that I was not interested. Still, Tom urged me to think more seriously about it.

I honestly tried **not** to give Tom's proposal a second thought.

When I told Liz about my meeting with Tom, I also told her that I was not about to leave our new, half-finished house and all the friends that we had made in the Atlanta area. I guess I went on and on for just a little bit too long about why I was not going to consider doing it. I must have given myself away somehow.

I caught the silent, assessing look that Liz gave me when I mentioned it for about the fifth time.

"What?" I said frowning.

"Oh, nothing," she said, "but don't try to tell me that this is the end of it. When would you ever refuse to change jobs as long as it means some kind of movement within General Motors? Don't try to tell me that you're not interested in doing it."

I protested of course, but as it was, Liz was quite correct.

It wasn't even a week later that Tom sent his clerk to fetch me again. "Joe Spielman really needs you in Kansas City," Tom said. "He figures that you can get some things done. You won't need to worry about losing anything on your new house. Argonaut will take care of that."

Then, he dangled the ***real*** carrot in front of my face:

"You know that Joe's got the Corvette plant, too. You'd go a long way toward getting into his good graces. I expect you'd get your shot at the Corvette plant in a year or two if you do this for him."

Then, my only thought was: "Ah, **hell**! How am I going to tell Liz **this**?"

When I told her that evening Liz said:

"I knew that whole thing wasn't over when you told me the first time, remember? When do they want you to transfer to the plant in Kansas City?"

"They want me there like last month," I joked.

But Liz was not in the mood for joking.

"Crissy is a senior. We'll have to stay here until she graduates—no question. We only have to think about David—he's got two more years of high school. But, if I know David, he'll be flexible. He's doing really well on the track team but knowing how easily David makes friends, I think he'd adjust to the move without too much of a problem. Anyway, we can sell the new house—I don't know—can we put the new house on the market while it's still being built?"

"Good God!" I exclaimed. I felt that I was the luckiest man in the world to have a wife like Liz. She had always willing to sacrifice anything just for my sake! I grabbed her in a bear hug that lifted her feet from the floor. I kissed her again and again and said:

"I love you, Baby! I really hate this for your sake. We were building your dream house. Now you won't even get to move into it.

I know how this hurts, but, you're right, I can't refuse the move if it's gonna' get me what I've always wanted."

Liz shrugged nonchalantly, but I knew that she was hurting. She had to be. She could not joke about our situation—no need for her to try. This sudden upheaval in her life had to be devastating—again. Liz swallowed hard and tried to show a brave face but I had already seen the light refracted on the unshed tears in her eyes. Still, it wasn't long before she said:

"Wherever you go, the kids, and I will go—eventually."

Not only would we be leaving the place where we had lived the longest and made the most friends, we would be leaving the place where we had lost our beloved little Muffy; we would be leaving the place where our kids had done the most of their growing up; we would be leaving the place where I had had the most success in my career and had made a name for myself in automobile manufacturing; we would be leaving the place where I had challenged myself the most by learning avionics and had owned and piloted my very own airplane; and we would be leaving the place where we were building the dream house that we had modified to be just the way that both of us wanted it to be.

Liz said that we were going to have challenging times ahead of us. She was the one who stubbornly refused to allow us to look back or break down about our coming discomfort. She reminded me of what I had once said: I could not rest on what I had already accomplished. She talked and talked to make the kids feel that their greatest accomplishments were still ahead of them—they could not worry about a little bump in the road right now. She was my rock and she spent more than a little time shoring all of us up and making the kids realize what we expected of them.

Finally, we all talked frankly about things that we had to do as we sat around the kitchen table on one afternoon soon after that. There were so many things that each one of us needed to consider; many adjustments that we all had to make in our lives; so many things that each one of us had to finish up. We would have the time.

I contacted Argonaut Realty right away since they were the arm of General Motors that was going to have to deal with our builder about the new house from now on. Argonaut was going to have to push to get our new house finished as quickly as possible before they would even consider putting it up for sale.

As it turned out, the house that we were living in was the one that Argonaut wanted to put up for sale right away. Our counselors at Argonaut Realty were quite frank about it. Then the local realtor declared that Argonaut had a certain policy that they always followed. He declared that they felt that they would have a better chance of selling the house now if it was empty. He needed to be able to show the house at any time day or night and it would be better for us if the house was clean and empty and we were not living in it. We tried hard not attach any racial motivations to it, but we couldn't help it. In the end, we didn't care one way or another—we just wanted the house to be sold.

We never even had the time to think about looking for another house in Kansas City. This whole thing, the immediacy of it, was putting us in one hell of a pickle. It meant that we needed to pack up the house and move out of it as soon as we could. We had to put everything except some of our clothes, into storage. We were going to have to "bite down" and set ourselves for a long, hard haul.

We decided that our only option was to lease an extended stay apartment for Liz and the kids in Sandy Springs. We found exactly what we needed in a complex on Roswell Road just a few blocks or so from the kids' high school.

The plant manager's secretary in the Fairfax plant found a small apartment for me near downtown Kansas City, Kansas in a nice, quiet neighborhood not far from the plant.

I agonized over the fact that it was going to be nerve-wracking time for all of us with no reprieve in sight at all.

The one bright spot that we had not counted on when we got ready to pack up our house: we were familiar with two of the guys who were the movers and packers. They were still operating their two big trucks and working for the moving company that General Motors always used to move their executives. When they showed up to pack up our house, we couldn't believe it! We were pleased to see them again after so much time had passed. We all laughed and hugged each other. They promised that they would personally see after the things that we had to put into storage.

The guys looked at Crissy and David in amazement. The kids had been young when they had last seen them over eleven years ago. They couldn't believe how much our kids had grown up and we were really surprised when the oldest packer showed us pictures of his four-year-old grandchild.

When they asked about Muffy we had to tell them our sad news. They sympathized and remembered how he had bristled and growled at them in Flint but had recognized them and had even seemed to tolerate them when we had moved from Flint to Saint Louis. We all laughed about how much Muffy had mellowed as he had grown older. He had even allowed the movers to pet him when they had come to move us from Saint Louis to Sandy Springs.

The kids proved to be both flexible and adaptable. They seemed to accept the adjustments that the family had to make really well. I was glad when Liz reported that she did not think that the upheaval in our lives affected her work in any fashion at all, but I wasn't sure that I believed her.

As much as I hate to say it, it did affect my attitude in a profoundly negative way—there were too many loose ends untied. I had left Doraville too soon with too much unfinished and too many of my pet projects incomplete. I really, really hated to do that. I had to keep reminding myself that I was making this sacrifice so I could eventually make my way to Corvette.

My Mom

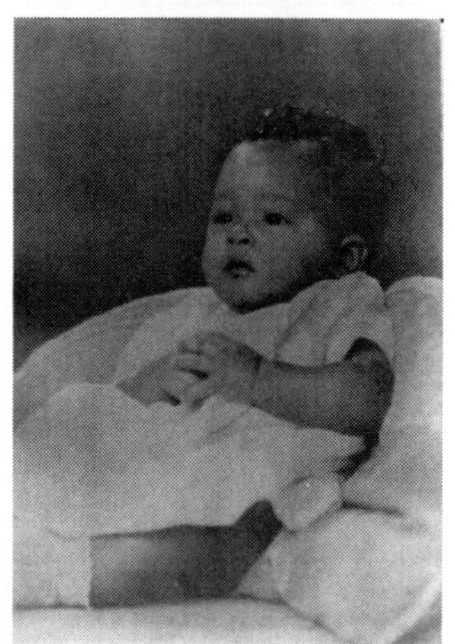

Baby Wil Cooksey

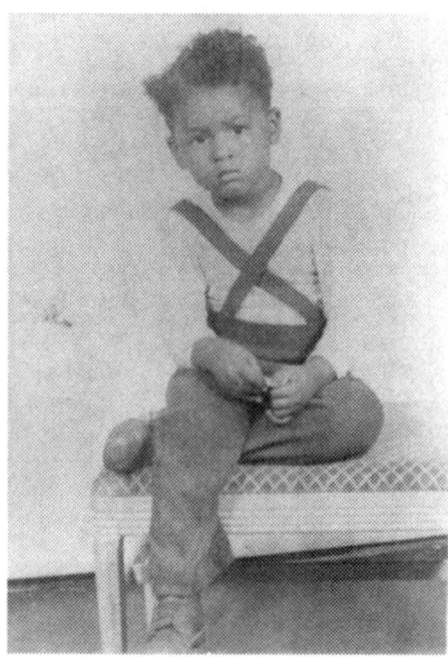

Young Wil Cooksey

1 Lt Cooksey 1968 Vietnam

Bronze Star award to Wil Cooksey while in Vietnam

1969 1st Corvette in front of my 1st house

Standing tall with Bob Morris, who hired me in 1972 to work at GMI

Wil and the General Motors Institute Team

Group photo of Corvette team

10 Best Award for Corvette

1998 UAW-GM Quality 500 Grand Prize Winner Celebration

Colin Powell gets ready to be the Pace car driver

Dan Gayle receives Corvette plant award

ICCC Trophy Awards for our car show

International Council Of Corvette Clubs

J.D. Power Award

General Motors Corvette Assembly Plant shop chairman Bryan Worley (left) and Plant Manager Wil Cooksey hold up J.D. Power awards today at the plant.

Corvette quality continues to rise

Bowling Green-built car wins second straight coveted award

By JIM WATERS
The Daily News

Even after more than 34 years on the job, Lorett Allen said Corvette's quality keeps getting better.

Allen, material operator of General Motors Corvette Assembly Plant, gathered with 600 of his fellow workers today in the plant's auditorium to celebrate the car's second consecutive Best in Segment award given by J.D. Power and Associates.

"Winning this award back-to-back is fantastic," Allen said. "This shows that all employees are dedicated to their jobs; everyone gives 110 percent."

While he understands Kentuckians' propensity for basketball, Guy Briggs, vice president and general manager of vehicle manufacturing for General Motors, said he was looking forward to next year and what "up in Detroit, we call a hat trick; you might call it a 'three-peat' here."

Along with the honors heaped on the local plant, the sole manufacturer of Corvettes [illegible]

See CORVETTE, 6A

6-19-02

JD Power Award celebration with UAW and GM management

Jim Caviesal and Wil Cooksey at Indy

Joe Spielman with Corvette Team and his new car

Liz and I with Colin Powell at Indy

Mike Yeager and Wil at FunFest

Motor Trend Award with Gerald Ellison ,Jack Evans and Wil Cooksey

NAI fly in at Tuskegee Alabama

Ron Fellows and Wil at LeMans France

Wil , Tom Wallace with Koos Petinger

Wil and Bill Quinn attend UAW-GM Race

Wil and Corvette Team at FunFest

Wil and Corvette Team with 1st 2008

Wil and Dave Hill at Indy

Wil and Ernest Foote at Black Engineer celebration in the plant

Wil and friend Sam Robinson

Wil shows off #427 Corvette

Wil and his race car

Wil and Liz

Wil and Liz at Sebring getting ready for a lap around the track

Wil and Liz on cruise ship

Wil and Liz visit horse farm

Wil and Liz with our corvette for racing

Wil and Liz with our yellow Corvette

Wil and Ron Zarella with JD Power award

Wil and the General Motors Institute Team

Wil and Tommy Morrison at Rolex 24 hour race

Wil at ICCC car show

Wil at Indy waiting to take a trip around the track

Wil Cooksey and Jack Evans and the 1997 BEYA

Wil is working in his office

Wil receives Educational Award from NAFEO

Wil shows off #427 Corvette

Wil with David Hill and Parnelli Jones

Wil with family

Wil with George W. Bush while he tours the Corvette plant.

Wil with Mom and some of our family

Wil, Liz and the Jones on cruise

Wil's Race Car

XLR training at phoenix raceway

Wil with Sisters and Brothers

GM Fairfax Assembly Plant—Kansas City, KS—Dreamscape Number 9

I wasted no time in getting straight into the heart of things as soon as I got to Fairfax. Bud Darnell made it clear to everyone when he introduced me in my first production meeting that I was to be completely in charge of all production. Not only did I sit in meetings with every department listening to reports for what seemed like hours, I toured the plant constantly until I learned who the people were and what all of their jobs were. I also learned every nook and cranny of that plant and just which jobs were done in every square inch of it. We were responsible for assembling the Pontiac Grand Prix—both the two-door and the four-door models with all of the variations of roof and body styles. Since I did not have my family to go home to at night, I spent hours after work with the second shift learning about leftover work and catch-up procedures and deciding what should be done about both. I learned all about the inspection procedures and decided what could best be handled after hours. Finally, I began to feel that I had a pretty good handle on the inner as well as the outer workings of the plant.

I learned that the assembly plant was named Fairfax because of the old Fairfax airport and airplane factory that was still sitting right next to it on the property. During World War II the plant that now housed General Motors Fairfax Assembly had originally been built to produce F84F jet fighters. As late as the war in Vietnam, part of the old assembly plant had still been turning out B-25 bombers. General Motors had purchased the plant somewhere in the 1950s and had begun to produce Pontiac cars in one of the old buildings. Later GM had built the new facility. Art Thomas, superintendent of trim, took me across the river where we could view the panorama of the new plant and everything surrounding it from the top tier of a hotel parking garage. When I looked down upon the property, I could see that the plant seemed to be built on a portion of the old airfield that still looked to be partially operational. I wondered if small aircraft and helicopters had ever been used to fly needed parts into the Fairfax plant in emergencies. Art wasn't so sure about that.

When I was being shown around the Fairfax plant for the first time, I was told that the plant was running three shifts. I was really surprised to hear that. I was glad to quickly discover that it was not quite the case. In my experience in General Motors, it was the plan in plants three times as large as Fairfax that the third shift was always used for maintenance, equipment repair, and clean-up while all the major machinery was turned off and not in use. The much smaller Fairfax plant was no exception but the attitude and culture of the plant were by no means similar to that of the huge plants. How they viewed things and how they thought of themselves was simply much different. The larger plants like the one I had just left in Doraville had totally different cultures, they were three times as busy, and they were producing multiple models of 3 or 4 different kinds of products, whereas Fairfax only produced one product, one brand—the Pontiac Grand Prix. There were only about 5,000 employees and most of their jobs were on the assembly lines during the first two shifts. Since they liked to think of themselves as running three shifts, rather than two shifts and maintenance as the larger plants did, that was okay by me.

Since the rebuilt Fairfax plant was one of General Motors' smaller, newer facilities, the newness also seemed to be reflected in the updated attitude of the workers as well as the practices that were being used. The daily work had been set up to run under the "Team Concept," that is, one supervisor ran several groups each one having one team leader. The team leaders supervised the team members who were the line workers or parts assemblers. Each group of workers (or each team) always worked on one job or on one project. This concept certainly seemed to be working fairly well at this plant in all of the places where it had been fully instituted and I was really pleased to see that. Fairfax was one of the most up-to-date, modern, and well-run concepts in all of the General Motors plants that I had ever visited or worked inside. One of my jobs as I saw it was to get the "Team Concept" to work even better in all areas and on all of the shifts. So, I set about getting that going right away.

I was truly amazed at how well the workers on both shifts responded to me and how my ideas were well received right away on both shifts. Since neither the supervisors nor the workers knew when I would show up or where I would show up, that seemed to keep them on their toes. I was glad to find that this smaller plant seemed to be so very versatile and the workers seemed so eager to please. They were a real joy to manage. Their eager co-operation kept me on my toes, too.

I always tried to make sure that I had something to bring and to add to the program. I found that I was easily able to actually try out some of the new ideas that I had never been able to get going in Doraville and hadn't a prayer of ever getting started in Saint Louis. Some of the methods and practices that I had tried to update in Doraville seemed to take forever to get going, but they had eventually, sluggishly gotten started in some places. Soon enough I found that newer, more innovative ideas were much, much easier to manage on the smaller scale in Fairfax.

I made sure that everyone knew that I was there to listen and learn from them anywhere and at any time. I wanted everyone to feel that I was always approachable and that my door was always open. I made sure to let the upper management as well as the line workers know that anyone was free to stop me at any time whenever they saw me, and that I was always willing to consult with anyone who had a problem or idea no matter where I was headed or what I needed to get done right then.

My sense of humor seemed to intrigue the workers as well as the management team. I had hoped to give the impression that I was a good-natured guy, and I always tried to have a ready smile and a good answer if there was a problem. I couldn't deny it when Art Thomas, accused me of always comparing their small Fairfax plant to the huge plant that I had just left in Doraville. He contended that I always did it in an unfavorable way. But, I laughed heartily and promised with an elaborate apology that I would never do it again. He laughed, too, and went on to tell me that Jeff "Smiley" Watkins, the night shift superintendent, had made it well known to everybody that if he heard "Doraville" come out of my mouth just one more time, he was going to run away screaming.

The next afternoon while the staff was sitting around the table in the plant manager's conference room I made sure I found a reason to mention Doraville at the very beginning of our production meeting. Then, I turned to Smiley.

"Aren't you gonna' scream and run away, Smiley" I deadpanned.

The room went absolutely silent while poor ol' Smiley turned as red as the crimson crayon in a kid's box of Crayolas.

"Gotcha!" I laughed.

Bud Darnell threw back his head and laughed and so did everybody else. That seemed to break the ice. I felt that a few people really might begin to warm up to me and my sense of humor at that moment. Actually, I soon began to feel that their attitudes became a whole lot less stand-offish.

Bud Darnell told me that Gus Barnes, the former plant manager always believed that all the people in management should dress a certain way. To me they looked too up-tight and too stiff to work in an assembly plant. It seemed like they were going to church or somewhere formal: dark suits, ties and white dress shirts were still the norm among the upper management guys when I got to Fairfax. Bud told me that Gus had felt that style of dress affected their attitudes as well as their sense of the jobs that they had to do.

I quickly gained a reputation as a relaxed but snappy dresser despite my size. My particular style profoundly disrupted the stuffy style of the Fairfax boardroom.

I favored neatly pressed and creased dress pants and long-sleeved stiffly starched dress shirts in plain white as well as white with pin stripes, and certain subdued colors: light blue, mint green, light yellow and grey. I kept my shirt collar open and the cuffs my shirt neatly folded back. I seldom wore a tie. I think that everyone soon began to realize that my style was much more suitable every day for a hands-on, hard-working man like me. I have always liked to wear a thin, gold chain around my neck and some adornment on my hands and wrists. A gold watch, a thin bracelet and a man-sized diamond ring on the little finger next to the ever-present gold wedding band were part of my style. I liked a close shave with a liberal splash of mossy-smelling after-shave lotion on my face and a light touch of cologne of the same scent on my chest and shoulders.

Back when I had first arrived in Atlanta, I heard about a retail store that carried really beautiful men and women's casual and dress shoes in their downtown store—Friedman's Shoes. I found that the shop had shoes made of various leathers as well as exotic skins in just about every make, style, and color. They specialized in fitting large-sized feet like mine. Friedman's stylish shoes, boots and belts really pleased my tastes. (I still shop from the catalogs that they continue to send me to this very day and I still try to make a trip to their downtown shop whenever I visit in Atlanta).

I was really flattered when I saw that many of the supervisors and upper level management guys immediately adopted my style of dress and grooming. Even my constantly trimmed, back-combed hairstyle seemed to have an effect on some of them. Others took on my methods of energetic, hands-on supervision including my habit of constantly being out on the floor making personal appearances in places in the plant where I was not necessarily expected to turn up. Some supervisors seemed even to mimic my habit of Army-style intelligence gathering: standing silently with arms folded, thoroughly assessing a mechanical problem or a situation involving people that I had been told about before I made a final decision about it.

I was becoming known as a quiet, ever-present stickler, and a hard driver who always wanted things to go a certain way. I have never cared to whom good ideas belonged to as long as the ideas worked to our benefit when we tried them out. Whenever I concluded that someone else had a better method of doing things or an easier approach to solving a problem than I had, we would go with it and only revert to my way as a final determiner if their method proved not to work as well.

I have to admit that being strapped for money did not usually bother me so much; after all I had grown up that way. But paying for two houses and two apartments at the same time really made my family a lot worse off than just mildly cash-strapped. Our finances were purely blown to hell. I juggled credit cards and raised the limits on each one so that I could make ping-pong, back and forth payments with each one. I also needed to have ready money to pay the costs for incidentals and pop-up expenses for building the new house. Every one of our savings accounts including those with General Motors had to be borrowed against just to pay for the expenses that we were incurring each month.

I certainly did not want Liz and the kids to feel the pinch, but they had to. Nobody was driven to eating ramen noodles for every meal or to having absolutely no cash at all for small things after the bills were paid but we all were aware that we were pretty near penniless. Crissy got herself a job after school at a Wendy's Restaurant close to the school to help to pay some of the extra expenses for her senior class trip, the band outing, and her graduation pictures. We were really proud of her for doing that. Both the kids and Liz cut back on some of the things that they wanted but were able do without like new clothes for the season. I sacrificed on guilty pleasures like beer and liquor and expensive cuts of meat to save money every day but I was not about to cut back on the expense of flying home at least one week-end a month to be with my family. Both Liz and I knew that we had to be careful with what we spent every day until one of the houses was sold. We didn't know how long we would be obliged to watch every penny but extreme frugality soon became our way of life.

We were getting pretty anxious. Then, someone connected to General Motors saw the spec papers on our new house and made an offer for it. Argonaut wanted us to consider it, but the offer was way too low and I knew that Argonaut was likely to be really slow about compensating me for any such severe loss that is, if they compensated me at all. We finally decided to refuse the offer but at the same time I felt very depressed thinking that the family had to try to hold like this for an undetermined time. I spent some sleepless nights worrying about our predicament and hoping against hope that another offer would come along soon.

Whenever Liz and I discussed it, she supported the decision to wait. If she had not been so adamant that she and the kids would be just fine for the next few months in the a tiny, three bedroom, cramped apartment I might have thought about giving in and taking a loss just to free up even a small amount of money.

One Sunday morning just before Liz was to take me down to the airport to board a plane back to Kansas City our builder called and told me that he had met a guy who had been watching the house in River Green as it was being built. The builder did not usually get involved with the sales of his houses, he left that to the real estate agents, but he said that this guy really loved the house and loved that spot right across from the clubhouse where the house was being built. The builder had talked to the guy himself, showed him the plans, and told him about our first Argonaut fiasco. The man was ready to buy: no dickering, no dealing—just our asking price whatever that might be. That was surely music to my ears! I was overjoyed to tell Liz about it.

Our potential buyer was really afraid Argonaut was going to be difficult to deal with so he was ready to make the deal with me as soon as I could get back into town again. Now, Liz and I felt a whole lot better about refusing Argonaut's first offer and holding out for a higher price for ourselves. It had proven to be a good decision. This time, when Liz drove me down to the ever-expanding Hartsfield Airport to fly back to Kansas City we were actually happy and smiling when we kissed good-bye. We could see some light at the end of that dark tunnel we were trapped inside and we were pretty sure that it was not the headlight of an oncoming freight train this time.

The old saying "when it rains, it pours" came true for us. We got a good, solid offer on the house in Sandy Springs. Maybe now, our penny-pinching, depressing poverty, and anxious prayers were finally paying off. We were still renting the two apartments, but General Motors had finally agreed to pay for the cost of my apartment at least. At long last, it would be much easier for our budget to recover with those two houses off our backs.

Liz took four days off from school and flew up to Kansas City so that we could house hunt. She had made strict arrangements with the kids. They could not have any visitors: rule one. They must always get on the bus or walk to school—no driving: rule two. Liz had given two friends gas money to drive Crissy home to the apartment from work at night. Neither Crissy nor David was to visit their friends' houses or go anywhere unnecessarily while Liz was gone. Liz had pointed out to them that she would be gone for only a day or two, so, surely, they could last for that long. Liz's friends were charged with keeping close eyes on the kids for us.

I had already told Liz about the simple layout of the Kansas City Airport, but when she flew into it, she was really surprised by the ease of getting from the airplane to baggage claim then out to the passenger pick-up zone. After both of us had been dealing so long with the colossal, ever-changing, ultra-busy Hartsfield airport in

Atlanta, I guess it wasn't any wonder that both of us found the easy, non-confusing Kansas City airport to be such a joy to navigate.

Our real estate agent was John Amos, a fascinating man who knew the city like the back of his hand. He showed us where a person could be driving down 95th street in Kansas City, Kansas one second and in the next second the street simply changed names to Bannister street in Kansas City, Missouri. He was really delighted when we laughed heartily at his *Wizard of Oz* punch line:

"'*Well, Toto, we're not in Kansas anymore*,'" he quoted. Then he said: "We're in Missouri now."

He told us stories and showed us many things of interest in Kansas City, Missouri and Kansas City, Kansas. We were really impressed with Amos' in-car telephone which was the first time that we had ever seen a true portable car telephone, it was an analog contraption wired right into the cigarette lighter and used just like a regular telephone—not just a two-way communicator. He could call anyone anywhere on it and he easily received calls from everywhere on it, too. I was fascinated. I determined that I had to have one of those versatile telephones to put into my car.

One of the places that Amos took us was the famous Gates Barbeque Restaurant in downtown Kansas City, Kansas where the jovial clerks greeted us with their signature, "Hi, may I help you?"

We had heard about the greeting from General Motors people who had visited the plant in Kansas City, so we were delighted to hear it for ourselves.

We drove through the Country Club Plaza in Kansas City, Missouri where there were fountains, statues, shops and stores and so many attractions that we simply did not have the time to see it all. We saw the Truman Sports Complex where the Royals' Arrowhead stadium and the Chief's Kauffman stadium were built side-by side. Finally, we had to get busy house hunting. I had promised Liz a dream house and I was determined to deliver, so, for the next day or so, we looked at many houses that were for sale.

Finally, on the day before Liz was scheduled to leave, Amos took us down Roe Avenue. We were looking about at the well-planned, well-laid-out enclave that we were passing through when Amos said:

"Look! See that house way up on that hill? You can see it from here. That's where we're going."

"That thing looks huge!" Liz exclaimed. "Is it a *house*?"

"It has so much glass," I said. "Does it have any yard? Is that a rocky hill all around it?"

Amos just smiled. "Wait until you see it! It hasn't got much lawn at all but it has three floors. All of it is well-planned living space."

That was the house that we bought. I felt that I had fulfilled my promise to Liz. I gave her a dream house after all.

The house was right in the middle of the other huge houses all around it on the street, yet it felt isolated. It really seemed like a giant fortress with a four-car garage. A whole lot of glass blocks on the huge circular front of the house let in light yet maintained the inside privacy. Amos was correct: there was hardly any lawn at all except for the grassy expanse at the front of the house. It was thick and healthy-looking. The back yard was mostly slate and rocks that had once lain below the grass and soil all the way down to the edge of the cliff. Now a lot of the grass and soil had been washed away and huge rock ledges made up the side of the steep, rugged cliff just behind where our house sat. It literally towered high above the street below.

When the furniture arrived from storage, it seemed like a drop in the bucket in that huge place. I had never before seen a house with four attached garages, but there they were: two were turned toward the street and two more faced the house next door. I parked my Caprice company car in the bay of the garage nearest the door that led into the house through the kitchen.

The place was ultra-modern inside. There were loads of etched glass panels that ran up the bannisters of the stairs from the first floor to the top floor and stylized plastic tubing edged the stairs downstairs to the bottom floor. Five huge bedrooms, each one with its own bath, were the main attractions. Three bedrooms were on the top floor. A master bedroom almost the size of our house in Saint Louis was on the back and a guestroom with a bath was on the front corner of the house on the ground floor.

A two storied great room with thick, light-colored carpeting dominated the middle area of the house. A half bath with ultra-modern black fixtures was just off the hallway of the wide open great room. Black and gold wallpaper and shiny black ceramic tiles on the floor finished off the dark, polished look of it. The house had a lot of bathrooms.

There was a sitting room just off the kitchen and it was large enough for a couch, lamp table, and chair. Still, there was an eating area in the kitchen. A butler's pantry led through to a formal dining room at the front of the house. When I stood in the circular two-story entryway and looked up at the huge imported crystal chandelier I figured that it had to be hung up there by multiple workers using a construction lift. It was a glass monstrosity with way too many light bulbs in it. I was thinking what a pain changing any of the bulbs would be, but Liz absolutely loved the thing! So, who was I to complain? It was her dream house.

The ceilings in every room were high, even on the top and bottom floors. The below ground rooms did not seem to be below the ground because of the long bank of full length windows on one side and the ceiling heights. There was a double-sided fireplace right in the middle of the lower level. This level also sported several large closets and a big open black and white tiled floor that covered half the basement. I could only guess that it was intended as a dance floor.

I felt like a pea in a barrel when I gave up my cramped, extended-stay apartment and moved into the house. I had the kids' bedroom furniture put into two of the upstairs bedrooms. I had the movers to put what had been our master bedroom furniture into the larger upstairs bedroom at the front of the house and that is where I settled in for the time being. I had the movers to put the guest bedroom furniture into the smaller bedroom on the first floor. I was not about to attempt to pick out furniture for the master bedroom or the great room on the first floor without Liz's input. Both of those huge rooms remained empty after I had moved into the house. I did, however, order plantation shutters for all of the bedroom windows, but that was the extent of my decorating efforts.

I let it be known at work that I had moved permanently into a house in Leawood. I was surprised to find that many of the people who worked at the GM plant lived in and around my neighborhood. We all got together and went to a Chief's football game. At the end of football season we got together for a Super Bowl party at Bud Darnell's house. A general superintendent, named Stuart lived two houses down the street and we all sometimes gathered at either his house or my house to have an occasional beer. Some of us went out to the stadium together to see the Royals warm up for the up-coming baseball season.

Liz came for a three-day visit and after living in a cramped apartment for months, she could enjoy the spaciousness of the new house with me. She had another purpose for being there, however. She had sent the Kansas City Board of Education a letter of application and they had arranged a job interview with her. They wanted to offer her a job teaching English at Sumner Academy, a magnet school in downtown Kansas City. The school drew scholars from all over the city and all of the instructors at the school were themselves scholars, each with their own specialty or field of study. Liz was thrilled when she was offered a job there. She would to be ready to start there for the coming fall. The school was located in the same area as the Fairfax plant in downtown Kansas City.

While Liz was in town, we got the chance to go shopping for furniture and we bought a modern bedroom suite for the master bedroom and a long curved modern sectional couch in white to go in the huge, open common room in the middle of the house. Soon, we hoped to have the huge house looking and feeling a little less empty and more like a family home.

I really missed Liz when she had to head back down to Sandy Springs, but we consoled each other over the telephone after she got back to Sandy Springs that it would not be long until we would have the family together again under one roof.

The end of the school year finally came. Liz's nephew, Wally, who had recently married a lovely girl, Bernadette, came to town bearing a gift for Crissy's graduation. They only stayed for the ceremony because we were already packed and ready to get out of town at first light the next day.

Our two-car convoy headed out with Crissy and me leading in the Corvette. Liz and David followed in the Chevy Suburban. We were leaving a place that had been good to us that we really felt was our home. David was super-hyped about the move but Crissy was really weepy. I would have hated for her to be in the car with Liz because then both of them might have been weepy together and that would never do.

We spent the summer finishing our house in Kansas City. We found various pieces of furniture for all of the various rooms. We loved sitting out on the upper deck and enjoying the panoramic view. We could see for miles out over the rooftops of the houses below the high hill even from the deck off the lower level.

The kids seemed to go in totally opposite directions: Crissy spent hours in her room while David quickly connected with a group of tenth grade boys who would be his classmates at Blue Valley North High School in the fall. He joined up with the track team and he used the Suburban to drive some of the members of the track team to various other places to the summer track meets. Our house was always filled with teenage boys who were his track mates and whose appetites for snacks were simply overwhelming. We nicknamed them "The Chew Crew."

July 4th we saw the fireworks displays in three surrounding townships right from our decks. We delighted in watching the balloons fly by for the big Balloon Classic held to be held in a field outside Garden City, Kansas. They passed by right over the roofs of the houses along the street below our deck and we could see the people in the baskets attached below the colorful balloons. Every one we saw, we made sure to wave to them.

We attended the ICCC convention that year in Birmingham. They gave us a prize for traveling the longest distance to get to the convention of any of the members. We also had the newest Corvette and both Liz and I won trophies in the drag racing event.

Liz's cousins, Pauline and Nadine Scales visited us from Holly Springs. They really wanted to see Kansas City. Liz took them all over the place, but they really liked seeing where the Royals played baseball and the Hallmark Plaza with statues and fountains. They really seemed to enjoy sitting out on our upper deck and looking out over two states: Kansas and Missouri.

When summer was almost over and fall was moving in we were busy. Many of our fellow members from ICCC visited and some of Liz's teacher friends from Georgia came by for overnight stays while on vacations and driving tours. We had visits from many of our relatives: my sisters Barbara and her husband Rathel, Liz's sister, Florestine her husband Walter and their mother all came to see us. Many of the people who visited us were amazed that we had bought such a huge, ultra-modern house.

Liz and David fell right in to the social life in Kansas City. They joined Jack and Jill of America and Liz met a young lady who had been one of her students when she had first started teaching eleventh grade in the city schools of Memphis nearly eighteen years ago. Now, the young woman and her husband had kids of David's age and they all came together in the social club. Liz complained that seeing them made her feel that she was really getting old.

Crissy continued to remain isolated and did not seem interested in anything except to persistently make phone calls to her classmates and friends back in Sandy Springs. When the bills for the telephone calls topped $200 we put a stop to the calls and demanded that she should come out of isolation and get ready to go to work or enroll in Johnson County Community College. We weren't sure what Crissy had planned for herself but going to school was the only thing that we saw as a solution to her becoming a complete hermit.

We met many of our neighbors who had been living in the neighborhood for quite a while. Former football and baseball great Bo Jackson lived down the street with his wife and kids. They loved our Chevy Suburban because of its exterior spare tire. Bo's wife said that they thought it was really stylish.

Our next door neighbor's wife was a teacher so she and Liz seemed to have a lot in common except that she was an exercise advocate. Liz studiously tried to avoid her as she power-walked or jogged around the neighborhood. Liz stopped answering the door before breakfast because she knew that it just might be our neighbor trying to get Liz out on a walk. I laughed at Liz and told her that she must be exercise phobic.

Both Liz and I had to make the long drive up to Kansas City each day and we absolutely cringed at the traffic and the long haul to get home in the afternoon after work. Both the kids would be attending school in Leawood but they would be going in different directions each day. So, I needed to get a good used car so that the kids would have a way to get back and forth to school each day and to practice and after-school activities each evening.

I went over to a car dealer in Kansas City, Missouri to see what I might be able to find. I was met by a very dapper salesman, Lonnie Cobb who immediately said that I looked very familiar to him and both of us laughed about that. I let him know that I had seen a Pontiac on the lot that Liz and I had decided to buy. I thought it might be a good car for the kids to use.

When I introduced myself, Lonnie became very excited.

"That's why you look so familiar," he exclaimed.

He said that his mother's maiden name was Cooksey and that her family was from Texas. He proclaimed that I looked a whole lot like his youngest brother. We decided then and there that we had to be cousins—distant, maybe, but cousins.

A few weeks later, when I met Lonnie's brother, I found that the brother was a big, tall man who liked to wear cowboy boots and I had to admit that he and I did look a lot alike. We immediately accepted each other as cousins and both of us declared that we were going to try to find out from our older relatives just how close kin we actually were. We made a vow that we would get together with our families for a reunion as soon as we could. We kept that vow and we have visited each other since then.

I almost always marked the passage of time by the seasons especially now that we lived in a place where seasonal changes were so distinct. Seasonal rotation had not been quite like this in Georgia. Further south, the seasons seemed to overrun each other. We were truly in the mid-United States and the weather was distinctly different. The fall in Kansas really meant falling leaves and cooler weather. And tornadoes! We had heard much in the news about the mid-western weather. It also meant that everyone in the house got busy with the start of school. Now, every day, all of us were running off in different directions to school and to work.

I was growing far more settled in at the Fairfax plant. I enjoyed tremendously the things that we were getting accomplished and the apparent progress we were making. The way that my staff and the workers had accepted me, my methods, and my requirements made going to work each day no less than pure joy.

We slid into 1991 model change smoothly and we had no major problems with the Pontiac Grand Prix. The previous preparations that I had carefully overseen and put into place paid off in excellent fashion. Bud Darnell, seeing the seamless transition, was so gratified that he told me that he was confident enough with my stewardship that he was going to take a much needed and much overdue vacation. He said that he had not felt free to take a vacation away from the plant in well over two years. He talked about a lodge in the Minnesota woods that he shared ownership of with his brothers. He spoke wistfully about going fishing in the clear streams; hiking in the surrounding forests; cutting down dead trees from among the tall, pointed evergreens for firewood; frost on the bushes in the early mornings; and cool nights in front of a big, roaring fire in a log-sized fireplace that could also be used for cooking. I wished him well and promised that the plant would be fine in his absence. Actually, I had been totally responsible for the day-to-day running of the Fairfax plant almost from the first minute that I stepped in as production manager, so I did not expect anything to come up that I could not handle.

Christmas came that year along with a fairly light snow season. Liz bought home a huge 10-foot artificial tree that she had selected because she hoped that it would not be dwarfed by the big window and high ceiling of the common room. We had fun decorating the big tree. Liz found a picture frame, put a picture of Muffy in it and hung it on the tree. I had to use a step-ladder to put the star on the top.

One thing that was not a joy that season was the discovery that Crissy had not been attending her classes. A late evening call from her freshman counselor revealed to us that she had failed all of the three classes in which she was enrolled. She admitted to us then that she had been spending most of her days in the student lounge with a crowd of like-minded people without much ambition and a penchant for smoking cigarettes and not attending classes. She had never smoked at home, but she admitted that most of her extra money had been going toward financing her newly acquired habit.

I fairly hit the ceiling and went on through! The utter waste of money was enough to make Liz and I both want to wring Crissy's neck! I knew that sometimes kids growing up have a difficult time "finding themselves", but by contrast, my dirt poor childhood never allowed any room for me to waste money or time "finding myself" like that, so there was no way that I could understand Crissy's attitude at all. I had always wanted to give my children nothing less than a satin smooth way to go. They hadn't had to work their childhoods away like I had to do—except to pay for some luxury that they merely wanted. By contrast, I was called upon to help feed my family. My kids had never had any periods of homelessness; no debilitating poverty; and no doing without the things that were basic for living. I figured it had to be overindulgence and too much leniency that caused Crissy's attitude to be the way it was. We vowed to give Crissy one more chance to straighten up.

When the next semester ended and Crissy's grades were still below acceptable levels, since she had to leave school, she declared that she was going to look for a job and become independent. It was not too long after that she found herself a job. Then, her friends came to our house one evening to help her pack her things to move out and into an apartment that they all shared in downtown Kansas City, Kansas. That was the first time that we had ever met any of them.

Liz was heartbroken, I was disappointed, but I was still very angry over the complete waste of money. I firmly declared that I was only going to allow five minutes for Liz and David to cry about Crissy then we needed to get on with our lives and leave our daughter to whatever life that she had chosen for herself.

David's love of sports earned him spots on both the varsity football team and track and field teams at Blue Valley North High School. We had already spent time during the fall going to David's football games. Then, we attended his track meets in the spring and drove around the region to the meets in the summer with the AAU (Amateur Athletics Union) track team coached by Al Hobson. David and a classmate at Blue Valley North, Nate Hill ran with Marques Browne and Maurice Greene who later went on to Olympic greatness. Maurice's brothers and runners from Kansas City schools made up the

2nd group. They were all doing really well with the amateur team. We were hoping that David's talent and willingness to stick to his training program might earn him a scholarship to one of the large universities in Kansas.

Our hopes seemed dashed when David came home with his SAT scores. He was terribly sad because the scores were 4 points less than what he needed to get into the University of Kansas.

Liz's natural "teacher" instincts" made her spring into action. She enrolled David in SAT prep classes set up by parents at Blue Valley North. She brought home self-help tutoring books for math and English and started immediately to tutor David on the grammar and composition portions of the test while I worked with him on math and science. Liz took extra time with David and some of his friends around our kitchen table on week-ends and sometimes after school. It was no surprise when the boys took the tests again all of them passed by quite comfortable margins.

After months of planning, we began work on the 1993 model of the Pontiac Grand Prix. Our goal was to start production of the new car without stopping the assembly line at all after we moved the last 1992 model off the line. We had made the decision in an earlier production meeting to go ahead and try a rolling transition this time. We consoled ourselves that if it was not successful perhaps at least we would know what we had done wrong and use that knowledge for the next model year.

My tight scrutiny and close supervision were hardly necessary. The changeover to the new model was so seamless, so successful that Bud was ecstatic. We even began sooner than we ever had during a changeover period assembling the variations and different styles of our Grand Prix. I was proud of the fact that we were still making improvements even though we had figured that we were already better than just good at what we were accomplishing. The usual problems with fuel door fits, two-door and four-door passenger door fits and headlight fits were at a minimum. Even the paint shop people seemed to be more than successful at their jobs during the changeover.

Bud sent his secretary to find me one afternoon while I was down in the repair section of the plant watching the repairmen wrestle with door fit problems on some of the two-door sedans that were coming to the final line. As soon as I sat down in his office, Bud looked at me solemnly and asked:

"Ready to leave?"

I frowned and stared at him. "What does that mean . . . ?"

"Joe Spielman wants you at the plant in Bowling Green right away," Bud said resignedly. "I know that's the height of your ambition—to manage the Corvette plant. I sure hate to see you go right now, but . . . are you ready?"

I looked away. I didn't want Bud to see the intense joy and anticipation that must have been burning like a fire in my eyes right then.

"I hate to leave Fairfax right now," I said truthfully, "We've got some things going on that I had hoped to see through to the end . . . but, yeah, I'm ready . . ."

Liz got home a bit later than usual that evening. I was watching television in my chair in the bedroom when I heard her come in and set her school things on the floor in the kitchen. She was singing somewhat off-key a popular song that she must have been listening to on her car radio. I knew she always stopped at the kitchen counter to go through the mail, so I got up and went out to the kitchen to tell her the news. When I told her, she laughed, ran into my arms, and hugged me mightily. She knew it was my dream to manage the Corvette plant and she shared my happiness that the dream had finally come true. Finally, though, she sat down on the settee in the kitchen as if she was really tired.

"I'll have to tell—" she started. She stopped, sighed heavily, and was quiet for a long time.

Then she said:

"Since I'll be leaving at the end of the school year, I really need to let them know ahead of time. That will give them plenty of time to find someone to replace me. They should appreciate that."

"I know," I said.

I sat down beside her and put my arm around her shoulders to warm her because she had folded her arms around herself as if she were cold. I gently kissed the soft hair at her temple. Then I said:

"Crissy is off on her own and David's been accepted to run track at the University of Kansas. That's all he talks about. I know he'll want to stay here when school is out to participate in AAU track with Al Hobson for the last time this summer before he goes on to the university. Maybe we can find a way to work it out for him."

"We won't have to worry until school is out." Liz said slowly. I could tell that her mind had already gone ahead to search for a solution. "But . . . we need to start looking right now to find a logical way for him to stay . . ."

"We will," I said. "You know what? Soon enough, it's gonna' be just you and me, Babe."

That was absolutely the wrong thing for me to say!

Liz must have been feeling sadness already because we would have to leave both of our children in Kansas not to mention the new relatives and friends we had found. She simply could not manage to give me a "chin up" or a "brave face" this time. The tears had already started spilling down her cheeks. As usual, she didn't make a sound. I couldn't help but feel responsible, so I sat holding her, rocking her in my arms until her tears stopped. I knew she was going to have to get used to the fact that her children were grown up. It wasn't long before she whispered to me what she had said long ago, the first time I had uprooted her and taken her so far away from all the things that were familiar to her. It was the same as it was over twenty years ago:

"Wherever you go, I will go."

The first thing that I did was to get in touch with the Corvette plant in Bowling Green, Kentucky. A telephone operator put me in touch with Nick Willingham in Production Control and Logistics. I told him who I was, and then I needed to tell him not to ship the new 40th Anniversary Corvette that I had ordered.

"Can you pull it off the line and keep it there?" I asked. "Just park it for me in the plant manager's parking space, will you? Thanks."

I still have that car in my garage today.

Once again I got myself physically and mentally ready to become a regular commuter. This time I had to fly on Sunday evening from the airport in Kansas City to the airport in Nashville. Because there was no commercial airport in Bowling Green, I was obliged to rent a car in Nashville and drive north up I-65 into Kentucky. I got off the freeway just inside Bowling Green city limits, turned left and drove down the main thoroughfare, Scottsville Road, to the Executive Inn and got myself a room there. The large motel had the most amenities of any lodgings in town in 1993.

I met Jack Evans, the regional manufacturing manager at General Motors, in the motel bar as we had previously arranged to do. We planned to have dinner at Rafferty's further down on Scottsville Road.

Jack had called me at Fairfax last week to let me know that he would be in Bowling Green today and was prepared to introduce me to the management team and to the line workers tomorrow. I was not ready to begin work just yet. I really needed to tie up a few loose ends in Kansas City then I needed to find some kind of temporary living arrangements in Bowling Green. This was a very small town so I knew that there were not a lot of apartments or temporary-stay units to rent as I had found in the large urban areas. I was not about to spend the next few months in a motel room. I was hoping that I might find a small furnished house to rent. My problems were solved for me after I had toured the plant and then went visiting in the city.

I went by to see my old friend and former General Motors superintendent Sam Robinson. He had been among the first to move to Bowling Green from Saint Louis to help to set up the Corvette operations. He had since taken an early retirement package from the company, but he and his wife, Hazel, were still living in town and had opened a monogram shop in a strip mall along Scottsville Road. I had visited at his house and he and Hazel had visited at mine while Liz and I were still in Atlanta. We had only recently talked and he knew that I needed a place to stay in Bowling Green. He generously offered to let me rent an empty upstairs bedroom/bath in his house that had been his son's living quarters. He promised to let me rent the room for as long as I needed it.

I now had things all set up even better than I could have hoped. I now could feel that I was primed and ready to make my move to Bowling Green. I drove down to the airport in Nashville and flew back to Kansas City. When I returned to Bowling Green in a week, I planned to hit the ground in a dead-out sprint as the new plant manager of the General Motors Corvette operation.

Corvette Assembly Plant—Bowling Green, KY—Awakening! Number 10

I was now working at my dream job. I should also say that I was now doing just what I was meant to do. Finally, I had gotten to Corvette!

Joe Spielman had kept his word. He had taken special care to make inquiries of Sam and others because he was very concerned to know if the atmosphere and attitudes within the city and in the plant would be conducive to a black man coming in to take over the top job at the General Motors Corvette plant.

Joe had to be well aware that some residents in and around the city of Bowling Green still harbored a simmering, deep-seated anger toward General Motors and the Corvette plant because those people had anticipated jobs being brought to the city for the benefit of the local residents. Instead, General Motors people had followed the jobs from Saint Louis to Bowling Green leaving only a very few jobs for the locals. This had caused strong anger and retaliation from the locals who felt deceived and cheated by General Motors particularly since tax breaks and incentives had been offered beforehand by the city to the company for re-locating here.

Tales were still told by the first arrivals of anger and retaliation, even by law officials. They told horror stories of how the General Motors people were often arrested and hauled into court for public drunkenness and the like. Back in those days, new arrivals who were sent to Bowling Green from other plants in other cities still felt that they had much to fear in retaliation from the still-irate Bowling Green residents.

Joe was also concerned about the people present in the plant society who were proponents of racial prejudice and bigotry—those who might resent and resist having a black man in charge of their livelihood as well as their workplace. He was concerned about sending me to face any traditional prejudiced attitudes from inside the plant as well as those from residents of the city and the region.

But I had lived long enough to know that the darkest elements of society would always be present no matter where I went or what

I did. I felt that I could not stop to worry over it. I was not about to try to single-handedly wring evil from anyone's soul. I certainly was not going to pause in my appointed mission because of it. I had a job that had been entrusted into my hands and I had to get that job accomplished. I was bound and determined not to let anything or anybody weigh me down or stop me from accomplishing my job under any circumstances. Failure was not an option.

What Joe had not let me know was that Corvette was floundering, barely limping along at a snail's pace with the present production with almost no chance of getting a new product for the next year at the start of 1996. Joe had shown that he had confidence enough in me and my methods and abilities that he felt safe putting his faith in me. That was enough. I knew that I had to put the job on my shoulders and take it the rest of the way on my own.

I was gratified that many of the people, who had worked with me in Saint Louis and had transferred to Bowling Green years ago, gathered around to welcome me to the city as well as to the plant. I was happy that they seemed to regard me as a rediscovered friend. Yet, I harbored no illusions. I could not forget that among them were many of the same people who were bred in that horrible nightmare—the workforce in Saint Louis. I was sure that practically every one of them had brought their same old habits and dispositions with them to Bowling Green. I knew well enough that a change of location does not mean a great "Sea Change" in attitudes or in human nature over the years—not by a long shot.

Barbara Meyer who had been the secretary for the retired plant manager, Paul Schnoes, came into my office to help me empty my boxes and to place my things on the desk and into the credenza. She assured me that even though Paul was retired he was still living in town. She said that Paul had said that he would be glad to answer any questions or address any concerns that I might have. I was glad to hear that. Remembering my protocol, I asked if she would stay on as my secretary. She quickly replied that she would more than happy to serve me just as faithfully as she had served Paul.

Barbara placed a packet of notes on my desk and I sat down to look at them. It did not take me long to notice something: there was a well-written note possibly from someone in the hourly workforce complaining that the managers did not follow the rules that the

UAW had agreed to in the last negotiated contract. Safety rules were being violated by lazy workers and non-caring supervisors, the note complained. There were notes that went even further: these notes named names and complained that the union members were abusing safety rules right and left all the time.

I was glad not to be blindsided with this and I guessed that was Barbara's sole intention. I couldn't help but feel as I read these notes that I needed to burrow beneath all this to get to the real concerns. But this was going to take time. There were items on the notes that were bound to be smokescreens used to cover the very real and very important issues. The UAW was likely to only pretend to care about safety because some of them did not want to do certain jobs at all. There were very likely to be small issues that were used to cover the larger issues of insubordination and refusal to complete certain tasks. I also wondered if the UAW was not using the safety issues to cover up the main issues of sloppy work, the even graver, more important issue of missed work, and, worst of all, absenteeism from work.

Good God! I thought. Was I going to encounter a viper's nest with the UAW here in Bowling Green? I really needed to be careful and to use more than a little cunning. Truth be told, there were likely to be icebergs floating on this calm-appearing ocean that seemed small on top of the water where the naked eye could easily see but were monster-sized beneath the surface of the water where they were hidden from view. I could only guess that it had to be large doses of insidiousness and hidden dangers that had damaged and sunk the careers of other plant managers in General Motors as well as in other industries that carried larger workforces. It might have seemed inconsequential, but I was sure that others had been lured into complacency by disregard of the real facts. I could only wonder how many faked smiles, insincere well-wishes and handshakes I had already encountered. I knew that I needed to work gradually toward building real trust—trust between the UAW and the management team; trust between my lowest level supervisors and the workers; trust between my management organization and me; trust between the regional coordinator and me. This would need to be worked on gradually at first, then, sped up whenever I was sure that a strong enough platform had been laid to sustain it. This could only come with time and very careful planning.

I called Barbara into my office and asked her to sit down. I knew that she had to be in the first layer in my foundation if I was to be successful in my quest to build trust. I saw wariness in her eyes, so I knew that I had to begin right away trying to sweep away her fears. I was not going to start by asking questions about people and seek to undermine her regard for them or their way of doing things. I let her know right away that I was not looking for her opinions pro or con about anything or about anyone. I respected all that had been done before my time, but now was my time and I expected her to help me to achieve my own goals rather than re-hash anyone else's goals.

I saw what had to be relief in Barbara's expression. Her face became more and more a picture of complete openness. She did not want to be pushed into a corner but she seemed to want to be honest. I was glad of that.

"Plant safety and absenteeism," she said immediately when I asked what things were going to be my biggest challenges in her opinion.

"We've got a problem with some of the doctors around here who give bogus statements to the hourly people so they can deceive their supervisors," she admitted, "So what can the supervisors do?"

I could well imagine. This was nothing new. That had been a problem in varying degrees in every one of the larger plants where I had worked over the years, but here in this small community, it should have been harder to pull that off. Barbara also said that employee morale was at an all-time low. They were not sure that a new product for the plant would be forthcoming. General Motors was holding off giving the new Corvette to Bowling Green because of the old-time attitudes of many in the UAW, product quality, and lack of co-operation.

Barbara gave me as much information about the plant as I needed over the next half-hour or so. The rest I would find out for myself. I felt like it would be easy enough for me to move around and get a handle on who did what, how and what methods that were being used to get it done, when they had to get it done and where it needed to be done over the next few weeks. Evidence was what I needed—evidence to back up what I had already heard. I needed evidence that I could gather with my own eyes, with my own devices. I needed evidence of who, what, when, where, why and how—evidence that was strong enough to sustain me when I had to make tough decisions.

I could not wait to get back to Sam's house to ask him what he knew, get his opinions, solicit his advice, and to use him as my sounding board. He would have in-depth knowledge about which members of management and which workers were pushing which issues and talk about what was in the contract with the UAW. He would know just what it was that the union was demanding. Sam and I sat up talking until far into the night long after everyone else was in bed. Finally, both of us needed to get to bed. I needed to rise early to get to work before the plant was scheduled for start up the next day.

I was in my office at the plant long before the line was scheduled to start. I took off my suit coat, hung it in the closet, unbuttoned the cuffs of my shirt and turned them back. I hooked my communication devices onto my belt. Now I was ready. I walked out of my office and onto the production floor.

This is what I vowed to do as long as I was plant manager, the same as I had done for my entire career in management—go right out onto the front lines from this point on. I intended to fly straight into the teeth of each and every monster. I intended to take my quest to build trust and integrity straight to the people. I vowed that I would learn their names and what their jobs were—every single one of them. There was no way that we could ever expect to build a quality product at that plant if I just sat back in my office and did not have first-level involvement in everything. That wasn't going to happen.

The first people I encountered were workers who were the ones who came in early to start up the machines and the early-morning maintenance workers who had to be there to repair any breakage that might occur at start-up. One of them with blonde hair and skin so pale that he looked dangerously anemic saw and recognized me.

"Hey look. That's the new old man," he said in a stage whisper and they all turned to look at me.

"Damn good-lookin' big 'ol bastard, ain't he?"

"Knew him when he was in Saint Louis," another said, "He was always a real regular fella, always out on the floor. I remember they said he knew all his worker's names and—geeze! Is he comin' over here—?"

I walked straight up to them and put my hand out:

"'Morning," I said, "How's it going? I'm Wil Cooksey . . ."

Two of them shook my hand tentatively; only one of them reached out confidently.

He seemed to be the oldest among them and the most sure of himself. They all told me their names. I looked straight at the older one because I thought I had seen him before in Saint Louis. So I took a chance:

"I remember seeing you. You were in repair in Saint Louis weren't you?" I asked.

"Nah," he said, "I worked over there on the frame line with your brother back then. I use to see you all the time. That's probably where you seen me, too."

"Oh, yeah, yeah," I said dramatically although I still didn't quite recall. "Frame line, yeah. Couldn't remember where in that plant I saw you before, but I knew I remembered your face."

"So you still recognize my face with 15 more years of age on it," he said laughing. "Either you've got a darn good memory or I ain't aging all that fast."

"You seem to be aging pretty good," I said.

I could tell that he was pleased that I had acknowledged him.

"How's your baby brother doin'?" He asked me. "Is he still in Saint Louis? Reckon he moved to Wentzville to the new plant didn't he?"

"He's still in Saint Louis," I said. "He was laid off during the cutbacks so he started selling cars. I think he likes what he's doing now pretty well."

"Oh, I think I would like that better, too," one of the others said. He seemed eager now to join the conversation. "I'd like that a whole lot better than I do working on this factory floor, I bet."

"So would I," the other one said, "Bet your brother is glad that he don't have to get up before day to go to work no more."

"Nope," I laughed as I began to move on, "He's at work sometimes 'til 9 o'clock at night, or later."

They laughed and then they all seemed to speak at once:

"Aw, naw! I wouldn't like that neither! No way . . ."

"Man! I couldn't handle them kinda' hours **at** all. That's a lot worse than this . . ."

"I'd much rather come in early, put in my eight and get on off. Even with overtime though, that's better any day!"

I moved on quickly but more of the line workers, supervisors and superintendents seeing that I had stopped to talk with the others came up eagerly to greet me and to talk. Word seemed to have spread quickly that I was on the floor and those who did not get the chance to meet me when I was at the plant previously came over to me now. I wanted to watch the start-up but I did not hesitate to stop and shake hands and talk . . . talk and shake hands . . . shake hands and talk . . .

Soon enough the whistle blew for the line to start. The switch was thrown and power was turned on, but there was absolutely no movement where I was standing. There was a whole lot of rushing around at the line as if to make sure that there were enough people present to begin the work. From experience, I knew this was possible but it amazed me that it always seemed to happen at the last minute. There was far too much standing around and looking and waiting long after actual start-up time. The noise level had steadily ratcheted up. The line supervisors seemed to be trying to gather people up—maybe utility people—to fill positions that had no workers in them. It must have been the vicious result of absenteeism.

After all these years working at as many locations as I had worked and seeing as many lines start up as I had seen, nothing that happened here could have been a surprise for me. I waited for what seemed like ten minutes before the line actually started to inch along like a half-dead snail. I thought that I was prepared for that God-awful pace as the line lumbered forward, but I was not. How could General Motors justify running this plant, keeping it open and employing workers at the Bowling Green location if the daily production of the cars was of this low volume? It would hurt to see it happen to the Corvette plant but since the production amount was so low, but I could not dispute the fact that this location might need to be shut down or get in some other new product in order to survive.

When things began to settle down I was left standing with only supervisors around me watching the slow movement of the line. I could see that some of the workers were trying hard to appear to be busy but I knew that this was only for my benefit. Well, I had news for them, damn it! They were going to have to do it every day, I said silently to myself. I would have been willing to bet that they could start up a game of bid whist, finish it and still get their jobs done before even one car passed by their location at this rate. I did not want anyone to think that they could fool me, but I was not about to say anything or interject anything or let anyone know just what I was thinking—at least not yet. I had already seen much more than they expected or wanted me to see on just my first day out here, in just this small amount of time.

I walked over to look at the section of cars on the final line then I went straight on over to repair. The repair area would give the truest picture of how well the plant was doing than all the other areas along the line.

The repair bay was filled to capacity with cars and I knew that there had to be many others in the repair yard outside. That was far too many cars in repair and this could only mean that there were not enough cars going straight on through in the "finished" mode to the shipping line. There had to be some good reason for this. I was determined to get the real story on it, too. I looked around and saw that there were repairmen working on the cars, but I was not about to ask them anything except what the major problems were that they saw coming through every day. I wanted facts and figures on that but I did not want any opinions and I was not about to give any myself—not yet—not to anyone.

I walked over to a snazzy-looking, red coupe wondering why it was there. I leaned over to look at the repair slip. I quickly put my hand over my belt buckle and caught back the end of my tie to make sure that nothing abrasive on my clothing would touch the car. I knew that I needed to get myself a belt buckle cover to come over here. When I leaned down and ran my hand along the rear quarter panel of the car, I was horrified. I could feel someone behind me. I turned to find a guy who had to be a repairman. He was a younger, quite muscular, white guy with a slim, good-looking face, hazel eyes, and sandy hair. His jaws were covered by a sandy shadow. His clear eyes searched my face for a long moment. He studied my expression and must have seen my disgust as I looked at the car. Neither one of us spoke at first. Maybe he was making up his mind whether or not to be a "Whistle blower." Finally, it seemed that he had made up his mind.

"It's not right, is it?" he said indicating the right rear quarter panel of the red car that I had been examining. He took off his right glove.

"That job's in repair because of the door fit—not the paint job. It oughta' be here because of that paint. Look at those pits right there. As soon as we get the door fit, they're gonna' ship it out with those pits in the paint like that."

He told me then that the pits in a Corvette paint job were caused by gases from the fiberglass body escaping from beneath the paint before it dried. They were labeled by various designations: "pits" "poppers," "craters" and "blow outs." For the serious Corvette lover who wanted a show car, a paint job with pin-hole blemishes and a rough texture like this in the paint job was a serious flaw—nothing short of a disaster.

We talked for a while about other serious and not so serious flaws in quality, dirt in the paint, and other things that needed to be taken care of that would make the paint job much better. He showed me a few things caused by worker carelessness that should not be overlooked that could be handled right on the line. I walked around some of the other cars looking to see if there were any more with "poppers."

I turned around from my inspection to find that the repairman was gone. He had probably slipped inside a car or quickly melted behind one of the walls in the area. I did not look for him because Bob Shell, the superintendent of Paint and the Body Shop was approaching where I stood. I knew Bob from Saint Louis. He had been among the first people to transfer from Saint Louis to Bowling Green years ago at the beginning. We greeted each other.

"What about these pits in the paint, Bob?" I asked. "Are we getting a hell of a lot of 'em?"

"Unusual if we *don't* get 'em," Bob said. "Craters in the paint happen nine out of ten times. We've given so many reports to headquarters that it's not funny. I think they just don't want to invest the money it would take to really fix the problem."

"How would you propose to fix it?" I asked.

"Just a prime coat on the fiberglass body in a clean environment," Bob said simply. "That needs to be done before these panels are shipped to us. We've looked into it and our suppliers say they can do it easy enough, at just a little more cost. Headquarters won't go for it, though. They won't spend the money."

"We've got a clean room. Maybe we can make it better ourselves. We need to talk about that. Let's get your guys to try that special coating on something we've already got. You coat the panels to use for examples yourself. Then maybe we can work on getting the money from HQ for the suppliers to coat the panels. Think you can get hold of enough coating and put it on maybe four cars, different colors just to show the difference? Are you willing to do that?" I asked.

"Yeahhh," he said slowly. "So we just want to show it off, huh? I can't promise when we can get it done or—"

"Do what you can," I said moving quickly away. "You take care of that and just let me know when you get it done."

I went back to my office with so much on my mind that I knew I needed to write it all down in order to remember it. I had filled almost two pages of my writing pad with "to do" notes before I knew it. I was still writing when Barbara reminded me that I had told her that I intended to meet with my staff after lunch and the rest of the management team after the line went down today. I told her that I certainly did. I expected that I would be meeting with them until I had a full report from every one of them no matter how long it took.

Ron Boyd, the production manager came into my office and we sat down to plan our strategy before the start of the meeting. We needed to be on the same page, looking for the same things, and trying to get the same things from the workers. I was not ready to divide our duties just yet because I expected that we would be more effective if we handled things that suited each one of us the best. I did not expect that he shared my philosophy about being out in the plant so much, few managers did, but I did expect for him to handle whatever he choose for his projects, then we would work together on the rest.

Both Ron and I were unsure of our ground. There had been rumors that the assistant plant manager positions were going to be phased out in General Motors. We were forced to talk about it, share our thoughts about it. I did not want to speculate, but I asked Ron what he would want to do if his job did get phased out. He was quite sure about it: he already knew that he would want to transfer to another plant or he said that he would leave General Motors rather than drop below his present rank. I knew that the plans were made in HQ already, Joe had told me. A small operation like Corvette was sure to be one of the first to lose its assistant plant manager. Ron and I agreed that he should not wait until the plans were made for sure.

That night when I got back to the house, Sam was my sounding board once again. He'd had enough experience with all of the people in the plant that he could tell me things that I needed to know about who had said this or that as soon as I asked him about it. I felt relieved being able to say what I was really thinking and unload to him. Also, I really needed Sam to add his thoughts and knowledge to my fact finding before I got ready to make up my mind.

I was well aware that I had a very long way to go. I had already thought about where I was going to start. I had to get to know the people and I knew that was going to take some time. I had to get to know the culture of my organization, what made it tick, and where everyone fit into it. I wanted to know what the nuances of my organization were, see the relationship between the UAW and management, and know what each part of the organization contributed to the running of the plant. I wanted every one of the members of the organization to feel the weight of responsibility on his or her shoulders for making things operate at 100% efficiency. I wanted to train every one of the workers in the plant not only on their own job but on the job of someone else as well in my quest to make the plant more productive. I was determined to make that happen.

I had to quickly get used to the attention of the press. The local newspaper, *The Bowling Green Daily News* used a large photograph of me in my office and gave me a good write-up. They told my story in their April 12, 1993 edition. *The Nashville Tennessean* newspaper featured me in a large and splashy color picture on the front page of the Business Section and pointed out that I had graduated as an electrical engineer from Tennessee State University in 1966. They wrote about the production of the plant and speculated about the future.

I also got quite a bit of television time in Bowling Green, too. Gene Birk the anchorman on WBKO News gave my story quite a bit of air time. The station sent two new interns out to do an interview with me, take pictures and move around to grab quick interviews with others in management. They showed many of the workers in the plant on their jobs and talked about the Corvette quite extensively on the evening news.

I was anxious to get back to my family in Kansas City. By now I had become a very efficient commuter. Two years ago, I had grown proficient at navigating the giant, ever-changing airport in Atlanta; then, I had grown even more experienced as I learned the quickest way to get through the airport in Kansas City. Now, I figured I had become nothing less than an expert when I quickly learned the ropes in Nashville. I drove my car down from Bowling Green to Nashville International Airport, parked in the satellite parking lot, took the bus to the terminal, got off, checked my bag at the counter outside, got my boarding pass, got on the airplane and flew back to Kansas City.

Liz knew just where to pick me up outside the baggage claim in Kansas City. Then, we drove down on I-435 to Leawood. During the drive, Liz told me all about what had gone on at home during the previous two weeks that we had not talked about over the telephone. I told her everything that I had been doing in Bowling Green up to that present time.

We talked about David and how he was doing in school. Finally, we talked about Crissy and her foray into adult independence. I knew that Liz would always find that to be painful because she still felt that Crissy had not been ready to go off on her own when she had. Whenever I could, I tried to convince Liz not to agonize about it, although I knew from experience that it was impossible not to worry since our daughter was not living under our roof anymore.

On Saturday we hung out with some of the friends and our new family that both Liz and I had found in Kansas City and had grown close to. We had promised to host a barbeque on our upper deck before we left Kansas City for good. We cooked chicken and ribs and basted them with Gates barbecue sauce. We knew that we would really hate to leave Kansas City because of the friends that we had made. It was almost impossible not to feel sadness because we had grown to feel so much at home in the city.

Back when we had first gotten to Kansas City, Liz had located some of her mother's relatives who, the family legends declared, had fled to Kansas during the dark of night because some of the males had dared to fight back against the constant persecution in Mississippi during the early 1940's. Liz had never met any of them until we had moved to Kansas and she had started working at Sumner Academy. Somehow through family communications, they had discovered Liz and the whole Kansas City family had turned out to meet her, she said. She told me that she was absolutely overjoyed to meet them and really did feel immediately close to them because they were a "long lost" part of her mother's family.

It was a funny thing, I had been waiting for my entire career at General Motors just to get to the Corvette plant, but I felt just like Liz did, I hated to move away from Kansas City. Both of us had found parts of our families there. Then too, we would be leaving both of our children in Kansas City. I could only hope that as soon as school was out and I could get Liz moved down to Bowling Green, the sooner she might be able to get over the feelings of great upheaval and loss.

Usually, kids are the ones who move away from their parents in order to get a chance at education and the promise of good employment. Kids are supposed to grow up and leave home to go to college, perhaps, or the kids have to get out into the world to search for upward mobility and prosperity. But we had a true role reversal going on: because of my employment, Liz and I had to leave our children, our friends as well as our new-found family behind. It was true that I had finally achieved my dream job, yet, it was impossible for me to feel good about leaving Kansas City.

When I got back to Bowling Green, I wasted no time putting the plans in motion that I had made with the co-operation of my staff. My priorities were not set in stone. I kept it uppermost in my mind that my key had to be flexibility. I planned to shift my attention back and forth from whatever was in front of me and go on to something else whenever I most needed to do it. These methods had served me well in other plants and under other circumstances, so I saw no reason to change now.

My staff and I went out into the plant to inspect the special units that Bob Shell had gotten the paint shop to do. They had done four of them, all coupes. There was a red, a black, a yellow and a white. The paint job on each of them was as near perfect as any that I had ever seen. We all walked around and around the cars giving as close an inspection as any of our plant inspectors might do. We walked over to a car with "poppers" and back again to Bob's specials. There was absolutely no comparison. We all felt that it was, indeed, a sad thing because every day we were sending those cars with the flawed paint jobs out to our prized Corvette customers. The undercoat on the cars that Bob had painted was done separately and by hand spraying in the paint shop. No way could this to be duplicated logistically in the plant before assembly. It made me know immediately what I wanted to say and just who I planned to say it to.

I knew that Russ McLean, Corvette Program Manager would be visiting the plant from corporation headquarters in Detroit later in the week. Russ and I had worked together in Doraville when he had been gaining experience as a production manager and before he had gone up to work at headquarters. He knew how I worked and I was pretty sure I knew his methods fairly well, too. I knew Russ was a man who would hold people's feet to the fire—he was good at holding people responsible for whatever they were assigned to do. I knew that he would put a name to a job and hold that person fully responsible for getting that job done. I felt that he and I worked a lot alike and I felt like I could depend on him, no matter what.

As soon as Russ walked into the plant, I was ready. First we sat down in my office and discussed everything from special projects to plant safety. We both held out little or no hope for the Master DOT program. It was a many-faceted plan that looked complex and un-workable on paper, so I very much feared that it was not going to be as good as it should have been when it was put into place and tested.

We both agonized over plant safety and health. There was an iceberg that I knew was bound to appear on my radar screen much sooner than later. I did not say so, but I planned to put some real teeth into that as soon as I had my feet firmly on the ground.

Finally, we got around to the issue that we were having with poppers in the paint. I wanted Russ to see the example cars. I knew that he always had been one to get out into the plant floor as much as possible, so I had no second thoughts about taking him out onto the floor now. He immediately began to stop and talk with people that he knew, but soon enough we were standing in front of the demonstration cars. He took his time going back and forth between the cars with "poppers" and the example cars just as I had hoped that he would.

"Ah, my goodness!" He said, "Has anybody from headquarters seen this—has Joe Spielman or anybody been down here?"

"No," I said.

"This is the kind of concrete information that Joe really needs to have. This kind of proof is what he needs—if not for the C4, at least for the C5," he said. "He really needs to see this."

I knew that changing the culture of the plant was not going to be a quick and easy job. I was all too aware that some of these workers in the Bowling Green plant with whom I was going to be dealing were born and bred in that briar patch that was Saint Louis. That thorny culture was wrapped around them and seemed to be thoroughly dug into their very souls.

I also knew that changing the culture of work environment was going to take time and a great deal of patience. I also knew that relationships between the UAW and management which had a long history of being adversarial since before the move from Saint Louis to Bowling Green was not about to be changed overnight. That did not mean that things were completely unstable, nor did it mean that it was going to be impossible to change. Relationships had to be strengthened if not rebuilt from the very ground up in order to be effective in the long term. I felt, of course, that no one in Detroit could decide what needed to be done to build trust or to strengthen relationships. We at the plant level were the best judges of what had to be done and we were the only ones who would ever be able to get anything done toward accomplishing that goal.

My immediate boss, Jack Evans, had expended much effort in getting me introduced to the workforce and established with upper management. Jack was a worrier, a micro-manager who expended much effort into making sure that things went according to a carefully laid plan. He spent a lot of time in checking and re-checking to see that all bases were properly covered and all leaks were properly plugged. I, of course, was supremely confident. I felt that I knew what I was about, what I needed to do and, of course, I felt that I did not need the constant supervision. I knew that I could stand alone in my position. Therefore, I did not always welcome Jack's constant worrying and constant checking up even though I was new, untried, and untested as a plant manager. I could well understand Jack's constant worry even though I resented it.

I felt that I always needed to leave myself room to maneuver and manipulate—to operate in my own way. I needed to follow my own devices. That is why I was not always receptive to Jack's close supervision. I understood that he wished to make sure that all "t's" were crossed and "i's" were dotted but I was becoming worn down by his obsessive checking and calling me constantly at all hours to make sure about this or that and wondering if I was aware of this or if I knew about that. I felt that he was too obsessive, too pressuring and too over-cautious. I resolved that sooner or later, I was going to have to go firmly to the wall and call his hand on it. After my experiences in Saint Louis and my long sojourn in Atlanta, I was more than confident that I was able to guard my back, take care of my people, and move forward at the same time.

The one thing that purely gave me the worst kind of headache was the issue of plant safety. Memos, bulletins and flat out mandates were coming into the plant in bundles and packages from the personnel department at headquarters. The people who worked at jobs where there was a danger of any kind were constantly aroused with various cautions. Places where there were moving parts, slipping dangers, dangers of falling equipment, loose equipment and tool dangers were constantly pointed out on sign cautions and pointed out in memos that were plastered up everywhere all around the plant. Still, every so often a complaint would get to me about safety violations out on the floor—especially, it seemed, from various observers who wished to remain anonymous.

I knew that sooner or later I was going to have to meet that monster head-on. I was afraid to wait much longer because of the information that was constantly coming to us about violations and accidents that had already happened at other plants. Those accidents could very well have happened at the Corvette plant, too. The equipment and the processes that were being used in those other plants were the very same as the ones that we were using. I was determined not to wait until something disastrous happened because of pure carelessness as well as accidentally on the part of any of the workers.

We had such a problem with theft of the 40th Anniversary Edition of badges and the matching discs for the wheel covers that special guards had to be used to prevent it. We were decisive about prosecuting thieves and even the accomplices were let go from the plant immediately whenever we had definite proof of their activities or their guilt.

The 40th Anniversary was not any more difficult for us at the assembly plant than any other Corvette, even though it had been said in many different places that it was. We were building more convertibles with the 40th Anniversary model than ever before. Many people thought this was because the convertible had a ruby red cloth top to match the body of the car. The ruby red leather seats with an embroidered logo that matched the car were new, and the 40th Anniversary badging on the sides of the car was special, too. Such color matching and special badging was, indeed, a first: a beautiful new innovation that had proven itself in a short amount of time.

There could be no doubt that this edition of the C4 Corvette was more than just popular. No matter what anyone said, the orders that were coming in steadily to the plant made us know that this was different. As time went on and we neared the end of the manufacturing run, we had to ultimately speed up the assembly line. The marketing people had to know the score too, and before we even thought about starting up the real work for the 1994, they had made the effects of their ad campaigns felt. They touted the exciting points about the keyless entry on the 40th anniversary model and the matching ruby red seats with the logo embroidered on the headrest as "brave" and "bold" innovations for the upcoming model year.

Before I was at the plant very long, Dan Gale called my office to invite me to come over to the Corvette Museum. In 1993, it was not yet the Museum that it is today. It was just then in the final planning stages. At that time it was located in Tower Place, a strip mall along Scottsville Road, and some of the items that were intended for use in the museum could be viewed in a larger area down the street in Greenwood Mall. I understood that after much wrangling, land had been secured to build the museum just across the street from the plant in a hay field along the freeway.

Dan was a true visionary who pitched the idea of the museum to anyone who would listen. He carried his ideas to Detroit to General Motors headquarters and to any corporation that he might get to come on as a corporate sponsor. I promised to do everything that I possibly could to help to bring the idea of the museum to fruition, from lending cars for exhibits, to letting spare parts and whole engines be used, to helping him bring in innovative cars on loan for exhibits. He was right: people might initially come to Bowling Green to visit other attractions as well as the Corvette plant, however, the museum would, indeed, serve to complete the overall attraction. There was no tourist attraction anywhere else to compete with the grand scale he had planned—nothing in the category to compete with a Corvette-themed museum to be found anywhere at all in the area around the city of Bowling Green, in Warren County, in the state of Kentucky or in any of the surrounding states either for that matter.

I was more than happy to participate in the ground-breaking ceremony for the museum on July 4, 1993. True, the site was a barren field in the middle of nowhere at the time, but Dan had convinced us all that the hay field in which we were standing quite near Interstate 65 would someday house a museum to show the history and progress of the car that we all loved.

Some evenings after work and on the week-ends when I did not fly back to Kansas City, Sam and I drove around Bowling Green and we located areas where Liz and I might find a house that we could purchase. At that time, there were few houses for sale of the caliber of the one in which we were living in Kansas City. Sam suggested that maybe I should buy a house with land around it to possibly compensate for the size of my house in Kansas City. He also told me that there were one or two people in the Bowling Green area whose hobbies seemed to be buying houses, fixing them up then re-selling them. We were hoping to find one of those houses that might be for sale at that time.

I had Liz to come down to Bowling Green so that we could look for a house in April. We knew that we did not want a big house, especially since the kids would not be living at home anymore, but we were afraid that taxes would absolutely chew us up if we did not find something that would cost the same or more than the house in Kansas City. Real estate agent Dot Fly took us all over Bowling Green and around Warren County to look for such a house.

Finally, we found a house out in Warren County built by a builder who had put a fence around the land and a gate across the blacktopped road that led to the house. It was owned at that time by Joe Campbell, who, as it happened, owned the Chevrolet dealership in town. We were surprised to find a tennis court and a swimming pool on the property. There was a barn and Neva Campbell, Joe's wife, owned a herd of cattle that grazed on the range around the fenced-in land. It seemed very much like the set-up that Sam and I had discussed on our house-hunting excursions around Warren County.

Joe and Neva were willing to sell us the house because Neva said that she was anxious to move back inside the city limits, so Liz and I promptly bought the place that same week-end. Liz seemed very happy that we would have space around the house and grounds with no one living anywhere close to us at all. So was I, but I had something else in mind. Neva and Joe had given me the idea that since I had the pasture space I might really enjoy giving cattle-raising a try. I had grown up a city boy and I knew absolutely nothing at all about having a real working farm so I began to think that it might be an enjoyable and profitable thing to do since the place was already set up with a cattle feeder, two electric water dispensers in the back fields, and a fairly large pond in the front pasture. There was a very nice barn on the property, too.

Liz had lived on a farm when she was young and many of her relatives in Mississippi were still predominately farming people although the majority of them lived in town and worked at other jobs while still working the land on the ancestral farms left to them by their parents and their families. Liz had grown up around animals and she told me that caring for them was not nearly as easy as it seemed to be offhand. It was smelly, dirty work, she declared. There was more than a little risk involved and she said that she was not at all enthusiastic about having farm animals around ever again in her lifetime. I assured her that I would do all of the work myself and she would never have to come into contact at all at any time with any of the cows. Liz shot me a quick, slanted look from the corners of her eyes that she thought I did not see. But I caught that look and I laughed at my wife because I was well aware of the skepticism that she was feeling.

"I'm gonna' show you," I promised. "Just you wait and see."

Almost a week after Liz got back to Kansas City, she called to tell me that Amos had already found a buyer for our house. She said that Amos had brought a man by that afternoon as soon as she got in from school. The buyer was a doctor from India, an American citizen now, and Liz said that he seemed to be a nice man and very, very much interested in everything about the house.

"He absolutely loves this place," Liz told me. She laughed. "He couldn't stop raving about the chandelier in the hall and the black guest bathroom. Amos says that he would buy this house tomorrow if he could."

"The hell he can!" I exploded. "I won't even consider it. I know you haven't forgotten what happened to us in Atlanta, have you?"

"How could I ever forget that?" Liz laughed merrily as if she **had** forgotten. "We were pushed out of our house way too soon because we didn't know any better. Plus we were building another house. It was an ordeal, but I can laugh about it now."

"Well, I ***can't*** laugh about it," I said grumpily. "I'll never do that to my family again!" I had made that vow and I really meant to keep it. I went on:

"I hate to tell the doctor but he'll just have to wait until we move out of the house. He could have a load of cash in a briefcase to bribe me; I still wouldn't consider it."

"I would!" Liz said still laughing at my grumpiness. I knew better because that had been one of the roughest things that we had ever gone through in our lives.

On a long week-end I decided that I would drive up to Kansas City from Bowling Green. I only wanted to try it out because I knew that Liz and I would eventually have to drive both cars down to Bowling Green in May. I left Bowling Green early in the morning and I found that I was still in pretty good shape when I finally made it to Kansas City that afternoon.

"Neither one of us is 20 years old anymore," Liz said. "But, I don't think it will be all that bad."

After I had only two days' rest, I started the trip back early on Sunday morning just to see how I would feel after a long round trip like that. Actually, that short turn-around wasn't so bad after all.

The next time I flew to Kansas City it was on a one-way ticket because I intended to drive my 1992 Quasar Blue Metallic Corvette back to Bowling Green so that I could trade it in for the 40th Anniversary model that I had been driving as my company car and now I was intending to buy it.

As soon as Liz picked me up from the airport, I found that a couple of things had happened:

Skip and Jerrien Hill who were the parents of Nate, David's friend and fellow school mate, had agreed to let David stay for the summer in their empty basement bedroom so that David would be able to participate with Nate in AAU field and track that summer before the two of them went on to the University of Kansas. David was always at the Hill's house anyway if Nate was not at ours.

We quickly agreed that we would allow David to move one of the twin beds out of his room and into the Hills' empty basement bedroom for his use. We were happy to pay Skip each month for room and board for David. Skip staunchly refused at first but we finally persuaded him to take the money. We were happy to have a handle on the problem of what to do with David during the summer track season before he was ready to enter the University of Kansas. We were overjoyed that Skip and Jerrien solved that problem for us and for David.

Our next big resolution was Crissy. She called us the next day after I was in Kansas City on that week-end in April. She wanted to come home. We were pretty sure that Crissy, no matter how much she claimed that she wanted independence, was not willing to be left alone in Kansas City without her family nearby—near enough to use as a fallback resource. Of course Liz felt strongly that we should allow Crissy to return home. After all, Liz argued, we had not been ready for Crissy to go out on her own when she had made that decision to go. Now that Crissy had her taste of emancipation, I figured that she had found being responsible for herself was not as easy as her friends had convinced her it would be. Before I left that week end, Crissy had re-installed herself into her old bedroom upstairs and was planning to move down to Bowling Green with us.

The return drive to Bowling Green in the Corvette seemed like a much shorter trip for me. I do not think I drove inside the speed limit at all on the open freeway (though I should not admit that now) and I felt much more accustomed to the drive. During the trip, I worked on making myself even more familiar with the best locations to make rest stops so that I could know this whenever I was ready to move the family from Kansas City to Bowling Green.

Soon enough, school was out for the summer and it was time to move my family to Bowling Green.

True to his word, the doctor purchased our house in Kansas City for exactly the price that we were asking. We could not have asked for better timing. It was the first time that we had ever completed a deal and sold our house just before we moved out of it. We were ecstatic about that. However, Liz and I really hated to leave Kansas City. We had to admit, everything about our sojourn in Kansas had been wonderful. We resolved to visit and re-connect with our relatives in Kansas City as soon as we possibly could.

We could not believe that our familiar moving man was back again when the Stevens moving vans pulled up to pack our furniture for the move. We were more than happy to see him again. Now, he was the manager and the three other movers worked for him. He told us that back at the office in Flint, when he saw our name to be packed and up moved so soon again, he was really surprised. He said that he came with his crew just to see what city we were about to move to next. He was carrying a little bit more weight and his wavy red hair was low cut now and his thick sideburns weren't bushy and red anymore but his sense of humor was still the same. He claimed that he had just let our old washing machine go last year and replaced it with a newer model. By now this was an inside joke between us and we knew better but we all enjoyed the good-natured fun of it just the same.

Since the University of Kansas preferred that the athletes not have a car during their freshman year on the campus, David and Crissy drove the old, blue Oldsmobile down to Bowling Green. Liz and I drove the suburban. We stayed the night in the Executive Inn and got up early the next morning and went to our new house to wait for the movers.

All of our movers declared that they liked the new house in Bowling Green much better than they liked the elaborate, modern glass and stone of the house that we left in Kansas City. Liz laughingly chided them and said that it was because the Bowling Green house was all on one floor and they did not have to lug furniture up and down from three floors as they had to do in the house in Kansas City. They laughed too, and admitted that this was true.

Just as soon as the furniture was installed into the house and Liz had gotten it all straightened around just the way she wanted, she began going to job interviews. She had set up interviews for herself ahead of time as she always did when we moved from one city to another. Liz was scheduled to go to the Board of Education of the public schools of Warren County, Bowling Green City Schools and to Western Kentucky University. Warren County immediately found a place for Liz to teach English and French at Drakes Creek Junior High School. Bowling Green City Schools seemed not to need English teachers, and the university was much slower to respond. By the time they came back to Liz with an offer, she had already signed a contract with Warren County. Liz truly wanted to work with the university students but she was steadfast that she would not try to back out of the contract that she had already made, even though Warren County might have given her a release from the contract that she had signed. She told me that teachers always needed to have the integrity to stay with any contract that they had already signed. I fully understood her point of view.

Crissy went looking for a job at the fast food restaurants in town. It wasn't long before she was hired at Wendy's. She promised us that she would enroll at the junior college as soon as the classes got started that she needed. She also promised faithfully that she would go to classes this time without fail.

Before long David took a flight back to Kansas City to get ready for the summer track season. He said that his schedule for the AAU track season was already set. Soon after he had gotten back, he sent us a packet containing an article from the Kansas City Star newspaper showing where he and Nate had participated in the All Star Dream Classic, a football game between the best high school varsity players among graduating seniors from Kansas City, Kansas against Kansas City, Missouri's best graduating senior players. The game had been held at the Kansas City Chief's Arrowhead Stadium. David said that it had been arranged to give the seniors in and around both Kansas City, Kansas and Kansas City, Missouri a chance to play again before they headed off to college.

The caption under the picture from the newspaper gave David's name and said that he was picking up a fumbled football but neither his number nor his face was visible in the picture. That was the only thing that he had gotten to do in the entire game, he told us. A newspaper photographer just happened to take a picture of his one play and it had been used in a Missouri newspaper. He said that the picture had been taken just before he had been tackled by a guy who had to weigh at least 500 pounds compared to David's slight 150 pounds!

Luckily the photographer hadn't caught anything else, David claimed, because the guy who had tackled him had been so fast that it had been unreal and David had been absolutely flattened like a pancake by the guy's tackle.

There were just too many players on both sides of the field, David said, and they all had been promised at least one turn on the field and that had been his one and only turn. David complained in the letter that the much bigger and much tougher Missouri players had routed the Kansas guys by a score of 17 to 2. It was a good thing, he said, that his full scholarship at the university was for track and field. Now, he would never have to worry about getting monster-tackled like that ever again. Liz and I laughed about that for weeks.

We were able to attend the 1993 ICCC convention in July without having to make a long drive to get to the city where it was being held. The Untouchables of Huntsville, Alabama put on a spectacular convention and we were overjoyed to be able to make the trip in less than two hours. Both Liz and I were glad that we were not too tired from the drive and we could enjoy touring the areas of the

Redstone arsenal that allowed visitors to go into it. Also, we were able to attend to the Untouchables' opening gala that night. During the week we were able to participate in the races, attend the picnic, enjoy hanging out, dancing, and playing bid whist practically all night on one evening that week with of our fellow Corvette enthusiasts.

James Lundy of Huntsville and the rest of my friends in the ICCC were overjoyed that I was now the plant manager of the Corvette plant. They all knew that it was a dream come true for me and they celebrated my victory as if it was their own. Many of them promised that they would regularly make special trips to Bowling Green to visit at the Corvette plant. They have since kept that promise.

Lundy, Elex Withers, John White, Phil Gatson, Emory Anderson and a few others who were the dyed-in-the-wool racers sat down to talk about racing one evening during the convention like we always did. I was saying that I would like to have a race car built to fit me since I had looked and looked and could never find one to really accommodate my size. I still had in my garage the excellent racing engine hand built by Lamar Walden just ready to be put into a race car that it would fit. Elex said that he could talk to a guy named Brent Eubanks who had built his race car. Eubanks had a shop located in Huntingdon, Tennessee down Interstate 40 between Nashville and Memphis. Lundy volunteered to go with me to Eubank's shop to talk to him about building a rail race car that would be fitted out just for me.

Thus, we began a year during which Lundy drove from Huntsville up to my house every other week-end then we made the trip from Bowling Green down to Nashville to Huntingdon, Tennessee to Brent Eubanks' shop—a trip of some 100 miles there, then 100 miles back. We kept that up faithfully until Brent finally set up my specially fitted rail race car.

Lundy celebrated with me when I eventually got the car after months and months of dealing first with Brent, then another builder, then with another company to finish the car up in Memphis. Clay's body shop, painters and re-finishers, of Russellville, Kentucky painted the car for me. I have to admit Bob's Body Shop in Louisville did a spectacular job of selecting the colors for the car, painting my name on it and painting a replica of the Corvette motif on the sides of the car.

In the end, Lundy and I racked up many, many miles trying to get the car done. John White from Memphis convinced me to buy a decent truck and trailer to haul the car to events after John found out the hard way that the old truck that I had bought would never do. He drove the truck from Memphis hauling the race car and it was a real ordeal for him handling the old truck. After that, I got a brand-new, heavy duty Chevrolet truck with dual tires on the back that was capable of hauling heavy loads like the trailer. I had years of excitement and fun hauling that car around and racing at the convention and at other events as well. Later, I was proud to have my car on display for some time in the front window of the National Corvette Museum.

We went into the manufacture of the 1994 Corvette during the fall of 1993 and problems with the exterior of the C4 would still occasionally crop up. Fits were the big item that definitely needed work: exterior fits like fender fits, door fits, hood fits, and bumper fascia were enough to keep the repairmen constantly busy. In some cases poor fits were not really noticeable to the naked eye of the casual observer, but to the true Corvette aficionado everything becomes noticeable sooner or later with the kind of cleaning and polishing that those experts are prone to practice.

The C4 "clamshell" type hood left very little room for chance. The headlights had to fit properly flush into the hood. The opening had to be uniform all around. It was such a problem that engineering had to get involved in really extensive re-fitting.

The gas door was problematic with the C4 and batches of them sometimes did not fit flush and had to be refitted or re-hung by the mechanics for the sake of precision. That would not seem to be such a big problem, but to the true Corvette aficionado who demanded that the gas door fit flush with the gap around it showing evenly all the way around, it was a problem.

When the passenger door of a unit was closed, those doors needed to have even gaps all the way around, too. This was a very big problem in more ways than one. There were just some aspects of the exterior of the car that simply had to be re-engineered to make the doors and other parts fit properly. Neither un-uniform gaps all around the door nor raised fits could be tolerated. Sometimes such things could not be left in the repairmen's hands. Door opening and closing efforts could be affected by door fit to the opening, glass fit to the door and the fit of the weather-strip above to the glass portion of the door. That was a real problem. We had made the interior of the Corvette air tight except for one vent in the rear tub. The problem was that if the door was slammed aggressively, there would be push back as the air was exhausted from the interior of the car. The only help that was ever proposed for this was indexing glass, that is, glass that did not close completely until after the door was closed. It was a good solution to the problem but it had to add more to the overall expense of the car.

Manufacturing capability needed to be such that the exterior appearance of the car would be sound. Re-design needed to be a part of the overall picture, too: if the way a design was laid out could not possibly pan out in reality, then re-design might be the only fix for the problem. Re-design was absolutely our last resort in the manufacturing cycle.

The interior of the car posed its own particular problems. The biggest headaches that the assemblers had were interior door panel fits and instrument panel fits. They had to simply do the best that they could to make the parts come together. Because General Motors did not want to spend mega bucks on a car that was, possibly, not going to be around for more than a year or so, the assemblers had to tweak this or that to get the best fit possible. I did my best to convince headquarters that it added value to the product to get the right parts from the right people all of the time. Finally, I got them to listen.

When I found that about the only place that I could get an increase in the overall operating budget without causing a howling fight with headquarters was in personnel, I used that tactic whenever I could and put more people into place. Then, we were able to use more hands to work on whatever needed the attention at that time to do our best to make the car better.

One of the maintenance guys who was about to retire wanted to get out of farming and he had heard from Bobby Thomas who also worked in maintenance at the plant that I wanted to get started with raising cows. Bobby, who owned a large herd of cattle himself, kept urging me to buy the cows and saying that I would soon see that raising cattle was easy and very rewarding. Thus, the two of them talked me into buying the guy's twelve head of cattle which consisted of nine breeding heifers, two steers, and a bull. They also convinced me to buy the retiree's farm tractor so that I could cut hay from the fields and stock it in the barn for the cow's winter food.

Liz did not hit the ceiling as I thought she would when the cattle were delivered to our pasture, but she was quick to remind me that her days of dealing with cattle were long ago past. I told her that this was my project and that she would not have to get involved at all, but I knew that Liz just did not believe me. As it was, the time would come in the future when I had to eat my words "without mayo."

Every day as soon as I sat down in my office before I walked out into the plant, the first thing that I did was to open my desk drawer and look again at the stack of notes that Barbara had reluctantly given me almost a year earlier. These notes pointed out more vividly the safety violations that were taking place on the line and especially in the overhead mechanical areas. By now I had really closely checked the credibility as well as the possible sources of these notes. I was not about to let anyone know that I was giving the information that much attention and consideration, even Barbara. I had absolutely no idea of the whistle blower's motivations, but I was inclined to believe that there was a very good reason for the great concern that was being shown here and it was not even that well-hidden. I knew in my heart that it was going to have to come to a head sooner or later.

I was aware that Russ McLean was going to visit the plant but I was not sure when. Together with Chevrolet engineer Dave Hill, Russ was going to try to lay the groundwork to install two very different systems at the plant, one for testing squeaks and rattles in the new cars and another for the purposes of quality control. Both systems were long overdue in my opinion. We needed to build in quality from the inside out and from the beginning to the very end of each and every product run. If we planned to accomplish this we needed new systems as well as new methods and new equipment.

The plant engineering department was going to have to carry the bulk of the work of re-tooling, rebuilding and re-installing. It was as simple as that. Our systems were by this time showing the age and stress factors that long and heavy use had put on them.

Our engineering department had to work with numerous outside contractors to get the bulk of our systems changed over to work more efficiently and more effectively but much of the work had to come from our in-plant workmen.

I was glad when Russ had finally convinced upper management to go ahead and install the groundwork for the new systems that we would need for building the new generation Corvette. I breathed a sigh of relief even if our future of building the C5 was not yet a done deal. We already had a fully functioning C5 planning team, but many of the people on the team had regular and necessary jobs that had to be attended to every day. I was working on a plan in my mind to change this just as soon as I could, even before be sure that we at least had a good chance of building the new car.

The way I saw it, we were going to have to see that our plant was producing cars that had quality built into every single unit well before we were told that the C5 was a done deal. What if we were producing only 12 cars an hour? If those were 12 quality cars that were going to customers who were going to be satisfied with them, then we were doing our jobs. Not only were we going to have to be an assembly plant, we were going to have to be a **quality** assembly plant. My job was going to have to be seeing to it that our plant became a **quality** assembly plant. We needed to bring man and machines together to see that we were building quality into every single unit, every single run. Then, I could feel that we could, logically, show that we were really ready to build the C5.

To that end, I resolved that we would continue to bring the general superintendent, every superintendent and department head together in a meeting to begin each day. We needed to know logically where they were and where we needed to go to get to the next level. Those meetings had long-ago proven to be very productive in many other assembly plants because everyone would know what everyone else was doing and what the next steps needed to be toward building a quality product that our Corvette customers would really want to own and drive.

The most difficult thing that I had to work on was to change the culture of the organization. During the next few months I set about working as hard as I could on that. I already knew from the standpoint that I was working with the old time Saint Louis union leadership that I was going to have a very, very "rough row to hoe." So, I followed my plan of watching and waiting, gathering information, keeping records and making sure I was involved on a daily basis with everything that was being done in the Corvette plant.

There were some workers who wanted nothing more than to do a good job wherever they had to do it and then to go home satisfied at the end of the day. Those people were by far the majority of the workers. There were those who cared deeply about the platform on which they were working, the people with whom they were working and the life that they were a part of. Others loved the product: they owned it, drove it and they very much wanted to see the product do well in the marketplace. There were those who kept to themselves, displayed obstinate and dysfunctional attitudes and seemed not to care if the whole organization was falling down around them just as long as no one within the organizational structure bothered them at all.

Then, there were the self-important, the hucksters. Those were the workers who were mere inches away from being modern-day outlaws. There were the union leaders who seemed to be people who were a world apart and saw themselves as living on the mountain top. Some of them were capable and intelligent people who put the needs of the union membership ahead of their own and worked diligently toward being the best stewards of the union's interest that they possibly could be. Others among the union's leadership cared only for their own interests, their hefty paychecks and their time spent on the job **not** doing the work—not building cars. They did anything but the business of General Motors and they spent all of their time at the union hall or rabble-rousing whenever they were in the plant. They wanted to be seen as important by the workers and by management while everyone concerned knew that rabble-rousing was their only occupations. They often represented very real and glaring weaknesses in the jobs that they (the union representatives) **should** have been doing for the workers and the self-aggrandizing jobs that they really were engaged in on a day-to-day basis. For better or worse, I set about exploiting any weakness that I found in the union organization as far as I could toward the business of getting cars built.

I wanted to know about any stress-related problems that the workers had with their own particular job that they were required to do every day. I wanted to know which jobs had far more "back-breaking" work connected to them than was normal. I especially intended to find the unfairness in the distribution of the jobs and what could be done to equally distribute the work. I knew the advantage of getting out on the assembly line and actually seeing what the workers were required to do on a day-to-day basis.

Because I was always out in the plant myself, I would often call the personnel in industrial engineering out to a job and get reports on how they could level out the work load among the workers long before the labor union got the chance to assess the "unfairness" issue at all. I held people accountable who were capable of doing something about the workloads even if it meant putting more personnel on the job. I did my own assessments, gathered my own intelligence and made my own judgments long before the union got around to filing a grievance for a worker's complaint about an unfair workload.

Oftentimes, I prodded my management group to take care of any items that might have caused a grievance long before the union representatives got around to working on it. As time went on, the personnel department found it rather difficult to convince the union representatives of our true intentions—we did not consider that we were co-opting the power of the union. The union tried hard to show that what we were doing was **not** making the handling of grievances more efficient. I disagreed, even the union members had to admit, that this was a great part of the job of management in the first place. Did we really need to have a union grievance filed to cause us to take care of our workers? No! We absolutely did not! There was not a lot that could be said about that.

We spent Christmas in Texas with my family and during that time I thought a great deal about the lack of camaraderie between my management staff not to mention my staff and the union workers. I knew that the workers organized parties among themselves. I wondered why the managers could not do the same. I decided that I would speak to Barbara and see if she could not organize the office workers and plan a party that would pull the entire staff together at Christmas for the next year.

It was in April, 1994 when all hell broke loose! I was walking down the final line when I was notified by one of the workers that there was a breakdown on the line. I was tempted to go over, but I decided that I would finish what I intended to do before I went over to the breakdown. After all, there were supervisors whose jobs were to take care of such things. They would report it to me later anyway. I was about to continue with what I had intended to do when my Number one "whistle blower" the sandy-haired repairman came looking for me.

"You need to go over there and take a look at the locks on that thing," he said and he promptly walked away.

Sure enough, when I made it to the breakdown, there were at least five repairmen working overhead. There were two upper level managers present and at least three supervisors watching from the floor. There were several workers in the break room already engaged in a card game during the work stoppage.

There was only one lock on the repair and at least five repairmen working.

I did not say a word to anyone. I stepped up a ways to see if the other four repairmen had locks in place anywhere.

It was easy for me to see that most of the repairmen were not wearing any kind of safety harness at all! Those would have been easy to spot because they should have been attached quite obviously with lines that reached down and were counterbalanced below. One of the repairmen that I could easily see was even crawling around on the pipes overhead without benefit of one piece of safety equipment!

It was obvious that every one of the repairmen scurrying about overhead had not bothered to strap on their harness and might not have even known the location of the necessary safety equipment. I looked at them for a moment and I became even more furious!

Still, I did not say a single word to any of the supervisors because I was not so sure what kind of scalding or profane words would have been likely to come out of my mouth at that point. I went back to my office and pulled out my notes and files and gave vent to my anger by slamming them down hard on my desk. I sent one of the clerks to call the personnel director to my office.

I soon entered into one of the lowest points of my entire career with General Motors.

First, there was my need to establish myself with everybody in the plant as a person of integrity. I needed to accept that everything that happened at that plant and under that roof was my responsibility. Obviously, I was more than willing to do that. I had all but killed myself to establish trust and integrity among the workers and management at the Bowling Green plant right from my very first day on the job!

Secondly, I had seen to it that every supervisor posted a chart of the problems that they were working on improving and checked them off when they had made those improvements for their workers. I had stressed over and over in the meetings to every supervisor that worker safety was of primary importance to everyone! I preached to them that they were to depend upon documentation, documentation, documentation to show unequivocally that they were following the rules. My staff and I had been talking daily about plant safety.

Thirdly, I had told the workers truthfully that I would go to the wall with my bosses to save every one of their jobs. Even in cases where retirement was an option, we would not push anybody out who still felt that they were capable of giving a good days work for their pay. If we worked a job down to the point that some people were not needed on that job, I favored moving workers into continuous improvement jobs or to jobs where they could be used in another way to benefit the corporation other than having them work forever on the line.

My reputation for fairness and square dealing had preceded me I knew. I encouraged doubters to check my record at other plants and to make it known to others under my command that I was a straight shooter. I was known for being on the front lines and out front every place that I had been. So, this was nothing new to anyone at that plant!

But, here I was about to allow my personnel people to "blow the whistle," "drop the dime," and "lower the boom" on my workers, repairmen and supervisors on the strength of records that had been collected on them—all of it without their knowledge. It was not underhanded at all—they had been warned in the past and warned by me numerous on top of numerous times in just the time I had been plant manager! They were all so very guilty that it made my teeth hurt and my head ache as if a stake had been driven into it just to think about the blatant and dangerous violations that these workers and supervisors had just done!

When I accepted what had to be done, I could not sleep at night. It was as if I had gone back to the dark days of the Vietnam war. This was all my nightmares come back to me in spades. I was really hoping against hope that it would not come to this crucial point so soon and in this manner. I had hoped that with the constant demands and warnings the worst offenders would change their ways before these blatant violations had to be brought to such a boiling head.

It was not as if the personnel and plant safety people hadn't issued warnings and handed out mandate after mandate. They had been begging, cajoling, posting, and hammering up warnings on the walls almost from the day that General Motors Bowling Green Assembly Plant had been opened. Personnel meant what they had preached and posted for so very long: plant safety was job **one** for everybody!

I backed their play over 100 percent! I had stated many, many times in all of our meetings:

"It is absolutely mandatory for all of us to follow the GM/UAW health and safety rules and practices at **all** times! There are to be no deviations and no shortcuts: each one of us **must** follow procedures just exactly as they are written. These have also been spoken and given out to all, over and over again for years and years!"

Yet and still, even after everyone had been told over and over, called in and warned, threatened with firing, they **still** would not take the time to comply on the most basic and important points of the safety procedures!

Cheryl Ollila was now the second personnel director at the plant since I had become plant manager. Cheryl had come in to replace Terry Urich. So it fell to Cheryl and the rest of her personnel department to fire the gun. We did not know it at the time, but that shot was destined to be heard everywhere all over the corporation.

I asked Barbara to gather up all of the notes that she had filed away—especially the old files that she had never shown to me. Then, I took all of my own notes and observations and put them with the inch-thick files that personnel had been collecting over all these years in Bowling Green. Some of the files were nearly fifteen years old. These files had never seen the light of day before.

When our personnel department was ready, they let headquarters know what we were planning to do.

GM's personnel department at headquarters was on top of our actions 100 percent! The top union leaders in Detroit at the United Auto Workers headquarters were behind us, too. They were certainly all about safety! They did not want any UAW workers in any plant anywhere to be hurt, maimed or killed because any of the workers had failed to follow the safety rules. If management had not posted and re-posted, reviewed and re-reviewed those rules of safety, then the UAW would have had a roaring problem with us! As it was the UAW had a roaring problem with its own people!

We were given more help than we could ever have wanted. The head man at General Motors Department of Labor Relations told us: "when you have named the management personnel who are responsible both directly and indirectly, **fire them, now**!"

Those harsh, inflexible words really upset every one of us!

We had not figured that the corporation would be quite so harsh on the supervisors! After all, they had **not** had any of the workers under their supervision at the Bowling Green Assembly Plant to be maimed or killed—at least, not yet!

Our first major concern was with those whose job it was to supervise the union members who worked on the dangerous jobs overhead. We were concerned about workers who worked with moving parts and machines of any kind that could sever limbs; we were concerned about workers who worked in hazardous areas that used high voltage electricity that could easily cause death; and we were concerned about those workers who dealt with chemicals that could that could burn, scar or cause extreme health damages to individuals. The supervisors who were responsible for the workers on those jobs were guilty of negligence and the lack of due diligence in the performance of their jobs. As supervisors, their lack of strict enforcement of the rules made them guilty, guilty, more than guilty!

It was, indeed, the supervisors' jobs to see to it that each maintenance and repair worker locked off all power sources to the equipment before he started to work on it so that nobody could inadvertently turn it on or start it up while the repairmen still had his hands or any part of his body either on it or in it. And, too, supervisors should see that each repairman put his individual lock in place to completely lock off robot cells, or any equipment that might prove to be self-starting. The locks were designed to prevent anyone from taking their own individual lock off the equipment and inadvertently turning it back on while another repairman who had not locked it off was still in harm's way.

There had been workers within our assembly plants and in other assembly-type plants that used machinery who had lost limbs, been seriously hurt, fallen to their deaths and been killed by equipment that had started to run while they were still inside of it or working on it without using the proper safety precautions. Other accidents had happened because repairmen were not properly belted for safety when they were working overhead and they had been hurt or maimed when they had fallen into moving machinery, or fallen to the concrete floor from overhead because they had failed to connect up safety harness or they failed to properly obey the rules of safety that were meant to protect their lives.

Our facts were clear: we had too many regular violations and too many regular violators. We knew that it was just a matter of time. We were not about to wait until it was too late!

Now it fell to Cheryl and her staff to call each of the known offenders into the meeting room for interviews before the full report was sent to headquarters. I sat in each and every meeting to let it be known that I fully supported the position of the personnel department. It was more than disappointing to me when each of our fellow supervisors who were the first to be interviewed gave their confessions or, worse, rendered their excuses:

"Yeah, I knew that they didn't have all the locks in place but I just didn't want to take up valuable time getting everything set up," one confessed.

"They've done it a hundred times before just like that," another one said, "and nothing's happened. So I figure that nothing was ever going to happen."

"Nothing's ever happened at any time at this place," said another, "We're better than that. So why in hell do y'all want to bother with it at all?"

"When are you new people going to get off our backs and let us get our jobs done?" Another wanted to know.

"Y'all should know that those signs and stuff you guys put up don't change how the workers gotta' get the jobs done around here!" Another protested angrily.

The truth of the matter was that our Personnel Department had the evidence by the loads and we were prepared to send every bit of it to the personnel office at headquarters. The trigger had been pulled, the gun fired, and the bullets had found their marks.

Our fellow members of management at the Corvette plant were furious at us. They had confessed to their sins, they had not tried to refute the evidence and they had set themselves up to suffer our punishment, perhaps, whatever that entailed, but they considered that we were "selling them out" by reporting their negligence to Headquarters!

"Fire them! Make an example of them for every other workplace!" the head of personnel at headquarters kept screaming at us. "Get rid of them! We do not need managers on our payrolls who won't direct their people to follow orders even when the orders have been written and re-written—when they are as plain as day and that **specific**! Any fool on earth should know that their job is to make their people understand and follow the rules!"

I went home every night bearing that boulder squarely upon my shoulders like the doomed character in Greek mythology I had read about in high school literature class. I did not want to have to be responsible for any harsh disciplinary measures like that. I certainly did not want to ruin the career of anyone. The whole thing was purely wreaking havoc on my nerves. But what else could I do? The die was cast.

Liz noticed my inability to sleep and tried to help me whenever she could. She went to the drugstore and asked the druggist for the strongest pain medicine that she could possibly get without a prescription for me. My jaw teeth had begun to ache as if there were alien devils jamming their pitchforks into my gums. Liz strongly advised me not to have the teeth extracted though I could see no other solution for the intense pain that I was suffering.

Liz tried her best to help me when the debilitating, stress-related headaches made me nearly blind in one eye. Many nights she sat up with me drinking coffee and talking. I had to wonder if she had a hard time staying awake at work the next day herself.

"You'll be sorry later if you get your teeth extracted," Liz warned me over and over. "That pain has got to be related to your nerves. Maybe your teeth will stop aching when this big mess at the plant is finally over."

As it was, Liz was quite correct: when my extreme stress abated so did the extreme toothaches and headaches.

Those who were proven to be guilty were even more stressed out than Cheryl and I were. They knew now that HQ was involved and that their careers were on the line. The members of our management team who were involved quickly turned their backs whenever I walked out into the plant and came anywhere near them. Or, they would sit sullen and silent in production meetings. The other managers did what they could to help. They came forward to support us when their guilty colleagues were openly rebellious. Many of them were aware that the problems were stemming from job levels above theirs, but they did not care—they wanted only to do their jobs and to do them well. They let us know that we had their support when we spoke to them because they surely knew that we were right. They managed to show their support and they gave us support when and where it really counted: they were more than diligent at their own work.

Some of those on our management team who had been called on the carpet began to say that we favored the union above our own fellow managers. They claimed that they were stabbed straight in their backs by our underhanded methods. However, after we began to interview the guilty union members, that talk seemed to die quickly away.

The union workers who had been found to be guilty of safety violations knew right away that they were all alone in their individual plights. They knew that the national and local unions backed us up 100 percent. The national labor union had made iron-clad safety agreements with management long ago. The local members were required to know what was in their national agreement: personal safety was everybody's job. They were responsible for their own personal safety, so who could they blame except themselves? They had been made aware of the rules long ago. We had warned them over and over but they had become far too careless and too accustomed to violating those rules.

Since the power of the UAW even at the local level was not behind any of the violators, many individuals felt isolated and betrayed. Some openly threatened us with retaliatory measures. I became really angry when certain individuals made physical threats toward Cheryl or toward my family. I let them know in no uncertain terms that all of our family members were strictly off limits. As an individual, I could take care of myself and so could the others but I was not going to have any of our family members who had absolutely nothing to do with anything that happened at the Corvette plant to be caught off guard, innocent and unaware while they went about their daily lives.

Many of the maintenance workers and repairmen who had to be disciplined refused to work at all, or they slowed down in a manner designed to put the worse hurt on us. But there were others, including my whistleblower who had tried to follow the right course from the very first. If anything he and his colleagues worked longer hours and took on double the work with harder tasks to make up for the missed work that the retaliatory group left behind. I cornered him one day in the repair yard and I let him know just how much I appreciated his hard work. I was very concerned for his safety. He assured me that he had been a Marine who was well-schooled and well trained in self-defense and he would be able to take care of himself if the need ever arose.

It was upon the advice of the UAW chairman of the shop committee, Eldon Renaud, that I first became acquainted with the legendary sheriff in Warren County, Sheriff "Peanuts" Gains. Sheriff Gaines was a reticent man when it came to his job. He did not have much to say when he found out about the predicaments of Cheryl and me and of our immediate staff, but he let us know immediately that he would never tolerate any threats to any of our family members. He took the lead role in working with the Warren County and Bowling Green city police departments to protect all of them. While he did not apprise us of his methods, he was true to his word. After I found some of the lights on my property broken, I would sometimes see a sheriff's cruiser or a city police car parked in a turnaround or on a slope near the house when we left or came in at night. There were the unmarked cars, too. I do not know if any of the threats were ever acted upon other than having garbage dumped on lawns, lights broken or if any attempt was ever made toward anyone else on the personnel staff, but I do know that all of our families did receive police protection for quite a while.

Neither the members of management nor the union workers who were involved had any idea even to this very day how hard I had to fight headquarters in order to keep all of my people in place. I was on the telephone for hours on end each and every day in an attempt to talk through our situation with my immediate superiors and solicit their help to deal with the real fire-breathers in personnel up in Detroit at Headquarters. I finally had to agree to harsh disciplines for all of my management people—for those who had violated the rules themselves and for those who had condoned the unsafe actions of their workers in more than one case. I finally agreed to some fines and to send the violators home for two weeks without pay.

We were told later that some union workers made the trip up to Detroit to plead their cases before their National Labor Union. Their pleas were summarily rejected just as we knew that they would be. Their union was dead-set against them. The complainants very likely learned in Detroit that I was the one who had already pleaded their cases down to either fines and/or suspensions without pay. If I had not done that, many of Bowling Green's workers and the members of management would have been fired right there on the spot. GM's upper level personnel department was looking for a good, clear-cut case like ours with good, solid evidence such as that which we had gathered on which to hang their hats when they were dealing with the other assembly plants in other cities where safety rules violators became an issue.

Even with the concessions that we had convinced corporate headquarters to make, we still became pariahs in the Bowling Green plant with many of the violators viciously hating our guts. But we were the ideals, the shining example, and "poster children" up at headquarters. We soon became the model for the entire corporation.

In spite of all of the upheaval and mental suffering that "The Case" had caused to me, to Cheryl, and to the rest of the personnel staff, I was gratified that we had made such an impact before there was a single accident where any worker in the Corvette plant was hurt, maimed, or killed because of their own gross negligence.

We began systematically to work with personnel in small group meetings basically to settle things down and to try to get more co-operation from the workforce aimed at improving attitudes. We tried to make sure that the groups did not contain too many radical thinkers in any single group or any of the disciplined repairmen or their UAW sympathizers. Our purpose, we stressed over and over, was to get our workforce to work together to make our plant an example of co-operation between the hourly workers and management. We were convinced that this was the only way that we were going to make sure that HQ brought a new product into the plant. We found that some of the workers would turn their backs to the speaker in any group if workforce versatility or any other of our ideas were mentioned but, overall, most of the workers were co-operative and listened attentively.

If we found that there was someone or a group who did not want to talk in the meetings, we would not single them out, but we would always try to seek them out where they worked and try to get them to talk about anything that might be of concern to them. Thus we began to organize what we later called diagonal slice meetings. We hoped that we accomplished more in the meetings than just to afford the workers gripe session opportunities. We wanted to make sure that everyone felt that his or her opinions were important. We made sure that Jane Bolin who edited the in-house newspaper, *The Vette Gazette*, published the problems that were brought up in the diagonal slice meetings, and then gave perfect examples of the methods we planned to use to deal with them.

Jeff Gordon came to lend his considerable star power to help the UAW and GM joint venture to create excitement for the new 1996 car that was to be raffled off at the NASCAR Sprint Cup series that September. I introduced the visitors to the plant from UAW headquarters and GM headquarters in Detroit. I also introduced Jeff for a short speech to the visitors before he received several golf shirts and other gifts from us all. He signed the Sebring Silver Metallic coupe that would be given away and inspected the badging and decals that had been attached to the car in the body shop. We crowded out into the yard and Jeff got into the car and made a few passes and did a few harmless doughnuts to delight the crowd.

Liz and I attended the race as guests of the UAW/GM joint venture. We got a tour of the newly renovated Charlotte Motor Speedway in Concorde, North Carolina just outside of Charlotte. We were told that there was an apartment building along one of the turns and we thought it would be pretty good for an avid race fan to be able to sit on the balcony and see any of the races whenever they felt like it. We saw Jeff score enough points to be the Sprint Cup winner to end the series. Although we weren't too sure, Liz and I thought we had a pretty good handle on how the points for the Sprint Cup were scored.

We witnessed the raffle and saw our Corvette given away to a screaming fan. I though the guy's wife would surely faint. Everybody seemed to wonder what would eventually be done with the car.

Russ McLean, true to his word, had gotten the track built according to test track specifications in the land out in back of the plant to test for squeaks and rattles. Along with the rumble road, a torque twist track, "in phase" track and "out phase" tracks were also installed. The track was very effective for detecting squeaks and rattles. Once detected, then "quiet room" diagnostics could be performed in the sound proofed rooms that we had set up in the plant. The "quiet rooms" were well insulated rooms where the car could be taken and diagnosed with a stethoscope called an "engine ear" that was capable of magnifying sound up to ten times more so that the human ear could easily hear it. Even the smallest clue of where there was a squeak or rattle could be detected by the engine ear. The normal areas that were worked on to prevent squeaks and rattles in the cars were top panels, instrument panels and interior trim areas. In these areas the touching and rubbing together of metal-to-metal and metal-to-plastic was likely to be the culprit. Many times we could take care of such things well ahead of time by putting in Velcro strips and chips before the car got to the final line.

We knew that we had made great strides in fitting, trimming and diagnosing for unwanted sounds when we were asked to receive visitors from other plants to review our system. Over 100 people came through our plant from other GM plants and we sat them down in small groups to discuss our methods with them.

I finally got Russ McLean and Dave Hill to give the body and paint shop some consideration. Bob Shell had told me over and over that he was tired of trying to do 21st Century work with an 1800's vintage body shop and even older tools and methods. He claimed that his newest tool was a hand paint sprayer. It was not really as bad as that but I knew that if we were going to be successful in making a push to build the C5 Corvette, we had to have an up-to-date body shop. Joe Spielman had already gotten approval to pay for the panel coating, which had made a 100% difference in the look of the paint on the body of the car, now we wanted him to get us the money to renovate both the paint and the body shops. We figured that the car magazines were giving us enough praise nowadays to warrant more consideration.

We needed to improve our processes and we could no longer afford to do it piecemeal. Previously, one of the businesses in the neighborhood next door to the shipping company had been burning loads of ash-filled trash and even that damaged the paint on the vehicles that were loaded on the carriers waiting to be shipped. We almost had to wrap each car individually in plastic to see that each one made it to the dealers without paint damage. Also, when cars were left in the yard outside, sometimes they were damaged by the weather. Extreme sun and heat could badly damage our paint. We sent painted panels to the southernmost coast of Florida to test the effect of continuous exposure to the sun's most direct rays on the paint. We hoped that every bit of research that we did helped us take the necessary steps to find a workable remedy and to pursue continuous improvement.

The paint shop was a big project of mine. We were able to install electronic robots in the paint shop to replace the hydraulic units and install paint measuring tools to provide more even coverage and improve our entire process. The Byk Gardener tool was a device used to "feel" surface imperfections and give a good measurement for the thickness of paint on our sample cars. Then, the DuPont representative had shown us that their new 2-step clear coat process offered greatly improved gloss retention and resistance to environmental damages such as acid rain, bug juice, tree sap, and bird droppings. In order for the coating to be effective, the paint had to be free of lint, dust particles, ash, crumbs, hair, and other air-borne floaters. Thus, the new, renovated paint shop needed to be installed with a totally dust and dirt free "Clean Room" before the new process could be useful at all. We started renovating the paint shop on weekends while all other processes were down. We were overjoyed to see the paint guys from DuPont in the plant almost every day to make sure that the new mechanical appliances that were used to apply their clear-coats were effectively installed.

When Liz's school got out for the summer she went to Holly Springs to visit her mother. Almost as soon as she left, Dr. James Becker, head of the department of teacher education at Western Kentucky University called to let Liz know that he was prepared to offer her a position in the education department at the university. He wanted her to come in the next day to meet with everyone in the department. I called Liz at her mother's house right away but, as usual, Liz had gone somewhere. I finally caught up with Liz at her sister's house in Memphis. After I had delivered the message to her, Liz said the she would start for home as soon as she could get her bags packed.

Walter called me back while she was packing and told me that he was not happy that Liz would be driving alone so late in the evening so his daughter had volunteered to ride along with her. I was really glad that both he and his daughter, who was named for her Aunt Liz and called, "Little Libby" were so thoughtful.

Liz went to the interview the next day and was hired as an instructor in the education department at Western Kentucky University. She certainly seemed to be happy that she would now be teaching college students—grown-ups. I could only hope that she was satisfied with the decision that she had made.

On September 2, 1994 after all the years of fund-raising, gathering up artifacts, putting together exhibits and sweating blood since late in 1988, Dan Gale and The National Corvette Museum Foundation held it's ribbon-cutting ceremony for the initial building of the National Corvette Museum.

I admit, the towering round structure with its skin of bright yellow was not much to look at when it first went up—not at first. Then, the spire of red had gone on top of it to point toward the sky. As the building and the grounds around it were prepared, the dream became much more down-to-earth reality. I was told that some of the workers at the GM plant had contributed to the museum during the earlier stages of its inception by making payroll deductions toward lifetime membership. I paid the membership for myself and Liz during my first years as manager of the Corvette plant. Since my Lifetime Member number is 509, I was gratified to believe that 508 people had already become lifetime members before I did.

We watched the structure as it went up over the months and I must say that it was rather impressive right from the beginning. I had already seen the artist's drawings of it. Everyone agreed that the architects who had designed the building had done a super job. The overall design was conceived to mimic sweeping speed and the tail lights of an earlier Corvette design. It won architectural awards for the innovative concept. The design was given press time on the pages of several architectural magazines. Everyone in town, especially the banks, wanted something to do with it the museum these days.

On the opening day for the museum, it was hard not to get caught up in the excitement of it all. The museum looked absolutely perfect, and the September weather was perfect for all of the festivities. The mayor of the city and the county executives came out to speak to the crowds, the national president of the UAW came, and I came across the street to speak for the Corvette plant and all of the workers.

The dream of Dan Gale and all of his supporters had finally come true. It was a banner day for everyone on the board, the workers at the museum and for all of the workers at the plant. We had held meeting after meeting to get everyone ready for the day. We planned to offer constant tours through the Corvette plant for those people who came in early for the ribbon cutting ceremony. Literally thousands of Corvette owners packed the freeway and backed the traffic up for miles and miles on either side of Interstate 65 and on the off-ramps leading to the museum. We used signs to direct them to park on the grounds of the plant and hired busses to transport them over to the museum. It worked so well that we decided that it might work for the next big event, too. We concluded that the museum and the plant needed to form a partnership to make that happen.

Finally, all the hard work for the museum had paid off. I was happy for Dan and his supporters and happy for my own situation at work, too. I felt that many of the nay-sayers and the older, more calloused union die-hards may have been moved to a more softened position about working more closely with management now that we had done the work to put them more out front for the scores of museum visitors who came across from the museum to the Corvette plant to watch them work. Many of the workers had some experience with meeting and talking to visitors, but they had never been put on display in quite the way we conspired to show them off. They simply had to get used to it and many of them really seemed to bask in it.

We had been stressing so much to the plant workers that they needed to keep their areas clean. They needed to help the sanitation people to do the jobs. There had been occasional lapses, but now with so many more museum visitors out and about in the plant, many of our workers had seen fit to spruce their work areas without having to be asked to do it. I was hoping that this was only the beginning.

By that time, my rookie luster as the Corvette plant manager had almost completely worn off. As I had hoped from the beginning, I was now being seen by the Corvette community as well as the Bowling Green business community as someone who knew how to handle the workers, the plant, and my role in the community as a business leader. I was invited to be a member of the board of one of the banks in town and to work on the board of Greenview Hospital. I was receiving invitations to participate in the business of the city and I also got requests to visit many venues in many different places outside of the city as well.

That fall, Mike and Laurie Yager invited me to be their guest at their Corvette Parts and Accessories "Funfest" in Effingham, Illinois. I wanted very much to attend but, in truth, I was not confident enough to leave my floundering organization to operate on its own even for a week-end. We had too much going on with classes and trainings that we were trying out during the week-ends. I really felt that I needed to be present in case any hole needed to be plugged or any fire needed to be put out. I was so involved in everything that happened at the plant every day at that point that I felt that I really needed to be there to see that everything was going as it should.

One of the things that had purely given our assemblers on the line headaches in fitting prior to 1994 was the rear window in the soft tops of the convertibles. On all previous models, the window had always been plastic. There had been more than a few complaints about it over the years. The plastic tended to become cloudy depending upon the suppliers or, ultimately, the owner's location. It tended to get creases and folds depending on the length of time it was stored in the "down" position and retain those creases long after the soft top was raised. There had been numerous complaints about that. But now, the designers in Detroit had decided to try a new glass rear window for the convertibles with a built-in defogger grid. We were scheduled to put it on the 1994 convertible tops. We soon found that the tops made little if any difference to our installers. While there was no problem in that regard, we found that the windows sometimes prevented the cloth top from folding down quite as smoothly as everyone was previously accustomed to. Finally, we concluded that the rewards were much greater than any drawbacks.

Some of the painters had been constantly complaining about the new 1994 Copper Metallic color. They simply could not get perfectly matching paint on all of the panels. Often panels simply could not be matched no matter what the painters did. As soon as the copper cars were assembled and were taken out in the sun, the differences in the painted panels became clearly obvious. Changing and swapping panels did not always work, constant re-painting was too time-consuming, never a sure thing, and thus, far too costly. We finally had to cease using the Copper Metallic color. All of the Copper Metallic Corvettes that were painted and shipped out were snapped up as quickly as they hit the dealers' floors. The color became a collector's item. The knowledgeable customers wanted it because of the difficulty to produce it and because no more were scheduled to be produced. The Copper Metallic Corvette became a rarity even before the last one left the plant.

Another color that we were told to delete from the next year paint roster for the Corvette was the Black Rose Metallic. It had never been a popular color for the car and I do not think that it was ever meant to replace regular black by any stretch of the imagination. The color had been somewhat of a success on larger Cadillac sedans, but that did not mean that our sports car owners would accept that color on their cars. By far, they did not.

I was happy that the plant had ***not*** been asked to place the decals on the twenty-five or so convertibles that were to be used for the inaugural "Brickyard 400" race at Indianapolis. The work was done by a Detroit-based company who moved their operations to Bowling Green into a building that they leased in order to handle the business of putting the decals on our cars and other business that came their way. We were only too glad to have the car hauling business next door to transport the cars over to the new decal and detailing operation. The car haulers would simply wait until the decal assembling was done, and then they put the cars back on the trucks to resume their trip up to Indianapolis.

When I had first started work at General Mills back in the '60s, I learned the value of having a well-organized and well-run quality department. I oversaw the reorganization of each quality department in each plant that I had worked in since then according to what I had learned in my engineering classes. I was still new to the industry back in those days, and I was still wet behind the ears. In 1993, when I came to the Corvette plant, I was no longer inexperienced and I saw the value of re-working and re-setting a whole new quality department.

At that time, I could not see how everybody was responsible for quality when no one department was really responsible for it. The quality people could not logically make reports against the departments to which they themselves belonged or held allegiance to. That just did not work. A quality person had to be independent, and therefore make reports straight to the plant manager or some member of the plant manager's staff.

Cliff Mitchell had been made responsible for quality well before I came to the plant, but he was a member of management and also a plant liaison to headquarters. He was expected to attend to his headquarters duties as well as do the plant job. It was obvious to me that our quality control section had to become its own separate department headed by someone who was only responsible for that duty in order to make quality control as effective as it needed to be.

I put Mitch Thomas in charge of quality control and gave him a staff. This department would report straight to the plant manager thus having no allegiance to any one department. Also the quality department was to be held responsible for training staff and making sure that quality was tracked through all departments. I wanted to make sure that the quality department stood alone in its mission, that it carried its own goals and responsibilities, and that it never became too empathetic to any other department. This type of quality control operation with its traditional methodology became much more effective in making sure that we were producing the kind of product that we were charged to produce at all times. If a department was not getting its job done and finished in station, then the quality department needed to make sure that the quality of the product was not compromised because of that, even if it meant that the line had to be stopped in order to get any particular problem handled.

Rod Michelson eventually took over as head of the department and he was instrumental in bringing other refinements to quality control. Under his leadership other plants studied our quality methods over several months and with the number of new refinements that we made, we became more and more confident of the effectiveness of our innovations as time passed.

One innovation that seemed to be effective was our use of "trainers" on the job to assist when help was needed with repairs or anything else in getting the vehicles off the line in a quality manner. These trainers were usually repairmen who were well-versed on many of the jobs to be done toward getting a good vehicle build. I needed to make sure that they were determined to do a good job. To me, the natural choices for those jobs were my dedicated, sandy-haired repairman and his fellows who had worked so hard to make sure the jobs were being done during our previous troubles with slowdowns during the worker safety crisis. These men tackled their new jobs with just as much passion and dedication as they had shown previously. I let them know that I was very proud of their work. I made sure that those workers were put on their own levels of compensation, too.

Right from the beginning of my tenure, I started to ram heads with the old-time union leaders. Our confrontations could sometimes get pretty heated in the confines of my office. I had said to members of the union and to members of management as well that if they were not confident enough in General Motors products to purchase and drive the cars and trucks then they should not be allowed to park their foreign-made vehicles close to the plant. "Billy Jack" Jackson, one of the top union leaders, declared that he and any other GM employee should be able to drive what they wanted and should be allowed to park wherever they saw fit to park. I was equally determined that the union leaders especially should feel compelled to drive what they produced—if not a Corvette, then at least, a General Motors product of some kind.

Billy Jack was determined to flout the rules. He would often park right out front in a "No Parking" zone just to be contrary. Soon, I'd had enough. I told the clerk to call a wrecking company in town to come and haul away any car that was illegally parked on plant property anywhere. Soon after that, during a productive sweep by the wrecking company, Billy Jack's pick-up truck and several others were hauled away.

Billy Jack fumed, cussed and stomped in fury. He declared that he had valuable cargo in his vehicle, including a loaded gun in the glove box. He said that when he retrieved his vehicle, everything had best still be inside. He continued to rant and rave for at least several hours and was almost apoplectic, but he had learned the hard way that I really meant business.

Eldon Renaud, who was also a union official, was determined to fight fire with fire. He called all of the towing businesses in Bowling Green and warned them never to come to the plant again. He warned them of the dire consequences of butting heads with the UAW. When I was told of this, I had the clerks to call other towing and wrecking businesses as far away as Nashville to see who we could get to take the job. Soon enough, we located a towing company in Nashville who had no fear at all. Hearing this, Eldon had to scramble to get the non-GM illegally parked vehicles out of harm's way. He wanted to know if the towing company was willing to tow the vehicles to the union hall rather than to Nashville. The towing companies were not inclined to listen or to comply to his request. They were only interested in collecting the fees that would be charged for the return of the vehicles.

I had told the union members often enough that I was not inclined to let up. They now knew what their options were: if any worker wished to drive a non-General Motors vehicle, they needed to be prepared to park in the most distant parking lot and walk down to work at the plant from there.

Really bold and decisive moves had to be made toward assuring that the C5 would be kept and built right in Bowling Green. While there had been a C5 workgroup that was already formed before I came to the plant, much work still needed to be done yet and the people who were working in the group needed to be given the time to do it. I saw that the path previously taken by some of the week-end work groups to get the job done had only been moderately effective. They needed bolstering as well as time to get some real work done.

Now, I fell back to my previous areas of success, that is, I used my ability to get auxiliary people into the plant to train on the jobs of the C5 workgroup or "Project 96" people as we were now calling them. That way I could cover the jobs of the 96 /C5 workgroup while they dedicated their time and effort toward getting that job done satisfactorily. That gave them not only time, but a totally new direction. Their previous direction had been to work on the total package all at once. Our new idea was to get them to work on ways to reduce costs for some of the items that we knew would be needed; deal with items of quality, reliability and efficiency that we knew would be part of any production product; and deal with the relationships between design, feasibility and dependability. That way, we could more easily work with each of the areas singly until a satisfactory solution had been reached, then, move on to another.

We designed those responsibilities between union members as well as members of management. That way, the union workers could feel that they had just as much of a stake in the planning as management did. We decided once again to hold classes whenever necessary to train the temporary workers as well as the members of the union who wished to learn something about another job other than the single job on which they ordinarily worked.

Finally, we re-introduced the Master Dot planning process. This time, planning components were identified and names were assigned to each component. Regular follow-up meetings were held and progress was recorded. If a due date was missed, then the assignee had to come up with a recovery plan. Holding each person or group accountable for each event yielded excellent results. Each team was charged to help each other accomplish their individual tasks.

Don Hackworth, Group Vice-President of manufacturing came to visit the plant. Our review of the overall plan with him was quite lively. We all enjoyed the discussions that we had when we revealed our set up to him, presented our ideas and told him how we planned to handle our challenge. Don soon realized without a doubt that the Bowling Green Assembly plant was up for the challenge of building the new C5. Our progress in the plant was the results of many hours work just the same as the Vehicle Development Process (VDP) that they had in headquarters. Don was quite satisfied that all of the problems that we had experienced in the plant with the C4 had been anticipated and addressed by our work group and the solutions that we had come up with would be applied fruitfully to the new design for the C5.

Members of our workgroup were sent to Detroit to assist Dave Hill's team in making sure that the new product would be built in a quality manner. We sent the hourly as well as the management groups and leased quarters for them so that they could stay in Detroit to work closely every day with the people who were responsible for the engineering of the C5. Our team was charged to bring realism to the engineers especially from the viewpoint of those who had to actually put their hands on the product and do the rest of the assembly work on the cars in the plant. Whenever the work group found that their viewpoints were not being listened to or taken seriously, they were charged to report directly to me immediately. Then I got involved by telephone or by going up to Detroit myself to meet with engineers and designers. I would add more push to the corrections that the workgroup had pointed out. We were determined to leave no stone unturned to make the launch of the C5 successful.

To this point, I suppose I had proven myself and my leadership abilities to everyone at headquarters, because Don designated me as the final word when it came to determining if the plant was ready to ship the new C5 Corvettes to the customers. This authority had never been given to any plant manager. I presume it was because my engineering background, quality control and reliability training, and deep involvement in every aspect of manufacture in the plant. My philosophy had always been that the manufacturer has to have continuous improvement every year, that is, the new manufacturing run always needed to be better than the previous year. All known problems needed to be addressed and every weakness known and handled to the point that any weakness we found could be turned on and turned off to assure identification (just as we had done with squeaks and rattles) before any new model could ever be produced.

I realized that another big thing that I needed to do was to get myself and my staff well-known to Corvette lovers, Corvette customers, and to people who ran the established Corvette events around the country like Chip and Bill Miller in Carlisle, Mike and Laurie Yager in Effingham and staunch enthusiasts like Charlie and Jim Robertson and their group in Florida and Buzz and Ruth Marston out on the west coast. It was a big ambition, but I felt that the premise was right. People needed to think that we who were responsible for building the Corvette loved and trusted the car just as much or more than they did. I encouraged my staff to appear at Corvette rallies and meetings around the country no matter how far away. Bill and Cindy Bubliz's Bloomington Gold rally in Arizona was far away but it was a big Corvette draw; and the club rally right down in Nashville was close and although it was a relatively small one, the people in it were very important. If an invitation had been extended beforehand, I always tried to make sure that someone from the plant personnel would be there. That way we could be sure that many Corvette customers could attend the event for the sole purpose of closely consulting with actual plant engineers and other members on my staff who were totally familiar with the build of their car. I wanted all of them to be there to consult with our most avid Corvette customers.

Finally, we decided in a staff meeting that as many knowledgeable people as possible would be obligated to attend any event that the Corvette Museum put on.

I cannot remember who got the bright idea to get the famous "Snake Skinner" into the plant. The engineers at HQ had re-built and souped-up a Corvette and made it into a race car. It was lighter because they had removed some of the inside insulation and weight and they had bored out the engine to drive up the RPMs. It was commonly known as the "Snake Skinner" because it had been used at the test track to try to beat the race times posted by the Dodge Viper. That car was the forerunner of all the Corvettes that had been made into race cars since then.

It was decided that since I was the drag racer among us it should naturally fall to me to be the driver of the "Snake Skinner." I agreed to race it in a series of exhibition runs at Dallas Jones' Beech Bend Drag Strip at the Buick Grand Nationals.

I made at least six runs and had beaten every car, then I missed a gear and the car that I was competing with caught up to me and beat me to the end of the track. The car that had beaten me was driven by a woman. She seemed to be almost apologetic because she knew that something had happened to the Snake Skinner. I denied that anything had happened, because it was totally my fault. Everyone had to understand that it was not at all the fault of the race car. I only pretended that it mattered a whole lot to my male ego, but it really didn't. Finally, I was more than good-natured about it. Our total intention was to get out there and let the people know that we at the factory believed in and really trusted our product. It was all in good fun but I had a hard time living that one down in the plant, nevertheless.

When the holiday season rolled around, Barbara gathered a planning group to set up a Christmas party for the staff and superintendents. They planned to hold it at the old hotel building on the by-pass that Holiday Inn had recently sold. The building was shortly after burned to the ground and the new owners were accused of arson.

A few of the superintendents declared that they would not be present at that first Christmas party because they were yet stewing over the still-lingering effects of the plant "Safety Crisis." I did my best to nip that small insurrection in the bud by declaring that all of my staff should try to get all of their people to come. Everyone who attended got a huge kick out of the six-foot-six black Santa Claus who confessed that his racing abilities had been compromised by missing a gear on his sleigh on the way to town from the North Pole.

The Planning Committee gave ourselves a pat on the back after it was over. I have to admit that the party was not only a considered success, it was the beginning of the annual Christmas parties and staff get-togethers that seemed to grow, draw the staff together and become more and more expected among all of them from that point on.

The next big challenge in the plant was to begin building the 1995 Corvette. All of the refinements that we had made on the car in the previous year were in effect so it was nothing short of an easy build. It was as if people who had not noticed the Corvette up to this point had suddenly come around and were seeing it for the very first time. Everything seemed to make a difference, even the restyled air vents along the front quarter were talked about in many of the sports car magazines.

The not-so-splashy ZR-1's that had never been that big of a hit, were suddenly getting the attention they had never gotten before since the announcement had been made by Headquarters that the ZR-1 would be discontinued after this assembly run was over.

In January of 1995, as soon as the New Year began, we officially began building the third Pace Car that Corvette had ever built for the Indianapolis 500 race. It was not easy because the paint process was scheduled to take twice the production time of any other vehicle. Each car had to go through the paint process twice: first the Artic White was applied to the whole vehicle; then, the white paint was baked and finished; then, the bottom half of the cars were masked off and the Dark Purple Metallic was applied to the upper half of each car. The cars were then hauled over to the decal company so that they could put on the elaborate flying red and white side stripes of the Indy 500 fender-to-fender decals, and then apply the red-and-white striping completely around the front hood of the car. The interior of the cars were completely black with two-toned black and purple leather seats with the French stitching of the Indy 500 badge embroidered into the headrest. Our total production run was 527 Indy cars. We had refined our processing and had gotten steadily better at painting those cars, but it was cause for celebration when the last one of those cars was finally finished in the plant and shipped over to the decal company.

87 of the Indy cars were sent to Indianapolis and Jim Perkins, Chevrolet general manager drove the Pace Car for the race. Liz and I attended our first Indianapolis 500 as guests of Chevrolet. We sat in Chevrolet's skybox and we enjoyed immensely meeting the celebrities. Rapper/actor Ice-T was one of them. We ate the excellent food that had been catered, and we watched the pace car doing its duty out in the front of the pack. Jim got the race started and made several passes around the track before he pulled off the track for the race to begin. Jim himself pulled out onto the track to lead the slowdowns whenever there was a caution flag on the track for an accident with body pieces littering the track or oil spillage. It was truly thrilling to see our product on display to such a huge audience. I was supremely confident that none of the rest of the 400 or so 1995 Pace Cars that had been built in our factory and shipped to dealers around the country would remain in their showrooms for very long.

We held another celebration at the plant with the top officials of Mercury Marine of Stillwater, Oklahoma in attendance when we built the last of the ZR-1's and drove them out of the factory. Mercury Marine had built and serviced ZR-1 engines since the late 1990s. The ZR-1 had never created much of a stir in the Corvette community and had been the least touted, but it been the first of the high-powered engines that had been created for Corvette. This more expensive option was largely by-passed by most buyers. Except for the fender flares, five-spoke wheel covers, heavy duty suspension, and wider stance on wider tires, the ZR-1 did not appear to be different enough to warrant its higher price tag. There was no special badging, no fanfare, nothing. It was informally called "King of the Hill" because of its higher powered engine, but that was all.

It had hung on until 1995, and then the company had shipped the last of the engines to the plant to be stored until another use was found for them. The flash and dash that could be obtained on the lesser-priced models of the Corvette was far more preferred by the everyday customers. We made a huge ceremony out of driving the last ZR-1 off the final line. We rented smoke machines and got together a good crowd of workers to shout and cheer while the plant and newspaper photographers snapped pictures to complete the hoopla. General Manager Jim Perkins and Chief Engineer Dave McLellan were on hand for the ceremonies. Jim waved the checkered flag while Billy Jackson, UAW rep, rode shotgun and I drove the car through the smoke and into Corvette history. The last red ZR-1 coupe went straight over to be displayed at the Corvette Museum. The heyday was ended for the ZR-1, but it was a true forerunner of high-powered engines of the future and the banner that was displayed in the window read: "The Legend Lives."

I was told by a member of his staff that Vice President Jack Smith had been invited to the Kentucky Derby but he would not be able to attend. He had suggested that the Governor's Office should invite me instead since I ran the Corvette operations in Kentucky. I said I would be willing to attend if invited, but I thought no more about it. Around the first of April, I was surprised to get an invitation from Gene Strong, Secretary of the Economic Development Cabinet of the state of Kentucky. He called my office to make sure that I had gotten his invitation to the Derby. I had already sent the letter back to say that I would be more than happy to come. I told him that I had to pull out my tuxedo to make sure that I could still fit into it. He laughed and took care to tell me that the week-end activities would be purely fun—no business allowed. I was excited and geared up to have a really fun week-end. Of course, Liz was excited, too. She used the opportunity as an excuse to buy two new outfits, one with a matching flowered hat since we had heard much ado about women wearing elaborate bonnets to the derby.

We drove up to Frankfort on Thursday evening and checked in at the Holiday Inn. The next morning we met the other thirty or so guests. We went to breakfast then on a tour of Gainsborough Farm to see the stock of breeding mares and their offspring. We got to see the champion Derby horses that were kept on the farm in luxurious quarters. Their sole jobs were stand at stud to sire more derby champions. Some of the men made semi-tasteful jokes about how they envied the pampered life of a stud, and, of course, I joined right into the fun.

We went to the Old State Capitol for lunch and wrapped up the day with dinner and a night of dancing at the Governor's Mansion.

On Saturday morning we walked across to the Derby Train that took us from Frankfort to Churchill Downs in Louisville. It was a wonderful trip with all of the ladies in their summer frocks and hats and all of the men in suits and ties. The train wound speedily through the Kentucky foothills and all of the riders got busy trying to figure out how we were going to bet our money once we got to the track.

We met many celebrities on "Millionaires Row" at Churchill Downs. Dave Thomas founder of Wendy's came by and signed our programs. We felt really special being among the people who really knew all about the horses and were winning money on the various races, but we were not so lucky. Liz only won a couple of dollars, but I lost my entire stash that I had set aside for betting in the other races that were run well before the Derby race even started. I had given up until Gene gave me a tip on the last race. I won almost enough money on that race to break even.

The Good-by Breakfast the next morning was excellent. We got to thank Gene for inviting us and we got to mingle, exchange addresses and say good-by to many of the new people that we met. We all were hoping that we would get to come back again. In fact, we went back six more times: twice to represent Jack Smith who had been invited and could not make it, then we were invited four more times because I was GM plant manager in Bowling Green. We enjoyed it even more every time that we went. Liz remembered the protocol for us and was always sure to send a note to thank Gene and those members who had made the derby trip such a memorable one for us.

During the summer, I visited Bloomington Gold, a car meet in Bloomington, Illinois. Then I went down to the Petit Le Mans at Road Atlanta race track in Atlanta, Georgia. I hung out with Tommy Morrison and his crew and watched as the perils of racing visited an awful calamity upon poor Tommy. Corvette did not do so well in that race at all.

I found that in trying to connect effectively with Corvette customers I could be gone from the plant constantly and almost every week-end during the summer months. Yet and still, I was determined to keep it up if I could. As it was I hardly saw Liz at all because she had started taking evening classes after work driving up to the University of Louisville to begin the work toward her doctorate degree. I had promised to be supportive while she worked on her degree. I helped her to find someone to keep the house clean and I certainly did all that I could do in every other way to keep my promise to her.

When we started our regular runs of the 1996 Corvette it was, by this time, very routine. This would be the last year for the C4 and the sales were projected to be very sluggish because it was generally thought that everyone was tired and worn out because the C4 body style had been around for so long. They would now be anticipating the C5 and ignoring anything else that came out of the Corvette plant right now.

Since we no longer had the ZR-1, it was decided in Headquarters and brought down to us by new Chief Engineer, Dave Hill, that we would start to produce two special models for 1996, the Grand Sport and the Collector's Edition as soon as we could in order to try to generate some Corvette lovers' interest and enthusiasm. The press releases went out and press conferences were held to let the public and the dealers know that something new and very exciting was on the way from Corvette. We planned to offer fresh new paint, new horsepower, new electronics, new Z51 handling package and new tires—all that and even more.

It was generally thought amongst us at the plant that our paint and body shop had really proven itself with that 1995 Pace Car. It seemed now that they were invincible and could do anything. Few in the corporation and none in the public knew that the two-toned paint on the previous Indy pace car had nearly brought our paint shop to its knees. If not for the body side molding, painting that car might not have been the beautiful job that it turned out to be for us.

So now, we were very happy. We were cheering because we were told that the Grand Sport (which would have been a complete horror for our paint shop) would be done completely with decals by our outside company.

But not so!

We had celebrated too soon. Somehow, somewhere in HQ, the decision was made that the two-toned car would be **painted**! All of the work would be have to be done right in the paint and body shop at the Corvette plant!

We could not take the time to sit down and cry. I had to rally the troops and to keep their spirits up! We definitely had a good reason to update the paint shop because of what was coming: the grand sport would be a very difficult two-process job just like the 1995 pace car had been. But, this time, the stripe thought to be the "second color" (it was technically the first) would be going in a new direction—straight down-the-middle of the vehicle!

We consoled the paint shop that since we knew these specifics ahead of time they would have the time, maybe, to do a good job with it. They would definitely have all of the support and help plus all of the new equipment, re-tooling and machining that I could rake, scrape, and muster for them.

No doubt the paint shop would have to run the Grand Sport bodies normally through the painting process and get the white paint on first. It had to be that way. The middle of the car body was to be masked off and the Admiral Blue paint coat would then be applied to each side. After the drying process was completed, edging strips would have to be applied where the white color met the blue because those painted edges were, of course, far less than perfect because accidental paint overruns simply could not be avoided.

With the coming paint shop ordeal on all of our minds, we wondered how in the world the marketing department at HQ would set up the cost of those cars. We knew that there was a process, of course, but we had to think that the Grand Sport convertibles might naturally cost less money than the coupes because there was far less area to paint and process on the convertibles than on those coupes.

The appearance of the bold white stripe down the middle of the darker Admiral Blue coupe must have reminded some of our hunters and wildlife enthusiasts of the white stripe down the middle on a skunk's fur because they immediately tagged the Grand Sport with the moniker: "skunk car."

The Z-16 Grand Sport option included an LT4 engine, black five-spoke wheels with black brake calipers, red lettering on the engine that designated it a "Grand Sport," two red hash marks on the left fender, and black insides or a black and red option which included black floor mats and perforated seat covers with "Grand Sport" embroidered on the head rests. The car was heralded in many sports car magazines as "jaunty," "spry," "sporty" "young at heart" not to mention "fresh" "new" "upbeat" "lively" and "dashing."

We did a total production of 1,000 of those cars and there was a real celebration when the last of them went out of the doors of the plant! Not surprisingly, we were told by our informal and formal surveys that sales of our "skunk car" were "sweet" indeed. Every one of those cars was ordered long before the last car left the plant.

By the same token, the "Collector Edition" was a "sweetheart" to assemble and produce after our experience with the "Skunk Car." Once again we used the 5-spoke wheels which belonged to the old ZR-1 painted a silver color to best match the body of the car. Engineering notified our suppliers and we pulled forward many of the things that had been planned for the interior of the C5 in order to make the "Collector Edition" unique. The badging on the front shell was unique and the removal of wiring bundles which allowed for wider interiors and wider seats made for more mainstream comfort. The real name of the color for the "Collector Edition" was actually "Sebring Silver." Except for the clear reds: Bright Red and Torch Red, the Sebring Silver, the "Collector Edition," proved to be the best seller of any Corvette body color to that point.

All of our hard work at the plant had paid off at last. In the 1996 Annual *Subscriber Survey* of American built vehicles, readers finally gave the 1996 Corvette the top spot. The closest that we had gotten in past years had been third or fourth. We had been coming in second to the Dodge Viper for the last two years in a row. Now we were finally on top!

We needed to work together as one team of engineering, manufacturing, design and marketing to get the C5 done. Joe Spielman, Vice-President of Manufacturing, Russ McLean, Program Manager, Dave Hill, Chief Engineer, and I as the Corvette Plant Manager were all charged to work closely together to spearhead the entire operation and to bring it to a close with a final product. Tadge Jeuchter who was a GM engineer came down to the plant from Detroit and found housing to stay and work with us until we completed our mission.

Our C5 workgroup in the plant were standing on their heads in deep, deep mud. They were super busy and super stressed now that time was drawing near for the C5 to be produced. Since our previous successes were behind us we had to understand what we needed to do next. Everyone agreed that we had to make the introduction of the 1997 fifth generation the best ever.

Months ago, each area had been compelled to produce a list of customer "must haves" vs. customer "wants." Then, the workgroup took each list of items and turned it into "things that were needed" and "things that had to be improved" on the new model.

My staff and I considered ourselves to be the voices of the customer since we went among them so often at various Corvette events. Not surprisingly, our list included the following: two drink cup holders; improved seating; better paint; more precise panel fits; improved exhaust appearance and tone; more colors; improved glass and door fits; more horsepower; better-looking wheels; improved stereo equipment; On-Star guidance equipment; compass in rear-view mirrors; and better hatch closings.

From all of the intelligence that they had pulled together over the months and from all quarters, the C5 team developed a list that included the items that had to be of great concern on the new car in terms of the specifications from engineering and quality build. This list included: door and window fits; headlight cover fit; hood fit; deck fit; fender fit; two cup holders; deck lid pull down; step-over entry; size of foot wells; instrument panel fit; tail light fit; roof panel fit; and various trim fits.

Finally, the leadership team began to meet on a regular basis to examine various concepts of the next generation Corvette design. A "Joe Spielman" corrugated paper cut-out was used as a model to make sure that the inside of the coupe could accommodate a driver of Joe's height and size. I was used as a model to make sure that the new car would accommodate someone with big feet—size 15 and larger. Russ had to concern himself with the logistics of building the new car.

Dave Hill and the engineering team working with Tadge Jeuchter at the plant had to oversee every aspect of the engineering of the new car. I was concerned with quality and build.

The team's first impression of the drawings and mock-ups were this: from the front, the Corvette design looked too much like the design of the Chevrolet Camaro. It was a boxy look that nobody wanted. That had to go!

Eventually, the designers gave the hood the smooth, rounded, downward swoop of a shark's snout. Someone said that the new design had a shark's "smile" as if it were ready to "bite the competition right in the ass!"

The original clay design was finessed until everyone signed off and the design was frozen against any future changes. At this point everyone had to begin to work at optimizing their assigned work responsibilities.

We had to take the time to mourn the passing of Zora Arkus-Duntov, former Chief Engineer with GM who had been there during the earlier years of Corvette. He had been an icon with Corvette racing in his blood. We all attended a memorial service held for him at the Corvette Museum across the street from the Corvette plant.

Our first job was to get the last of the C4 models out the door of the plant. It was arranged by Jim Perkins that Mike Yager, owner of Mid-America Motorworks would get the last C4 off the line. Mike wanted all of us to sign under his hood with white paint pens and to have a ceremony when the car came off the assembly line.

Mike wanted white-painted, 5-spoke wheels, two stripes on the left front fender, and a considerable amount of badging. We certainly took the time to give him just what he asked for. We let him start the car up and drive it off the final line himself, plus we gave him a send-off from the line with the sound of cheering and the blasts of many Corvette horns.

I think Mike was very proud of the little ceremony that we provided for him and I know that he still has that car in his "Garage Collection" on his Mid-America Motorworks campus in Effingham, Illinois.

As soon as the last C4 went out of the doors, we started to re-build and re-tool the plant for the production of the all-new Corvette. We went into production of the C5 amid much hoopla and anticipation. A white Corvette with the same markings as the last C4 that we made for Mike Yager was the first C5 that came off the line. The car magazines, bulletins and papers praised us for the newness and innovation of our new product. It was going to be an instant hit! This is what all of the publications proclaimed. All of the extensive research and dedicated personnel and all of the work that General Motors had used for the new Corvette were touted far and wide.

This car was going to be distinctive—it was to be all-new. Even the assembling of the parts for this car was all new. Everything, including the new hydro-formed frame rails had to be accounted for in assembling the new car. The rails were steel and very strong and this caused the underbody structure to be very stiff as one-piece construction tends to be. This was the stuff of hand-built race cars. The rear transaxle was rear-driven coming from the all-new engine. The rear-located transmission caused the interior of the car to be more open and roomy as did widening the wheelbase and relocating the bundles of wiring to the rear of the car behind the passenger and out of the way. There was plenty of room in both foot wells now and we were using another supplier for the seats—they were, by far, more comfortable.

I tended to think that there were too many hands on the parts and pieces. A lot of the assembly workers were getting too much assistance from the plant engineers as well the engineers who were in our plant from HQ in Detroit trying to make sure that the operators got everything right.

I knew though, when I saw way too many operators who were out of their standard positions, things were just not going right. This meant to me that the operators could not get their jobs done in their own positions and were walking out of their assigned spots to try to get their particular jobs finished up. Too many mistakes were being made because of unfamiliarity. Nobody wanted to admit defeat or to cry for help, but things were fast catching up to us and I could see very early that our operators were really panicking.

There was some insistence by the HQ engineers for us to go ahead and use some of the C4 parts and try to make them fit onto the new C5. We at the plant did not want to do that, but what choice did we have? The correct parts either had not been planned for or they were not available when the assemblers were in position to use them. Therein lay many of our problems in assembling that car. We even had problems using the same suppliers of parts because some of them were not ready to make the changes or set up for the re-tooling of the parts that the new car needed and it was not because they had not been informed by telephone or in hand-written specifications.

Although the 1997 General Motors Corvette appeared at first glance to be a flawlessly beautiful new product we had problems right from the beginning of the production run.

There was far too much variability between the cars coming off the line. The cars were looking far too different to the naked eye and for sure our discerning Corvette customers could notice the differences when they were together. There would sometimes be variation between the left and the right seats in an individual car. That was not as easy to fix as it seemed to be.

The most important thing of all was the variation between the painted panels on the cars. Of course, such variations in the outright appearance of those items would cause customer complaints, so those cars went straight to repair. A never-talked about secret is that anytime a car has to go through repair, more cost should be attached to the price of that car because more individual time is spent on it. That is why a car that has made it to the final line may have had more "hands-on" time spent on it than others. Surprisingly, this makes absolutely no difference in the overall pricing of the individual car. It is a headache and a truth that is not even considered.

We began to get reports from the testers that the door fits of our new coupes were causing very real problems. Many times after the vehicles had been started up and the inside of the car had become thoroughly pressurized, the windows would blow out of the frames with a startlingly loud "floop!" It was a bad enough problem that I raised an alarm with engineering at headquarters as soon as we started to test the cars. I raised such a commotion about it that Dave and his people arrived at the plant with a virtual bag full of "blow-out clips" in their hands to put on the windows of the C5. I did not like it but, grudgingly, I had to accept the "fix" because it seemed to handle the problem.

Still, I knew that we were headed for a disaster of epic proportions. The plant was fast filling up with repair and the repair yard was running over. The repairmen were putting in way too much overtime and they did not seem to be making any headway with the number of cars that were stacking up. They began to complain bitterly about the amounts of overtime that we were requiring from them.

Everybody was so busy that I finally sent one of the student interns from Western Kentucky University out to the repair yard with a clip board and a pen to write down the types and kinds of repair that was present on most of the cars so that we could get some idea of what items kept turning up over and over.

Most of the problems could only have one source. Nobody wanted to hear that the problem rested in any way with general assembly! Of course we were having the usual fit variations: trim fit variations, trim panels, the headlight doors, and the car door fit problems. Couple those with water leaks, wind noise, not to mention very unusual squeaks and rattles and that was more than problematic. Putting it all together, the fault had to be in the basic formulation of the parts: the frame and body just did not come together correctly.

Everybody knew that there was no "quick fix" for that problem.

When the repairmen could not quickly fix or repair this huge problem, we all knew that we were in trouble. No one department could be blamed or said to be the culprit when things were going this horribly wrong. Everybody knew that the assemblers could not be blamed if the parts they were getting were all wrong!

I was angry. I had spent practically my whole career working in the chassis department of three different General Motors plants! It was entirely possible that somebody knew the truth from the first. Somebody knew that we were going to need to get help and they should have admitted that to us long ago! It was disheartening to know that the people who were responsible were not coming clean. What looked good on paper in mock-ups and in drawings too often was not workable in real-life. I felt like the HQ engineers were "pissing up my leg and pretending it was raining everywhere." I am not proud to say that I told them that in just those words in one of the production meetings with the headquarters engineering guys. We had to face the truth: the very soul of our assembly process simply was not working! There was no cosmetic "fix" that would help us!

Some re-engineering desperately needed to be done right along with the back-breaking work that we were already grinding out.

Since we could not get quality-built cars off the assembly line, I made the decision to stop production of the new 1997 Chevrolet Corvette until engineering and tooling could get a good handle on what was going wrong.

When I gave the order to shut the line down, we all wanted to just sit down and cry our eyeballs out. Headquarters and Chief Engineer Dave Hill and his department were not happy—I might even say that they were livid and enraged! It wasn't as if Tadge Jeuchter and the rest of the engineers from HQ were not in it with us all the way up to their shoulder blades. They knew it: what had to be done, had to be done. Nobody could say that we hadn't worked our tails off for a hellish number of hours. Nobody could say that every one of us had not tried until we were exhausted to make it work. But I had to do what absolutely needed to be done and I was willing to accept the responsibility individually and singly right onto my own shoulders. We had nothing but cars that we could not get repaired without a total re-work after they came off that final line! That would never do!

Surprisingly, I got more support from headquarters than I expected after Tadge had seen to it that the other engineers saw and thoroughly accessed our situation. The entire plant seemed to breathe a sigh of relief then. It brought us all together more than any glowing success might have done. Nobody in the Chevrolet Corvette plant was willing to produce and put into our customers hands mediocre products with our names and reputations attached to them.

Of course we already knew that if the final line was not running correctly it was every department's business. Many of the workers whose jobs were halted went down to the final line to try to help out with the trouble on the final build process without being asked to do it. We were all in the murky soup together and we were determined to walk out of it with our heads held high just as soon as we possibly could.

First of all, we had to clean out whatever cars in the repair yard that could be fixed. We needed to notify dealers. We had to let suppliers know in no uncertain terms that they would be dropped from our lists if their parts could not be consistent in formation or if they could not re-tool those parts for us in time or if they could not figure out how to do it. We knew that many of them had lied to make us believe that they could supply certain parts when they had not completely retooled their shops to make our new parts. They very badly wanted that lucrative General Motors contract. They had hoped that they would be able to deliver parts to us but they were just not caught up and ready to do it.

The worst part of it all was that we were not able to satisfy our most avid Corvette customers after we had built them up to such a state of intense expectation. Our customers had waited so very patiently for the new car.

But we were not going to make it to our goal! We were not going to satisfy our customers! I really felt that **this** was one of the lowest points ever in my career as the General Motors Corvette plant manager.

At that same time, plant personnel director, Cheryl Ollila had spoken to me several times about the Black Engineer of the Year awards given each year by Tyrone Taborn's *US Black Engineer and Information Technology* magazine, The Council of Engineering Deans of the Historically Black Colleges and Universities (HBCUs) and Lockheed Martin. But my nose had been so firmly jammed against the grindstone for the past few months that I did not have the time to think about it at all. So, she gathered my biography and information on her own and sent it to the nominating committee. When the news came back that I had won the President's Award, it was a real surprise to me.

The awards program was scheduled over the course of three days. There were workshops and programs and a company recruitment fair held for college and high school students scheduled for Thursday and Friday of the days that the conference was being held. I really thought that I would be too busy in the plant with the new car to attend the ceremony, but everyone seemed to really want me to go. Just in case I couldn't go, the marketing and sales department had made up two life-sized cutouts of me and one of the scarce C5 Corvette in the red version to be used for the three days of display and for the ceremony.

However much Cheryl denied it, I still believe that she was the one who got upper management at General Motors Headquarters involved. Jack Evans called to inform me that everyone at headquarters wanted me to attend the ceremony in spite of the fact that things were not going well at the plant. So, at the last minute, Liz bought a new evening gown and I dusted off my old tuxedo. We flew to Baltimore so that I could attend the conference and accept the award in person.

The huge area of the Baltimore Convention Center near the Inner Harbor was used by many companies and the US armed services to set up their displays and to make presentations during the three days of the convention. Dan Clements, who worked in recruitment and acquisitions at headquarters, Lewis Cole, an engineer at headquarters, Angela Barber-Hatter, an engineer at headquarters, and Derek Lawrence, an engineer at tool and die set up the huge General Motors recruitment display and Mel Stuart, of talent acquisitions at headquarters came to Baltimore to guide us all during the programs and the three days of recruitment.

I was happy that my mother, my three sisters, my youngest brother and all their spouses came to Baltimore to see me accept the award. They all enjoyed a few days walking through the numerous displays at the convention center, relaxing in the numerous cafes and shopping in the colorful boutiques along the waterfront of the Inner Harbor in Baltimore and eating lunch in the colorful cafes while they were waiting for the day of the ceremony.

On the evening of the awards ceremony, I was to be introduced on the program by Jerry Ellison, Vice President of General Motors. Jack Evans and the engineering manager from GM headquarters attended also. I was pleased and proud that they had dusted off their tuxedos and took the time out of their busy schedules to make the trip to Baltimore, too. They hosted a dinner at a private restaurant in the city for my family and me before we all went over to the awards dinner. Then, Jerry diverted the General Motors aircraft to Bowling Green to fly Liz and me back home the next day. Flying in the company jet really reminded me of the freedom of flying myself in my own airplane and flying anywhere I wanted. Big difference though: my plane was not nearly so luxurious or so easy a trip as the large GM jet.

As soon as we were home, Cheryl and her group organized a celebration on the floor of the plant for me. They invited Liz to come out. Liz had to dismiss one of her university classes in order to get there in time.

The cafeteria provided cakes and refreshments on the floor of the plant. One of the cakes was decorated with a little red corvette on top. It was a wonderful and heartfelt celebration with an introduction by Cheryl to tell the story of my award. Cheryl introduced me and I thanked everyone for their well-wishes and told them about the ceremony in Baltimore. Then we had fruit punch and sandwiches out on the floor of the plant for everyone.

Jack Evans came to town for a second celebration of my award for the community members in Bowling Green. The second ceremony was to be held at the museum. State Senator Nick Kafoglis, the mayor of the city, the county commissioners and many dignitaries from Bowling Green and Warren County turned out to toast me for winning the honor. Many of my own good friends came out to celebrate with me: Abraham Williams of the Housing Authority and his wife Mildred, Drs. Harold and Cassandra Little and Dean Howard Bailey and his wife Kayla, from the faculty at Western Kentucky University, Rick and Dr. Cassandra "Cookie" Starks and many of the teacher education faculty at Western who worked with Liz came out including Dr. Sam Evans, the assistant dean of education and his wife, Mary, Dr. Chris Wagner a professor of administration and his wife Elaine and Dr. Nancy LaPosser from the Education Leadership department. The museum workers went up and down the aisles handing out glasses and made it possible for everyone to toast me with a glass of champagne. The evening really made me feel special. Everyone seemed to have enjoyed the program and especially the champagne toast.

No sooner than the toasts were over, even before the hoopla died down, I had to get right back to the business of trying to get the 1997 model Corvette off the assembly line. We were almost building the car in repair, yet we were still winning awards even with our abbreviated production schedule. Our enduring bright spot was the LS-1 V-8 engine. It was a jewel. We won awards for the design of the car, for the interior, for the exterior, for the crossed flags in the design of the new emblem, for the hatchback design, and for the wider wheel base that had been pioneered first by Oldsmobile. But the biggest award winner was the performance of our car on the racetrack right out of the factory or off the showroom floor. Many of the old-time racers were more than happy to take the car to the track and put it through its paces. They absolutely loved that stiffness of the hydro-formed frame, the ease of the active handling package, but most of all they loved the performance of that LS-1 V-8 engine.

That year, we held the plant Christmas party at the museum for the first time. We did not know if it was going to be an annual thing but I think everyone rather hoped that it would be. We contracted with a fairly new place, Cambridge Deli, to deliver food for the party and we really did enjoy the ease of just letting them handle everything. They did a super job. I found out later that Mike Hughes, the owner of Cambridge Deli, had been a GM employee who had worked at the Corvette plant in the past. Now, he had become one of Bowling Green's finest restaurant owners, caterers and businessmen.

By the time that last 1997 Corvette went through our plant doors, the department of engineering at HQ had practically beaten our gremlins down to earth. Our persistence at the plant had caused everyone involved to work harder and stay at it longer to get things right. Between us all, we fought off the C-5 problems using back-breaking hard labor. We had built only 9,752 coupes that were certifiable to be sent to the dealers and everyone in the plant felt very much like we had built one side of the Roman coliseum brick by brick and by hand, while we fought an uphill battle with Hannibal's elephant army coming down on top of us. The last of the units that we built did serve to soften the barbs from some of our harshest critics because they were aware of our back-breaking work.

We had finally got all of our suppliers on board. At last they had re-tooled their workshops and seemed able to live up to the promises that they had made to us. I had already taken the time to go personally to each and every one of their shops and I told them eye-to-eye that they would be off our lists for good if we could not get the needed parts from them and soon. Afterwards our build became more and more perfect. Time and feverish change had overworked almost everyone in the plant, yet it had made us more confident. Our last few cars were as near perfect as we could make them right off the assembly line.

Surprisingly enough, the scarcity of the 1997 Corvette and the perfection of those last units had awakened a hunger in Corvette lovers for more! When we began building the 1998 models, General Motors Marketing announced via television, in all of the car magazines, and in the mainstream publications that we would be building a coupe and a convertible as well for the new model year. We started out producing more and more cars that were well-built enough for sale right off the line. I do not think there was a one of us in the plant who was not relieved and thankful that it seemed we had overcome that giant hurdle and we had settled down to producing quality built Corvettes at last.

Motor Trend magazine picked our convertible as its "car of the year" and featured a beautiful Light Carmine Red Metallic with a Light Oak convertible top on its cover. *Auto Week* gave us praise as well and wrote about how hard we had worked to overcome our build problems. The Corvette was voted North American Car of the Year at the North American International Auto Show in Detroit.

Most of the praise that was heaped on us was because of our processes. Many car magazines described and extolled them, but we were also praised for the beauty of our exterior paint. The interior seating and "heads up" display of the instrument panel was highly praised, too.

One of the automobile magazines claimed that we were building more cars with fewer people. This was essentially not true, we still used the same number of auto workers; it was just that the headquarters people who had been with us for so long while we were trying to get the new Corvette started had now gone back to their daily jobs in Detroit. The paint and parts people were not needed as constantly as they had been before. Our regular operators had learned to do their jobs in-station and on their own without the use of trainers. We had constantly offered training classes during the time we were down when the line was stopped. I was not about to let anyone go. None of our regular workers were inclined to refuse training anymore nor was the UAW balking at having their people to learn another job other than their own. The workers seemed to have come to the knowledge finally during the line shut-down that there was value to them and added stability to each job if the workers were able to help out anywhere in the plant and on any job wherever they were needed.

Another of the things that the automotive magazines were reporting and our chief engineer, Dave Hill, was pretty proud to claim: fewer hours were being spent to build each vehicle. This was essentially true—but not entirely. Sometimes, in order to get a quality build the first time and to get the build done correctly, I had to insist that more people were needed and we had to split some particular jobs. I did not care about hours or anything else. I always kept the customer uppermost in my mind. There was no way that I was going to stint on anything that was needed to make our customers happy.

We hadn't had this much demand as we now had for the convertibles in years. It was really surprising. Almost every other car that came down the line in our factory was a soft top. There was an added feature that all the car magazines were wild about: the convertible now featured a separate trunk accessible from outside of the car! Corvette had not had an outside trunk in years and years. The sales and marketing guys had put the publicity out there in print and pictures: the Corvette was capable of carrying two golf bags in the trunk. Very true: Two *small, soft* golf bags! Anyway, I do not really believe that all the publicity hype served to make the convertibles any more appealing than they already were. Our avid customers simply did not care at all about that! Those cars were selling because the public liked them very much and they were satisfied that the cars were well-built yet were more than a good and beautiful value for the money. A more appropriate hype might have been that there was not much of a rise at all in the factory price of this well-built beauty. Now, **that** was something that we in the factory were really proud to claim!

We celebrated when the news first came to us that we would be building the Indianapolis 500 Pace Car for 1998. It was the fourth time that Corvette had been chosen for the honor. The last time had been in 1995. We couldn't help but congratulate ourselves on the new Corvette and start to believe that we had finally arrived.

We were already painting a light purple metallic car that had not proven to be that big of a seller. The pace car was to be a darker purple color without the metallic flakes and our trusty decal company from Detroit with their facility in Bowling Green was all set to apply the decals on the car.

When we started to assemble that car we all said that it was going to be an outstanding pace car. The standard 5-spoke wheels were to be painted a bright yellow to match the decals which were to run from the indentations in the front quarter panel all the way to the rear quarter. A very modern, stylized rendition of the flying Corvette flag went from the bottoms of each door through a single white strip across the back just below the trunk. It had yellow seats with a black convertible top which was set to be standard. Strobe lights were added to the official pace cars for Indy but not to the pace car replicas that we built. We had the decal company to finish the rest of the pace cars by mid-summer and we shipped the last of them to the dealers around the country by Fall. In total, our marketing analysis reported that we had built 1,163 of the cars and all of them were sold.

Sure enough, our workers had begun to call the car the "Yellow Bird" because it was dark with the yellow-painted wheels. I have to admit, though that the car did not have a great-looking presence in the raw, before all the decals were put on. I was really glad that no one was allowed to see it that way.

Parnelli Jones a retired Indy car driver and racing legend out of California drove the Pace Car for the 1998 Indy 500 race. Again Liz and I were invited to be at the race and we enjoyed the hospitality of Chevrolet in their suite in the upstairs enclosed grandstand. Nobody could have missed the Chevrolet Corvette pace car with its distinctive yellow wheels. Liz and I listened to the comments among people in the suite about how gaudy the wheels looked and many other not-so-complimentary statements about the car. However, whenever I questioned some of the naysayers, there was not a one of those people who would not have welcomed the opportunity to own one of those "gaudy" pace cars if they had the extra money and were given the chance.

Liz and I went again to Tyrone Taborn's "Black Engineer of the Year" awards program in Baltimore in February of 1998. The Council of Engineering Deans of the Historically Black Colleges and Universities had a meeting which I attended. I learned that all of the traditionally black colleges needed to recruit and retain more students (that was certainly *not* new knowledge). I made a vow then and there to help them. I decided I would use some minority engineering students as interns in the plant whenever I could and I promised to help the engineering department of my Alma Mater, Tennessee State University, in any way that I could. Dean Decatur Rogers of the Department of Engineering at Tennessee State University certainly welcomed my help.

Dan Clements, Lewis Cole, Angela Barber Hatter, and Derek Lawrence came again for the second year to serve as primary recruiters for General Motors. This time we had a beautiful, new Corvette to serve as the backdrop to entice job-seekers to talk to us and give us their resumes. We allowed them to sit inside the car and we turned the ignition switch to the "on" position to show off the restyled "heads-up" instrument panel displays and to demonstrate the movement of the convertible top and the feature that automatically lowered the windows. It was a part of the anti-blowout feature that had been developed and used back in '96.

Tyrone Taborn, chairman of the conference, stopped by our display to ask me if I would be willing to serve on the selection committee later in the year to help to choose the next year's "Black Engineer." In spite of the busy schedule that I had been keeping, I agreed to do it since it only meant that I would only have to give up only one full week-end to get the job done.

One very low point that we had to endure was the infamous "Drug Bust" at the Corvette plant in May of 1998. The local newspaper, *The Bowling Green Daily News* and newspapers around the state including *The Courier-Journal* of Louisville heralded the plant "Drug Bust" to the disgust and the shame of all of us. It was a very low point for everybody at the plant. Fifteen and more workers were arrested on drug charges and many other innocent workers were pulled in and required to testify about what they had seen and when they had seen it. General Motors had long announced that there would be a zero-tolerance policy toward drug use and drug sales on GM property.

Undercover agents had long been working inside the plant and it was for certain that all of them could provide undisputable evidence. Those arrested were charged with selling and possessing everything from Methamphetamines, prescription tablets to marijuana. Their names and ages were splashed over the pages of the newspapers. None of them were youngsters by any stretch of the imagination.

Spokespeople at HQ in Detroit spoke to the press for all of us to tell the newspapers that most of the workers at the plant were, indeed, hard workers who were conscientious about doing a good job and building a quality product. There was no comment at the time from our UAW Local 2164 but all of us had to think that it was not unusual that any of this had happened as it seemed epidemic in auto plants across the country. Ours was not the only small operation that this had happened to either, nor was it different that the workers had been the ones to complain that their co-workers were using drugs. They were very upset because drug use had caused their counterparts to miss much of their assigned work.

During the summer of 1998, I attended many separate venues that featured the Corvette. Liz and I went to the races at Sebring and we saw that many Corvette owners were parking their cars together in a special spot. They were near the place where the Corvette Museum had set up a tent to sell merchandise. That may well have been the beginning of the Corvette Corrals that became extremely popular at the racing venues after that. We were still celebrating the unexpected win by Corvette on the Trans Am racing circuit in Long Beach California. I conducted an informal question-and-answer session there with the Corvette owners and signed my name under the hoods of some of the cars.

We took a poll in the next production meeting at the plant to decide which of the engineers would drive cars to some of the Corvette meetings that were to be held around the country and in Canada during the rest of the year. Several engineers and some other members of the staff wanted to go. Someone suggested that we hold a little seminar to brush up on our knowledge about the new Corvette because everyone knew well enough about their own particular jobs but they might be asked a question that they did not know about some other parts of the car besides those that their own department was responsible for. We all agreed that this was a very good idea.

In August, we all went to the huge Corvettes at Carlisle event held each summer at the fairgrounds at Carlisle, Pennsylvania. Chip Miller and Bill Miller were the co-organizers of the events held at the fairgrounds and they made sure a tent was set up on the huge fairgrounds for the engineers who drove up from Bowling Green and down from HQ in Detroit to show off the new cars and to talk about them with the people who wanted to gain more particular knowledge about the car. Liz and I flew into the airport in Harrisburg Pennsylvania. Barbara called Chevrolet Marketing to provide a Corvette for us when we got off the plane in Harrisburg and we drove over to Carlisle to the fairgrounds to meet up with the engineers at the General Motors tent.

The Carlisle event included sales of cars, presentations by technicians, car shows, swap meets, sales of parts for automobile restoration, and the raffle of a Corvette on Sunday to end the week. Chip and Bill provided a golf cart for Liz and me to get easily from place to place. We visited as many Corvette owners in the field as we could and I signed under the hoods of countless new Corvettes.

We went to the top of the hill overlooking the fairgrounds where Jake Drennon and Dan Adovasio had established an outpost for the Corvette C5 Registry. Many of the cars parked up there were our newest models. It was good for me to get among the members so that they could say what they were feeling about the new cars. It was Jake who told me about the water spotting on the cowl screen—the plastic panel that we used to close the opening between the hood and the bottom of the windshield wipers. He said that he had really buffed and rubbed to try to remove the spots to no avail. I told him then that I would definitely see what could be done about that.

Jake and Dan invited me to be the guest speaker at their C5 banquet that same evening. I was asked to speak about the present product. During my speech, I asked for a show of hands to find who else had experienced Jake's complaint that the spots on the cowl screen would not buff out. There were many who raised their hands. I knew then that this was reason enough to ask our supplier to reformulate the plastic compound material used to create the panels on the cowl screen. I knew that it was possible to make the panels more robust—especially on the darker cars. We decided to make the C5 registry one of the places we could use to find out the significant things that might be overlooked but needed to be changed on the new car.

The plant engineers and I tried to help generate interest in the "Miss Carlisle Beauty Contest" by going through a pretend rivalry with other audience members to be the judges of the contest. The contestants all joined in the fun. The purpose was to generate interest. There was money to be used in scholarships funds for the contestants and for other deserving college aspirants in the area as well.

The parade on Saturday was a real winner. It was led by Bill and Chip in their vintage Corvettes and followed by Dave and Karen Hill then Liz and me then all of the engineers from the plant and those from headquarters driving the newest Corvettes. The rest of the drivers who followed formed up in a long string of vintage Corvettes, restored Corvettes, re-worked and restyled Corvettes up to the newest models fresh from the showroom floors. The areas all around the streets were packed from the fairgrounds all the way to the downtown area where a band was playing and crowds of people were gathered along the streets to view the spectacle. Many of the celebrity participants went to dinner after the parade and all of us shared our battle stories.

I promised Chip and Bill that we would return to their Corvettes at Carlisle festival every year and they told me that they intended to give help and support to the Corvette Museum in Bowling Green.

For the first time since I had been plant manager of the Bowling Green facility I did not feel that I was tangled up in melted-together plastic knots working on the new 1999 Corvette. At last, I felt free and comfortable about getting out and visiting Corvette venues all around the country. I was finally able to go in the early Fall to Mike Yager's celebration of the Corvette held at his Mid-America Motorworks Parts and Accessories complex in Effingham, Illinois. He had been inviting me to attend the "Funfest" for Corvette lovers for the last two years but I had always been too busy to leave the plant while we were trying to get the new Corvette off the ground.

Finally, Liz and I would have a chance to attend the Funfest. Engineers Tom Hill and Carl Haas, and quality people, Tom Kelly and Mark Megehan and their wives all went along. We all drove the new C5's up to Mike's Mid-America Motorworks campus. We were to be met by some of the engineers from HQ. I was more than surprised and very flattered to find that Mike had set up a tribute to me on his "Wall of Fame" in the huge "My Garage Museum" building where his famous car collection was kept. He was aware of how swamped I had been and he had never told me about his "Wall of Fame" or used it as an incentive to lure me there to see it. I truly had to admire him for his patience and understanding.

Mike had chosen an eclectic group of cars to display in his collection but each one had a story to tell. I was truly blown away when I saw them but I think that the whole idea was to present an extremely impressive picture to visitors. The mix included everything from the cars that I had either only heard about or seen in the movies like the 1964 "World's Fair" Corvette, to the 1968 Le Mans race car, to the 1996 "Last C4" coupe that Mike had picked up from us at the factory over a year ago. All the famous vehicles were beautifully displayed and described there in Mike's "My Garage" display. Liz and I spent a long time inspecting the cars and reading the write-ups about them.

All of the engineers went into the field to judge the cars that the owner's had spent the morning washing and shining up to put into Mike's big car show. There was an absolutely huge field of them. The cars that we picked were considered "Celebrity Choice" and we were photographed with Mike and the winning cars as we handed out the awards to each of the proud owners.

Mike's Funfest was another Corvette celebration that I vowed never to miss again as long as I was I was plant manager at Corvette.

Wendell Strode had taken over the helm of the Corvette Museum and the museum began to noticeably move forward for the first time in a great while. Wendell had been a banker at one time. Members of the Strode family were well-respected and long-time residents of the community. Wendell and I sat down and talked about the direction that he wanted to take the museum and I gave him many ideas that I felt the plant could really help with to achieve the goals that he laid out. I felt that the Corvette plant manager should have a place on the museum's board of directors and so did Wendell. We decided to form a partnership so that the plant's influence could be the most beneficial to the progress of the museum. Wendell confided that the first-ever induction ceremony for the Corvette Hall of Fame that they were planning to hold would include six standout contributors to the Corvette hobby. It was going to take numerous volunteers along with the regular workers at the museum to make the induction ceremony as memorable as possible. The initial list of inductees that they had planned was an outstanding one including: Ed Cole, Zora Arkus-Duntov, Harley Earl, Bill Mitchell, Joe Pike, and Larry Shinoda.

On the night of the Hall of Fame ceremony, many of the relatives of the six inductees were present and spoke to the crowd that evening. Everybody who was present at the ceremony seemed to be thinking of the future and hoping that this would be the beginning of a long and illustrious tradition for the museum.

The museum held an auction and some of the things that were auctioned off included artifacts that had been used by the inductees. The plant donated some things that we had as auxiliary over at the plant including extra wheels, fenders and oil pans just to make sure that the museum had enough items for the auction. It was surely surprising that the visitors to the museum were willing to buy a single corvette tire or an extra fender or even an oil pan in order to help the museum raised much-needed funds.

We went into production of the 1999 model with orders for many of the new coupes as we were able to produce right from the very beginning. The Dual Removable Roof Panels that featured the body-color panels plus the blue-tint transparent panels seemed more than satisfactory for those who wanted a hardtop and the added flexibility of an open top. The "Heads Up" display onto the windshield was new and standard on the coupe and convertible.

Soon enough we began to build the less expensive and far less flexible fixed-roof, hardtop coupe that we had made plans for over three years ago. Most of the General Motors upper management people were never keen on the idea because many people were calling the car the "bargain basement" model. It was designed to be less expensive. It did not have its own quality build design from the very beginning. It just seemed to be a convertible with a light-weight hardtop stuck on it. For the Corvette lovers who were willing to accept the hardtop in order to get a Corvette into their garage without spending all of their money to do it, perhaps this was thought to be their answer.

I went out to the line and watched the workers set the roof onto the car by guiding the overhead lifts with the bonding glue already on the top. It purely put my teeth on edge because there was absolutely ***no*** room for error! If the roof was off-kilter at all, there was no taking that roof off and resetting it. If a mistake was made in getting the grooves and eyes to line up or if the line and catches were not done right the first time the unit was simply not salable. We could only hope that the workers we had trained were prepared for such hellish precision. The classes and pre-schooling that we had sent them through had been our attempt to see to it that they were absolutely ready. But, their ***real*** schooling was right here on the line!

Each one of the assemblers for the hardtop became specialists and irreplaceable because of that "inexpensive" car. I immediately decided to use extra people to train behind them because any amount of absenteeism caused by family problems, illness or court dates among our trained hardtop setters might very well have stopped the hardtop in its "inexpensive" tracks. We all said prayers that this would never happen. It was firmly against my principles to have a singular job like that where back-ups were required, but I made sure that there was a back-up in place at all times for assembling that car.

The majority of the line workers cringed when they saw one of the hardtops coming down the line because of the "knuckle biting precision" connected to it.

"Here comes another one of those 'Billy Bob' cars," they would say while everybody alternately went into nail-biting jitters and sweating the details.

The workers who were most skilled in lowering the top onto the "Billy Bob" car had to move quickly into place to see that the hard top was attached correctly so that the build could successfully be completed.

We did not dare to try to paint the hardtop before fixing it onto the car—that would have been a disaster of ultimate proportions. At first, the hardtop was sent off the line as soon as the top was attached then the entire prime coated surfaces were painted. Of course none of the glass could be attached before this was done, thus adding more special handling and work that had to be completed off the line. Everyone was glad when the build of the hardtop became more standard much later. We were able to accomplish this before the end of the 1999 build cycle was over.

I had been told that someone in upper management in Detroit had coined that not-so-complimentary "Billy Bob" moniker to indicate that the little hardtop was a real bargain for the everyday buyers who wanted to own a Corvette yet had really balked at the coupe and convertible prices. Lucky for us, the people who had previously expressed the desire for that "inexpensive hardtop" stepped up and bought it. Everything was limited about the car including the colors that we offered for it. As it was, we only built a little over 4,000 of the "Billy Bob" hardtop model out of a total of 33,300 cars for 1999, during the whole of the building run. But that was enough to keep it in the build cycle for 2000.

As for my part, I quickly joined the battle that Dave Hill, Tadge Jeuchter and the other engineers had going at HQ. Our research had shown that customers were not interested in cheapening the fixed roof models to death by putting smaller wheels and tires on them, cloth seats in them, hand-crank windows with manual locks, and hand-change outside mirrors on the doors. The color offerings for the car were limited enough. Somewhere in some car magazine the words "dinky" "ridiculous" and "cheap-looking" were used to describe the first three hard-top units that we turned out in this manner. Very quickly, the windfall of outcries and objections began to have an effect. In my considered opinion and (I am sure) the long held and valuable opinions of all true Corvette enthusiasts far and near: ugly nicknames, epithets and disparaging connotations have no business being associated with the Chevrolet Corvette—ever!

As "trouble free" as the C5 had finally gotten to be, we found some items presented persistent problems as we went into production of the 1999 model. But by Christmas we had overcome most of our problems and we were riding high. We had been selected as one of the "10 Best Cars" by *Car and Driver*. We had been picked as "America's

Best" by *Auto Week* and we were featured in any number of other car magazines and automobile sections of numerous newspapers.

I truly hated to see the personnel director, Cheryl Ollila leave to go back to work in Labor Relations at headquarters. I selected Bill Quinn to replace her. He moved his family to Bowling Green that Spring. Bill and I had quite a few years of solving problem in the plant, dealing with the union and the rest of the workforce before I received a call from headquarters requesting him to go to Fairfax to head the labor relations team there.

I set about interviewing candidates for the job and finally interviewed Theresa Lawrence. I was very surprised when I found out that Theresa was the wife of Derrick Lawrence whom I had met at Tyrone Taborn's Black Engineer of the Year Awards program. I had not met Theresa until she came to Bowling Green. I was happy that Derrick also wanted to transfer down to work at the plant. Theresa started to work right away trying to get the UAW to work with us.

I had been working since I had come to the plant to change the culture of the organization. Teresa's job was to carry on that work and to try to negotiate even more than what the PDs before her time had gotten started. Theresa's own pet projects seemed to be "team Concept" practices. We sent the UAW leaders to other plants to see how good the concepts worked there. That seemed to work pretty well when negotiation time came around. The union leaders themselves were talking about what was going on elsewhere and how well it seemed to be working out

I was truly determined that we would try to get the workers to stop smoking in the plant. It had not been an easy job at all. Finally Teresa thought that if we gave the workers somewhere outside to light up, we might be able to wean them off the cigarettes, especially with the coming of the winter season. It had been a chore to pull off, but it was even harder to get our high-paid UAW car builders not to fight to do the jobs around the plant like grass cutting and painting furniture.

Since our daughter Crissy had moved out of our house, she had started to work for Wendy's. I was very glad that she had found employment that she enjoyed, but Liz was not satisfied until Crissy had gotten herself back into college. Soon enough, we learned that Crissy was about to make us grandparents. I was dismayed, but as soon as the sweet little baby was born, she became a part of the family. Crissy named her Catrina Elizabeth after her grandmother. Grandchildren definitely have their own place that is hard to imagine being unfilled. I began to wonder immediately if there would be more.

Our car was used as a pace car at the 24 hour Le Mans races in France. I would have loved to have gone over to see our car displayed to the French people and to watch the races. I knew that Liz would have so much loved to go, but she was too deeply involved with teaching her classes, attending graduate school and seeing after our daughter and our new grandbaby to spend that amount of time away. I only considered the trip for a moment. I did not really want to go all the way to France if Liz couldn't go with me

There had been a lot talk for a long time about General Motors really getting back into racing with the newly-built C5 Corvette. Tom Wesoloski was tapped to manage the 1999 factory-sponsored racing team and the engineering and design team of Gary Pratt and Jim Miller were tapped to design, fabricate, and provide trackside support for the Corvette team. Although the car was touted as a production-based automobile, the racing model was re-designed as a GTS race car, the C5-R, which simply retained the standard frame with the hydro-formed rails, the production engine block, and the factory steering rack. The bored engine was given more horsepower. As for exterior changes, Pratt and Miller used carbon fiber to widen the body, they opened and bolted the headlights over with plastic but they left the tail lights essentially the same. When they were finished with all of the modifications, we were proud of saying that right off the factory floor, our production model made one gorgeous, tough-looking race car.

It was a surprise that the C5-R did very well in its debut performance at the Rolex 24 Hours at Daytona and we were happy and very encouraged by that. It had held its own in the GTS class with such overseas competitors as Porsche, Mazda and Audi. Our guys came in with a third place win right out of the box. I attended the race but I admit that I went to sleep in the corner of the Chevrolet suite during the 24 hours. I woke up to find that we were still looking pretty good. When the announcement was made that we had taken third place, I was proud of our performance in the C5-R's debut race. We did not really expect to do that well among the more seasoned factory autos. I bragged that I expected it, of course, but I didn't really, that was mostly bluster on my part. However, I was confident that Corvette was well on the way into GT racing once again.

It was after that third-place win at Daytona that our Corvette customers first started to look at our hardtop as a "racer" or a "stripped-down hot-rod." It might have been the ads that showed it out front. It made the other Corvette family members, the targa-topped coupe and the convertible, seem like the more sedate or luxury members of the family while the hardtop seemed to be far more "out there" in the limelight, a little more of a "street rod" maybe just a bit of a "macho thug." Besides the third-place win at Daytona, it may have been Dave Hill's own inspiration that made the public know that the new, scrappy little hardtop had arrived. Maybe it fit the song about the "Lil' Red Corvette" more than any other model, but it sold over 4,000 units and that was enough for us to keep it on the build list when we went into the year 2000.

By now, the C5 had become the darling of the more mature generation who had watched and loved the Corvette for at least two generations while they raised their families. And now, even though the Corvette had become much more expensive, with their kids gone, our customers could now afford to buy that two-seater sports car that they had dreamed about for so many years.

My staff, the engineers, and I had been out and about and out front at car shows from the smallest shows to the really huge ones. We had attended enough of the museum meetings, car rallies, car corrals, and enthusiast gatherings now that we were becoming well known to Corvette lovers far and wide by name and by the jobs that we did. We willingly got up close and personal with our customers: we kissed babies, petted dogs, inspected and admired the many changes and modifications that people had made to their cars, signed our names under car hoods, signed under trunk lids, signed engines, signed valve covers, took pictures with owners, took pictures with groups, autographed car models, autographed pictures of the car, autographed caps, autographed T-shirts, autographed posters of the car, and autographed books about the car. We had to make a list to designate who would be willing to give up a weekend to visit the gatherings, rallies and the races. I always made sure that I headed that list as often as I could. Most of my staff seemed to enjoy the travel to and from the events. I know that all of the staff was always ready to go the shows and rallies and to meet the Corvette owners from all over the country.

We began getting new wheels for the 2000 into the plant from a different manufacturer by late July, 1999. For those who had been longing for new wheels, these were their answer. These wheels were thicker cast aluminum with stronger edges. The flattened, five spoke wheels were changed at last: the wheel itself was thicker yet lighter and each wheel consisted of ten spokes within the perimeter of the wheel. We knew that our customers would be sure to order these but we still made sure that those fans who absolutely loved the old design were still able to get them on their cars.

The Corvette engineers had been trying for some time to work out a way to take some weight out of all of the models without compromising the integrity of the unit. The drive train and the trans-axel were targets. The engineers had succeeded to some extent with opening up the hardtop because we could move much of the wire bundles and other bulkiness and shift it to the rear of the seats. The fiberglass that the hardtop was made from was much lighter than the convertible top combinations and the fastback glass on the coupe. Some of the components that we had used for economy in the hardtop had proven to be good for all of the models. The engine, mimicking the racers bored-out lightness, had been another way to do it. The LS-1 345 horsepower still offered a wonderful power package and the racing program planned to continue using our base engine in the company sponsored racing program.

Our seat manufacturer introduced new, longer-lasting materials that they said would improve the durability of the seats, so that was changed for the 2000. The seats we now offered had a Torch Red color among them which was closer to our best-selling Torch Red for the car. We tried out the seats in a 1999 car and found that it was a better overall match so we offered the seat color as a suggested color for the 2000 Torch Red models.

Many complaints caused engineering to change the interior during the quest to make the car lighter and in doing so we changed the door pads and the size of the air bags. The seals around the windows got a change, too. That change had proven to be just what was needed to channel the water away from the door during heavy rains. Now it no longer poured down on the driver or the passenger from the channel at the top of the door where the trapped water was released when the door was opened. Our heavy water tests had proven that these changes were good. Likewise, the seals on the trunk lids and targa tops were changed for the better, too.

My secretary, Barbara Meyer, had recently retired to be with her husband and their new grandchild. My new secretary, Pam Danks who had replaced Barbara, informed me just as soon as I had gotten to work one Monday morning that there was something new in the paint shop that I really needed to see. I dropped my things onto my desk and walked out into the plant. I was really proud of our paint shop. They had really stepped up to the plate and proven themselves in more than one tough situation. The awards that they had gotten had made HQ really listen when they wanted to do any innovation. Phil Keinle, who was now superintendent in paint, met me and we walked over to the paint shop together. He wanted me to see how the new tinted clear coat that the guys from DuPont had encouraged us to use looked on a Millennium Yellow convertible and a Magnetic Red convertible.

Both those paint jobs were absolutely gorgeous! They looked as though an observer could almost fall into the depths of the paint. The red one was a beautiful Candy Apple that just begged to be on the cover of every car magazine out there! While I was in the outer area of the paint shop talking with Phil about the new processes, how they were working out and any replacements that were needed for the paint shop, the more I got to really take a good look at the car with the Millennium Yellow paint job on it.

Many people had been waiting to see the yellow color back in our 2000 run for the millennium. In the past we had reserved the yellow cars for a special run at the end of every build. I had heard from Tadge Juechter that surveys showed that the special paint job was a very sought after color. Thus, we decided to include the yellow into our regular build schedule.

I made up my mind. I knew that I had to have that Millennium Yellow car. It would be just what I needed to jump start my Corvette collection. I knew that I would have to try to catch Liz at a weak moment—maybe while she was truly preoccupied: it would have to be while she had her head stuck in a book alternately nodding off to sleep and snapping awake to study for an exam in one of her graduate classes, or if she was propped up in bed half-asleep while grading her students' lesson plans late at night. If any argument came up later from Liz about the expenditure of money for another new Corvette, I could always say:

"Well, you said it was okay!"

I admit it was shameless of me to take advantage of my wife that way but how could I be expected to resist when I knew that the only way I could get her to agree to letting me buy myself yet another Corvette was to sneak it on her in some underhanded way.

I had already convinced Liz that we needed to build a separate, free-standing garage because we had a truck parked out in the yard, a trailer in the yard that I used for hauling the race car, and a tractor which I left in the yard sometimes after I had been cutting hay for the cows for winter. Liz already had agreed that I could have the garage built (she had been groggy and really sleep deprived then, too). I figured that since I had the space, I might as well put another car into the bay beside the 40th Anniversary Corvette. So, I figured it was a done deal: I would put the Millennium Yellow Corvette into the garage beside the 40th.

After I had gotten the yellow car home, Liz promptly declared that since I still had an unfilled bay left in the garage, it was probably just a matter of time before I got the urge to put yet another car into it. That had better **not** happen, she warned me firmly, especially not in the underhanded way that it had happened this time.

One of the Holley Performance Products brand managers called my office several times and Pam finally caught up with me between meetings and connected us. He was wondering if I would allow him to put an after-market conversion on one of my cars or have one of my people to come over to evaluate their new exhaust system. The new exhaust was a conversion that would run from the catalytic converter all the way back and out through their stylish exhaust extensions at the back of the car. After I thought about it, I felt it would be best to let him put the new exhaust system on my own new Millennium Yellow convertible. I think that is what he had in mind anyway.

After the technicians had finished installing it, the system as a whole looked good and sounded absolutely wonderful whenever the car was started up. I only had one complaint that I gave them: the beautiful pipes were rather sharp to the touch along the edges. When the average Corvette owner was cleaning his car, he was very likely to run his hand against the sharp edges of those pipes. The managers at Holley assured me that the pipes that they were prepared to sell commercially would be far more finished along the edges. My overall evaluation was that the system was excellent because I loved the sound that those pipes made. I felt that the pipes should do very well as an after-market conversion. I wondered why such a system couldn't be added to the Corvette while the car was being assembled on the line even if it added a tiny bit more cost. After all, wasn't Corvette all about looking and sounding powerful? I vowed to talk that over with Dave as soon as I could.

When I finally caught up to Dave, he told me that the manufacturer could not put the pipes on in the build process at the factory because the federal noise standards for automobile companies would not allow our cars to pass the particular standards imposed on the exhaust system if we put on the pipes. He was convinced that we would just have to depend on the after-market guys to produce any pipes that were outside those standards.

One of the members of the Corvette Forum took pictures of my car parked in front of the plant. He wrote in his article in *Corvette Fever*:

"Even Wil Cooksey, the Corvette plant manager, hates those dinky exhaust pipes that come from the factory! See how he had them changed on his personal car!"

I let anyone who asked me know that the pipes were a Holley experiment put on my car to let everyone see them. Everyone would want those good-looking exhaust and pipes, I claimed. Those words really did prove to be the truth in the end.

When we went to the ICCC convention, James Lundy saw my new Millennium Yellow Corvette. When he heard those pipes, he declared that he very much wanted that car. Many of my ICCC friends argued that they wanted it, too, because of the paint as well as those pipes. Of course I promised my buddy Lundy that I would sell the car to him just as soon as I was able to let it go. I am sure that Holley got a few more sales after I allowed the guys at the convention and all the true Corvette lovers at other venues that I visited that summer to rev the engine on the car and listen to the throaty roar of those tail pipes!

Every plant under the General Motors banner always had an Employee Incentive Program where employees could submit suggestions that were designed to help improve the business. There had been one at Corvette since Saint Louis. The Corvette organization had given out televisions, toasters, alarm clocks, jackets, pressure cookers and all kinds of awards to the employees from the General Motors Chevrolet Incentives Program in the past. However, we had to understand that we were a small plant, unlike the other giant plants in General Motors with multiple products and huge budgets. Those plants had given out cars—smaller, less expensive cars—as employee incentives in the past. I suppose that is why someone suggested that just this one time, we should give out a car, too, as a reward for a cost-saving suggestion or a suggestion about improving quality. We had to consider though that any one of our products even the less expensive "Billy Bob" car would be a pretty expensive incentive for us. I really thought the idea was a good one, nevertheless.

I took the idea to Jim Campbell, the Chevrolet brand manager. I told him that we wanted to reward any employee who gave us a good enough suggestion that might help us to win the J. D. Power Platinum Award for Quality. I told Jim that our plant really intended to compete for that award. It would be a real feather in our caps if we won it. We wanted to be recognized as the best. We wanted that kind of publicity to help us with sales.

Jim agreed to pay for a giveaway car from his budget. It had to be special, Jim asserted and the person who won had to have a real cost-saving idea or a real important idea about improving quality for either the plant as a whole, the car, or the brand.

We had already decided that the car had to be different—very noticeably different. It had to be a one-of-a-kind paint job. We landed on Platinum Purple Metallic for the color to commemorate the J. D. Power Platinum Award. The car we selected was a hardtop. Phil Kienle's painters did a masterful job. They painted the car, masked it off and then, very carefully painted two platinum stripes only a few inches apart, right down the middle of the car. They also used the legendary 5-spoke ZR-1 wheels painted platinum. We left the car on display on the floor of the body shop for all of the employees to inspect.

The car was a great incentive. We had never seen the workers so inspired to come to work, to stay at work longer, to work together, or work so hard. In the past, whenever I had been out and about in the city, I had run into our employees from the Corvette plant getting haircuts, shopping in grocery stores, and browsing at the mall—all during working hours! Many times I would get a call from the owner of Chuck's Liquor Store during the hours that the plant was running that I had employees from the plant coming in to buy liquor during plant working hours.

Not so these days!

Since we were delaying the introduction of the 2001 models, we decided to give away the other incentive prizes and the car at the end of the 2000 model year on the day that we took the last of the 2000's of the line.

We gathered all of the workers in the body shop to announce the incentives winners and the winner of the car. The names of the successful suggestion makers were put in a barrel and rolled around many times. We drew names for a television, an electric toaster oven, jackets, caps and the other prizes. Then we drew Billy Phelps' name from the barrel for the car. He almost fainted but afterwards he was a real trooper. He allowed the museum to display the car for several months, and then he sold it to Bob McDorman in Columbus, Ohio, who owned a very large Chevrolet dealership and later became one of the Hall of Fame inductees at the Corvette Museum. Billy said that he intended to use his profits from the sale of that prize car to send his son to college. Everybody was happy for Billy and his son.

I was reminded that my son, David, had finally finished college by this time and he had knocked around in Kansas for a while doing this job and that until, finally, he had gone off to Atlanta to see if he could not find a job that might be more suited to him. I fully supported him in this idea since he had grown up in Atlanta. Then too, I was acquainted with quite a few people in the area that I knew I could count on to help him along if he needed it.

I had to become a commuter again. One of the management initiatives GM was to regularly bring the plant managers to Detroit to HQ in order to have us to make reports at the plant manager's meetings. There were not that many reports going on—at least not from the plant managers. Mostly we **heard** reports about the state of the business, about future needs, how to keep competitive, what was happening with the UAW (especially when negotiations were coming up), about sales, about marketing, about what future needs might be, and they told **us** how things were going in the plants. There always seemed to be something to take our time away from getting cars built.

The people at headquarters were not responsible to get cars off the line and to the dealers. Their business seemed to be holding meetings. They were really good at planning those. The plant managers resented being taken away from our business of getting the cars off the line and into the car dealers' showrooms. We did not need to hear all about the international UAW organization when our **only** business was dealing with the local UAW rank and file within our plants each and every workday. Even the managers who lived and worked in Detroit and vicinity resented being taken away from their daily business to discuss general business and the larger concerns of the company about the international UAW.

At last, we plant managers were delighted to hear that our travels would be minimized by using the internet and we would have net meetings where we could hold the business meetings from our computers in our offices right from our various plants. We were told that we could bring in our staffs to our offices for the meetings if need be.

That had not lasted long!

Too many times the meetings over the net at each plant were summarily interrupted by urgent plant business. Something was always happening in somebody's plant that demanded their immediate attention. Nobody could just sit still at their desks and listen while something important was happening out in their factory. All too often a plant manager would be obliged to get up and leave his desk and the electronically broadcast net meeting to take care of urgent plant business out on the floor of his own plant.

Soon enough, we were back to having the plant managers meetings at HQ in Detroit again. Once again we were required to make the trek to Detroit and stay at least overnight. Perhaps the upper managers really felt that they could not feel as powerful with us in our plants as they could having us sit before them in a group while they talked at us. One upper-level manager in particular actually garnered something close to very real hatred from all of us with his gestapo-like speeches and tactics. In his quest to secure our respect for his own importance, he was prone to resort to unnecessary blustering. His repertory included nothing short of fear-management tactics.

When I was traveling, my biggest problem was Liz. She hated it when I had to go off to Detroit. I joked that it was not because Liz missed me; it was because she was obligated to feed the cows while I was gone. I had sworn that Liz would never have to get involved with my cattle-raising project. Now, I had to eat those words. Liz said to me querulously:

"I knew damn well this was going to happen when you brought those cows in here!"

We both knew that the cattle had to be fed during the fall and winter when I was traveling. The feeders had to be filled each day when grass was not high enough. Hay was just not enough to completely sustain the cattle—they needed at least one good meal of grain a day.

Liz simply did not like to go into the barn where the grain for the cattle was stored. She did not complain too much at first—not until I had traded my first bull and got a new bull into the pasture.

Bobby Thomas had patiently explained to me when I first started the cattle raising project that every farmer always keeps and raises the female calves that are born to the heifers so as to breed them when they mature, thus increasing the size of his herd and his profits. However, the sire of those maturing female calves and all of the male calves that are born to the first bull needed to be rotated out, sold off, or made into steers and sold for slaughter. Then, a new bull not related to the offspring had to be brought in. Liz understood this only too well; she was familiar with the biological aspects of it. She had spent much of her childhood on a farm after all. The problem was that she was really terrified of the new bull. He had a tendency sometimes to look and behave just a bit too menacing.

Both Liz and I had become accustomed to the first bull that I owned. He was a plump red Herford with a sweet-looking white face. He very efficiently took care of his duties with the cows and his efforts had produced multiple female calves into my herd. We had nicknamed him "Gus" and he was as tame as a big puppy dog. He quickly became quite attached to anyone would feed him and a couple of times he had broken out of the fence just to lie in front of the garage doors to wait patiently until someone came out to put grain into the cattle-feeding troughs. We couldn't be really angry about his breaking the fence because he never went anywhere, he would follow docile and calm behind Liz or me back through the gate whenever either of us went to get food from the barn to feed the herd.

Not so with this new bull! He was simply not tame!

He was as black as a moonless night and he was unfriendly and mean as a water buffalo. He had come from a stock of animals that were absolute giants. He was as brash as he was big, and he was very impatient. He kept the entire herd of cows constantly stirred up and busy. If he was not occupied by either food or sex, he would stand belligerently and stare at whoever came anywhere near him with his head half-turned and lowered while he blew gusts of steamy breath through his nose. He did not like it if anyone dared to walk near the fence of his pasture. He broke the fence whenever he was inclined to do it and I always needed a lot of help from my friends wielding golf clubs, chairs or ropes to round him up.

The new bull seemed to tolerate me to a certain extent but he would always try to intimidate Liz. I kept on telling her that the bull wasn't so bad—he was just a normal, slightly rambunctious farm animal, in spite of the fact that he was so huge, had a fierce-looking face with rather small, red-veined eyes. Liz said that he always looked as if he had been grazing on wild-growing loco weed. Having his horns sawed-off did not help one bit—Liz still feared him and she did not want to go anywhere near him at any time.

Bobby Thomas came out and we took a good week or so stringing an electrically charged wire all the way around the cattle field. Bobby assured Liz that once the electricity was turned on, one burning zap against the bull's nose from the wire would surely be enough to contain him. That proved to be true, but it seemed to make him all the more belligerent. The more un-settled the bull behaved the more Liz feared him.

Things came to a head one week-end when I was gone up to Detroit for a meeting. When Liz got home from school, she looked about for the herd and determined that since they were nowhere to be seen, they were likely to be grazing in the back pasture next to the back water-feeder where I had moved a couple of bales of hay into the feeders for the winter. Liz decided that it might be a good time for her to get the trough feeders in front of the barn all filled up with the supplemental grain before the herd came up to the barn for the evening. She related this story to me:

She had filled up the first bucket of grain to carry to the troughs from the huge aluminum vat inside the barn where I kept the grain stored, and she was re-fastening the cattle gate that was held by a chain across the barn door. Just then she heard a deep, rumbling sound right behind her and at the same time felt a scalding gust of hot breath against the back of her neck. She claimed that she half-turned and was eye-to-eye with that huge, red-eyed, midnight menace standing right behind her. Liz had no idea where the big bull had been hiding but he had crept up on her as soundlessly as a cat and was poised as if he intended to be the first to get at that grain, or worse, as if he fully intended to intimidate Liz and forcefully take the grain away from her.

Liz said that a spurt of pure fear-laced adrenalin went shooting through her veins making her drop the bucket of grain and go leaping clear over the cattle gate without even re-opening it—a thing that neither of us would have believed she was capable of doing under normal circumstances. She claimed she fled through the cattle gate at the back of the barn and ran a zigzagged path to the gate in the back fence, unlatched it, and got out of there to the road. Meanwhile, the bull left the grain untouched to follow Liz around the barn. Liz said that the bull paced and forth back inside the fence and around the pond to track her progress as she walked all the way back around the fenced-in field and down the road to the house—a trip that she complained had taken her a pretty good amount of time to make.

Finally the bull went back to the bucket of grain after Liz had fled, and all the rest of the cattle had to go without any grain at all until I returned home late the next day. Liz told me the whole story and declared that she would not go back inside that fence or into that barn anymore. She claimed that the bull really had it in for her and she surely could not, in any way at all, abide that mean ol' devil!

By the 2000 season, Corvette was firmly entrenched in racing and the company's publicists in Detroit were taking full advantage of the news of race team's success. During the annual 12 Hours at Sebring, Florida, drivers Ron Fellows, Chris Kneifel and Justin Bell driving the C-5R No. 4 had taken 16th in the overall race and 5th in their class. The other car, No 3, driven by Andy Pilgrim, Kelly Collins and Franck Freon came in with a 24th overall in the race and 6th in their class.

Corvette took first place at Texas Motor Speedway in September in an ALMS series race, and then they scored again at Road Atlanta at the end of the month. Our publicity claimed that we were the only sports car that could come right off the assembly line and go right onto the racetrack and win.

How true.

GM's marketing department was shouting this news of the win in all of the car magazines. Apparently there was a lot of truth to the publicity that few if any modifications had to be made in our LS-1 engine for it to become completely race ready. Except for the 4th place finish in Le Mans, France, and 5th and 6th place in Sebring, the factory sponsored Corvette racing team never finished out of contention on the racetrack again for many years.

Our little "thug" of a hardtop completely earned its stripes with the latest racing news that year. Since the race team was using a version of the hardtop for racing, it had become a bona fide contender. When the 2001's came out, our "lil' scrappy" was no longer just a hardtop, it had morphed before the Corvette lovers' very eyes into the mighty Z06 carrying air-cooled brakes and a race-ready engine. The LS6 engine could produce 385 horsepower and it was capable of being a stand-out on its own as a true "muscle car." Now, for the racers, it rated a step above its coupe and convertible mates. It was now named

"Z06" to commemorate engineer Zora Arkus-Duntov's race prepared big block that he had campaigned in the 1960s.

The "inexpensive" little hardtop did not retain any of the trappings that we had nursed and felt so protective about for almost 2 years. When it had come off the engineers' drawing boards this time, it was an entirely re-worked automobile. Absolutely nothing was inexpensive about the Z06. Not only did it have a new racing-based name, our Z06 retained little of its hardtop precursor. It was all grown up, standing on its own, and flexing a mass of considerable racing muscle in its sleek, stout little body. It quickly became the darling of all of the car magazines and, as the workers on the line were fond of saying: "that 'Zee' is its own bad self." Our bad little "Zee" was our most expensive car in the 2001 lineup just edging out the convertible that had been the unquestioned price leader and the favorite new car since 1998. The Z06 was our awards winner now and that car was really about to change everything.

It had been decided in engineering design at HQ that all of the Z06s would carry only 6-speed manual transmissions. We were sent titanium exhaust systems for the Z06, but I was informed in a production meeting in Detroit that we would only be able to get those in limited supply. The exhaust systems were true racing equipment, we were able to see that when we got them into the plant. We could only hope that our supplier could produce more for us.

Even the tires on the Z06 had to be different. We had become accustomed to the firmer run-flats by this time, but the wider, softer street tires for the Z06 were by far more similar to racing tires—they were nothing like the run-flats. There was a different, more modern tire-inflator kit designed to be included by the plant inside the Z06. It was designed to plug and fill a flat tire until the driver could make it to a repair place. Many times our operators on the final line would forget to put the kit into the cars. The new car dealers were obliged to request the kits from the plant if the kits had been forgotten or left out by mistake.

I chose a black Z06 with black/red seats and black/red interior for evaluation purposes and then I drove it as a company car. I soon became far too accustomed to the power under my foot and the short racer-like throw of the shifter. I could not let that Z06 go back into the fleet.

Fortunately, Liz was by that time very deeply involved with her doctoral dissertation—she was too worn out and too overworked to argue when I pointed out that I needed to add the black Z06 that I was driving into my garage collection.

"I'll sell it later," I promised reasonably, "Didn't I sell Lundy the yellow one just like I said I would?"

"Oh, all right," Liz agreed. She needed to get rid of me so she could finish a paper for her class the next night at the University of Louisville. "As long as you actually plan to sell it . . ."

It never happened. I still own that Z06.

Jack Garrett from Tyler, Texas who had by now become president of ICCC found a mechanic who wished to test out a nitrous power booster and introduce it to the Corvette enthusiasts. I allowed him use the black Z06 for his tests. It really boosted the torque on the low end of the acceleration. I claimed to Liz that this had changed the car so drastically that I would never find a buyer for it. I know that Liz did not believe what I said—she was just too tired to put up a good argument.

Liz went off to Mexico to visit two of the students in her class who were doing their student teaching in Mexico City. Western Kentucky sent a group of teacher education professors to Mexico because another professor, Vicky Staton had written a grant to allow the teacher education students to do their practicum in Mexico. Alice Mikovich was coordinator of student teachers in the teacher education department and she helped out with the program. Two of the students had been enrolled in Liz's English methods class and were now teaching in a school where there were English learning and English-speaking students. There were others from other departments at Western who made up the rest of the rather large group who also went down to Mexico City to visit students. The program was an experimental one designed to give student teachers experience teaching in another country.

I was glad that Liz had gotten away from the university for a while, but I was quite uneasy about the trip. Liz was really under a lot of pressure to finish the work on her doctorate degree. She'd had so much bad luck with the people who were on her dissertation committee. Her original committee chairperson, an assistant dean in the department of education at the University of Louisville, had died unexpectedly. Then the next professor who headed Liz's committee seemed as sadistic as academic. Liz told me that she could go into screaming fits at the drop of a hat. I was hoping that the trip to Mexico would relax Liz and take her mind off her dissertation troubles—at least, for a little while.

David came home from Atlanta and declared that he wanted to change his life completely. He had thought about it and decided that he wanted to join the military just as I had done and he declared that he might stay with it and make a career of it. I counseled him as far as I could about the military life and we talked far into the night some nights with me telling him all about the Viet Nam combat experiences that I had never shared with anyone else. I did not try to sugar-coat anything. Quite contrary to what I had intended, the counsel that I gave to David seemed to make him all the more determined to follow in my footsteps, so I consoled myself that, perhaps, I had helped him make the right decision.

I contacted my neighbor across the street, Teddy Barlow, whom I had met at the race track long before I learned that he was my neighbor. He had a really nice race car that he had been running for some time. He knew who I was but we had only met when I had seen him at Beech Bend racetrack. He had told me one time when we were talking at the track that he was an Army recruiter.

Liz and I saw David off with Teddy about a month later to be sworn into the Army. Liz was not particularly happy to see her son leave to become a military man, but I could not help but feel that it might have been the best thing to help him to stop his wandering life—moving from job to job—and get his life firmly back onto the straight and narrow.

When Liz and I had gone to the Black Engineer of the Year Conference earlier in the year, I was very impressed when I learned more about AMIE (Advancing Minorities' Interest in Engineering). While Liz was gone to Mexico, I spent time working with AMIE for their upcoming conference. At that time I became acquainted with Myron Hardeman who was the executive director of AMIE and Pat Burgess who worked at Morgan State University in Baltimore and also worked for AMIE. They told me that AMIE had come about as a result of a concerted effort by Abbott Laboratories to encourage diversity in their own worldwide workforce. Now the AMIE group had grown to include many more corporations and many more people including the Council of Engineering Deans at HBCUs (Historically Black Colleges and Universities). I figured that I could help the group at the same time that I was working with Tyrone Taborn on the Black Engineer of the Year Conference. General Motors had already seen the worth of this. They were now aware that they could get some really good potential engineers from the recommendations of the alliances when they had first sent their recruiters to the conference. Now, I was charged with keeping in contact with the recruiters.

By far, our crowning achievement at General Motors and the Corvette plant in particular in 2001 was that we won first place in the Initial Quality Study (IQS) of J. D. Power for the Z06. We had been shooting for the award for the past three years.

We were awarded "Automobile of the Year" by *Automobile Magazine* for the Z06. Also, the Automobile Association of Canada awarded the Z06 "Car of the Year." That was an award that we had not expected at all.

The quest by engineering to make the Z06 lighter in weight eventually resulted in a lighter weight in the other two models of Corvette too. We won high praise for the glass mat battery which we put into all of the cars and the thinner glass of the windshield of the Z06 which eventually was used on the two other models.

The customers had complained that the exhaust pipes on all three models of the cars were "dinky" and "unattractive." Many buyers regularly had their whole exhaust systems completely changed out at Mike Yager's Funfest venue in Illinois, and at other such car parts shops in Florida and California. They also bought new pipes and exhausts in other speed shops all over the country. Usually the Corvette people swapped out their whole systems or they had the more attractive round tips like those in Mike's parts catalog hooked onto their exhaust pipes. It was toward the middle of the year when we changed the exhaust system and pipes on the Z06. We were always working to make all models of the cars more appealing to the customers.

Both the C5-R race cars that General Motors sponsored finished in first and second place in the Grand-Am 24 hour race at Daytona in February. For the rest of the racing season, the cars never finished any lower than 4th place in any race that they entered in the GTS class including the 24 hours of Le Mans in France.

General Motors Racing released a statement announcing that they would allow groups and companies to buy a race prepared Corvette C5-R built by Pratt-Miller a very well-known engineering and fabrication company out of Hudson, Michigan that had been building the GM race cars from the beginning and were handling the day-to-day aspects of GM racing. By this time Doug Fehan had taken over as the program manager of Corvette racing for General Motors. He was already working hard with Pratt and Miller to develop the next generation of the Corvette race car. He was very deeply involved with training race car drivers at many of the venues around GT racing.

I could only guess that it was thought that if individuals and groups were willing to sign papers and take road handling training courses and a driving/handling class at any of the driving schools around the country such as Bondurant Driving School in California they might be able to get hold of a race car such as the racer that the company owned. I did not know much about the program as we at the plant were not at all involved in it, but I could not help but think that the screening process that they used had to be a good one.

After all of Liz's mind-strapping hard work, she was thinking of dropping out of the doctoral program without finishing it.

When I came home one evening to find her crying at the dinner table with papers and books lying on the floor where she had flung them all around her, I was stunned. She had worked too long and too hard to end it like this. She had been driving up to the University of Louisville for classes two days a week for over two years now, leaving well before 5 o'clock in the morning and returning home sometimes close to 11 or 12 o'clock after her last evening class. She had sat up nights researching and writing the papers for the classes that she was taking, plus she had spent the rest of the time grading papers for the classes that she taught at Western. She had been doing this for at least the last three years.

First Jim Becker then later Vickie Staton, who had headed the education department at Western, had been absolutely wonderful to Liz. Carl Martray the dean of the education department had first encouraged them to schedule the classes that Liz taught so that she could have two days in the week free to drive back and forth to take graduate classes at the University of Louisville. Liz still taught a full load of classes and went on any trip scheduled by the education department.

I knew that Liz was overworked and over-anxious. It was hard on her but still she tried to spend time with our family. She got to travel with me once in a while, but usually her summers were chock a' block full of classes she taught and classes that she was taking. She spent every hour of her day reading, writing, or grading papers.

I was really furious when Liz told me that her dissertation committee had decided that she could not finish her dissertation by spring. That was when she had become really depressed, had herself a crying fit and had finally decided to just abandon the whole thing. She was ready to leave Western Kentucky University if she had to do it.

I got on the telephone and personally attempted to contact every one of the professors on Liz's committee. I intended to let them know just how hard she had worked and sacrificed to get her work done. I wanted them to say it straight to me if they had any obligation to help Liz get her degree finished and I wanted them to be able to tell me personally if they thought they had fulfilled their obligation. I enlisted my secretary, Pam's help in getting in touch with every person on Liz's committee to tell them that I intended to meet with them face to face for their explanation.

Professor Steve Miller who was the chairman of Liz's committee told me immediately that he was in favor of the spring date for Liz to finish her degree. He promised to work with Liz as late as necessary to get the work done in time. Professor Gene Fiene who was also on Liz's committee said the same. Professor Christopher Wagner was hospitalized at the time because he had suffered an asthma attack that spring, but I was mollified by the fact that he left the hospital and made it to the university in time to meet with me. He was weak from the ordeal he had just undergone but he promised that he would soon be back on his feet to work with Liz as much as was needed in order to meet the deadline. (It didn't hurt that Chris, a white-haired, distinguished-looking man was also a fun-loving Corvette owner who loved to go to funfest and claimed that he had posed as me in several occasions.) I was gratified that all of Liz's advisors were staunch academicians who believed in working closely with their doctorial candidates.

I was encouraged because Liz seemed to have renewed spirits after the meeting. Steve Miller and Liz's friend and colleague, Professor Jacqueline Schliefer stayed long hours after classes for several days during one week making sure that Liz got the work wrapped up. I went up to Liz's office at the university and sat with them one night while they wrote and corrected until well after midnight. Once was enough—it was too much for me. I took Jackie and Steve out for a special lunch at Rafferty's downtown when it was all finished. I think both of them were just as happy as Liz was to see it done.

Liz went through graduation ceremonies at two universities: The University of Louisville as well as Western Kentucky University. Chris Wagner, Gene Fiene, and Steve Miller participated in Liz's ceremonial hooding at Western. Then Steve Miller and Chris Wagner hooded Liz again at the ceremonies at the University of Louisville.

All of Liz's friends, relatives and colleagues turned out for her graduation. Liz's sister, Florestine, told Liz that as much as she had wanted to bring their mother up to Kentucky to see Liz get her doctorate degree, their mom was not able to make the trip. Their mom was by this time living in a nursing home because she needed constant assistance—she was unable to spend time either walking or on her feet. Teen, Walter, and Liz's cousins Pauline and Nadine came up from Memphis and Holly Springs for the ceremonies at both universities. James and Carolyn Lundy came up from Huntsville, Alabama and brought their family to Liz's graduation at the University of Louisville. They were part of our family, too.

By now, David had gotten married to a young lady named Levine Vassell who was also a member of the military. They came up from the post in Fort Campbell for Liz's graduation. The kids and I planned a surprise party for Liz at Raffety's for all of Liz's friends and colleagues.

I knew Liz was glad to celebrate and so was I. It was over at last. Both Liz and I could both breathe freely again.

2002 was truly a banner year for us at the Corvette plant. We won the J. D. Power Silver Award for being the industry's 2nd highest quality plant in North America. Not only that, we won the J. D. Power Initial Quality Study (IQS) for the second year in a row.

We won awards for the seats and the interior furnishings, and there was much buzz about the retro waterfall between the seats of the Corvette convertible. Most complimentary to us was the talk about our continuous improvement of the Z06 and our drive to make our sports car the most talked-about in the industry. The engineers had made improvements on the engine to make it a 5.7 liter LS6 V-8 engine. It got 20 more horsepower to bring it to 405. The engine cams were improved to make room for freer intake and exhaustion thus boosting the power of the engine.

The upshot of all of the under-the-hood changes was that the Z06 was faster, longer lasting without changing the oil as often, and gave a much better overall performance to the everyday driver. Many of the body changes were designed to give better ride and durability to the Z06, and to improve the handling and performance thus making the car more appealing to the non-racing conscious Corvette drivers.

On the strength of the last year's racing season *Automobile Magazine* named the Corvette the "Racing Car of the Year." The C5-R had absolutely dominated all of the cars in the GTS class during the last season and started the 2002 season with a 1st place win at the 12 Hours at Sebring in Florida. The Corvette team of Ron Fellows, Johnny O'Connell and Oliver Gavin handily won that race.

In June, we heard that Corvette's 2-car entry had dominated the field in the 24 hour race in Le Mans, France and had finished in first and second place in the GT class. Once again I only wished that I had gone to France to see the team win big but this time I just couldn't go. There was just too much activity at the museum and at the plant.

Corvette dominated the ALMS circuit for the rest of the year until October narrowing out the field among the regulars who were dropping out. We met and talked with the Flying Lizards race team and Liz laughingly told the guys who were English speakers how much she liked their name. We also met other race teams at the hotels that we were staying at and we made sure to wish them all luck. I am sure that they did not have the slightest idea who we were unless they had chanced to see us in the pits behind the race team where we could sometimes be found.

Liz and I were more than thrilled when Robin Pratt of the Pratt and Miller group provided me with my own race gear with my name on it. She loaned Liz a suit, too, so that both of us could go into the pits any time we wanted to really be close and see all of the action behind the scenes at the races. Robin played hostess for us and made us welcome in the compound that they had made between their big trucks on the race grounds.

Although we had been dealing with all the possibilities, we were finally told that the two-seater Cadillac Evoq concept car that had been talked about for over a year would certainly become a reality. We were absolutely thrilled when the word came from HQ that we would definitely be called upon to assemble the new Cadillac product in our plant. Now, we could no longer call ourselves "The Corvette Plant"—we were going to be a true General Motors Assembly Plant because we would be assembling more than one product.

In fact, we had received word some months ago, that there was a possibility that we would get two other two-seater cars that General Motors had on the horizon, the Pontiac Solstice and the Saturn Sky. It was not a sure thing even from the beginning, and we knew that if we had only a part of the assembly of either of the cars, we would definitely have to get busy adding to the existing space in the plant and getting in new personnel, too.

However, we quickly learned that we would not be building any additions to the plant with only the Cadillac two-seater sports car coming to us. We could look forward to being able to hire a very few more people to work on building the car, but that was all. Dave Hill who had currently been moved to become our new Vehicle Line Executive made our business case at HQ in Detroit.

Dave told the executive committee that we would be able to build the Cadillac, now named the XLR, with a minimum of new personnel; a minimum of new financing; a minimum of space within the existing structure of the plant; and a minimum of time to be used for our mission.

My job was to get union and management to work together for the benefit of the existing health of Corvette in Bowling Green as well as for the future of the new XLR operation. We needed to come up with a team operation that we had never had before between union and management and make that concept workable.

We had to convince the union workers to do the jobs and the complete the operations that crossed the traditional lines drawn by the UAW and agreed upon by management about operator responsibilities. The union stood firm about operators doing any of the work that included repairs on the machines that they used and operated. Bryan Worley, the union representative, and I worked out new rules and agreements that would allow the union to cross some of those lines that seemed inflexible and seemed to hinder the operators' abilities to produce the XLR at minimum cost. Our ultimate goal was to be competitive with the 2-seater Lexus SC430 in both styling and in price. I could tell from the prototypes that had been produced that this was going to be a very real possibility.

Dave Leon came down to Bowling Green from the engineering group in Detroit to set up and begin to build the new car. The workers who went with the Cadillac seemed very much like the Chosen Ones. Everyone who worked on the XLR was given a set of smocks with their names as well as the name of their product embroidered on them. Of course we claimed that this was to protect the workers' clothing as well as the car but none of the rest of the workers believed us.

We did everything possible to carve out the space that we needed to assemble the XLR using what we had allotted within our existing structure. We made the needed floor space available by shifting and moving offices and carving up the existing areas of the plant by erecting new walls and dividers. When the first modules which were to be assembled into brand new Cadillac XLRs arrived in the large trucks, we were ready.

The car was based on Corvette's Y platform—the C5 that was produced up until 2004. Unlike the Corvette though, this was a two–door coupe /convertible—this car had a power retractable hardtop that was designed to fit snugly into the trunk of the car.

Contrary to what the press had been saying, this was not just a Corvette in Cadillac skin. As the line workers had once said when the Z06 had matured long ago: "the XLR is its own self."

It was ultra, ultra-luxury/sport with plush seating and other inside appointments. The entire interior was different with highly polished Eucalyptus wood trim on the door handles, steering wheel and it made up the entire center console. It was entirely Cadillac-type luxury with a 4.6 liter *Northstar* V8 or 4.4 liter *Northstar* SC V8 both using a 6-speed automatic transmission.

Our "rolling bin" method of construction was very successful. The "kit carts" as we called them were each stocked with the exact number of pieces needed at the individual stations that we had set up. At the end of the building station, we had put together a car that was truly worthy of the Cadillac name.

We congratulated ourselves on a job very well done when slowly we rolled out the very first Cadillac XLRs. I took a black one from the first batch to be my own personal daily driver. It really matched my tastes for sportiness and luxury. When I brought it home to stay, Liz looked at me and sighed.

"I guess you're just hopeless," she said. "We'll never have any money to spend because you can't stop buying every car you're building."

The Indianapolis 500 Pace Car was ours once again in 2002. HQ made the decision and we were asked to pull ahead to April the 50th Anniversary Corvette paint, a dark burgundy with metallic paint chips and the special metallic coating that DuPont had provided. The public had no idea up to that point that the scheduled pace car was actually the 50th Anniversary model. Everybody thought that this was a special edition just for the race even with the 50th Anniversary badging. Many in the public as well as some people in General Motors thought that we would try to use a gold-colored paint for the 50th Anniversary edition that was scheduled to be released to the public in late August.

But, **not so**!

Even as much as I would have **loved** to see gold paint on the 50th I knew well enough what a disaster it might be. Both copper metallic and the gold metallic had been absolute failures for us in the past.

I was willing to bet DuPont breathed a huge sigh of relief when we did not ask them to provide gold paint for our 50th. I knew that our chief engineer, Dave Hill and his assistant, Tadge Jeuchter and Harlan Charles in marketing, too, had to fight quite a few roaring battles up at HQ over using that gold paint. I know they told them over and over in no uncertain terms that both copper and gold paints had given us nothing but trouble at the plant. The paint had shown inconsistency even when it was used on metal panels—not to mention the disaster that it was on our fiberglass panels.

I had to agree with Dave about the chances of inconsistency of the gold paint. I knew it well enough because I had reported it to them often enough in the past when we had tried to use that paint on the cars in the plant before. We dared not even try to use the gold; it would have been a disaster of major proportions.

Anyway, the more I looked at that Special Anniversary Red on the cars (technically it was called Xirallic Crystal Red), the more I grew to love it. I knew already that I needed to have that 50th Anniversary Corvette as part of my own little collection.

Our body shop painted three cars for Indy, two convertibles and one coupe, and we were sent shale-colored interiors for those cars (shale was designated as a color between beige and very light grey). The shale was used for the leather seats and the instrument panel. The door pads and the instrument panel were a bit of a darker shade. It was the first time the IP had ever been anything other than black. The two-toned shale-colored interior and the shale colored convertible top really sealed the deal for me and many, many other Corvette lovers who had waited so very patiently for the 50th Anniversary Edition.

The new, much stronger, spun-cast aluminum wheels which we were scheduled to use for all of the 2003 Corvettes were pulled forward for the Indy pace cars. The wheels were painted lightly champagne/gold for the 50th Anniversary and the wheel insets had the 50th badge on them, too. Strobe lights were added to the one car to be used as the pace car. We had already put the 50th Anniversary badging on all of the cars when we sent them out of the plant to the decal company. The golden flying flag decals the company put on the sides up to the hoods of the three cars were smaller compared to those that had decorated the sides of the previous pace cars. They also put

"Corvette" in large letters across the top of the windshield of the pace car.

Chevrolet invited Liz and me to the race and I was asked to go out onto the field to meet Jim Caviezel who was going to drive one of the convertibles to pace the race. He wanted to meet the people who had put together the car that he was driving. He had taken several practice runs in the convertible and he absolutely loved it! Even though I had been told that Jim Caviezel was famously reticent and that he was a person who never smiled at all, I was in the car right behind Jim during the parade of other Corvettes and he was actually smiling and waving to the crowd. He really seemed to be having a great time driving that car. He wanted very much to take one of the Corvettes home. When he was told that the winning driver would get to take one that did not have graphics on it, he told me that he wanted to know why he could not have one of the others.

During the 500 parade Liz and I got to ride with Chevrolet drivers around the track before the race. It was indeed quite a thrill for everybody

We went to a screening of one of Jim's new films during the week-end. We got to hang out for the evening at an IMAX theater in Indianapolis where Jim talked about his film and his career. He also said that he very much wanted to drive another Corvette at the Indy 500 and he was not alone in hoping that Chevrolet would be selected for another turn on the field as the pace car for another Indianapolis 500 in the future.

Helio Castroneves won the 500 on race day driving a Chevy-powered Dallara. He took a turn around the field after the win riding atop his biggest prize: a brand new 50th anniversary Corvette. Harlan Charles his wife Mai, Liz and I all presented the keys to Helio in the ceremony that was held right after the race was over.

When we started to produce the 2003 Corvettes and the 50th Anniversary color was introduced, we got an awful lot of negative feedback. But later, I got the feeling that the color of the car did not mean quite as much to true Corvette lovers as the fact that it was a 50th Anniversary Edition. Finally, they must have accepted that there would be no gold paint. We sold 11,632 of the anniversary edition that year. I am sure that the shale-colored interior was enough of a change to convince some people that this car was different. The number 50 combined with the Corvette symbol was embroidered on the headrests of the seats, put on the side of the front fender in the logo and added into the logo on the rear deck. Corvette marketing made several options standard equipment on the 50th: the different seats, the fog lamps, power seat on the passenger side, child-safety and airbag cut-off on the passenger side, dual-zone air conditioning and controls on all of the cars. We put a window shade and hookup under the hatchback glass on the coupe only.

We made some changes to the soft top itself for the convertibles and to the latching mechanisms. We changed the 350 horsepower engines somewhat, and gave the coupe and convertibles Magnetic Selective Ride Control. Technically, we began to use magnetized fluid in the shock absorbers. It was new and different at the time, but many cars use it now.

Although the 50th Anniversary paint and options package was not available on the Z06, the car got some attention of its own in 2003. The engine was bored again and the horsepower was upped to a startling 405. The headliners were made thicker, not to make it more stable as it seemed but because of federal regulations for cars capable of such speeds. The Z06 had a tough-looking black-out interior and got a Heads-Up Display (HUD) on the lower front windshield. The 6-speed, transmission with a short-throw shifter belonged singularly the Z06 as did the exhaust system. The engineers did not stint on anything with our feisty hardtop and it was the unquestioned leader in power as well as speed options.

Charlie and Jim Robertson had been urging us to come to their Circle City Corvettes Beach Caravan for quite a few years. Liz and I finally had a chance to attend. Every year Charlie had been sending us a Corvette teddy bear with a small sign around its neck that read:

"Hi Wil, Remember Circle City Beach Caravan!"

Since we had never made it, I figured that they did not expect us to attend at any time soon, but we surprised them all by attending their event. They directed us to drive to a small motel in Dothan, Alabama. From there, we drove down in a long caravan of Corvettes to Panama Beach in Florida. We stayed in a hotel on the beach; we all went into the water to swim; and they held an auction that night.

All in all, we had three full days of sun, fun, and beach activities. They had been conducting an auction of several items that the club had collected from several Corvette venues for several years to raise money for the museum. We promised Jim and Charlie that this would not be our only time to attend and that we would get them an item or two for their auction. We tried to make sure after that first time we attended to get down to their big activity whenever we could.

We were happy that the Lone Star Corvette Club invited us to visit them in Fort Worth, Texas later on in the month of May. Johnny and Edie Downs who were most ardent workers at the Corvette Museum invited us to be guests of their Lone Star Corvette Club. I couldn't have been happier. It was good because most of the activities were scheduled to happen in Fort Worth. I knew that Richard, Barbara, and Debra would want to visit the at the race track for the festivities.

The other guests, Dollie and Nick Cole, and Dick Gullstrand were at the activities and Liz and I spent time with each of them. We talked about the excellent organization of the Lone Star club and how they seemed to be drawing other clubs in with their activities. I made sure Johnny and Edie knew that Liz and I would always come whenever they invited us.

GM Racing was continuing to make a name for themselves in 2003 with a victory at Sebring. Then, they ground out a 2 and 3 finish at the 24 Hours of LeMans. Liz and I managed to make it to the Grand Prix at Road Atlanta where the two cars of the race team made it to 1 and 3 finishes. The race team had gotten brand new cars painted with all new graphics. The team seemed to struggle a bit by the time they made it back to Road Atlanta in the early Fall for the Petit LeMans but we made sure that they knew that we were proud of their successes.

In fact, everyone connected to Corvette was really glad for the success of the factory-sponsored race team. The team seemed to be firmly ingrained by now and fast moving up the ladder with consistent wins. The company of Pratt and Miller were doing a fine job with the racing nuts and bolts and the mechanics of the cars. By now, I think the race car drivers and Pratt-Miller were expecting some of us from the plant in Bowling Green as well as from Detroit to show up at the racetrack to visit with them for a short while every now and again. Whenever Liz and I went down to the track to visit, we would stay for a short while then we would quickly let them get back to the business of competing while we stood back out of their way and cheered them on. We would let any of the team sponsors with representatives at the track know that we recognized their contributions, too.

David and his wife, Levine had been stationed in Fort Campbell, Kentucky and they were able to come up to Bowling Green to visit us often. All of us had been watching the happenings in Iraq on the evening news for some time. Liz was devastated when she learned that David's Army unit was going to be deployed to Iraq—then, she was furious at me for encouraging David to join the Army in the first place. She just did not want to have to go through the horror of war again—especially with our son. It was too much of a reminder to Liz of the days when I had been sent off to war. She had only known me as a grown man though, and she seemed to feel that I had been a thoroughly trained combat soldier. She believed that as a result I had been well able to take care of myself. But, she could not accept that David was a grown man and a soldier who was able to do the same. I guess she only thought of our son as her baby and she felt protective of him as a mother. I had to figure that my mother must have felt the very same way about me back when I had been sent off to the war in Vietnam.

We lost a very dear friend of the Corvette hobby in 2004. When Chip Miller died, brought down by a little known and understood disease, Amyloidosis. All of us who knew him were determined to educate ourselves about the disorder, and to support the charitable foundation that had been set up in his name. Chip's son, Lance, stepped right into his father's shoes and seemed determined to carry on his father's legacy with business partner and friend Bill Miller. All of us at the plant wished Lance well and pledged to support him each year at the Corvettes at Carlisle event just as we had supported his father over the years.

Wendell Strode had discussed with me long ago the big 50th Anniversary celebration that the Corvette museum was planning. They had been working since the past September to hold the celebration in Nashville on the outside grounds of Adelphia stadium (since named LP Field). They planned to host caravans from all over the US, Canada, and any other countries who were willing to participate. We would host them in the plant and they would host them at the Museum. There were celebrations planned at waypoints all over the country but the museum would be the overall host in Nashville for the 50th Birthday Bash.

When June 25 came we were all ready. As it turned out there were caravans streaming in to Nashville every day. Then there were huge amounts of Corvettes lovers driving their cars back and forth between Nashville and Bowling Green daily up and down I-65 in a steady stream to visit at the plant and museum. There was special parking for the 50th Anniversary Corvettes at the plant, the museum and at the stadium in Nashville. With Chevrolet as our primary sponsor we tried to make the atmosphere as festive as possible. There were seminars that were conducted with speakers who were closest to the hobby. Then, for a fee, the museum allowed vendors to set up tents and sell their wares on the grounds of the museum as well as at the stadium in Nashville. There was a stage for bands to play music on the grounds as well as down by the river.

We had spent so much time planning that it turned out to be far better in reality than we had hoped. There were a few glitches along the way, but nothing major. The businesses in Bowling Green stood to benefit from having so many people in the city as well the businesses and hotels along I-65 between Bowling Green and Nashville.

With all of the celebrations for the 50th done, it was time now for us to turn our attention to the business that would fully occupy us in 2004.

This was to be the end of the C5 generation. There had not been an anniversary package on the Z06 so now, to make things equitable, we were obliged to do a super job on our hardtop model for the final hurrah of the C5.

The commemorative editions were offered in all three of the models this time: the coupe, convertible and the Z06 all wore the badging in honor of the racing success of the C5-R. The Z06 had a 350ci, 405 horsepower LS6 engine, 6-speed manual transmission, FE4 suspension, and heads-up display on the lower front windshield. The other models had a 346ci, 350 horsepower, LS1 engine, automatic transmission available, sport seats, 6-way power driver and passenger seats, fog-lamps and tire-pressure monitoring systems

The special LeMans Blue paint for the commemorative editions was by far our top selling paint, outstripping our ol' famous black. Torch Red, which was usually in second place behind black as a color contender, came in third place with the 2004.

The headrests on the seats were embroidered with the crossed-flag emblem with "Commemorative" inside the emblem. Other emblems recalled the LeMans wins—even the emblem on the waterfall between the convertible seats recalled the wins at the 24 hours of LeMans.

The Z06 hood was lighter in weight by over 10 pounds because carbon fiber was used for the hood much like the carbon fiber used to stretch and lighten the body of the C5-R. Most of the Z06s were given hood decals with a graphic herringbone pattern placed between red and silver. This was an indication to the buying public that carbon fiber had been used. Much was made in the press of this new lighter hood on our mass produced Z06 Corvette because carbon fiber use had its origins in aerospace technology. Our little Z06 land racer was already capable of speeds that were well on the way to allowing it to take flight—and now it had carbon fiber used in it like airplanes and rockets!

Probably because it was the end of the C5 era, we were once again chosen to build the pace car for the Indianapolis 500. We sent them one of our new Artic White convertibles and they sent it out themselves and had it painted blue on the rear quarter panel and decorated with red, white, and blue flying stripes. They used the polished aluminum five-spoke wheels. Film star Morgan Freeman was on the track to drive the pace car to start the race. When I met him, I was truly surprised how down-to-earth he truly seemed to be. I told him how well the elements of his personality really came across well on the screen and he seemed thrilled to hear that I thought so. I told him that my wife was also a native Mississippian. Both he and Liz really made the most of that.

We were asked to deliver 23 of the new Artic White Corvettes and 25 of the LeMans blue Corvettes to Indianapolis. These vehicles were used as "Festival" or "Track Vehicles." Previous race winners, film stars and other celebrities were allowed to drive these vehicles on the track before the race along with other "Support Vehicles." There were 33 or so of the red Chevrolet SSR pickup trucks with the convertible tops that were last year's pace vehicles. They were also decorated with red, white and blue flying stripes.

Liz and I went to Indianapolis for the race. I was gratified to see that the country's military personnel drove the cars along with the numerous celebrities. I rode in the car driven by last year's pace car driver, Jim Caviezel, who told me that he was glad to be back at the races again. He actually did enjoy meeting people out on the track in the festival atmosphere. He seemed to be enjoying himself driving the convertible and waving to the crowd.

For the first time since I had been coming to the races, I heard the announcer say:

"Lady and gentlemen, start your engines."

This time, they had a female in the race. It was Sarah Fischer who started the race but did not finish.

Buddy Rice won the 500 race driving a Panoz G-Force Honda. He was given the keys to one of the white Corvettes as part of his prize for winning. I really wondered if he intended to keep it and drive it but I did not get the chance to ask him.

I was hardly back to work when my youngest brother, Richard, called to tell me that our mother had been hospitalized. I went immediately to Fort Worth to be with my brothers and sisters at her bedside.

When Mom was almost well enough to go home, we all began to wonder if she could stay at home alone anymore. It was more than taxing for her to do the small things that she would have to do as a homeowner and none of us siblings were comfortable thinking of her in the house by herself. I was relieved when she agreed to go into an assisted living establishment for a while. I flew back home to Bowling Green thinking that everything was on the way to getting better.

I don't think there is any person who falls ill who ever thinks that they will be incapacitated any more than a short while. They always feel hopeful and anxious—constantly speaking of the time when they will be able to go home. My mother anticipated getting back to the things that she needed to get done at home and talked about getting on with her household chores right up until the end. All her children anticipated that she would soon get used to being in assisted living. That concern alone put us off guard for anything else.

When Richard called me with the news that our mother had died suddenly, neither of us could do anything but cry. We were not prepared by any stretch of the imagination. We wept together trying to comfort each other, but both of us, the oldest and the youngest of the siblings, needed more than comfort. No matter how long we had been independent and on our own, we seemed anchorless now, rudderless without our mother. Even though I had lived away from home for all of my adult life and had only spoken with my mother sporadically before she had fallen ill, she had truly been the bond of our family. One of the old Negro Spiritual hymns speaks mournfully about the bereft feeling of being both motherless and far from home, as if there are no worse circumstances on the face of the earth.

How true.

We buried my mother beside my brother David in a plot that she had reserved and paid for long ago. It did not surprise us that she had made such specific plans because we knew that she had become more than adept at anticipating circumstances and taking care of herself and her children after so many years, despite the fact that she had been married three times. Before her health had failed, Mom had been able to go on some pretty good vacations, take a cruise, learn how to use her new computer for e-mail, travel to meet all of her children's in-laws, and do many of the things that her working life had prevented her from doing for so very long. At her funeral, I gave a remembrance of how she had sat proudly behind my desk in my office at the Corvette plant, laughing gaily, issuing "pretend" orders, and mimicking me almost perfectly. All of my mother's children were aware of how long and how hard she had worked, but we were able to satisfy ourselves to a certain extent with the knowledge that she had finally been able to truly enjoy her life freely for a fairly long time after all of her children were grown.

We had been working hard to improve upon the three C6 concept cars for 2005 that we had kept shrouded inside the plant for more than two years, really, since about the end of 2002. Nobody was willing to go through the same troubles ever again or go through the absolute pain that we had gone through not so long ago when we had been trying so hard to come out with the C5 Corvette.

Although we were only intending to change a few things for the C6, we did not intend for those things to be a problem when the build got started. We retained the location of the engine at the front of the car; kept the time-tested hydro formed rails; kept the rear transmission; and changed some of the dimensions of the body of the car. We had listened when our customers had complained about the back end of the car. We wanted it to remain distinctive, but we wanted to slim it down enough so that it would be noticeable to our customers who had wanted it slimmed down for so long.

The length of the car was reduced by a little more than 5 inches and the width of the car was reduced by more than an inch. The inside dimensions of the car stayed practically the same because the wheelbase was widened and increased which allowed for more inside room. The new C6 had round rather than the standard oval tail lights. The C6 sported two, deeper cup holders on the center console. But here was the greatest change of all: the headlights were exposed after over forty years of the hide-away headlights!

For the last two years, Dave, Tadge, Harlan and all of the engineering, design and marketing team in Detroit had been fighting a monumental battle in HQ to get rid of the flip-up headlights! Disagreements had gone on at HQ for far too long. I had been asked for my input as far as manufacturing was concerned and I certainly sided with Dave and the rest. It was true that the hidden headlights had been part of the reason that the Corvette had gained legendary status, but it was time for them to go. When Dave had asked me to speak up, I had been glad to do it as a manufacturer but also as a Corvette enthusiast. It was a fact that General Motors would save money on the costs of labor as well as materials with the new lights and I told them this. There was a certain amount of waste and scrap connected with the hide-away lights. Warranty considerations always added up, too, and engineering and design couldn't give a proper upgrade for a new car with the flip-up lights. I also agreed strongly with Dave when he argued that high intensity lights were the future—they were modern as well as necessary.

Just like the C5-R had pioneered the exposed headlights on the race track, the C6 would bring them out on our street cars with greater refinements. The lights were high-intensity for both the high and low beams with the running lights, turning lights and the parking lights all under the C5-R type polycarbonate covers. No reflectors were needed below the covers, only the painted surfaces and the high intensity lights themselves. That was a big plus.

We got a late start building the new C6, but that did not mean that it was any trouble at all to build or any the less new and refined. It had an LS-2, 6.0 liter V-8 small block engine. It was the largest, most powerful small block among any American cars with any claims to speed and power in a long time. We built first the coupe, later we built the convertible with no Z06 in this production run. Still, we built more cars in a shorter period of time than ever since the Corvette was being built in two different locations in 1981—Saint Louis and Bowling Green.

Our C6 was all about horsepower and fuel economy all wrapped into the same package. The six-speed manual transmission was not an extra-cost option and the short-throw shift lever on the C6 was very much the same as the Z06 had always been. Even the automatic transmission had options and shift patterns with a stronger shift version than last year's C5.

Very much in the news were the wheels we used on the new car. The tires were 18x8.5" on the front and 19x10" on the rear and they were Goodyear Eagles. This had the effect of spearing the car downward to avoid lift when it was on the move. Combined with the higher spring rates and shocks, larger sway bars, larger cross–drilled brake rotors, combined with revised gear ratios, and flip down rear-view mirrors this car was totally aerodynamic, built for speed and road-gripping stability on the highway and on the racetrack, too.

One of my friends, an engineer in paint at the testing center in Detroit, knew that I would want to know right away that there was no truly red color listed on the paint schedule for the C6. My fondness for the red color for the Corvette was well-known. When I got that call, I immediately went over to the paint shop. Sure enough no red color was listed on the painting schedule for the new car. I took a look at the second list of the colors that the paint shop was scheduled to do later, and then I hastened back to my office.

I called Dave Hill on the telephone. He was quick to tell me that we might add a bright red to the colors for the Corvette sometime later on in the run.

"It wasn't there when we introduced the cars," he said. "It's far too ***rude*** a color for the new car, anyway, don't you think?"

"***Rude?***" I repeated incredulously. "Corvette is a ***sports*** car—not a family sedan! Corvette people want that bright red. What about that song by Prince? It doesn't say anything about a little dark mulberry or a little dark maroon Corvette. The song says ***red***!"

"Song?" Dave asked coolly. "Since when do we paint our cars to fit ***song lyrics***?"

"We've still got a ton of Torch Red left in the paint vats in the paint shop," I said, "We could just go on and add that to the list couldn't we?"

"No," Dave said flatly. "It's your call what you do with that old paint, but we're not going to use that old Torch Red on these new cars."

I walked back over to the paint department.

"Don't tank up the Torch Red just yet," I told Phil Keinle, "Not until I talk to Joe."

I got on the phone in the paint shop to call Joe Spielman.

"No red at all?" Joe was obviously surprised. "We aren't painting any red?"

"Precision and Monterey Red are scheduled for later," I told him, "But those two are too dark—they're more ***maroon***. They aren't really ***red.*** Torch Red is the only true bright red that we've got. I don't know why Dave wants to take it out when we haven't got any other. We've got a ton of Torch that's still in the vats."

"I'm going to talk to Dave," Joe stated heatedly. "And to Bob Lutz, too."

We painted one Torch Red 2005 car and shipped it up to Detroit for Joe Spielman. He showed off that car everywhere he went in Detroit, on the east coast and down in Florida. He never failed to say how absolutely gorgeous the new C6 looked in the Torch Red color.

Meanwhile, we cleaned out the vats and sent the Torch Red paints down to the Saturn plant in Tennessee

Soon enough I got a call from Dave Hill.

"We're going to start shipping the Precision Red to the plant for the C6 right now," he said "We're still working on a new bright red paint that we'll use later."

That was Dave. He was used to winning hard-fought huge battles and all out wars up at HQ. He wasn't about to back down to our tiny, plant-level insurrection.

Once again we built the pace car for the Indianapolis 500. Our racing-ready Victory Red convertible was given "Machine Silver Metallic" paint right down the center of the hood, across the top, and down across the trunk with titanium and black accent stripes. The Indy 500 decals were placed on the sides of the car. The windshield featured the slogan "An American Revolution" across the top. A Chevy bowtie was featured on the hood. Much was made about the fact that Corvette was the only American car to leave the assembly line with a 400 horsepower motor capable of 186 mph in 4.1 seconds. Also, a lot was said in the press about the rear and front tires and even more was said about the selective ride control and the Z51 performance package of the coupe.

General Colin Powell who was going to drive the pace car was himself a Corvette owner. He spent time with Liz and me and the rest of the HQ personnel and their wives before the race. General Powell told me that I had the best job in the world since I could pick out and drive any Corvette that I wanted. I told him about the Cadillac XLR that we were building and said that he might want to take a look at it, too. He was accompanied by his son who was quick to tell us that General Powell really thought the world of his new Corvette and would not let anyone else drive it so maybe the son might get the XLR if anybody was offering a deal on one. We told him that we would see what we could do.

I actually told C5-R race car driver, Olivier Beretta the same thing. He very much wanted to drive one of the new Corvettes to see if he wanted to buy one, so I told him that I would be glad to let him test-drive the company car that I was driving while we were down at

Road Atlanta. From the moment that Beretta hit the driver's seat of my car with me as his passenger, he had me gripping the armrests, holding onto the handle on the front IP, and grabbing for anything else that was handy to grab. I think my fingerprints are still prominent in the roof of that car. It is still in my garage even to this day.

Beretta did everything that was "do-able" with an automobile. He drove around and around and carved elaborate doughnuts on the grounds of Road Atlanta. When we went onto the streets outside the racetrack he still scared the liver out of me even though I knew that we were never really unsafe. He had already proven that he was one hell of a good driver, so I reminded him through my chattering teeth that his test drive was absolutely over.

Someone from *Corvette Fever* took a picture of Beretta and me in the Corvette just after we got back from our little spin—he wore a big smile and I wore ashy lips and a sweaty forehead. I kept my promise to help him to get a Corvette shipped overseas so that he could use it as his daily driver.

Beretta gave me the huge 1st place medal that he won the next day in the Road Atlanta race. My new secretary, Lynn Herron had it framed with his card, an IMSA patch, with the picture of the two of us in the car, and I hung it on my office wall right across from my desk.

When we lost a museum supporter as well as avid Corvette racing supporter, Roman Sabadaszka, none of us could believe the suddenness of his death. He and his wife Marilyn had been on the scene at every one of the Museum's activities for many years. Marilyn knew that I had let my 50th Anniversary Corvette go to a friend of mine, J. C. Moore of Huntsville Untouchables Corvette Club. I agreed to buy the Sabadaszka's car from Marilyn because I knew that Roman had added great-sounding tailpipes and kept that car in tip-top condition. The car I call "Roman's Favorite" is in my garage collection and it is one of my very favorite Corvettes to drive.

We began manufacturing the 2006 Corvette in September of 2005. The new 2006 Cadillac XLR came later. The Z06 "big block" engine was all the news. Actually, the engine was not the legendary big block of the old days; it was a new small-block based with 4.125-inch cylinders bores in an aluminum block with pressed-in steel cylinder liners, titanium connecting rods and intake valves.

Once again our Z06 was made of legendary stuff. Our engineers at HQ kept right on improving it. It was a race car now pure and simple. It had the same Gen IV 427-cid V8 with lightweight reciprocating components that redlined at 7,000 rpm. The front fascia was given a larger grille with a cold air scoop while the rear end was rounded down and softened. Like the race cars, more carbon fiber was used in the Z06 to lighten its weight. The large, 19-inch rear wheels combined with the 18-inch front wheels made the car seem to spear downward at the front just like the race car.

To further add to its growing legend as a racer, the Z06 was used as the pace car at Indianapolis. Legendary, seven-time Tour de France bicycling champion Lance Armstrong was tapped to be the driver. This was the 17th time that a Chevrolet had served as the pace car at Indy, the eighth time that a Corvette was used as the pace car and the very first time ever that a Z06 was used.

There was to be only one Artic White Z06 with the red and blue badging the Indy 500 logo on the sides and the large Chevrolet bowtie on the hood. Strobe lights were added in the running lights and a light strip was put across the hardtop. We had **never** painted a white Z06, but there was nothing else different between the pace car and the Z06s on the Chevrolet car lots except the lights, the badging, and the paint. The Z06 came off the assembly line racing-ready with a 505 horsepower engine capable of 198 mph and a 0-60 mph time of 3.7 seconds every single time on the clock.

We delivered a large amount of the LeMans blue convertible Corvettes to the track for the Festival celebrations and they were used along with red Chevrolet SSR vehicles. Liz and I were supposed to ride in one of those Corvettes for the Festival Parade behind the pace car but somehow we missed the window of opportunity to get the car that was intended for us. I had been summarily dragged to a press conference which had caused me to be late. We were quickly ushered into a room with Dolly Cole who was also late and with other celebrities in the same predicament as we were. Gene Simmons whom we did not recognize at first without his Kiss makeup truly surprised us because he spoke to us immediately and called me over to where he was seated comfortably on a couch. He shook my hand and I was surprised that he knew who I was. I was pretty sure it was because he had seen my name on a guest list or something and I was the only other face that was left to put with the name. Since I was a Corvette builder, he said he was wondering why I didn't see to it that I had one of my own for the parade. When I told him why I had missed it, he laughed.

"That's the story of our lives: missing deadlines," he said amiably.

We were shown through a huge mass of waiting people and told to climb up the ladder to the top of the huge float that had a giant figure of a helmeted race car driver holding an oversized replica of the Indy 500 trophy with the faces of the winners on it. The float was decorated with beautiful festival streamers and draped with a huge replica of the black and white checkered flag. The whole thing was pulled along by the duplicate of an Indy race car and was right in the middle of the parade. Since Liz and I really weren't supposed to be there, we weren't waving to the cheering crowds. The other occupants of the float urged us to wave to the crowds. One of the celebrities whom I vaguely remembered seeing somewhere turned and said to me:

"You really should wave to 'em, Mr. Cooksey. They know who you are. They're probably Corvette owners just like I am."

Liz and I both stared at him, and then we gave each other an "oops!" stare. Maybe the people along the route were, indeed, a Corvette crowd and maybe they did, indeed, know who I was. Of course I did ***not*** want to disappoint them! Liz and I got busy waving enthusiastically to the crowd along the parade route after that.

The racing team had really used their new C6-R race cars to great effect in 2005. They had broken a number of records during the previous race season. The cars had won everything possible in the GTS class now they made the switch to the GT1 class. The newspapers and the sports car magazines proclaimed that the factory-sponsored race team had done exceptionally well.

Now, the 2006 race season was about to start. Liz and I made it to Sebring for the opening of the season. It was a good, hard-fought race. The #4 car with Gavin, Beretta and Magnussen finished first and the #3 Corvette with Fellows, O'Connell and Papis finished in the fourth position.

I was determined to include more of the races into my schedule because now the presence of Corvette on the race track had brought Corvette owners together to show off their cars more than ever at the tracks. It had now become a wonderfully organized thing. Jack Morton Worldwide had taken over the Corvette Corrals. They had made the corrals into a very comfortable place to be at the racetracks. The huge tents that they used were truly welcoming to the Corvette owners. There was food provided in the tents, handouts, racing schedules, and visits by the race car drivers. They organized programs that featured talks by celebrities like Corvette racing program manager, Doug Fehan; legendary race car drivers, Ron Fellows, Johnny O'Connell and Olivier Beretta; race car builders Pratt and Miller; and the factory guys like Tadge Jeuchter, Harlan Charles, and me. All this made the programs very informative and more than worthwhile. There was always one of the newest Corvettes on display in the corrals, and sometimes, concept cars from Detroit were brought out and shown off.

For the last few years, the Corvette Museum had been doing well. Everyone at the plant and in the whole Bowling Green community was really overjoyed to see the progress that the museum was making. I had been on the board of the Corvette Museum for a few years now. First I had served because the Museum needed the help and I was determined to do all that I could to help keep them afloat. Then I was appointed to the board by then mayor, Eldon Renaud who was also a GM employee. Eldon and I had known and trusted each other since we had worked together in the plant in Saint Louis. I was again appointed to the board by Mayor Elaine Walker when she was elected because she said that she was interested in keeping the hard workers on the board and I guess I conveniently filled that bill.

I don't know when it happened that the Corvette Museum board and the Corvette plant recognized the symbiotic relationship that had quite naturally developed between the museum and the plant. The plant manager was to have a permanent position on the board since the plant was in a position to help the Corvette Museum and, of course, there was some *quid pro quo* with the Museum being able to assist the plant at various times, too. Museum Delivery for buyers of new Corvettes was one of the events that the plant was able to co-operate with the museum to establish. Then there was the *Automobile Build Scrapbook* and the more extensive plant tours that the plant co-operated with the Museum in sponsoring for buyers who received Museum delivery in order to make more impact. I think both Wendell and I felt that this was the right thing to do.

The Museum board went to Spring Mountain Motor Resort and Driving School and the board members all stayed at the resort and participated in the numerous activities that the resort offered. We got a chance to tour the resort and we went to the nearby town. After the board held our meeting all of us who wanted to participate in the driving experience got to drive one of the 200 and more vehicles that were available at the school. We all had just as much fun riding in the people mover as we did driving the cars around the track ourselves.

Another driving experience that Liz and I had the previous year with the Museum board was a trip to Bondurant School of High Performance Driving in Chandler, Arizona. We held the board meeting early the next day, then we went out to have driving lessons from the instructors. Of course we all chose to drive the Corvettes. Everyone seemed delighted with the experience and we learned that the weather in the desert did, indeed, cool off drastically at night.

I suppose that after I had been on the board for so long, the board members decided to put me to work. I was elected chairman of the Museum Board for the next year. Everyone joked that I had been on the board for ten years or more and it was about time that I finally had to do some work.

These days whenever I drove to the plant, walked inside from my car, and if no one stopped me for any reason, I would hasten straight to my desk, sit down and stretch out my left leg as much as I could. It was always a real relief to take a load off my painful left knee.

This was something that I hadn't shared with anyone except Liz. I had been the "Iron Man" to my family, my friends and my colleagues for a long time. I never missed a day of work. I had helped to jump start the physical fitness programs at the plant: I had climbed the ropes, done the exercises, run through all the courses and led the way toward walking for fitness and health—not to mention the fact that I was always out in the plant walking all over the Corvette side and spending horribly long hours on my feet over in the XLR section when it was starting up. I had spent a great number of hours on my feet standing and walking at rallies, car shows and programs.

For my entire career, the good health of my body had been my greatest asset. But now, my left knee and my right hip joint had begun to make a lie of my health claims. I had begun to feel like I had a demon trying to get out through my kneecap and lately that demon had begun to use his pitchfork on the joint socket of my hip. Standing and walking on those concrete floors out there in the plant had become very painful to me. I had tried to compensate by throwing my weight quickly from the left knee to avoid the excruciating pain whenever I stepped down on my left side. That, in turn, had caused me to put way too much stress on my right hip.

Now my right hip joint had become the very bane of my whole existence. The orthopedic doctors had already told me that the cartilages in both my knees were deteriorating but most of the cartilage of my right hip joint was all but gone.

When the pain was at its very worse, I could not help but remember how my mother had spent her life walking on those hard, concrete floors at John Peter Smith Hospital where she had been a nurse for over three decades. The cartilage of her knees had been worn right down until she had bone against rubbing against bone. Her knees had begun to pain her very badly toward the end of her career. She had needed to have surgery on both of her knees to gain some measure of relief.

My sister Barbara and I were very much like my mother in that respect—our heritage included the misery of bone rubbing against bone in our knees too. My doctor had been giving me shots periodically in my both my knees to give me some relief.

Finally, I'd had enough of the crippling pain. I scheduled the surgery on my left knee with Dr. Shinar of Vanderbilt Hospital in Nashville taking care of the operation.

"Your hip is in the worst shape," he told me. "We need to get that out of the way first."

That is what we decided to do. My younger brother, Richard, and my sister, Barbara, who was one of the twins, came up to be with me when Dr. Shinar did the operation. Richard stayed with a friend in Nashville and either he or Barbara or Liz took turns staying with me in the hospital room. Richard stayed with me each night and Barbara went back up to Bowling Green with Liz. They worked the schedule out pretty good so that one of them was there with me all the time.

I let the nurses give me the drugs that Dr. Shinar had prescribed because it felt really good not to have pain. When Richard helped me to stand up to go to the bathroom or take a sponge bath I could tell I needed the drugs, but I refused to take anything on the third day because the pain had begun to lessen. On the fourth day both Barbara and Richard left to go back to Fort Worth. The fifth day, Liz took me back to up Bowing Green.

It wasn't long before my hip began to give me trouble. It felt as if it were moving around on its own with no help at all from me. I had to go back to the hospital again to have Dr. Shinar remove the prosthesis in my hip and put in another one that extended further down into my leg bone. Again Richard and Barbara came up to alternate staying with me while Liz drove back and forth between Vanderbilt hospital and her university classes in Bowling Green.

It wasn't an easy decision, but I was determined **not** to have each of my kneecaps replaced in separate operations. My friends and family really made me feel as if I would be doing something wrong, but I truly wanted to get it over with. The fact that Dr. Shinar thought it would be workable for me to do it all at one time made me finally decide. Still, it was a very hard decision to make. I just wasn't sure if I would be putting my health into jeopardy by subjecting myself to going under the knife to have such an extensive operation.

Liz and Crissy did not feel comfortable with the arrangements I had made. Liz called Barbara and Richard and told them that she would buy their airplane tickets if they came back to be with me during the operation. The doctors who worked on my knees told me later some things that all of us would rather not have known. The doctors said that the operation had been extremely taxing for them and that it had been a very nerve-wracking and bloody undertaking for them. My knees were extremely sore and I felt sick and exhausted from being sedated for such a long time. I felt pulled apart like a worn out football in a pro football game: kicked around and manhandled by giants with my laces coming undone.

This time Barbara and Richard stayed longer. They were always on hand to walk behind me whenever the nurses got me up onto my feet and made me walk down the hall and around the nurses' stand. Finally, I began to feel more like myself; Barbara and Richard went home to Fort Worth; and the doctors declared that I needed to go to rehab. So I checked into SKY Rehabilitation Center in Bowling Green for a while. Before I left, I was admonished to use my walking cane to get around because there had been so much trauma to my right knee and right hip. I was set to have a pretty long recovery.

When I got back to work, I wanted to get right out to the XLR side of the plant to see how they were doing. I was greeted and wished well as I traversed the plant on my cane. Both the male and female workers came up to hug me or shake my hand, and to see how well I was getting around. Many of them had already filled my house with cards and letters, flowers and plants, foodstuffs and goodies. Liz had already sorted through those and she had decided what I should and should not consume.

There were two reasons that I really needed to get over to the XLR side of the plant: I wanted to see how the conveyor system that we had bought from a factory in Louisville was working out, and I wanted to get a handle on how we were doing with the XLR-V. The ultra-luxury/supercharged sports car had been shown to the world at the New York International Auto Show and in a Super Bowl commercial in January of 2005. The MVP of the Super Bowl, Dion Branch, had been awarded a new, shiny red XLR as part of his winnings.

The XLR-V had finally gone on sale to the public in early 2006. I wanted to know from Dave Leon just how well the sales were going. We already had an anger issue going with marketing at HQ because we simply did not think that the XLR was getting enough publicity. The car was General Motors' most expensive luxury/sports car and it should have been selling more and appealing more to the established customers of the higher-priced luxury imports.

Motor Trend magazine had given the XLR high ratings in Jack Keebler's column. *Car and Driver* magazine had said very favorable things about the tests that the XLR had undergone and passed. Much had been made of the XLR-V's supercharged engine and it had been very favorably compared to other popular sports cars both foreign and domestic.

While the XLR did use some of the same things that the Corvette used, like the larger brakes from the Z51 Corvette package and the same sized wheels the car used, but unlike the Corvette and more like the Cadillac, the XLR had four intercoolers built into the intake manifold and a six-speed automatic transmission. We wanted the fact to be known that this automobile was a *Cadillac*, right down to the supercharged *Northstar* engine.

Dave Leon and I decided that we had to try to get HQ to give our XLR more much-needed publicity. Both of us were committed to trying to see what could be done in the future.

Dave Hill had made his retirement official and now Tom Wallace had taken over as chief engineer. Before Dave left the scene completely, Tom and I decided that we were going to have a bit of fun with him at the next museum celebration. With the co-operation of Dave's wife, Karen, we decided to dress up in a pair of red and green plaid slacks to mimic the ones that Dave often wore to the Museum gatherings. Everybody had seen Dave in the slacks at one time or another. He had been photographed wearing them time and time again. Karen had found some plaid material and sewed the slacks for us. Karen had told us that she would get Dave to agree to the fun but neither Tom nor I thought that he would do it. Sure enough, he was wearing his signature slacks at the C5/C6 celebration for the museum held at Holiday Inn on Scottsville Road.

What I did not know was that Tom had found a cane like mine and both of us came out of the crowd limping along on our canes, wearing Dave's signature red and green plaid slacks while Dave was making his farewell speech.

The crowd went wild. Everybody thought it was hilarious. Even Dave could not help cracking up. A lot of people got busy snapping pictures. The three of us posed for as many snapshots as they wanted. Although Dave has always been known for his reticence, we saw him laughing out loud, dancing, and having a whale of a time that night at the party. When the group's official magazine *The C5/C6 Registry* came out, there we were on the front cover: Dave, Tom, and me wearing Dave's signature plaid slacks with Jake and Dan cheering us on.

When we had gone up to Corvettes of Carlisle the year before, Tom Wallace and I had noticed that Lance was still doing all of the conventional fairground car events that his father, Chip, and partner, Bill Miller, had traditionally done, but he had started to do some things that would be sure to appeal to the younger crowd like himself as well. He wanted to generate some interest in car performance by having a "burnout" contest. He asked if Tom Wallace could help him out. A spectator had volunteered to give Tom his car to try a burnout. Tom had been afraid that the spectator's car would be harmed if he had really stepped on it so the burnout had not gone so well. Tom had felt a bit embarrassed but we all were glad that the spectator's car had not been damaged. We had promised Lance: "Wait until next year." We planned to have our own car and to show the fair goers a for-real "burnout."

Tom and I got together and we planned for next year's contest we would bring to the Corvettes at Carlisle show a "Test Mule"—a car that was normally used at the proving grounds to run tests on all the important elements of the vehicle and the tires. We even thought about getting some tires that would make multi-colored smoke come out when Tom made them spin. That would make a true spectacle!

The next year even before we got to the Carlisle Fairgrounds, I had sent e-mails to Lance and made all kinds of boastful claims about what Tom planned to do. Lance e-mailed me back that he was really hyped for Tom's burnout.

Liz and I got to Carlisle and sure enough, when we got to the fairgrounds the next day, the Z06 "Test Mule" had already arrived from the test track on a flat-bed truck just as Tom had promised. When I inspected it, I saw that our "Test Mule" was a car that was designed especially for a burnout: it had 505 horsepower redlining at 7000 rpm with a switch to turn the traction control on and off—just the thing to give one hellacious burnout! It had a line lock system control that was handled by another separate switch which locked down the front brakes with a release for the brakes on the rear wheels so that they could spin freely but could not pull because of the front lockdown. There was even a system designed to spray water on the tires. I was really pleased that Tom had gotten the guys at the proving grounds to do such a good job on the "burnout" car. This should be great, I thought, this will really show people what our Corvettes in general and the Z06 in particular can do!

I hadn't even settled myself in a chair at the tent where the Corvette brand was displaying our newest cars for the visitors before I got a call from Tom. He was still stuck in Detroit and wasn't going to make it for the burnout contest. I needed to carry on for him, he said. He couldn't find the soft wheels that gave off the colored smoke, he said, so he had left the old tires on the car. Maybe I could make a good enough showing on the old run-flats, he said.

Good God! I thought, Run Flats!? Those steel-belted tires were as hard as rocks! I was not at all prepared to drive the car myself but especially not with those wear-proof Run Flats! Even if they were old and worn, how in the world could Run-Flats make a spectacle of any kind? I certainly had no experience with that at all! Oh well, I thought resigned, I can't disappoint Tom or let our product down.

Lance was surprised when he saw me behind the wheel when I drove into the three-sided concrete box in front to the grandstands for the contest, but he recovered pretty quickly and announced my name on the loudspeaker. Then, he signaled for the guy on the big lift vehicle behind me to box me in from the open side with another concrete barricade. I knew just how Lance always set this up so I was pretty confident that the Carlisle group had the know-how to make the exhibition perfectly safe for those spectators who wanted to be close to the car.

I started slowly, revving only through two gears, dragging just a bit and spraying water on the tires until I saw that the smoke was started pretty good. Then, I revved the engine more until the smoke covered me completely and drove everyone watching over the edge of the concrete box much further away. I sprayed some more water on the tires, grabbed another gear and, above the roaring engine, I could hear the loud cheering of the crowd. I hoped that the smoke was covering them up, too. The run-flats were old but I didn't intend to run them to complete destruction. However, I heard the loud "Bang!" a lot sooner than I expected. I got off the gas immediately.

As the smoke drifted away, Lance ran up to the car to congratulate me over the top of the barrier. As soon as the barrier was removed, I took off the line lock and backed the still-mobile Z06 out of the concrete box. The car still drove like a dream—that "Test Mule" still boasted the proud heart of a Z06! It was like a purebred racehorse at the end of the sixth race at the Kentucky Derby—it wasn't even breathing hard!

"Oh, my!" Lance kept saying over the loudspeaker, "Oh, my, my, my! Wil Cooksey!"

A guy with a microphone and another with a big television camera indicated that I should let down the window. I answered all the questions that he asked me and told him I had to grab another, higher gear because the engine had maxed out the lower gear. Then I got out of the car to take a look at the destroyed tire.

I hadn't anticipated that the steel belting would fly off and do that kind of destruction to the quarter panel of the car: the belts flying off the tire had made quite a hole in the right rear quarter. Surprising, but even with the shredded tire and the hole in the rear quarter that car was still standing tall and looking good!

The people who were standing around were amazed that the car was still drivable on those Goodyear run-flat tires. Many wanted to make sure that those were the same tires as their cars had. I told them that even though the tires were old they were still so good and dependable that a driver could easily make it to a car repair garage even with a blow-out.

Many people just wanted to inspect the car to see that powerful Z06 engine to make sure that it was the same as theirs. I told them that I personally owned a Z06 myself and intended to get another one if my wife would allow it. Some of the people wondered then about the extensiveness of the tests that the cars underwent in the development processes and I was glad to talk to them about that too, while other spectators stood around bemoaning the shape that the car was in until it was hoisted by the two workers onto the flat bed of the truck, tied down, and driven away—headed back to the proving grounds in Detroit.

I'm sure that many more people became avid fans of the car after that. But, there were those with little information who were absolutely furious that I had "destroyed" that dream car. That "Test Mule" would be right back out on the test track by the very next day with a change of tires and, maybe, a replaced rear quarter. That particular "dream" car was destined to be "rode hard and put away wet" and even more "misused" for a very long time by our test drivers. This was all in the interest of future Corvette chassis and drivetrain development.

For the last few years, whenever Liz and I had gone to the east coast for the Corvettes at Carlisle, we always went a day early so that we could go to a meeting of the Liberty Region Corvette Club in Pennsylvania in Allentown where we would first have dinner with Will and Dee Abney, and Robin and Ed Proctor and some of the rest of the Liberty Region Corvette Club. Later in the evening, they came together with clubs from all over the region for the big meeting. I always talked to their gathering and answered questions and I would always give them titillating hints about all of our new products. Liz and I would have dinner with the group and we would spend the night at a hotel there. Then the next day we would all drive down to the fairgrounds at Carlisle. The Members of the Liberty Region group were avid fans of the Corvette and we tremendously enjoyed meeting with all of the people who made up the group.

When Liz and I had driven my company car up to the fairgrounds at Carlisle all of the guys who had attended decided that we would have a bit of adventure. Steve Grilli who had become my new quality manager at the plant was an avid motorcycle rider. He and his wife, Lucy had been riding for a long time. Jeff Webb, who was the area manager of body and paint at the plant and his wife Marie each owned and rode their own motorcycles, too. J. P. LaLonde the plant engineer and Carl Haas also an engineer were bike riders, too. Hearing those guys all tell me about their motorcycle adventures made me want to join their ranks.

So, all of the people who had come up to Carlisle from the Bowling Green plant made the side trip to York, Pennsylvania on our way back to Bowling Green. We toured the Harley-Davison plant there. That was when I saw and fell in love with the Harley 100th Anniversary bike. I was bound and determined that I was going to get that Harley 100th Anniversary bike for myself!

However, I knew better than to mention this to Liz because I figured it would have infuriated her. If I had told her my plans right then it would have been like riding all the way back to Bowling Green with an un-caged Bengal tiger occupying the seat beside me in my

Corvette. I had visions of Liz with bared canine teeth and un-sheathed feline claws during that long trip home. That did not appear to my imagination as a very pretty picture of my wife. I told myself that is why I kept quiet about it all the way back to Bowling Green.

I'd like to think that I approached motorcycle ownership quite logically. I bought a few books and enrolled in motorcycle safety courses and operator's classes. Liz was really not as angry and disagreeable as I had thought she would be. We had been married long enough that she knew my tendencies toward multiplicity and hyperactivity a whole lot better than I thought she did. She even said that she would ride with me when I finally got the motorcycle. It wasn't long before I found a 100th Anniversary Harley Davison bike just like I wanted, brought it home and put it in the garage.

Steve Grilli, Jeff Webb, Carl Haas, J. P. LaLonde, and I began to go on jaunts around Warren County on the less traveled roads. We would leave on Saturday morning and stop at a restaurant that served breakfast. After we'd eaten, we'd finish up our ride by the afternoon. Soon enough, we started to discuss going out to Sturgis, South Dakota for the huge bike week rally. Every biker should experience Sturgis at least once they all argued. Sturgis was a kind of Mecca for all real bikers, they assured me.

Carl Haas was the "iron man" a "dyed-in-the-wool" rider who had ridden his bike almost everywhere and who would venture out alone to go as far North as Canada and South to Florida whenever his urge to ride took over. Steve Grilli was a long-time rider who would much rather ride on a bike than drive in a car. Jeff Webb was a long-time rider, too; he approached riding more as a hobby than anything. Then, there was J. P. LaLonde our French/Canadian who had ridden bikes as a youngster and had recently taken up the hobby again after a few years when he came down to work in the states and had become a U. S. Citizen. Every one of them had been to Sturgis at least once or to other bike rallies in Florida, California and other places.

I was the only raw rookie of the group.

We planned for a trip to the bike rally in Sturgis. Liz had something going at the university and would not be able to join us, but Lucy planned on joining her husband Steve and Marie would be joining her husband Jeff. I would be alone, but that would probably be best for my first time, I figured. The guys borrowed a van from the plant and used my new enclosed trailer to take our bikes up to Sturgis. I took an airplane flight and met them in Rapid City where we had secured rooms at a Days Inn for the rest of the week.

When we went out on our first run into downtown Sturgis that night, the guys all laughed and made fun of me as I rode around and walked around bug-eyed and open-mouthed at the sights and sounds inside and outside of the city. I was absolutely astonished by what I saw. I quickly put on my dark glasses to cover my buggy eyes, and tied my bandana like a mask to cover the lower part of my face to shield my blown-away expression that night. The participants were having such free-wheeling fun that it was hard for me to believe that most of these people probably had perfectly normal lives back at home. We hung out with many fellow General Motors employees that we knew or had worked with at one time or another. If most of the others were part-time bikers like we were, it was certain they had normal lives and conservative jobs back at home just like we did.

There were races and exhibitions, shows and extravaganzas, and the ever-present clothes-shedding drinking games at the bars. I was willing to bet that those who were not first-timers had just as much fun laughing at us open-mouthed, gawking rookies as they did participating in the fun and games themselves.

Toward the end of our vacation I began to notice that, like me, the open-mouthed gawkers were starting to fit in with the hardened veterans. We were hardly noticing those who were dare devils anymore, or those who were scantily clad, or even the ones who were out and out exhibitionists. We newbies became more and more the hard-core bikers with each day that passed.

We all decided that we wanted to go on several road trips around the area. We saw the un-finished Crazy Horse sculpture; looked into the depths of the canyons; visited the park and photographed the iconic president's faces sculptured on Mount Rushmore; and we rode through the nature-made earthen sculptures in the desert on the way to the Devil's Tower. We went to the bike exhibitions in Deadwood, rode through Custer state Park, rode through the sudden downpours of rain and took pictures as close as we dared to the free-ranging buffalo. We knew that if any of those beasts had decided to run at us, no way could we have escaped onto our motorcycles in time. That made the experience all the more thrilling.

I took photograph after photograph. I made sure to show them to Liz when I got home. I figured the pictures would cause Liz to re-arrange her summer class schedule immediately, especially when she saw those pictures I took of the smiling, pasty-wearing, skimpily clad and unclad girls wearing body paint and posing for pictures at the bar. I was right. Liz looked at me with her brows raised:

"I'm going with you next year," she said drily.

Buzz and Ruth Marston always invited Liz and me out to the west coast to the race at Laguna Seca. The race was often the last competition of the season for the Corvette race team. The track was a good one and the Corvette Corral was always well attended. The Corvettes were given a chance to go onto the track and to do one at least one hot lap. Doug Fehan, the race car drivers, and the Pratt-Miller development team always came over to the hospitality tent to talk to the car owners and sign autographs. Tadge and Harland always showed up to represent the engineers in Detroit and I represented the Corvette assembly team in Bowling Green. There were always 1990's Corvettes as well as new cars that I had not signed, so I always went out into the field of the Laguna Seca Corvette corral to sign under as many Corvette hoods and on as many valve covers as I could.

I have absolutely no idea which of the enthusiasts and clubs were the first to form up their own car corrals and begin to park and participate in activities at the race track but I do know that many of the major automobile brands had begun now to use Jack Morton Worldwide to run their car corrals at the races or they used another similar company to organize a set up the logistics of their corrals. Like Corvette, the other brands with racing vehicles usually had large tents set up on the grounds of the racetrack with large fields around them and the car owners all parked their cars around that tent. Sometimes they had car judging and gave prizes and recognitions. I always took part in the judging if I was asked to do it.

Along with the Corvette corral Porsche, Mercedes Benz, Bentley, Maserati, and Mazda each had car owners' corrals set up at the track, too. The car owners gravitated between the tents, the race viewing area, the rest areas and the huge area where the Corvette Museum as well as other race-dedicated vendors like Piloti Racing Shoes were set up to sell their wares.

Buzz and Ruth's club, the Western States Corvette Council usually featured a program during the week-end of the race to put a spot light on all of the out of town visitors to have them to meet and greet guests and members of the clubs. One time their dinner was held at an animal enclosure and they had Tadge to ride into the tent on a huge elephant to the utter astonishment of everyone at the gathering. It took us a while to get over that one. We all were absolutely in awe of Tadge. I thought I knew Tadge pretty well, but I never thought he'd be brave enough to do that.

The Western States Corvette Council members were also huge Museum supporters and we participated in their fund-raising programs for the museum. Liz and I always wished we could stay longer on the west coast, but we had to get back to Bowling Green in time to be at work on Monday morning.

The big excitement for the 2007 Corvette was the new Atomic Orange color that we were going to use on all three editions. Tom let me know that we were going to replace the Daytona Sunset Orange Metallic and add a special tint coat on the Atomic Orange units that we painted in order to give an extra special depth to the color. We were going to make the color available as soon as the 2007s came out and we were pleased that the color started being ordered right away.

Surprisingly, the Indianapolis 500 chose the Corvette as their Pace Car for a record ninth time! We were overjoyed! It did not surprise me when Harland called to tell me that the Atomic Orange was going to be used for the pace car for Indy, but, as it turned out he had an even bigger surprise: it had been decided in Marketing that we were going to put the pace cars up for sale this time. We needed to get 500 of the cars over to the decal company at their new warehouse in Bowling Green just as soon as we could. That was going to take some doing. It would be the first time since 1995 that we would be offering the Indy Pace Car for general sale.

The interior of the Pace Car would be completely blacked out. The special seats would be perforated leather with a decorated Indy 500 on the headrests. Tom told us to go ahead and use the wheels for the pace car that were the same as the ones that we had been previewing for the 2008 in Sterling Silver.

I had heard that Patrick Dempsey would be on board to drive the pace car at the Indy 500 race. It was a little–known fact among many Corvette owners that Dempsey was a race car owner and driver who had competed with two other drivers in the 24 Hours of Le Mans, Laguna Seca, and at Daytona. I think all of the dyed-in-the-wool racers wanted to meet him after they found that out. So did I, but, I did not get the chance to meet him. I was really interested in what a real race car driver thought of our car after he had gotten a chance to drive it.

We would also be building another special edition. Race car driver Ron Fellows would be honored with his own special edition Corvette: ALMS (American LeMans Series) GT1 Z06. It would be only the second time in history that we had painted a white Z06 at the plant and the first time in history that we had a signed special edition. The cars were scheduled to have Corvette lettered across the top of the windshield and we would put on the red front fender stripes. Ron was to sign his name on all of the limited edition cars. We were scheduled to build 300 cars for sale in the USA, 33 for sale in Canada and 66 for foreign markets—anyplace outside the continental United States. Ron was at the auto show in Chicago on February 1st when his signature Z06 was unveiled to the public.

The interior of Ron's signature series was blacked out to just below the windows, just below the IP (instrument panel) and on the floor. There were areas of red along the bottom of the IP and on the bottoms of the doors and the edges of the seats. The center console was red leather-covered top and sides. The series was indeed unique in more ways than one.

All of the Z06 models now sported 505 horsepower with a LS-7 engine. The vent on the front of the hood was actually necessary for cooling. The seats were usually one color but it was decided that we were going to offer the special seats with closed embroidery on the backs. The dealers were going to be allowed to offer the option to buyers to request an override for an extra cost of $590. That meant that they could have the seats of their choice installed or whatever combination of interior colors they wanted. Many buyers took advantage of the option in order to make their hardtop, their convertible and, this time, their Z06, unique.

The new convertibles and coupes could have the Z-51 performance package with the larger stabilizer bars, enhanced cooling, and larger cross-drilled brake rotors. The cross-drilled brake rotors were included when the optional Magnetic Selective Ride-Control suspension was ordered. This system featured magneto-rheological damping to allow the ride control to be turned on and off.

The C6-R racing season started with some important changes. Ron Fellows was intending to retire. He had teamed with Magnussen and O'Connell for the very last time to race. Gavin, Beretta, and Papis had teamed together for the next racing season. Pratt and Miller Engineering had the cars ready for the 2007 season and they were once again offering to build and modify race cars for the public.

Liz and I always stayed at our time-sharing condo in Orlando in early May and we drove down for the Sebring 12-hour endurance race that always kicked off the racing season. We saw Gavin, Beretta, and Papis come in first among the GT1 class. Magnussen and O'Connell came in second. Doug Fehan told the crowd at the meeting in Sebring that the circuit that the Corvette racers were now running had been re-configured and many new races in new places had been added. In the past, Liz and I had been able to go to three or four races each year, but no matter how much we loved racing our work schedules kept us from being able to make many of the races.

I had a big problem. I always saw Johnny and Edie Downs regularly at the Corvette Museum because Johnny was a member of the Museum board and Edie worked in the Museum helping to see that everything went well with merchandise sales and other functions. Johnny and Edie's Lone Star Classic in the Dallas/Fort Worth area was being held at the same time that Charley and Jim Robertson's Beach Caravan was being held in Panama City, Florida. I admit, I didn't toss a coin because I always got the chance to visit with Barbara, Debra, and Richard and their families on the last day of the Classic, so I had to tell Charley and Jim that I would not make it to the Beach Caravan and I told them about my family in Fort Worth. I knew that their club was highly mobile and I would be able to see most of the members at Sebring and at other functions at the racetrack or the Museum.

It was good how each of the Lone Star club members took care of different aspects of the events right down to the last detail. The husband/wife teams seemed to work really well. Johnnie and Edie picked us up at the airport and got us set up with a car to move around. Robert and Linda Shellberg took care that we knew how we fit into the program, showed us out into the city and saw that we had good directions. Terry and Linda Walker took care of our working through the activity schedule. Craig and Laura Satterfield saw that we went to dinner and lunch and always fed us royally. Bill Armstrong came to take Liz and me to the airport to catch our flight home to Bowling Green.

Not only did each of the Lone Star members take care of their work diligently, the club always invited members of other clubs around the area to join them at their classic. We had become accustomed by this time to seeing more and more of the members of the ICCC participating with the club. Many of the members of ICCC joined in the huge caravan of cars around the edge of downtown Fort Worth to the Stockyards area where Lone Star gave out awards. They also participated in the big car show at Texas Motor Speedway, the gymkhana and the speedway rides. It was good the see the ICCC working co-operatively with Lone Star. Everyone seemed to have a wonderful time.

I made a promise to Liz at the beginning of 2007—I intended to take her to France for the Le Mans race in June. We had spent months making plans for it. We had decided that we would spend some time in Paris before we went on down to Le Mans. General Motors would pay for my travel and room and board in Paris and Le Mans but I would be obliged to pay for travel and all incidentals for Liz. That was fine with me. All I needed to know what arrangements that would be made for me so I could arrange Liz's accommodations to match with mine.

Liz and I flew from Nashville to Detroit where we met the race team, Group Marketing Manager for GM, Gary Claudio, who was an avid race supporter, and VLE Tom Wallace whose fiancée Karla was working in GM overseas operations.

The Air France flight was really wonderful. Liz hated the idea that we would be over the water so long, but she seemed to get over it pretty quickly. She promptly went to sleep and hardly opened her eyes until we were in France.

Our arrival was flawless except Liz left her fanny pack with a couple of hundred dollars on the plane and she was not allowed to go back to get it. When the pack was finally brought out to Liz, the money that she had looked forward to exchanging for French dollars was gone. We were both angry, but we were happy that her credit card was still there.

We checked into the Novotel Paris Les Halles which was a beautiful hotel less than a half-mile from the Louvre. We settled quickly into the hotel and went out riding the Metro like natives to the stop next to the Louvre. We were both anxious to see the Mona Lisa and Liz told me I would be really surprised when I saw how small it was. All the pictures that I had seen in books over the years had led me to believe that the painting itself would be larger than life. When I saw it from the closest vantage point that the guards would allow us to have, I had to admit that Liz was correct. It was a lot smaller than I expected it to be.

I was intrigued by the huge carvings and stone renderings of Greek gods and goddesses fighting with serpents, monsters and dragons on the first floor of the Louvre in the "Large Format" galleries. The huge wall-sized paintings and statues on the second floor where the French, Dutch, and German art were located were the same ones that I had been seeing in books and newspapers since I was a kid. Liz was surprised that I recognized and could even name one or two of them.

Liz was really excited that I could be so intrigued with the paintings and sculptures, and I was really kind of smug because my wife of over forty years had found out something new about me. I could have spent another day wandering through those halls and looking at the antiquities and paintings that had been so famous for such a long time. We stayed there until closing but we did not get to see much of the huge museum. We found out that we had spent our time mostly in the Denon gallery but I promised Liz that I would bring her back to view the rest of the paintings and antiquities one day.

We spent time walking along the streets of Paris and visiting the well-known tourist attractions Notre Dame Cathedral, Rue de Rivoli, and Pompidou Centre. We walked along the Seine River and looked at the barges going and coming very close to one another. We rode the metro to the Eiffel Tower. We only considered for a minute going up in it, but in the end we didn't because Liz claimed to be tired, but I think she was just trying to be sensitive to my tired and sore knees.

The next day we went to the Arc de Triomphe, the Bastille and Montmartre. As we were walking along an unknown street near downtown we were surprised to find a small cemetery that was said to belong to Benjamin Franklin but Liz said that it was probably more of a memorial because Franklin was once ambassador to France. We took pictures of it. We ate at Au Diable Des Lombards more than once because the people there spoke English better than we did and their food was good. Soon enough though, we were met by a GM representative who took us to the train station to go down to the Le Mans race.

One of the GM employees picked us up and took us to our hotel in Le Mans. All of the GM employees had rooms there and had set up an informational stand near the desk. We had a full itinerary from the moment that we got to the hotel. We were given credentials and it was a whirlwind of activity up until the race. Before the start of the race, we did not wander far from the GM pavilion because sudden downpours of rain kept us pretty contained. But we did get into the race area and out into the stadium. We stayed at the track until so late that we were dead on our feet. Tom and Karla grabbed sleeping bags and bedded down at the racetrack. Liz and I wimped out and went back to the hotel to go to bed. We came back to the track early in the morning to find that Gavin, Papis and Beretta had been sidelined in car #64. Magnussen and O'Connell came in second overall in car #63.

It had been a hard-fought and quite satisfying race. Liz and I participated in all of the racing festivities, and then we headed back to the United States with an experience under our belts that we would never forget. I had walked so much in Paris, then up and down at Le Mans that my right leg really needed rest but I couldn't help but think that the experience had been worth the sacrifice. I would just have to do my best and lean on my cane more than ever to get around.

When I got back to the plant, I knew I needed to get over to the XLR to see how well the group was holding up. We had done all that it seemed possible for us to do. We had crossed all of the T's and dotted all of the I's but the Cadillac XLR seemed to be on its last legs. Try as we might, Dave Leon and I could not seem to see any kind of light at the end of the tunnel after we started to produce the 2007's. Sales were going down and it seemed as though the car was headed for the brand graveyard. We sold only a meager 1,750 of the XLRs and the XLR-V's combined in 2007. It seemed that nothing was going to save the car. There was not much of a market for our luxury sports car that cost over ninety thousand dollars for the very cheapest model.

Finding General Motors vice president Joe Spielman sitting in one of the chairs in my office one morning after I had been out on the floor was a pleasant surprise. Joe had always been a regular visitor to the Corvette plant. Everybody knew that the Corvette was Joe's favorite car and, naturally, this was his favorite plant. He was a familiar visitor and he had always gone out on the floor, so he had been acquainted with many of the superintendents and the hourly workers for many years.

Joe waited until I had settled myself behind my desk before he said:

"I'm gonna' retire."

I was not surprised although I could not imagine Corvette without Joe but above all I could not imagine Joe without Corvette. I thought of some really rather trite traditions: ham and cheese, bacon and eggs, hot dogs and baseball, but there was nothing trite about Joe Spielman and Corvette.

"Why so soon?" I asked. "You're not quite retirement age yet, are you?"

"Not quite, but I've got the years in, though," Joe said. "Anyway, it's time—past time."

I didn't know what to say to that but I knew that there was another, more profound reason that Joe had decided to retire and both of us knew just what that was. Much of the power and decision-making of plant managers and product managers had been eroded of late by the upper levels of management who wanted to be entirely in charge everything—they not only wanted control of the entire company and all of the workers, they wanted complete control of all aspects of management, too. As if he knew the question that I was not asking and the reason that I was not asking it, Joe went on:

"I can't stand the fair-haired boys who go overseas and stay for a coupla' years doing God-knows-what," he grumbled sourly. "When they come back home, they promptly start to screw everything up over here. They seem to think that just being overseas gives them a profound knowledge and destiny and a magic anointment to lord it over everybody else."

I had heard a lot about that. My headquarters sources had been telling me for a long time that Joe was not happy so I already had some idea what and who was at the source of the dissatisfaction.

"Well . . .," I said, "Maybe they're figuring to buy in now since they haven't been a part of the success like we have."

"They haven't been a part of anything!" Joe exploded. "They want my job. They're spitting on our success and they're gonna' kill this company. Just wait and see!"

I thought of a good analogy for what was going on here: if you cut a big tree down from the top, it staggers on with its life. But if you cut the tree down from the bottom, that's the end of the big magnificent tree. If the roots are healthy maybe they will put out new sprouts. They are small and puny, more easily handled and a less costly to maintain than the single mature tree. Together those sprouts will be a lot more dependent, and much more subservient.

"Maybe it's just a matter of simple economics," I said aloud.

"Yeah," Joe said fiercely. "Economics rather than people! I'm a man who cares about people, therefore I need to be watched and second guessed! Damned them and the horse they rode in on!"

I was quiet for a minute.

"What are you thinking?" Joe asked. "Want to go out now, too? I know you aren't 65 yet are you? I was thinking I might get to choose who comes in here after you if you go before I do."

"I'm going out in March or so next year," I said. "I have to be 65 and eight months before I can get full Social Security benefits. Liz and I already checked on that. I've been paying Social Security since I was

14 years old. Taxes, too. Only time I didn't pay was when I was over in Vietnam." I snorted bitterly. "But I was paying then, too—you can be sure of that. Still am—in various ways."

"I know you're a Vietnam veteran," Joe said softly. "Are you getting veteran's benefits?"

"No," I said, "I guess I have to be chewing up the walls or something to be eligible to get any veteran's benefits. My hearing's affected from being so close on 8 big guns when my men fired 'em. I don't know if they even allow benefits for that. I kinda' doubt it."

I had the vicious nightmares only once in a while now, so I did not mention those.

Joe laughed. "I never have thought about you and me having this kind of a conversation. Have you?"

"No, but I guess it had to come, though," I said, "Time keeps marching on."

Presently, we got up and went out into the plant. Joe was greeted by many people on the line who had known him for a long time. That had always been Joe Spielman's problem on the corporate scene: he was too much of a "down-to-earth" and "for-real" guy. There was none of that "ivory tower" self-importance and phony-ness about him at all. He did not go along with the smarmy "corporate think" ideas—he thought for himself and truly believed that the workers who built the cars were very important. He was saying "Goodbye" and letting them see him in his capacity as a vice-president of General Motors for the last time. Joe made sure to tell them that he would be back—he would always come back as a Corvette customer.

I was well aware of what was happening to Joe. When I had been in Detroit for a manufacturing meeting almost four months ago, Tim Lee, vice president of manufacturing had called me aside to give me a heads-up about his intention to continually move all of the plant managers around to different plants. I supposed that since I had been on the job for General Motors for over thirty years and had been serving as the Corvette plant manager for over fifteen years, he thought that I deserved to be told. He did not give a reason, nor did I ask him for one. I told him simply that it would be a waste of General Motor's money to move me since I planned on retiring in a year and six months anyway. As much as I loved Corvette and loved my job, I planned to retire from it. I did not plan on dying at my desk or falling dead in my traces with General Motors' harness still on my back. I wanted to be able to do all the enjoyable things that working all of my life simply had never allowed me a chance to do. I wanted to go to the races in Long Beach, Saint Petersburg, Arizona and Lime Rock; I wanted to go to the car shows in Colorado, Ohio and Canada; I wanted to visit relatives all around the country; I wanted to take trips overseas to visit the old countries; and I wanted to see Africa for myself. Most of all, I wanted to be able to take naps in the middle of the day or whenever I felt like doing it.

When I told him my plans for retirement, he laughed and said that he understood that well enough.

I thought I would try to make him see that his plan to move the plant managers around just would not work for Corvette. I thought I could give him a rationale why that was:

"It's a special culture and the people who work at Corvette are special," I said. "The plant manager needs to stay in the plant long enough to build a good relationship with those people."

I could tell from the expression on his face that he was not receptive at all to any of my input.

Harlan Charles came down to my office from the design studio in Detroit before the end of August. He was interested in running something by me, he said. He wondered if I could include a special edition Corvette into the upcoming build schedule. It would need to be a Z06 and they all felt that a very special Crystal Red paint would be good for it. It needed to carry a black "stinger" on the hood very much like the old sting rays carried during the 1960's. He leaned over the front of my desk and opened up the poster that he was carrying. I could see a beautiful rendition that Kirk Bennion had produced in photographs and paints showing the hood of the old Sting Ray right next to the new version that he was proposing.

"Sounds terrific!" I said enthusiastically, "We've really needed something special like that! This is sure to keep the real Corvette lovers' blood going."

I stood up from my chair so that I could lean over my desk and spread the large drawing out in order to see all of it. When I had unrolled it completely, my mouth dropped open!

A stylish rendition of both the cars' hoods was there side by side. There was a picture of the 1967 427 Sting Ray. Two views of the ten-spoke wheels that we had been guarding in the storerooms for the 2009 Z06 were right there along with a picture of the proposed interior of the car and an explanation of the specifications. A picture of my smiling face sprang out at me, along with the caption along the top of the poster which read, "Special Edition Corvette 427 Z06" and along the bottom was printed: "Congratulations Wil" in large letters.

I stared at the large poster. It had been signed by Harlan Charles, Kirk Bennion and Tadge Jeuchter.

When I looked up at Harland, he was standing there with his arms folded and he had a large, bright Cheshire Cat smile on his face. I expected him to slowly disappear, fading away and leaving behind only his handsome black curls and that self-satisfied smile like the magnificent feline of *Alice in Wonderland* fame.

"You'll sign them all, of course," He went on briskly, "They'll have those "spider" chrome wheels and the special trim and graphics package. We'll do 505 in this special run . . . to honor the popular retiring Corvette plant manager."

The surprise had weakened my artificial knees and caused me to sit down heavily in my chair.

"Wow!' I breathed. "I don't know what to say! Wow!"

"So what do you think?" Harlan asked. "Will you be willing to sign under the center console covers and number all 505 of them?"

"Of course I will!" I laughed. "You know I will!"

Harland laughed, too. "Franklin Mint wants to do a number of model cars of your edition—I don't know how many, but they'll want you to sign those, too. They'll talk to you about that sometime late next year. Somebody will be getting in touch with you in the next few months."

"Sure," I said. "Wow!"

I got up from my chair then and extended my hand to Harlan where he stood across the desk from me.

"Can I keep the poster," I asked. "I want to have it framed."

"Sure," he said as he shook my hand warmly. He gave me that self-satisfied grin again, and he joked:

"Well, I think my work here is done!"

2008 was set to be a banner year for special editions.

We were given the Indy 500 Pace Car again for a record 10th time! This time Indy wanted us to do two pace cars for them that were capable of burning Ethanol fuel (E-85). Both were to have Z06 bodies but the Ethanol engine was put into both of them. They were both given the special light bar across the top and both were painted "Gold Rush Green" which was a "flip-flop" green/gold/ color that used the special effects paint that had been developed by PPG. Neither of these two cars was scheduled to be offered for sale to the general public.

The other Indy Pace Cars that we sent to them were black. There were coupes and convertibles, but only 1 coupe and 2 convertibles were fitted out with the strobes that were tied into the light system for use in pacing the race. The black pace cars were models designed to honor the 30th anniversary of the Indianapolis 500 and they were scheduled to be offered for sale all over the country right after the 2008 race.

The Indy logo was a wide white band along the door ending in the black and white checkerboard at the back with Chevrolet across the top of the windshield at the front. We built 234 coupes and 266 convertibles that were sent to our logo company and they were offered for sale by Chevrolet dealers. There was a small controversy about the tops for the convertibles. We were only sent the black tops toward the end of the run and those who wanted the gray were unable to get them.

A black Z06 was also sent to Indy to be given the logos and the badges that they had put on the other coupes and convertibles. This car was intended for Emerson Fittipaldi who was a racing icon. He had driven the Pace Car for the 2008 race. He had been promised an Indy Pace Car to drive and the Z06 with all of the Indy badges on it was the car that he wanted.

Hertz car rentals wanted us to build and paint 500 Velocity Yellow cars for their Fun Club during the summer. They had requested us to give them the distinctive Corvette seven-spoke wheels to put on the cars and to have them done in a chrome finish. Hertz had the black fender stripes added by an outside company to make the cars even more distinctive. We in the factory certainly had no problem with that.

Frankly, I was planning to wait until the fall of 2008 to order myself a new and innovative ZR-1 that I had already previewed on the drawing boards in the design studio in Detroit over a year ago. The ZR-1 was intended to be offered for sale in 2009 and it was surely going to be a beast! It was going to have a new LS3 engine and over 600 horsepower! It was going to have a distinctive clear opening through the hood right above the engine. It was going to be capable of increasing horsepower to 640 or above with the exhaust cap option. We were set to have a versatile build of the ZR-1in the factory, meaning with a few tweaks here and there a Corvette buyer who was a racing fanatic would really be able to do something special with that car right off the assembly line. Taking driving lessons at one of the driving schools out west was required of anyone who purchased the car. The car was going to have the kind of raw horsepower right out of the factory that I could not wait to get my hands on.

It was **not** to be.

No way would I buy anything else except the new 505 horsepower Z06. We were geared up to build and paint the Wil Cooksey Edition Corvette in Crystal Red with the black "Stinger" on the hood for the spring of 2008. I was scheduled to get # 001 out of 505 and to sign under the center console cover of every one of the cars. I tried to walk every inch of the way down the assembly line with Wil Cooksey #001 but I was so busy that I could not find the time to do it. In any case, I was more than confident that the assemblers on the line would take extra good care of my car for me.

It was the first time in a long time that Liz did not object to buying another Corvette at all. I was willing to bet that my wife had been really proud of me and my accomplishments for all of these years and finally she admitted to it!

I was already planning a whole new garage to house my namesake car—a large building to be built on the edge of the field right across from the house. The building would have to accommodate not only my small collection of cars, but it would have to reach two stories high in order to house my racing trailer and have an upstairs storage section to accommodate Liz's large collection of cloth and sewing machines that had completely taken over the guest house by this time. I figured that Liz could not object so fiercely about the cost and size of the new building since she would have a small part of it, too.

I hired George Schiff for the job. He was a general contractor in charge of a multitude of jobs at the plant and around the region. He found a builder who was scheduled to prepare the grounds and to lay the foundation for the building. It soon proved to be no easy task. None of the sub-contractors could seem to handle getting the garage built—various things went wrong. After about two or three false starts, it was George himself who got good workers together and finally got the project going in the right direction.

Lynn, Theresa and many of the people on my staff had been pulling together a celebration dinner to be held in March for my retirement. The place that they planned to have it was Holiday Inn University Plaza Convention Center. They kept me notified on a daily basis about who was set to attend.

During the week that the party was to be held, it seemed that the weather had conspired to keep everyone away. It was so cold and snow flurries started to fall around the middle of the week. I was afraid that the bad weather would keep all of the out-of-town relatives and friends from braving the drive up I-65 to Bowling Green. I knew that a few travelers from the North like Joe Spielman, Mike Yager, Tom Wallace, Tadge Jeuchter and Harlan Charles might have a big problem getting into the city. All my ICCC friends who were coming from the East might be spared. The clubs from Atlanta had hired a bus to bring them in.

Nobody agonized over the weather more than Liz did. She was distraught when an unrelenting snow started to fall on March 6. When David finally flew in to Nashville from Olympia, Washington, she began to feel relieved and hopeful that everybody else might be able to make it, too.

Presently, our house filled up with relatives: my sister, Barbara and her husband Rathel; my sister Janet and her husband, Ronald; Janet and Ron's children Dawn, her husband, Robert, and older son, Ronnie; my younger brother Richard and his wife Felecia. All the relatives took pillows and blankets and slept in various rooms. Whoever got to the kitchen first that Saturday morning was charged to start cooking breakfast for everyone.

Our dear friends Curtis and Sharon Sullivan filled their house with our guests, too. Liz's sister Florestine and her husband, Walter

Evans, and cousins, Nadine, Pauline and Andrea Scales, bunked at the Sullivan's house. Luckily, the Sullivans only lived down the road from us in a neighborhood closer to the river.

On the night of the program, after the meal was finished, Tom Wallace served as master of ceremonies for the evening celebration.

Tadge and Harlan presented me with a huge bill for the Z06 that I had "destroyed" during my burnout in Carlyle and they also gave me the run-flat Goodyear tire that I had demolished.

Mike and Laurie Yager brought me a huge framed collage made up of pictures that had been taken of us at Funfest. To the delight of the crowd, Mike used a knife the size of a small poniard to take the wrapping from the picture.

Pete Clark was dressed in his Irish outfit: Green suit with a black bowler hat. He represented the hourly employees who sent me a fitting tribute.

Sheriff "Peanuts" Gains told a few stories of our trials and tribulations together.

Joe Spielman recounted a few of the battles that we had gone through as a company and he wished me a happy retirement.

Finally our son, David and Ronnie Madison, looking nothing like their true military selves brought a huge basket full of items put together by Janet and Barbara to the stage. Among a few other items, they pulled mineral oil, castor oil, Ex-Lax and suntan lotion from the basket and declared that I would need these items during my retirement to help me to rest, relax and "keep things moving along."

We had an evening of dancing with music by my friend who served as DJ, Ray Fox. Finally, the out-of-town guest went upstairs to their rooms while the rest of us had to brave the snowy, uncooperative weather outside to get home. I felt like it was real and official now—I was about to become a retiree.

I found a new motorcycle on Ebay that a guy in Indiana was advertising. It was a 2006 Harley Davison Screaming Eagle Road King with a green/black specialty paint job. Soon enough, I drove up to Indiana, made the deal and brought that bike home and parked it in my back garage right alongside the 100th Anniversary Harley. I spent many enjoyable hours on Saturday mornings riding the Green Machine through the Kentucky countryside with all of my buddies.

The new motorcycle was so much fun to ride that I put a protective cover on the gunmetal/blue Harley and hardly ever touched it anymore.

Liz was adamant that I should sell the gunmetal/blue motorcycle since I never rode anymore. I noticed that each time George Schiff came out to inspect the work on the new building, he always found a reason to go over to my back garage. It did not take me long to figure that he was admiring the beauty and lines of my 100th Anniversary motorcycle. He finally confessed that he really wanted that bike. If I ever offered it for sale, he really wanted to buy it he said. It all seemed meant to be and to be fate-inspired to work out exactly right. I made a deal to sell the 100th Anniversary Harley Road King to George.

I retired from General Motors on March 31, 2008. I had spent almost all of my lifetime working, but I had never spent one minute of my time even thinking of ***not*** working. No matter what people say, no one can be *really* ready to retire especially if they have been working for over fifty years. Finally, with the help of Lynn and two maintenance workers, I began to gather up all of my belongings; get the walls cleared of my pictures, awards and plaques; and finish the last of my correspondences. I went to the departments in the plant and said my good-byes to all of the plant employees. I went down to the final line to bid "goodbye" to Ernest Foote who was the "official new car starter."

When I picked up the last of my belongings, I fully intended to ride off into the sunset in my namesake "Cooksey Corvette" with no worries either physical or financial for the rest of my life.

General Motors, Incorporated filed for Chapter eleven bankruptcy in December of 2008, just eight months after the date of my retirement.

Of course, the first place that the major American auto industry companies, GM, Chrysler, and Ford seemed to land upon to avoid disastrous demise and free-fall into bankruptcy was to reduce promised company contributions to pension funds, renege on stock options, and cut the health care benefits for those who were already retired. The subsequent move was to prod workers at or near retirement age to leave their jobs. There were to be no new workers hired to fill the vacated positions. The salaries of some of the lower-level executives were cut.

Then, the top executives of the three major American auto companies went to US Senate hearings hats-in-hands to appeal for industry bailouts. Riding in private company-owned aircraft and chauffeured limousines to Senate hearings certainly did not help the causes of the petitioners, nor did the fact that the car companies top executives were continuing to take their million dollar salaries and bonuses while the lower level executives and some of the union rank and file were sweating cuts and losses to pension plans and company-promised dollar-for-dollar matches to their retirement plans. These events held a prominent place in the daily news broadcasts for many weeks.

Each day, after Liz had gone to teach her classes at the university, I sat at home alone and watched the news with complete dismay. I dug the worthless General Motors stocks out of my safe and let them lie uselessly on the desk in my home office for several weeks. I busied myself with everything that I thought I needed to do in the course of every day. Finally, I picked up the General Motors stocks, put them back in my safe and tried not to think about them anymore.

It was surprising how busy my schedule was after I retired. I became active in the graduate chapter of my fraternity once again. I went to the board meetings of Greenview Hospital. I went to the board meeting of the Corvette Museum to serve in my role as chairman. Liz and I went to the quarterly meetings of the ICCC. Liz and I went down to the Lone Star Corvette Classic in Fort Worth. We went to Carlisle and up to Funfest. We went out to Laguna Seca to the last Alms race of the season. I was so busy that I had to wonder how I had ever had time to work.

It was the motorcycle trip to Sturgis, South Dakota that foreshowed the coming disaster.

My fellow motorcycle enthusiasts and I decided to use my truck and trailer to take all the bikes out to Sturgis. Liz, Jo Ann LaLonde and I all took an airplane out to Sturgis and met the guys there. The first thing that they told me was that the tie-downs in the trailer had broken loose from my bike and it had fallen against the side of the trailer. Steve Grilli, J.P. LaLonde, Jeff Webb and Carl Haas had taken turns riding my bike all the way to Sturgis. There was no discernible damage to my bike except a few scrapes and scratches to the paint.

We spent the rest of our vacation enjoying the sight and sounds of Sturgis. We saw many sights, enjoyed the food, and watched the shock on both Liz's and Jo Ann's faces as they marveled at the uncensored dress codes and unfettered fun. Liz snapped picture after picture in the bars and diners in the city of Sturgis, and on our rides to visit the monuments.

Only once did I hear an unusual noise in my bike and have to pull off the highway to check the mechanics, I did not stop riding while I was in Sturgis, but I made up my mind to get everything checked out as soon as I got home. Even after it was repaired, I could still feel the unease that seem to run through the bike as I rode it but I tried not to think about it. When I thought about it later, I wished fervently that I had paid closer attention.

The horrible accident happened when Corvette enthusiasts were in town for a Museum event. I had promised Ernie Richardson that we would go out for a ride if he brought his bike to town. Steve, Jeff, and Carl came by the house to pick me up and we met up with Ernie to get out on the highway.

We were enjoying riding in formation with Steve in the lead. Suddenly, there was a noise and my steering column locked down completely! I could not move it. We had just gone into a gentle curve but I was unable to follow it. I was only able to hold the bike in a straight line, and it left the road and headed downhill and into an open field in front of a house with garage sale signs in the yard.

I do not remember my body flying through the air or the ditch that I jammed my right leg into. I do not remember the sound of my bike crashing ahead and landing in the yard among the garage sale items. I do remember the pain when I became conscious: pain along my back where the rough terrain scraped the skin from it; pain where sticks and bushes gauged my side; aching agony in my jammed ankle and foot; and a burning center of pain in my right thigh. I felt like a large block of concrete had been dropped on me crushing me up into a million pieces. I hurt so badly it seemed impossible for me to move or speak. I knew that I badly needed to go to sleep to avoid the excruciating pain,

I barely remember my friends' voices as they kept prodding me to answer their questions. I realized afterwards that they were trying to make me stay conscious until the ambulance came that would take me to the hospital.

The semester had ended for Liz and she was intending to head to Tennessee and Mississippi to visit her relatives. I had already kissed her good-by and told her to be careful driving before I had gone out on my ride. Luckily, Steve's telephone call from the field in Glasgow had caught her before she left the house. Steve sent his daughter Lillian and her fiancé, Steve Mekolon, to pick Liz up and to bring her to T.J. Sampson hospital in Glasgow where the ambulance had taken me.

As soon as Liz was by my side the hospital personnel in charge of trauma and emergency at T. J. Sampson decided that it would be best to take me to the much larger Vanderbilt Hospital in Nashville where there were more personnel and equipment to take care of injuries like the ones I had sustained. They had done all they could to stop the bleeding, check lung function and for other internal injuries and to stabilize me, but they were well aware of their limitations—they were not equipped to handle the setting of the break in my large thigh bone. Lillian and Steve went to take Liz home to get her own car to drive down to Nashville. Liz told me later that she called Crissy and Catrina to come to Nashville with her.

By the time Liz drove down to Vanderbilt Hospital the personnel in surgery had already taken me in. I was told later that Doctor O'Bremskey and the staff doctors began surgery on my leg just as soon as they could. Their difficulty was not just the large size of my thigh bone, but also fact that it had broken just below the steel hip replacement prosthesis that had been inserted into it.

I do not know what procedure was used or anything else, even when they told me about it, but I was barely able to endure the pain. It never let up until I was sedated.

They had used pins, screws, nails and every kind of hardware imaginable to make the bone and the artificial knee attached to it stay in place. Even days later, I had to be moved from the bed to a wheelchair because I was unable to put any weight at all on my leg.

After about a week of staying in bed and taking pain killers, I was going crazy. I had never been ill, hurt or disabled before. The knee replacements and two hip replacements had only slowed me down for a fraction of time. I had accepted long ago that I was borderline hyperactive but constant work, travel and activity had kept me busy for all of my life. Staying occupied had never been much of a problem for me. Now I was down and all but out. When Liz and I discussed it later, she told me just how close it had been. I had barely made it. This was, indeed, the longest journey that Liz and I had ever made together.

Nothing went well after the surgery. I was taken back to the hospital, X-Rayed, examined and finally, I was told that I would be fine and just needed to rest. They said that all parts of my body seemed to be healing nicely. I tried to tell them that the pain had never gone from my leg and that I was not happy with the way the leg was healing, but nobody seemed inclined to listen.

By the time I got back to the hospital, my foot seemed to be literally hanging from a useless leg and turning in the wrong direction when I tried to stand. I knew that the leg was really healing up wrong because I could not put even the least amount of weight on it without quite a lot of pain.

I was told at that time that Doctor O'Bremskey was absent from the hospital because he was really ill himself. The female intern who spoke to me really did upset me. She sat frowning and looking as if she had been sucking on sour persimmons all day. She did not even look at my leg before she told me that nothing could or would be done for me. Since I had quite large bones, such a break as mine seldom healed correctly, she informed me. She even suggested that I might need to get myself a built-up shoe. I saw Liz staring at her as if she were about to leap at her. I knew that Liz was really angry. So was I. We got up from our chairs and got out of there without another word.

By the time that O'Bremskey had returned to Vanderbilt Hospital, the bolts, pins and screws in my thigh had broken completely away. My injured lower leg was now dangling like it did not belong to the rest of my body. My thigh bone seemed to be desperately trying to knit back incorrectly in that position and there was still a large amount of pain associated with it.

Doctor O'Bremskey was very apologetic. He gave me a list of several bone surgeons who would be willing to help me, but I had already gotten a recommendation from Polly Spann-Kershaw the wife of one of my brother Richard's friends who was a nurse at Saint Joseph's hospital in Nashville. Doctor Craig Morrison who was a bone surgeon at Saint Joseph took matters into his capable hands right away. In an hours-long operation, he and his assistants used wires, screws, and splints to make sure the bone was set correctly this time. I had never heard of this before but they used my newly-produced bone marrow to pack the bone into place.

Once again Richard and Barbara came to Nashville to hold vigil with Liz at my bedside. This time nothing was easy. The anesthesia made me really sick. My windpipe was bruised from the many alien pipes and drains that had been inserted into it during the long process of the operation. Richard told me that I passed out once after the operation was finished and if not for his quick action to roll me onto my side, I might have choked on my own rising vomit or aspirated it into my windpipe. I was really lucky that Richard was there.

This time, I did not recover so quickly at all. I guess my poor body was just tired from all of the surgery. This time the road was a long and hard one.

When I finally got out of Saint Joseph's Hospital in Nashville, I was brought back to SKY Rehabilitation Center in Bowling Green. Since I always had someone with me at the rehabilitation facility, Liz felt that she could leave my side to go back to teaching her classes at the university. When I came home from rehab Liz's sister, Florestine, came up from Memphis to stay with me. Teen brought a little round bell designed to set on a teacher's desk that had such a loud ring she could hear from anywhere in the house. She told me to use the bell to let her know if I needed help.

When Liz got home from class that first afternoon, Teen declared that I had been an ideal patient all day. I had never used the bell once, but the minute that Liz got home, I was using the bell constantly. When Liz figured out that I was only using the bell to call for her, she promptly snatched the bell right out from under my hand on the night stand.

"Gimme' this damn bell!" she demanded. I never saw the bell again.

No one could believe that I who had been such an active person for all of my life was now rendered inactive. I was not able to participate in any of the many activities that had motivated my life for all of the past years. My house filled up with plants and flowers in funeral imitation. I told Liz that when I had visitors, it was as if they were coming by to "view the corpse." Liz laughed merrily, plumped up the pillows behind me, and refused to allow me to let my spirits flag down.

Jack Garrett who was then president of the ICCC drove up to sit beside my bed and try to cheer me up. He took Liz's treasurer's records because it was certain that Liz and I wouldn't be attending the ICCC convention that summer.

Roger Reed and Earl Kinnard brought over food from the *Shake Rag Restaurant* which they had revived in the *Old Shake Rag* district, a long-ago black enclave on the North side of Bowling Green.

Frankie Lovings brought over a large basket of cards and goodies from the plant workers. I had already gotten telephone calls from many of them. They really seemed concerned about my health.

Eddie and Carolyn Jones came by to let me know that they were enjoying their retirement from the Corvette plant. They had since sold their house in Bowling Green and returned to live Saint Louis months ago. They had heard about my accident and came by while they were visiting friends in Bowling Green.

I was up and sitting in a wheelchair by the time John White came by the house to wish me well. He had driven up from Memphis and was on his way to Louisville for a car show. I had watched him when he was a high-speed drag racer in the past, driving Elex Withers' custom built, high horsepower Corvette. At that time, he had been a lot less cautious. He never said so, but I could see that he sympathized with me much more than most people. He had lived an active, daredevil life, too, but his activities had been curtailed to a certain extent by too-many near-misses and life-threatening incidents involving gasoline engines. I never said so, but I am sure that both of us were thankful that fate had been good to him—he could have been sitting in a wheelchair just like I was.

The president-elect of the museum board, Buzz Marston, had to take over the board meetings before my term as chairman was up and before the time came for him to be the chair because I was unable to carry on my duties. I really wanted to go to the board meetings but I knew that I couldn't, not in the shape that I was.

I was glad that Wendell Strode came by to let me know how they were getting along at the Corvette Museum. He brought me news of the past board meeting and delivered to me a packet of mail addressed to me that had been sent to the museum.

Liz got me a metal bathing seat to put in my shower so that I didn't have to stand and I could stay there under the water for as long as I wanted. Soon enough I was able to take care of myself completely and move around on my own in my wheelchair. Finally, I was able to get around on my walker. Before long, I could stand up on my crutches, but I was not able to go on trips of any length of time just yet or sit in meetings. After a few months my back and arm were almost completely healed except I would still have the deep scars. Still, I was feeling so much better. My right foot and ankle seemed to be healing well, and I could touch the floor with my right foot without collapsing in pain. My thigh seemed firm and stable at last. Both Liz and I and the whole family were glad that my lower leg below the break was not dangling anymore. Only a few people got to see the ugly car that runs from my waistline to my knee down the side of my right leg. It took over a year to heal after the final operation because most of the tissue was gone from the many operations. But I swore that I would never complain about it. To this very day, I have kept that promise

Liz and I seemed to have come through this crisis and made it to the other side at last. My only problem was that Liz had been feeding me too well while I was immobilized. I had gained far too much weight. Liz had to go shopping so that I would have something to wear outside the house.

By spring, 2010, I was able to put some weight on my right leg. I could use a cane to walk because after all of the trauma, my right leg had healed up a full half-inch shorter than the left. I was finally able to resume many of my normal activities. I attended board meetings again at the bank and at the Corvette Museum. I decided to run for president of the ICCC once again and I won. I began driving again with caution. Liz and I shared driving when we visited some of the places that we liked to go.

Mike Callihan, president of the Gunnison, Colorado Car Club had spoken to me some time ago and told me that the club had chosen me to receive the Lee Iacocca Award that had been created in 2006 by Lee Iacocca himself to honor "classic car collectors and their passion for maintaining an American tradition." I had not been unable to go out to Colorado to receive the award the previous fall because I was hurt. I really wanted to receive the award in person. So I let Mike know in March of 2010 that I intended to be present that August.

Liz was excited to be going to Colorado. She said that she had never been to Colorado at all before even though two of her father's younger brothers, Elmore and Emmon had lived in Denver since they had both done a stint in Colorado in the Army during the early 1950s.

We flew into the large airport in Denver, then we took a smaller plane to the Gunnison-Crested Butte Regional Airport. I had always heard that there was really a great difference in the air in the much higher elevations of the Northwest around the Rocky Mountains. Liz had been an asthma sufferer for all of her life and she said that her lung function seemed to improve greatly as soon as we were outside the airplane.

Mike picked us up and took us to a rustic inn. Both Liz and I laughed at ourselves as we got really winded just climbing the stairs to the second floor—we figured it would take time, but we knew we would soon become accustomed to breathing in the thin air. We enjoyed looking out of the windows at the wide vistas and the distant mountain ranges that seemed much closer than they really were. We met many of the club members at a cook-out they held on the low banks of what they called a wood side "creek." That creek was high and overflowing its banks in some places. It surely looked like a river to me especially when a guy that someone said was a Native American came floating by on a flat-bottomed fishing boat.

I signed under the hoods of many of the Corvettes and spoke at the huge downtown car show and rally that took over the whole town of Gunnison. The club presented the trophy to me at their gathering. Liz and I had a wonderful time looking at all of the cars and seeing all the people who had dressed up in period costumes for the events.

Boyce Grenard was at the show and at dinner that evening. Liz and I were really glad to see him. I knew that he was retired from the United States Air Force. He had been a member of the ICCC for many years although his overseas assignments now kept him from being at a lot of the ICCC quarterly meetings. He was working as a sensor operator in overseas operations and was stationed at Colorado Springs Defense Space Center. He had driven his Corvette over to Gunnison for the show because he had heard that Liz and I were planning to be there. I knew that he was not allowed to tell us much about his work but I told him all about what my son, David, was doing. Boyce, Mike and the rest of the guys in the Gunnison group really hated to hear that the Army had stationed our son in what had become a combat area of Iraq yet again.

When we left Gunnison, I promised Mike that I would return to their "Cool Cars, Cool Mountains Car Show" again just as soon as I got the chance. I had really enjoyed seeing all the cars and meeting all of the people. I figured that since I was retired, I surely might get the chance to go back in the near future.

Being retired from a company that had gone bankrupt was no picnic, though. I had already found that out fairly quickly. All of the General Motors, Inc. assets were, obviously, being used in ways other than taking care of their former salaried employees. My common stock was no good—I had already accepted that, but I am sure I was not alone in believing that General Motors was top-heavy with non-labor people. They had to be instrumental in causing the quick slide of the company from one of the top automotive builders in the United States to bankruptcy. I am sure that I was not alone in wondering if they were set to suffer some of the losses that the people in the lower echelons of management and labor were suffering. When Joe Spielman came through Bowling Green driving his new, red Corvette Z06, on his way back to Florida, he visited first at the Corvette plant then he came by the house to see me. Both of us had made plans for our futures but we also had painful complaints and regrets about our great stock losses.

Liz and I went to Mike Yager's Funfest in Illinois as usual in September. We were at an autograph session when I started to talk to Dave McClellan, former Corvette Chief Engineer and VLE back during the days of the first Corvette advances such as the original ZR-1and powerful engine advances. Dave was now on retainer and working for the CODA Automotive, a former Mitsubishi car manufacturer with offices in Santa Monica, California and in China. He wondered if I had done any consulting or any other work since I had been retired. He had not heard about my motorcycle accident. I told him that I was still recovering, but I seldom talked about my motorcycle accident because I did not like to think about being that close to my demise. He said that he could see my point.

Dave had an idea in mind when he talked to me—he wanted to recruit me to become a manufacturing consultant for CODA. I only mulled it over for a bit before I figured that I was well enough to do it. So, I left home on October 19 and went off to Los Angeles California to the American headquarters to review the product and get myself familiar with manufacturing and build specifications.

I quickly learned that CODA was an affiliate company established in 2009 by Miles Automotive and Battery Systems in partnership with the Chinese Hafei and Qingyuan Electric Vehicles. From the beginning the CODA vehicle was intended to be powered by an electric battery system.

Apparently CODA initially had several investors, many of them United States based companies. The initial vehicle was to be an all-electric, five—passenger, four-door sedan powered by a battery pack that could be used up to 88 miles on a single charge. I understood that the car used both energy sources: gasoline and ion battery power to deliver 73 miles on one gallon of gas. I was not satisfied with the workability of the idea about the delivery. I was truly leery about how the diversity of that combination of power delivered to the engine might work.

Dave and I went to Santa Monica where there were vehicles that had been partially put together in the assembly plant in China. These vehicles were finished up in the plant in Santa Monica, and then offered for sale. I inspected their operation and said nothing. I certainly did not want to be the bearer of gloom and doom or bad news. Neither did Dave although I knew that he had a very strong opinion since he was an engineer by profession. He had worked as Chief Engineer for General Motors and Corvette for many years. I was an engineer by training, too. I had never had any occasion to work solely in engineering but I had used my engineering skills almost every day in manufacturing.

Finally, we went to Harbin, China to where the body assembly and chassis were done. We noticed that there were areas of the plant that seemed to be off-limits to us. The car was scheduled to be shown to the world at the Los Angeles Auto show on November 19-28, 2010 and that seemed to be the main focus. Dave was obviously helping to oversee personnel and getting the right people into the right places. I asked as many questions as I could of the people who were English speakers and gave suggestions about the simpler processes at first until I got out onto the assembly line to see where the real work was done.

I watched the assembly line with dismay, consulted with the "overseers" and process engineers, and stood at the "final line" to watch the processes until I finally had to speak up. None of the people seemed to be capable of getting their jobs done in station. Too many people were required to walk out of their place to get an assembly completed to the point that it could go off the assembly line. Efficiency was not even considered.

When I finally got out to the repair yard, I could not believe what I saw. None of the cars coming off the line were finished to the point that they could be shipped to Los Angeles. None of them seemed to have the needed mechanics done or to be ready to have the final padding and trim put on them. I did not see any repairmen busily working on these cars and there were literally hundreds of them setting in repair for way too many varied reasons. That is all they seemed to be assembling—cars that needed to be repaired!

I went over to the paint shop. I wanted to inspect the "Clean Room" but was unable to do it because there was not a "clean suit" that was large enough to fit me although all the suits that I saw were labeled "extra-large." I was head-and-shoulders taller than the tallest of the Chinese workers and two times bigger than they. Whenever I walked out of a meeting with people all around me, I could not help but feel self-conscious.

To be honest I felt like Gulliver in Lilliput. This was too much like my patrols in Vietnam with the Vietnamese regulars. I was feeling vulnerable all of the time unless I was sitting down. Then, it wasn't too much better. When Dave and I talked in the evenings, he felt pretty much the same as I did. Neither one of us were inclined to go for a ride in the rickshaws or to spend time walking on the overcrowded streets.

Both Dave and I took pages and pages of notes and observations. Both of us were dreading to deliver them to upper management or to anybody for that matter. When we took the train for Shanghai to the battery plant, we had further reason to be dismayed. Why were we visiting here at all? I wondered. There were no batteries being made that could possibly be used in the electric cars at that time. We saw the production of batteries for hand-held devices going forward, but there were none of the large, car-sized cells that were scheduled for use in the CODA operation. I saw no indications or plans for the large batteries that the cars needed.

When I called Liz from Shanghai, China to tell her that I would be coming home soon, unfortunately, I did not get in touch with her right away. Then I remembered, Liz had told me that she was going to drive to Atlanta. It was time for the quarterly meeting of the ICCC. I caught up with Liz while she and the secretary of the ICCC, Gigi Bohannon, and Rosa Barker who was the corresponding secretary were busy signing up members for the upcoming year.

I was really looking forward to taking over the duties of president of the ICCC once again. It was unfortunate that the final meeting of 2010 had fallen at a time when I had gone off to China. The newly-elected vice-president, Randolph Jackson, had to preside in my absence.

When I returned a week later I figured that I was surely going to enjoy having the duty of presiding at the ICCC once again Most of all, I figured that I would enjoy having women, Rosa and Gigi plus my own wife, on my executive board. I told Liz that I would be glad to be able to order someone around again. Liz quickly turned up her nose in disdain and stuck her tongue out at me.

The trip to China had been wonderful. I felt like I was still able to be of some service and that I was able to put the knowledge that I had gained over my 30 years at General Motors to some good use. It had been strenuous and all of the walking had made me realize that I was not completely healed yet no matter what I wanted so much to believe. Now I realized that age, great use and misuse of my body had conspired against me. I really needed to slow down and rest more often despite the fact that my mind was still speeding along at 250 mph in the fast lane. Mental pursuits—rather than physical—would have to occupy my time now.

It was just at the beginning of 2013 when Joe Spielman called me to see if I wanted go up to Detroit to meet him. He intended to go over to the Design Dome and to the Tech Center to check out the new C7 Corvette. I quickly packed my bag for the week-end and flew to Detroit to join Joe and all of our old friends at the Design Dome. We inspected every inch of the 2014 Corvette Sting Ray. We talked to the team and told them about our experiences. We measured the car and looked at the specifications for every model. We looked at color samples for the body, looked at color samples for the seats, the tire specifications and build sheets. When we finished we knew as much about this Corvette as we had known about the ones that we had nurtured and built in days past when we were working. We all agreed: this car was a sure-fire winner!

I was back at home when the telephone call came from Jack Matukas who was now Chairman of the Board of the National Corvette Museum. Why the hell was I not in Detroit for the unveiling of the new Corvette, he wondered.

"I was just up there last week," I laughed. "Joe Spielman and I already previewed it. It's a beast! It's gonna' be great! Don't you think so?"

"Yeah," he said, "but I've got something important to tell you. We had our board meeting last night and guess what! It was unanimous: you were voted into the Corvette Hall of Fame!"

Somehow I managed to finish the telephone call politely. I really don't know what else I said to Jack after that. I sat down in a chair at the kitchen table because the kitchen was where I happened to be when I got the telephone call.

I don't know why Liz came into the room right then; I guess she knew that I had been talking on the phone to someone. When she looked at my face, she rushed over to me. Her eyes were wide with concern.

"What is it? What's the matter," she asked anxiously.

When I did not answer, she demanded:

"Who was that on the phone? What's happened? Tell me **something**!"

Liz could only stand helplessly looking at the tears that had started to run out of my eyes and down my face. She had only known me to cry like that when something very bad had happened, so I guess she was really frightened.

"That was Jack Matukas . . . on the phone," I said wiping my face with my hands. But the tears were still falling. "He wanted to tell me . . . the board just elected me to the Corvette Hall of Fame. I'll be the first of my race . . ."

Standing and watching me, wringing her hands helplessly Liz had started to cry, too. Then she leaned down and threw her arms around my neck with her face against mine. Our tears mingled.

"That's wonderful news!" Liz said laughing and crying at the same time.

I pulled her into my arms and she sat down on my lap, careful that she was sitting on my good leg. She put her arms around my neck. I wrapped my arms around her, buried my face against her neck. I really cried then.

"I guess now's the time," Liz laughed merrily in spite of both of our tears. "You've worked so hard all your life. Your family appreciates you. We know what you've done. Now the Museum Hall of Fame will give everyone else a chance to recognize what you've done too."

She laughed again and kissed my forehead.

"I guess it's time for you to cry."

INDEX

CPSIA information can be obtained at www.ICGtesting.com
Printed in the USA
LVOW12s0247190414

382347LV00001BA/1/P